ALMA MATER

Words and Music by Nancy Cook Mackaman

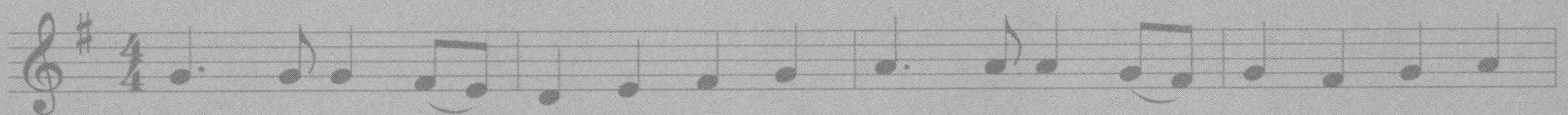

Through the years with ho – nor glow – ing, Love for you is____ ev – er grow – ing

From our hearts for – ev – er flow – ing, Mis – sou – ri S & T!

Wrought in sil – ver____ forged in gold, Al – ways in our hearts we'll hold,

U M Rol – la, M S M, Mis – sou – ri S & T!

FORGED IN GOLD

Fonts: Tungsten (Hoefler & Co.), Orgon Slab (Hoftype) and TSTAR Mono Round (Gestalten)
Paper: 100 lb. House Matte Text 3 (body), 100 lb. Accent Opaque Smooth Text (endpaper), 100 lb. Litho Label C1S (cover), 100 lb. House Litho Label (dust jacket)

Printed by Walsworth Publishing Co.
ISBN: 978-1-7349627-0-3

Lead author and editor: Larry Gragg
Contributors: Andrew Careaga, Debra Griffith, Mindy Limback, Jack Ridley, Mary Helen Stoltz
Layout Design: Jake Otto, Lindsay Stanford, Lishia Stevens

Cover: Detail from Norwood Hall exterior

Inside front cover: Students line up for the St. Pat's parade in 1911 as the Rolla Building and Old Chemistry Building loom in the distance. The image is part of a collection of amateur images donated to the university.

Inside back cover: Built in the 19th century, the Rolla Building continues to serve students today. The graceful 16,580-square-foot structure has undergone renovations over the years to make it more functional and comfortable, but it maintains its historic charm.

FORGED IN GOLD

Missouri S&T's first 150 years

Larry Gragg

Walsworth®

CONTENTS

A symbol of authority since medieval times, a university mace is carried before the president or chancellor and dignitaries during commencement or other ceremonial academic processions. Crafted by Jeff Heniff in the Rock Mechanics and Explosives Research Center using the university's specialized water jet technology, the Missouri S&T mace features the university's historic emblem in its crown. Its shaft is crafted from a red oak that was removed from campus to clear land for the 2008 expansion of Toomey Hall.

FROM THE AUTHOR

In 1871, Gustavus Duncan, the first student to enroll at the Missouri School of Mines and Metallurgy, traveled 10 miles a day on horseback from the tiny railroad stop at Arlington. He was one of just 32 students from Rolla and surrounding counties who took classes at the new college. From these humble beginnings, the Miner campus emerged in the 21st century as one of the nation's top technological research universities. In the subsequent 14 decades after Duncan enrolled, over 75,000 Miners graduated, and in 2019, Missouri S&T had almost 8,000 students on campus from 44 states and 58 countries. Moreover, students from 38 states and nine countries were taking distance courses from S&T.

This book is the story of that remarkable change. Chapter one is a chronological account of the campus's development. The remaining chapters each have a specific theme, from students and faculty to Miners' service in war and the extraordinary impact alumni have had on the world and beyond. Collectively, the chapters detail the many challenges the Miner campus overcame and its enduring commitment as a land-grant university. The Miner story is largely a positive one, a saga of affording Missouri residents access to an excellent institution of higher education and the efforts of faculty and staff to promote the success of those admitted. Yet, it is also a story of the difficulties that many groups, notably women and African-Americans, have had in gaining acceptance on the campus.

This is a history that I could not have written without the help of many people. In the Notes on Sources, you will see the names of all who permitted me to interview them. Some faculty members, staff and alumni like David Rogers, Leon Hall, Deanne Jackson, Caprice Moore, Will Zwikelmaier, John Gallagher and Keith Wedge shared information about the campus's history. Professor Jerry Cohen kindly translated a portion of a memoir of a UMR faculty member from East Germany. Several people reviewed portions or all of the book and offered suggestions for improvement: Andrew Careaga, Jack Ridley, Doris Gragg, Elizabeth Cummins, Paul Worsey, Harvest Collier, Jack Carney, C. Peter Magrath, Stephen Owens, Connie Goodridge, Linda Bramel, and Petra DeWitt. Debra Griffith, the campus archivist, deserves special thanks. She truly was indispensable in assisting me with the multitude of sources in the campus archives. It has been a delight to work with all the good people at Marketing and Communications at S&T. Mindy Limback, Mary Helen Stoltz, Jake Otto, Lindsay Stanford, Lishia Stevens, Terry Barner, and Tom Wagner all contributed to the volume and were consistently supportive of my work. Andrew Careaga asked me to write a new history of the campus and kept me on track to complete the manuscript on time. This truly was a team effort!

Sincerely,

Larry Gragg

FORGED IN GOLD

CHAPTER 1

GROWTH OF A MINER CAMPUS

In the 1870s, Rolla seemed an unlikely location for a new college. There were only about 1,400 residents in a community with more saloons than houses of worship. There were no paved streets, sewers, or water mains. To visitors there seemed to be as many dogs, hogs, horses, ducks, and geese as humans walking the dusty streets. Yet, it became the home of the University of Missouri School of Mines and Metallurgy in 1871. Over the following 150 years, it evolved from a "country academy" to a respected technological research university. From its origins in a single building that was shared with the public school, this school of mines evolved to become a complex institution with dozens of buildings and degree programs and a virtual presence around the globe. Despite two name changes over its 150-year history and the growth of academic programs beyond mining and metallurgical engineering, graduates continue to identify with their university's heritage and proudly call themselves Miners.

A view of Rolla in the 1910s from the south. The Phelps County Courthouse is at the center of the photo and the cupola of the Rolla Building, Missouri S&T's first structure, is visible in the distance, near the plume of smoke coming from the campus's mining and metallurgy building.

ORIGINS

In 1862, President Abraham Lincoln signed the Morrill Act, a piece of legislation that offered states land grants so that they could fund colleges for "agriculture and the mechanic arts." For over seven years, legislators in Missouri debated how to accomplish this. As historians Lawrence Christensen and Jack Ridley explained, "The indecision was whether to establish a mining school in the mineral district of southeast Missouri or to create an agricultural and mechanic college as part of the state university at Columbia, which was established in 1839." The two sides finally reached a compromise on February 24, 1870. There would be an agricultural and mechanical college on the Columbia campus, and there would be a mines and metallurgy school in southeast Missouri. Although there would be a physical separation from the Columbia campus, legislators decided that the "school of mines" would be under the administration of the University of Missouri's board of curators and president.

In 1839, state legislators had determined the location of the University of Missouri on the basis of which mid-Missouri county offered the highest bid in cash and land. Boone County won out. Members of the board of curators followed the same approach in determining where to locate the school of mines and metallurgy. Because Phelps County offered the most in bonds and land, the board members made it the location, a decision endorsed by state legislators on March 10, 1871.

FORMAL OPENING OF THE SCHOOL OF MINES.

The City Crowded with Visitors.

LARGE ATTENDANCE AT THE MEETING.

ETC., ETC., ETC.,

The formal opening of the Missouri School of Mines took place on Thursday last. The event had been looked forward to with interest for weeks previously by our own citizens and those of adjoining towns and counties. For two days there arrived by every train, stage, and private conveyance, large numbers of people desirous of witnessing the opening exercises.

ITS INAUGURATION.

The act of the legislature two sessions ago, authorized the establishment of the School of Mines, as a branch of the State University. Over a year was spent in examining into the merits of the various locations proposed. The principal bids, as well as the principal claims, to being selected as the point of location, were this and Iron county. The bids of this county amounted to $126,000 in bonds and lands, while the bids of Iron county amounted to $110,500. The donation and appropriations of one-fourth of the twenty-five per cent. of the State school funds to the State University, was authorized, together with 83,000 acres of agricultural lands. The final location of the School of Mines was decided in favor of this county in June last. A short time after Prof. Chas. P. Williams was appointed Director.

THE ATTENDANCE

was large, notwithstanding a heavy snow storm prevailed all day. The numbers were greatly augmented by visitors from elsewhere. Prominent among which were Col A J Seay, Franklin county; Mr Samuels, Calloway county; Hon Daniel E Davis, of Pulaski county; Hon B Smith, of Cuba; Messrs E W Murtfeldt, A Todd, H T Mudd, Geo J Bennett, J H Tice, C C Simmons, H C Lynch, Ed Wyman, Prof. Riley, Enos Clark, A J Conant, C C Bland, S G Williams, and Col Switzler, of Boone county.

THE EXERCISES.

During the forenoon the dedication of the new public school house, in which the School of Mines will be temporarily placed, took place. At two o'clock, after the arrival of the trains from the east and west, the inauguration of the School of Mines was opened in the large upper room of the public school building. Hon Elijah Perry, of this city, presided. The meeting was opened by prayer by Rev Andrew Luce, pastor of the Presbyterian Church. Then followed an appropriate selection, sung by the Rolla Quintette Club, and an air by the Rolla Brass Band. The chairman then informed the assembly that they would be addressed by Dr. Daniel Read, President of the State University, of which the School of Mines was a branch. Upon being introduced, Dr Read came forward and delivered a short address. He stated that to an unreflecting mind this meeting seemed of little moment, yet it made a part of the history of the great State of Missouri. He alluded to the fact that the people of Rolla had competed with other counties for the location of the School of Mines in their midst, and had made the splendid gift of $130,000 for the purpose. He concluded his remarks by alluding to the rapid strides being made subject of the moral and intellectual training of the young. The audience then dispersed.

AT NIGHT

a large concourse assembled in the the M E Church to listen to remarks from Col Switzler, Mr Wyman, Mr Mudd, Prof. Read, Mr Forrest Sheppard, Mr Conant, Mr. Albert Todd.

PLAN OF THE PROPOSED BUILDING.

Messrs. Barnett and Piquenard, the celebrated architects of St. Louis, have the plans for the building to be occupied by the school of mines. The size of the building is to be sixty by one hundred and thirty feet, three stories in height, in the Italian style of architecture, fitted up with laboratories, reading rooms, and a museum. The establishment of this institution in our city gives to us a valuable acquisition. It places our name before the world in connection with the valuable mineral resources of our State. Learned men abroad will hear of us. Capitalists will hear of Rolla as the place where true information as to prospects of investment in mining. They will come here to seek information. As our resources for wealth are demonstrated capital will seek investment here. Then our citizens will receive back with interest, the money they have spent to secure its location.

The board of curators hired an architect to design a building for the school and accepted a bid from a contractor for its construction. However, the Phelps County bonds that would have funded the project failed to sell, and the board canceled the contract. In the meantime, university president Daniel Read and a committee of the board of curators began a search for the first director of what came to be known as the University of Missouri School of Mines and Metallurgy, or MSM.

They consulted "some of the most outstanding scientific men of the nation" for recommendations, but they quickly focused their attention upon Charles P. Williams, who was a professor of chemistry at Delaware College and the state chemist. Williams had written a letter of application in April 1871, and Read traveled to Delaware to interview him.

Read liked what he heard and recommended to the curators that they hire Williams as the first director, which they did. Williams arrived in early September and placed an advertisement in the local and St. Louis newspapers promoting the opening of the new college, with classes to begin on November 6. Read and Williams negotiated the lease of the top two floors of an about-to-be completed building, intended for the Rolla public schools as a temporary solution for their need of a building. However, because of the failure of the Phelps County bonds, the board of curators dropped plans to build a college building and negotiated the purchase of the public school building for $25,000. Soon to be known as the Rolla Building, it remained the solitary campus structure for MSM's first 14 years.

Classes indeed did begin on November 6 with 13 students. During a heavy snowfall 17 days later, MSM held a grand dedication ceremony on the second floor of the Rolla Building with speeches from Read and Williams to a crowd that included state legislators and members of the board of curators.

The Rolla Herald account of the formal opening of MSM.

Above left: The Rolla Building was MSM's only building for 14 years.

Above right: Charles P. Williams was the first director of MSM.

Right: A cancelled $1,000 university bond issued on March 29, 1872, one of a series of 201 bonds issued and signed by Missouri Governor Benjamin Gratz Brown and State Auditor Daniel Draper.

THE STATE OF MISSOURI
$1000.
UNITED STATES AMERICA
$1000.
ONE THOUSAND DOLLARS

FROM 'COUNTRY ACADEMY' TO REPUTABLE MINES AND METALLURGY SCHOOL, 1871–1914

Above: MSM faculty (from left) Colonel J.W. Abert, Professor N.W. Allen, Director C.P. Williams, Professor Wm. Cooch, and Captain R.W. Douthat in 1873.

Opposite: 1894 map of the MSM campus.

THE EARLY YEARS, 1871–96

MSM was a rare type of institution in 1870s America. Fewer than 10 schools nationwide offered instruction in mining engineering when MSM opened, so there were few models for Williams to follow as he developed the curriculum for the new institution. He established a three-year degree program with a strong foundation in mathematics and the sciences and their practical applications, a curriculum requisite "for the engineer, or the general technologist." Building on the Williams approach, for several years campus leaders promoted MSM as "a school of Technology, with Civil and Mine Engineering and Metallurgy, as specialties."

However, because so few of them had attended high school, most of the students arriving at MSM were not prepared for the rigors of the curriculum Williams put in place. Consequently, there were three courses of study. The "regular" course was for the well-prepared students. A "preparatory" course, focused upon arithmetic and elementary algebra, was

available to help ill-prepared students make the transition into the regular course of study. Finally, there was a category labeled as "special" for students who faced no entrance requirements and who could take any sequence of courses as they worked toward a certificate of proficiency rather than a degree. Over the next 20 years, the school attracted many more preparatory and special students than regular ones. For example, in Williams' six years as director, only 24 percent were regular students. Moreover, total enrollment figures remained low, ranging between a high of 110 and a low of 43. The campus only awarded an average of three degrees a year between 1874 and 1893. Between 1887 and 1890 only one student earned a degree at MSM.

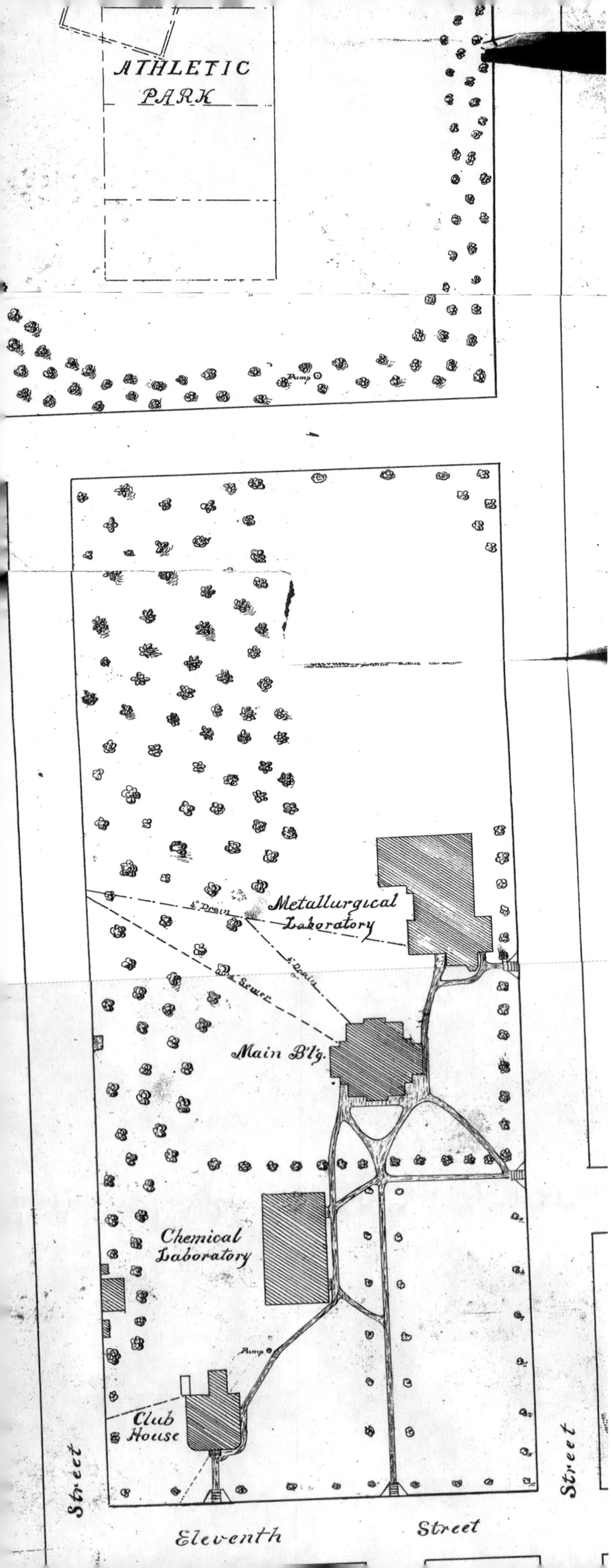

Williams, who served as director for six years, was able to hire two faculty members to share the teaching responsibilities — William Cooch, with whom Williams had taught at Delaware College, and Nelson W. Allen, who was a senior at the University of Missouri. Within two years, MSM's faculty had grown to five members. Over the next two decades, however, faculty turnover was common. Between 1878 and 1883, for example, there were four different mathematics professors. Some stability had emerged by the 1893–94 academic year when the campus had seven faculty members, but two of them had to teach a wide range of subjects. Paul J. Wilkins offered classes in German I and II, arithmetic, elementary algebra, and zoology, and Thomas L. Rubey taught English literature, psychology, general history, U.S. history, grammar, and English history.

Lack of adequate facilities accompanied the low enrollments and faculty instability. The campus added only three buildings in the first 25 years — a chemistry laboratory building in 1885, a dormitory called the "Club House" in 1889, and a mining and metallurgical building, which also served as a power plant, in 1895. When he arrived in 1897 as MSM's new director,

George Ladd bemoaned the poor condition of the four structures. He wrote that the club house was closed, and that two of the other buildings "were in bad repair."

"One of my first acts was to put tie-rods through the Mining Building to keep some of the walls from falling," Ladd wrote. "They were badly cracked." Professor Elmo G. Harris, who arrived in 1891, recalled "a row of outhouses ... distributed along State Street" and observed that "the waterworks for the School of Mines consisted of an old wire hand pump installed on an old well." The only "fire protection consisted of a wooden bucket and a tin dipper placed by the east front door of the Rolla building." Aware of these challenges facing the Rolla campus, the president of the Michigan School of Mines (now Michigan Technological University) claimed that MSM was "unworthy of being called a mining school. It is merely a country academy."

"... the waterworks for the School of Mines consisted of an old wire hand pump installed on an old well."

1890 photo of the Club House, Chemistry Building, and the Rolla Building.

Pipe fitting research, 1911.

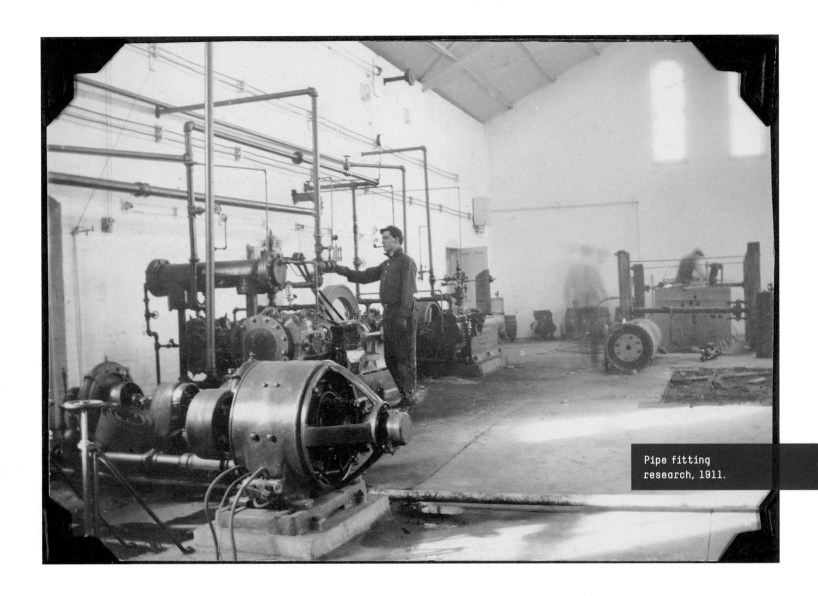

A MINER RENAISSANCE, 1897–1913

The directors who followed Williams — Charles Wait, William Echols, Elmo G. Harris, and Walter Richards — all struggled with low state appropriations and the challenge of attracting more students prepared for the rigors of the curriculum, but that all changed when the board of curators named George Ladd as director in 1897. A geologist with a Ph.D. from Harvard University, Ladd was a resolute six-foot-two-inch leader who acknowledged that he was "willful" and "quick-tempered." Intolerant of opposition, he belittled those who challenged him, once calling a local clergyman "a vicious, hypnotized, half-wit tiny-church preacher."

Ladd was determined to transform MSM, a school with "very little in the way of equipment; poor buildings; and an utterly inadequate income." He consistently challenged all efforts of the board of curators to limit the curriculum offered by MSM, and he cultivated the support of state legislators, select members of the board of curators, local power brokers, and the state's governors. One of his local supporters was Charles L. Woods, publisher of *The Rolla Herald*. Woods published articles Ladd wrote and assisted him in getting statewide circulation of glowing accounts of MSM. Once Ladd brought the entire state legislature to Rolla, wining and dining them, and effectively made the case that the campus was under-funded.

Ladd's efforts led to substantial achievements. He increased enrollment from 130 in 1896 to 210 in 1907, even though he raised admissions standards, and more students graduated. The number of degrees awarded improved from an average in the low single digits to an average of nearly 16 degrees a year. State appropriations more than tripled, enabling Ladd to nearly triple the number of faculty. He also added two wings and a second story to the chemistry building, constructed Mechanical Hall, Norwood Hall, a workshop, and a small gymnasium, and began construction of an ore-dressing building. Ladd persuaded state legislators to move the Missouri Geological Survey to the MSM campus.

Director George Ladd.

NORWOOD HALL, MISSOURI SCHOOL OF MINES ROLLA, MO.

Above and left: Mechanical Hall opened in 1902 and Norwood Hall the following year. Director Lewis Young continued Director George Ladd's push for the construction of new buildings.

Opposite top: 1899 handwritten notebook of Elmo Golightly Harris, former director, civil engineering professor and department chair.

Opposite bottom: Petrography Lab held in Norwood Hall, in 1910. Vachel McNutt, future alumnus of distinction, is second from right.

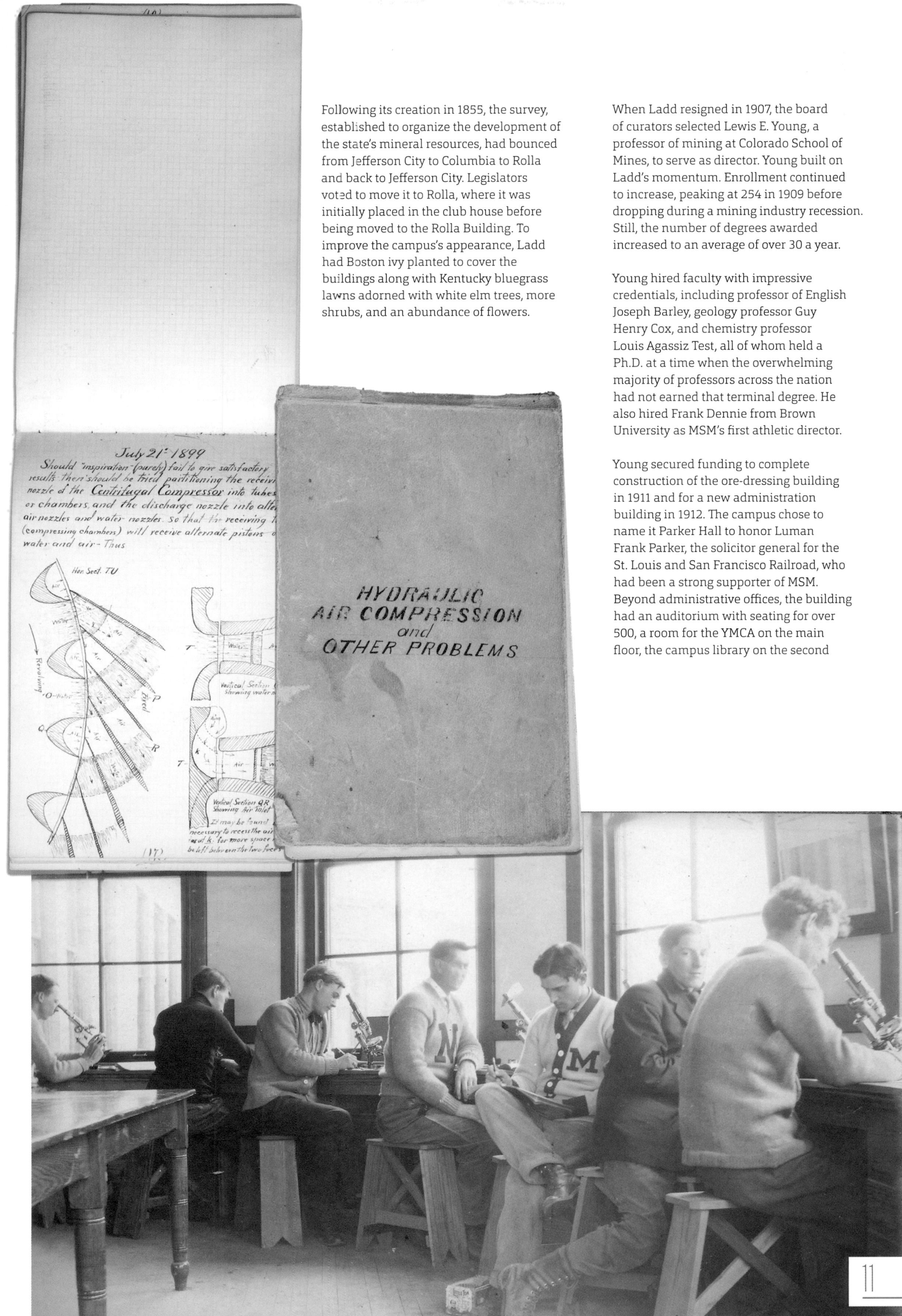

Following its creation in 1855, the survey, established to organize the development of the state's mineral resources, had bounced from Jefferson City to Columbia to Rolla and back to Jefferson City. Legislators voted to move it to Rolla, where it was initially placed in the club house before being moved to the Rolla Building. To improve the campus's appearance, Ladd had Boston ivy planted to cover the buildings along with Kentucky bluegrass lawns adorned with white elm trees, more shrubs, and an abundance of flowers.

When Ladd resigned in 1907, the board of curators selected Lewis E. Young, a professor of mining at Colorado School of Mines, to serve as director. Young built on Ladd's momentum. Enrollment continued to increase, peaking at 254 in 1909 before dropping during a mining industry recession. Still, the number of degrees awarded increased to an average of over 30 a year.

Young hired faculty with impressive credentials, including professor of English Joseph Barley, geology professor Guy Henry Cox, and chemistry professor Louis Agassiz Test, all of whom held a Ph.D. at a time when the overwhelming majority of professors across the nation had not earned that terminal degree. He also hired Frank Dennie from Brown University as MSM's first athletic director.

Young secured funding to complete construction of the ore-dressing building in 1911 and for a new administration building in 1912. The campus chose to name it Parker Hall to honor Luman Frank Parker, the solicitor general for the St. Louis and San Francisco Railroad, who had been a strong supporter of MSM. Beyond administrative offices, the building had an auditorium with seating for over 500, a room for the YMCA on the main floor, the campus library on the second

Director Lewis E. Young.

Parker Hall opened in 1912.

Jackling Gymnasium opened in 1915.

floor, and a materials testing laboratory in the basement. Young also developed plans for a new gymnasium, which became a reality in 1915 with the opening of Jackling Gymnasium. The building was named for one of the school's most prominent alumni, Daniel C. Jackling, a pioneer in the mining industry. In 1909, Young established a state mining experiment station to promote research on the challenges facing the state's mining industry. The *Bulletin of the School of Mines and Metallurgy, Technical Series* provided an outlet for reporting the results of research projects completed at the station.

During the Ladd and Young years, MSM eclipsed other mining institutions in enrollment. In 1901, Ladd reported to the board of curators that Colorado School of Mines had 234 students and Michigan School of Mines had 122 while MSM had 178. When Young resigned in 1913, MSM had 240 students compared to 217 at the Colorado School of Mines and 138 at the Michigan School of Mines. By 1920 MSM had more students enrolled in mining and metallurgical engineering than any other institution in the country.

Ladd and Young also improved MSM's reputation. In 1908, Victor C. Alderson, president of Colorado School of Mines, assessed the status of mining education in the country in an article published in the school's quarterly journal. Alderson concluded that, "on the whole, mining education was below the standard set by other kinds of engineering education." However, he noted that the "great private schools, like Columbia, Harvard and Massachusetts Institute of Technology were flourishing" and "the state mining schools of Michigan, Minnesota, Colorado, Missouri and California were doing excellent work."

THE

MISSOURI MINER

Missouri School of Mines and Metallurgy, Rolla, Mo.

Vol. 1, No. 8 Friday, March 19, 1915 Price 5 Cents.

HOUSE PASSES BILL 522.

School of Mines Directed to Confer Degrees in Mechanical, Electrical and Chemical Engineering.

St. Louis Globe Democrat, March 18, 1915.

Jefferson City, Mo., March 17.—After over three hours of heated discussion, during which Representative Frank H. Farris criticized A. Ross Hill, president of Missouri University, and members of the Board of Curators, the House passed the Buford bill, establishing courses in mechanical, electrical and chemical engineering at the Rolla School of Mines by a vote of 106 to 26."

The Board of Curators with the exception of Dr. S. L. Baysinger, vigorously opposed the bill from its introduction. Dr. Hill appeared before the House Committee on Education to fight it. In spite of the opposition, the Legislature saw fit to pass the bill.

It is a great victory for the School of Mines. For many days the faculty, students and citizens have anxiously awaited the outcome of the long fight. Coming as it did in the midst of the great St. Patrick's Day festivities it made that day one of still greater celebration. Bells were rung and whistles were blown and on all sides everyone was spreading the great news.

The bill, as yet, has not been signed by Gov. Major. As soon as this is done the victory for the School of Mines will be complete.

M. S. M. PAYS HOMAGE TO ST. PATRICK

J. J Doyle Represents The Patron Saint.

The 1915 visit of St. Patrick is over. The celebration held in his honor last Wednesday was generally conceded to be the most successful St. Patrick's Day celebration that has ever been held at the School of Mines.

For weeks the students had planned

Left: *Missouri Miner* account of the passage of the Buford Act in 1915.

Bottom: Albert Ross Hill, president of the University of Missouri (1908–21).

BECOMING A PREMIER UNDERGRADUATE ENGINEERING SCHOOL, 1915–63

THE SIGNIFICANCE OF THE BUFORD ACT

Ladd and Young had built a premier school of mines and metallurgy, but many on the campus sought to broaden the degree offerings at MSM, specifically to add ceramic, mechanical, electrical, and chemical engineering. As Jonas Viles, an early historian of the University of Missouri, explained, "The basic difficulty" for the MSM campus was "that a mere school of mines, a specialized branch of engineering," could have no reasonable hope "for any very considerable enrollment." However, university presidents Richard Jesse (1891–1908) and Albert Ross Hill (1908–21) and most members of the board of curators opposed those efforts since the Columbia campus was already offering degrees in all those disciplines except ceramic engineering, and the two presidents sought to avoid a duplication of degree offerings on the two campuses.

At the state capital, Rolla-area legislators Frank Farris and Carter Buford championed the idea of permitting MSM to offer more degrees in engineering. There were intense debates pitting the supporters of MSM against the supporters of the Columbia campus. After the legislature passed the bill with overwhelming support in both the House and Senate and Governor Elliot Major signed the Buford Act in 1915, the campus rapidly announced the requirements for degrees in electrical, mechanical, and chemical engineering and its intention to offer degrees in those disciplines.

Yet, the board of curators refused to comply with the new law. The matter ended up in the Missouri Supreme Court, which ruled "that all the engineering science is not only akin to but is in aid to the mining engineer, and for this reason … the Buford Act is not only a just and proper law, but a law that must be put in force."

Initially, there was slight interest in these new majors at MSM. In the 1919–20 academic year, there were only 26 students majoring in chemical engineering, six in electrical engineering, and five in mechanical engineering. Yet, when the campus aggressively promoted the new degree programs, a clear shift in enrollment resulted. A decade later, the number of students majoring in those three degree programs totaled 172, easily eclipsing the 127 students majoring in mining and metallurgical engineering. When campus enrollment peaked at 931 in 1940, just before the outbreak of World War II, only a third of the students were majoring in mining or metallurgical engineering.

MSM was no longer primarily a school of mining and metallurgy, and there was little prospect that it would recover that identity. Through the early 1960s there were fewer than 800 senior metallurgy majors at 50 institutions across the country, and even though MSM had the most with 63, that number was insignificant compared to the 3,000 majors in civil, mechanical, electrical, chemical, and ceramic engineering at MSM in 1963. By the 1969–70 academic year, the campus granted more undergraduate degrees in engineering than any other university in the nation, except for one: Purdue University. That year the campus led the nation in the number of civil engineering degrees awarded and was third-highest in the number of mechanical engineering degrees awarded.

769 B.S. Degrees Granted

UMR Ranks 2nd In Nation For Number Of Degrees Granted

The University of Missouri-Rolla was second among the nation's 275 colleges and universities which teach engineering in the number of bachelor's degrees in engineering granted during the 1969-70 academic year. UMR's total of 769 B.S. degrees was exceeded only by Purdue University with 910. The Rolla campus ranked seventh the year before.

Most of UMR's undergraduate engineering departments were among the nation's top ten. Civil engineering remained in the number one spot. Mechanical engineering was third and ceramic engineering tied for third; metallurgical engineering, fourth; petroleum engineering, tied for fourth; mining and geological engineering, tied for seventh; electrical engineering, tied for eighth; and chemical engineering, tenth.

In total M.S. engineering degrees, UMR was 12th of 197 graduate engineering schools (up from 22nd the year before). Several UMR departments also rated high in master's degrees. Both metallurgical engineering and mining and geological engineering were second; chemical engineering was fourth; petroleum engineering was tied for fourth; engineering management (listed under the category of industrial engineering) was seventh, civil engineering tied for 11th and mechanical engineering was 14th.

In doctorates UMR, with relatively new Ph.D. programs, was 42nd among 123 institutions.

UMR's standing was reported in statistics on 1969-70 degrees compiled by the Engineering Manpower Commission and published in the February, 1971, issue of Engineering Education.

More News & Views

Missouri Miner story on UMR as a premier undergraduate engineering university.

ACCREDITATION

From 1913, MSM, as a division of the University of Missouri, was accredited by the North Central Association. Beginning in 1972, the NCA granted accreditation to the campus — then known as the University of Missouri-Rolla, or UMR — as an "operationally separate" campus. Engineering programs across the nation sought accreditation through the Engineers' Council for Professional Development, or ECPD, which was established in 1932. Although accreditation by ECPD was voluntary, institutions hastened to gain the council's endorsement. By 1937, ceramic, civil, electrical, metallurgical, and mining engineering at MSM all had earned ECPD accreditation. Chemical and mechanical engineering struggled. For example, in 1943, ECPD officials informed the campus that they could not accredit chemical engineering because "the present staff engaged in teaching Chemical Engineering subjects is too inexperienced and is inadequate for proper professional training." However, by 1951, all the degree programs had gained ECPD accreditation. In 1980, ECPD changed its name to the Accreditation Board for Engineering and Technology, or ABET, and UMR and Missouri S&T engineering degree programs consistently gained its accreditation.

A student uses a drill while others observe and try to avoid the scalding steam cloud (1897).

Charles Fulton, director of MSM (1920–37), completed negotiations with the U.S. Bureau of Mines to locate an experiment station at MSM. Subsequently, the campus named the building to honor Fulton's efforts.

GROWING RESEARCH MISSION

Along with more engineering degree options, MSM slowly developed a research mission, an effort initially aided by the establishment of a Bureau of Mines experiment station on campus. In 1910, the federal government created the Bureau of Mines within the Department of Interior in the wake of several mining accidents, notably one three years earlier in West Virginia that killed over 300 miners. Initially, the bureau's task was to develop ways to minimize accidents, but eventually expanded its mission to conduct research into mineral products throughout the nation. The 1915 Foster Act authorized the bureau to establish mining experiment stations.

MSM Director Austin McRae (1915–20) began negotiations with the Bureau of Mines to bring one of the experiment stations to MSM. With the endorsement of the board of curators, Director Charles Fulton (1920–37) reached an agreement in 1920, leading to the establishment of the Mississippi Valley Experiment Station. Initially, the bureau began operations in the Metallurgy Building (known as the Interdisciplinary Engineering Building in 2020), but, with an appropriation of $100,000 from the state legislature, the campus completed construction on a new building in 1923 (named Fulton Hall in 1957) and relocated the bureau there.

In its first two decades, the station focused upon improving the recovery of Missouri lead and zinc from ore. During World War II, researchers focused upon manganese and aluminum to assist the war effort. The researchers' needs led to the construction of two additional buildings on 13th street and the leasing of three metal buildings near 14th street and U.S. Highway 66. The campus's need for the space in the experiment station building led to the construction of a new Bureau of Mines building on Bishop Avenue, which served as the agency's local headquarters from 1947 through 1996, when the federal government dissolved the agency.

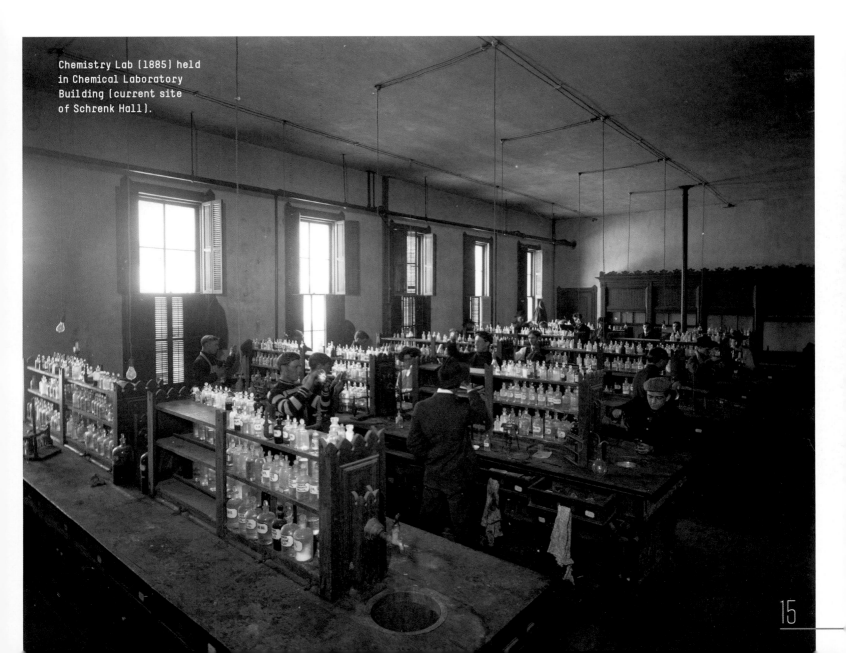

Chemistry Lab (1885) held in Chemical Laboratory Building (current site of Schrenk Hall).

The Mine Experiment Station building opened on the MSM campus in 1923.

"The Bureau of Mines Experiment Station 'increased research opportunities and closer connections to government and industry.'"

As Missouri S&T historian Jeffrey Schramm has noted, the Bureau of Mines Experiment Station offered students and faculty "increased research opportunities and closer connections to government and industry" just as the addition of the Missouri Geological Survey had done. Similarly, only two years after the establishment of the ceramic engineering program in 1926, the Missouri Clay Testing and Research Laboratories provided research opportunities for faculty and students. Beyond the laboratories for each department there were no other expansions of research facilities until the early 1960s when the campus established a computer center, and the board of curators approved funding for the Materials Research Center, the campus's first official research center.

With the increase in research facilities came more graduate students. Through 1920 it was possible to obtain a master's degree in science at MSM, but only 10 students had done so. Slowly, the number of graduate students increased to 25 by the end of World War II but escalated to over 360 by the time the University of Missouri System was formed in 1963. Among them was a growing number of Ph.D. students. From the mid-1920s, MSM students could take courses toward a Ph.D, but the University of Missouri graduate school granted the degree. By 1951, however, the graduate school in Columbia authorized the departments of ceramic engineering, geology, mining, and metallurgical engineering to offer graduate work that led to a Ph.D. Over the next 12 years, chemical engineering, engineering physics, and electrical engineering joined them.

As historians Lawrence Christensen and Jack Ridley discovered, these developments slowly elevated faculty research output. "From 1951 to 1953," they wrote, "30 faculty members in 11 departments produced 93 publications." By 1960, "64 faculty and 89 graduate students were involved in research activities." Collectively, these researchers had attracted $75,000 in federal funding.

Right: Merl Baker, chancellor of the University of Missouri-Rolla (1963-73), supported a more significant role for humanities instruction at UMR.

Below: Elmer Ellis, president of the University of Missouri (1955-66), pushed Dean Curtis Laws Wilson to hire more faculty members in the humanities with advanced degrees.

MORE DEGREE OFFERINGS

By 1963 — the year the four-campus University of Missouri System was formed — the campus had broadened its degree offerings to include a petroleum refining option in chemical engineering, a nuclear engineering option in metallurgical engineering, and a petroleum engineering option in mining engineering, as well as bachelor of science degrees in applied mathematics, chemistry, geology, and physics.

In addition, the campus sought to improve its instruction in the humanities and social sciences. In the 1920s, Director Charles Fulton concluded that the campus should place a greater emphasis upon "culture" for the engineering students. In addition to existing courses in English and history, he supported offering several social science courses — economics, sociology, and psychology — and even approved the hiring of Warren Scott Boyce, who had a Ph.D. in economics from Columbia University, as the chair of economics. While it did not offer degrees in those disciplines, the campus established the humanities and social studies department in 1946.

Still, a 1962 accreditation team raised grave concerns about instruction in the humanities at MSM. They found that too many of the instructors had only a bachelor's degree, and too many of them had large classes. University of Missouri President Elmer Ellis (1955–66) immediately responded by authorizing the hiring of Roscoe Goslin, who had a master's degree from the University of Missouri, to teach American history, economics, and sociology, and Jack Bobbitt, a Ph.D. candidate at the University of Missouri who had been teaching at the University of Montana, to teach American literature and composition.

When he arrived on campus in 1963 to succeed Curtis Laws Wilson as dean of MSM, Merl Baker told the campus that the humanities would serve an "even greater purpose in the future" during his tenure as dean, then chancellor. He argued that "today's engineer" needed a "more liberal base than yesterday's engineer," who essentially only "needed a great deal of technical knowledge."

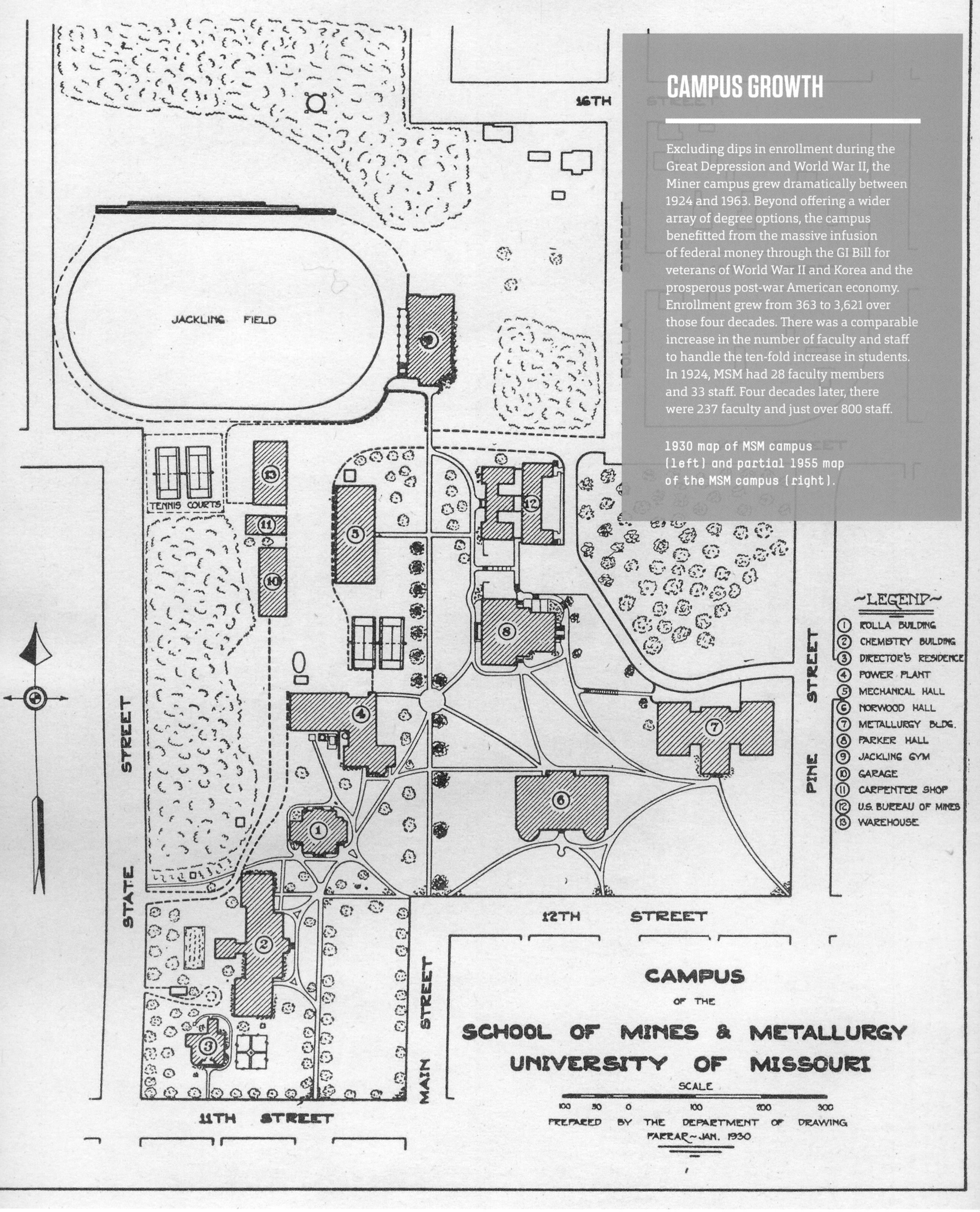

CAMPUS GROWTH

Excluding dips in enrollment during the Great Depression and World War II, the Miner campus grew dramatically between 1924 and 1963. Beyond offering a wider array of degree options, the campus benefitted from the massive infusion of federal money through the GI Bill for veterans of World War II and Korea and the prosperous post-war American economy. Enrollment grew from 363 to 3,621 over those four decades. There was a comparable increase in the number of faculty and staff to handle the ten-fold increase in students. In 1924, MSM had 28 faculty members and 33 staff. Four decades later, there were 237 faculty and just over 800 staff.

1930 map of MSM campus (left) and partial 1955 map of the MSM campus (right).

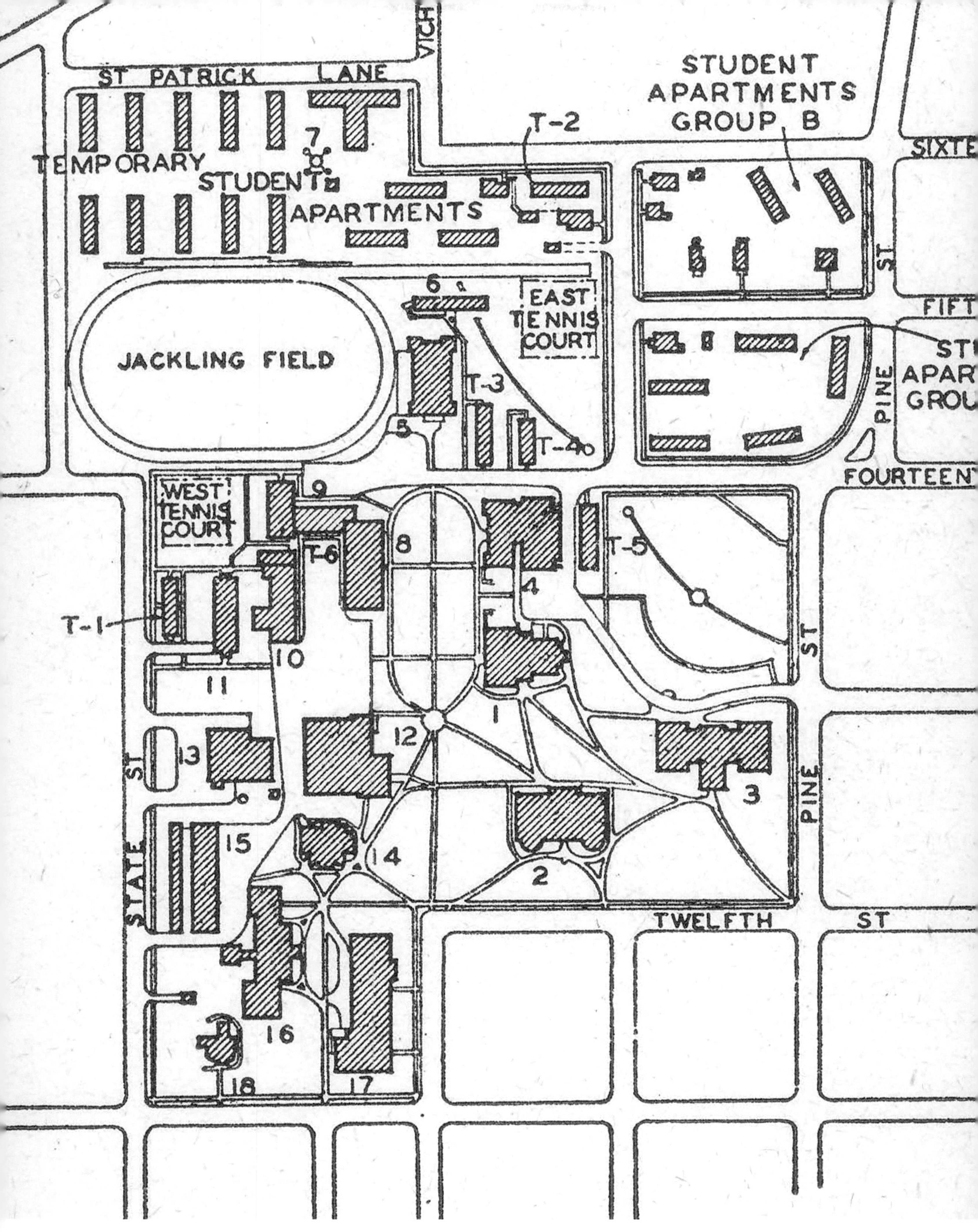
ST PATRICK LANE
VICH
STUDENT APARTMENTS GROUP B
T-2
TEMPORARY STUDENT APARTMENTS
7
SIXTE
ST
6
EAST TENNIS COURT
FIFT
JACKLING FIELD
T-3
5
T-4
PINE
FOURTEENT
9
WEST TENNIS COURT
8
T-6
T-5
4
T-1
10
11
ST
1
12
13
3
STATE ST
PINE
15
14
2
TWELFTH ST
16
18
17

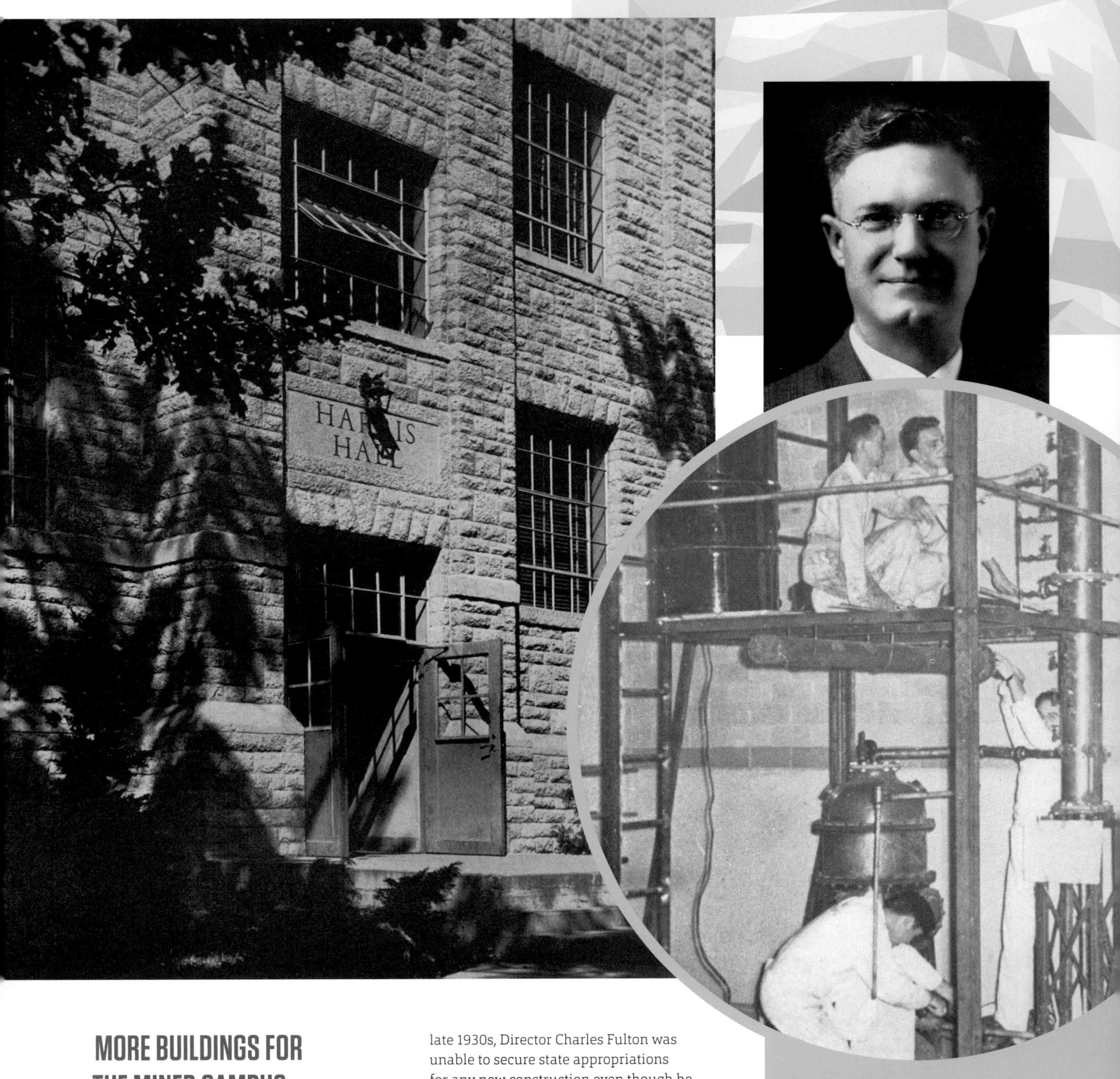

MORE BUILDINGS FOR THE MINER CAMPUS

The greatest challenge for campus leaders was providing a proper infrastructure for an institution that grew from just over 400 students, faculty, and staff to one with nearly 5,000 in four decades. In 1924, MSM had only eight academic buildings, and, according to historians Christensen and Ridley, "the campus was rather bleak and disheveled." Although enrollment more than doubled between 1923 and late 1930s, Director Charles Fulton was unable to secure state appropriations for any new construction even though he had developed plans for three buildings to address the needs of chemical, civil, electrical, and mechanical engineering. His successor William Chedsey (1937–41), however, secured $80,000 from the federal government through the New Deal program called the Works Progress Administration, along with $50,000 in state funding, for the construction of Harris Hall, which became the home of civil engineering for almost two decades after its completion in 1940. Chedsey, with the help of State Representative John

Left: Harris Hall opened in 1940.

Top: William Chedsey, director of MSM (1937–41), successfully gained funding from the federal and state government for the construction of Harris Hall.

Bottom: Chemical engineering students (1942).

J. Daily and State Senator Emery Allison, also gained a state appropriation for the first unit of a chemical engineering building, which was completed in 1941.

In the wake of the wave of veterans attending MSM after World War II and the Korean War, Dean Curtis Laws Wilson (1941–63) was able to convince Presidents Frederick Middlebush (1935–54) and Elmer Ellis (1955–66) of the need for a dramatic building program. Drawing upon federal grants and funds, state bond issues, and state appropriations, the campus saw the completion of a new power plant, four dormitories with a cafeteria, a student union building, apartments for married students and other families, the south wing of the chemical engineering building, an expansion of Fulton Hall, and new buildings for physics, civil engineering, mechanical engineering, and electrical engineering, as well as a building for the state's first nuclear reactor. In all, the expenditures totaled about $20 million.

The sheer magnitude of the increase in the size of the campus was impressive given the constant challenges in obtaining sufficient state appropriations and the substantial dislocations of the Great Depression years and World War II.

Top: Curtis Laws Wilson, dean of MSM (1941–63), faced the challenge of providing accommodations and classroom space for the thousands of veterans who came to MSM after World War II.

Middle: Frederick Middlebush, president of the University of Missouri (1935–54).

Surplus barracks, delivered during the 1946–47 academic year, helped the university during its housing crunch. The barracks were removed in 1960–61.

David Law describes the organization of Russian industry to his Russian Civilization class (1969).

BECOMING A TECHNOLOGICAL RESEARCH UNIVERSITY, 1964–2020

DIVERSIFIED DEGREE PORTFOLIO

The expansion of degree offerings that began after the passage of the Buford Act in 1915 continued through the last third of the institution's history. While it remained fundamentally an engineering university built on the foundation of its programs in mining and metallurgy, the campus inched ever-closer to becoming a comprehensive university.

Between 1966 and 1978, the campus added bachelor's degrees in computer science, English, history, psychology, philosophy, economics, and life sciences. The university also created the nation's first engineering management degree program in 1966. By the second decade of the 21st century, S&T offered degrees in 40 disciplines, including business and management systems, information science and technology, and technical communication, in addition to a teacher certification program.

Beginning with the establishment of the graduate engineering center in St. Louis in 1964, UMR and S&T extended its instructional reach beyond the campus. Following an experiment in 1966 to offer a course with the University of Missouri-St. Louis via a telephone line, UMR was able to offer more distance courses 20 years later once it had uplinked with the National Technological University. Under the direction of engineering management professor Bernie Sarchet, the link enabled UMR to offer video courses to 26 sites. By 2008, S&T offered distance graduate certificate programs in 29 disciplines and master's degrees in 10 disciplines, as well as non-credit development courses. It also began a cooperative engineering program with Missouri State University in

Springfield, where students could earn S&T degrees in civil, electrical, and mechanical engineering while taking virtually all their coursework on the Springfield campus.

The greater variety of degree programs helped minimize but not eliminate some dramatic swings in on-campus enrollment since 1964. Between 1953 and 1970, enrollment increased from just under 1,200 to over 5,400. Over the following four years, however, enrollment dropped by 25 percent, only to rapidly rebound to a then-record enrollment of 7,200 students in 1982. Between 1985 and 2004, the campus saw either drops or only slight increases with enrollment settling to a low of 4,393 students in 2000. Recessions, fluctuations in the demand for engineering majors, fewer Missouri high school graduates, and diminishing state appropriations that could be used for scholarships all played a role in the years when enrollment tumbled.

In 2000, incoming Chancellor Gary Thomas said his three priorities for the campus were "enrollment, enrollment, enrollment." He created the new position of dean of enrollment management, and under successive deans Jay Goff, Laura Stoll, and Tim Albers, enrollment increased dramatically after 2005. The campus deployed more sophisticated marketing techniques and emphasized recruitment of students beyond the state of Missouri. The 2008 name change to Missouri University of Science and Technology helped the campus distinguish itself from the other University of Missouri institutions and brought focus to campus marketing efforts. In just over a decade, enrollment increased to 7,948.

1870
1880 — 71
1890 — 69
1900 — 167
1910 — 229
1920 — 393
1930 — 598
1940 — 907
1950 — 1,685
1960 — 3,091
1970 — 5,411
1980 — 6,182
1990 — 4,826
2000 — 4,393
2010 — 6,511
2020

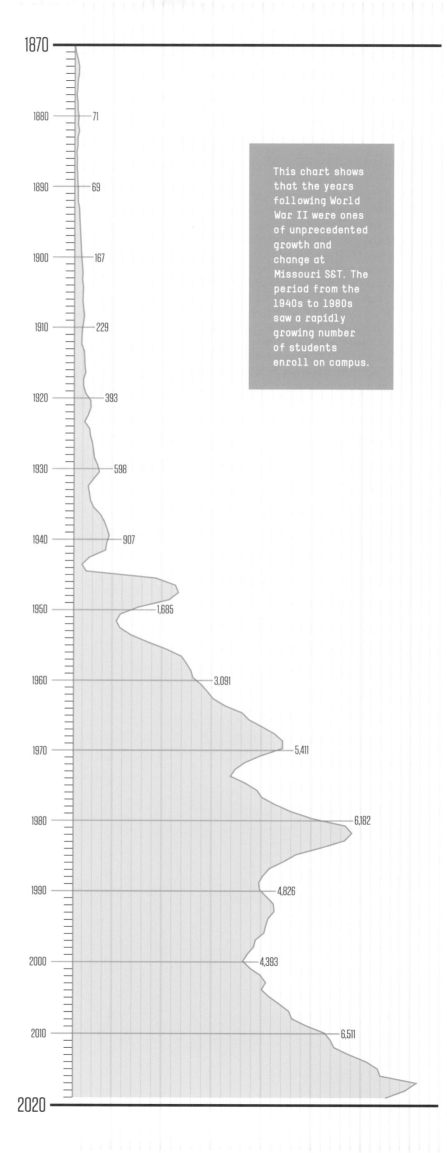

This chart shows that the years following World War II were ones of unprecedented growth and change at Missouri S&T. The period from the 1940s to 1980s saw a rapidly growing number of students enroll on campus.

STUDENT SUPPORT AND ACTIVE LEARNING

Steadily, the campus built a network of student support offices and programs. In the 1960s, UMR added a student financial aid office and a counseling and testing center and expanded the dean of students' office and student health department. In the 21st century, the campus added an office of undergraduate studies to promote student retention. The division of student affairs added programs to assist students with disabilities and wellness challenges and added student involvement programs to support the broader service learning activities. The campus created an office of student diversity initiatives to promote a more welcoming environment for women, underrepresented minority groups and the LGBTQ community. The university also established a chief diversity officer position to lead these efforts.

Building upon the Miner tradition of "hands-on" learning, the campus began to offer a variety of "experiential learning" opportunities, including funded undergraduate research with professors, study-abroad programs, service learning courses, and a wide range of design team activities ranging from solar car and solar house teams to a human-powered vehicle and Mars rover team. Several of these teams achieved success in national and international design competitions, including the solar car team, which won two national championships (in 1999 and 2003), and the Mars Rover Design Team, which won the international University Rover Challenge in 2017.

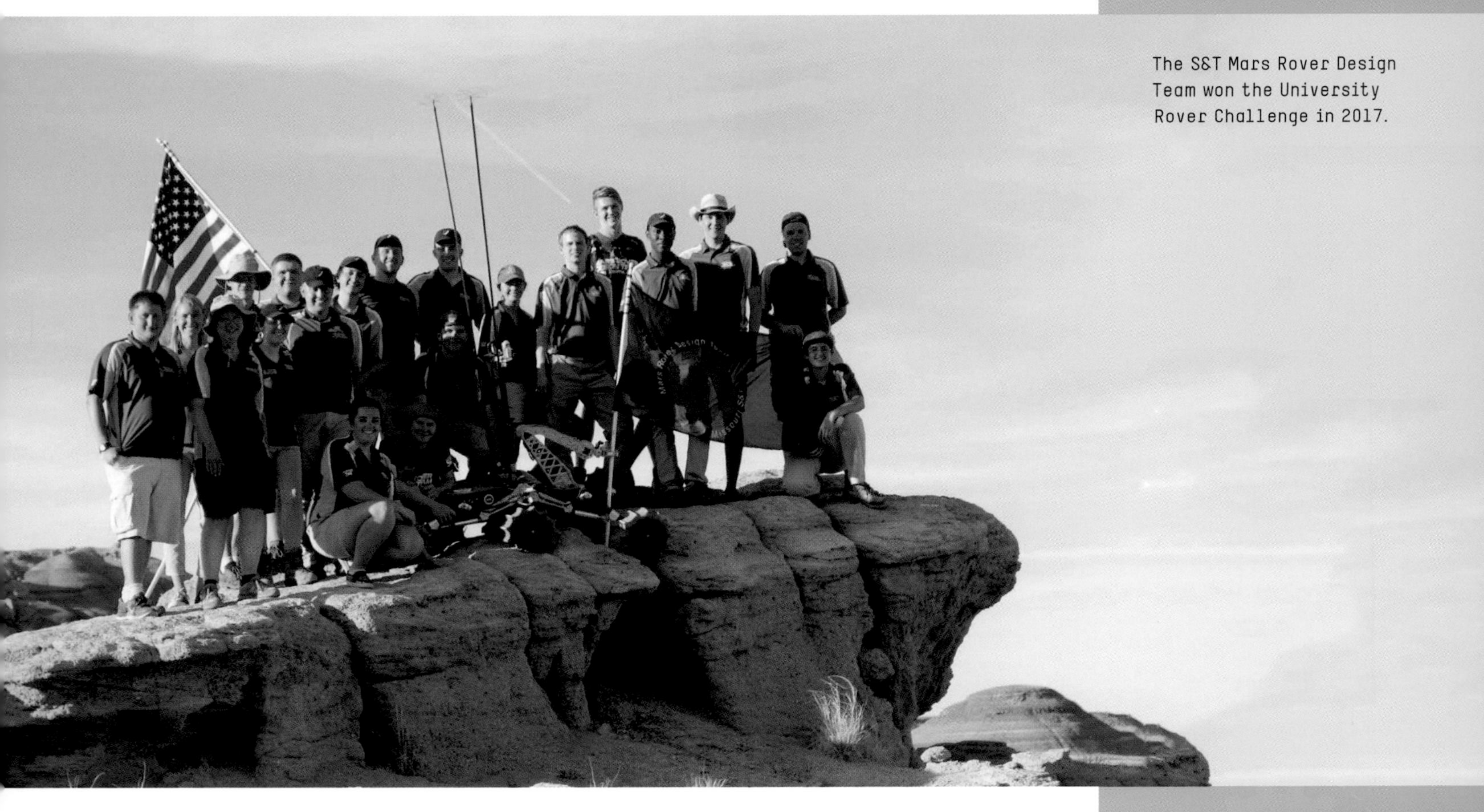

The S&T Mars Rover Design Team won the University Rover Challenge in 2017.

BECOMING A TECHNOLOGICAL RESEARCH UNIVERSITY

When President Elmer Ellis hired Merl Baker to lead MSM in 1963, he gave him the charge of increasing external grants and expanding Ph.D. programs. That move led to a more than half-century effort to move the campus into the ranks of technological research universities. Baker took over a campus where most faculty were focused upon teaching and undergraduate student success. Moreover, only 44 percent of faculty members held doctorates. When Baker stepped down in 1973, over 80 percent of the faculty had a doctorate. In 2008, 99 percent of tenured and tenure-track faculty had a doctorate.

As did his successors, Baker encouraged the establishment of more research centers. Beginning with Chancellor Joseph Marchello (1978–85), UMR began appointing Curators' professors who received financial support for research, and later, with external funding from companies and donors, endowed research professorships. Baker also promoted the establishment of more doctoral degree programs on campus, a trend that continued through the 21st century with 22 by 2020.

Baker and his successors developed UMR and S&T into a major research institution. External funding increased from $2 million in 1973 to $15 million in 1998 and $32 million in 2006. The faculty published 700 articles and 21 books in the 1972–73 academic year, and those numbers increased annually. The number of doctoral students increased virtually each year, reaching a total of 624 in 2016.

Project Under Way

A research project on infrared emissions from jet and rocket engine exhausts that may help minimize the detectability of jet aircraft and missiles is being carried out at UMR.

According to Dr. H. Frederick Nelson, professor of aerospace engineering at UMR and director of the project, there are three phases of aircraft of missile detection — visual, radar and infrared.

"In this project, we are interpreting the infrared signals from jet and rocket exhausts," he said. "We feel that the reduction of infrared signals will have a stong influence on our missile and aircraft capabilities."

The project, which is being conducted under the Missouri Research Assistance Act, has received a total of $18,313 in funding from the McDonnell-Douglas Corp. and matching funds provided by the University of Missouri under provisions of the act.

Nelson joined the UMR faculty in 1968. He holds a B.S. degree in aerospace engineering from Iowa State University and M.S. and Ph.D. degrees in aeronautical engineering from Purdue University.

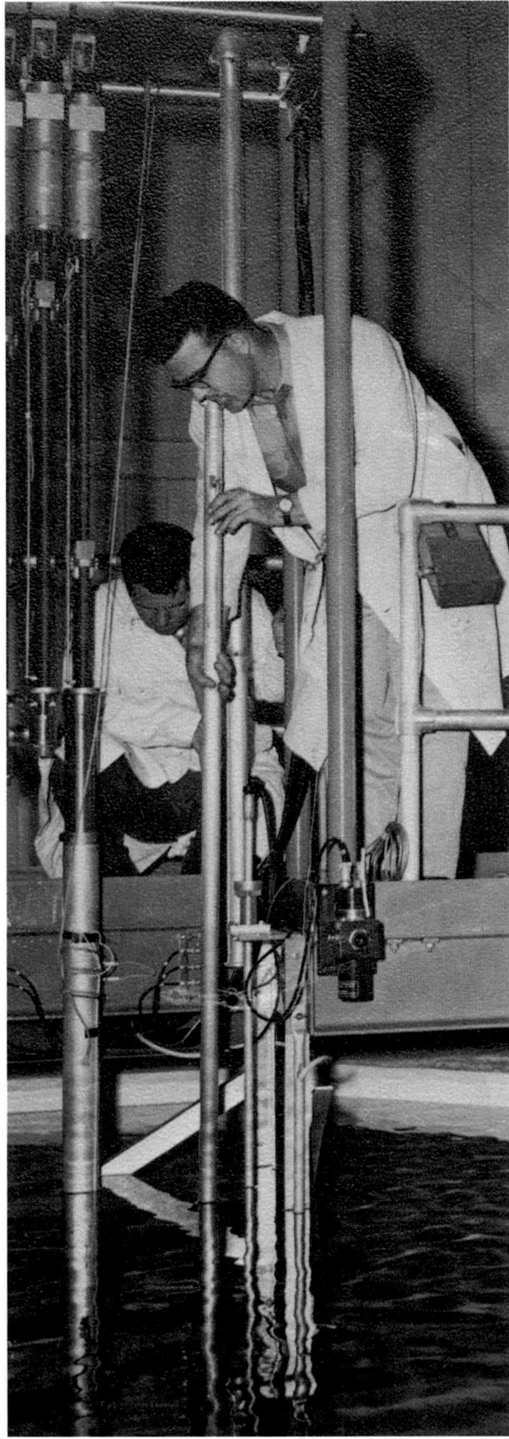

Above: The Missouri S&T Reactor was the first nuclear reactor built in Missouri.

Above left: Aerospace engineering research by H. Frederick Nelson received funding from the McDonnell-Douglas Corp in 1984.

Left: A student in 1974 investigates the boiling process.

MORE BUILDINGS

To accommodate the increasing number of students, the campus purchased the privately developed Thomas Jefferson Residence Hall and added a second tower. Beginning in 2005 it opened a series of residential colleges (later called residential commons). To provide working space for the staff, and to provide faculty with offices and laboratories, the campus had added and expanded many structures after 1964. In the 1960s, the campus opened the materials research building, a new library, and a multi-purpose building for athletics and intramural sports. During the following decade came a humanities-social sciences building, a new student union building, a mathematics and computer science building, an engineering research laboratory building, and a new chemistry-chemical engineering building to replace "Old Chem," which burned in 1969. Also, the iconic "puck," a round concrete platform near the old student union, appeared in the early 1970s and quickly became a centerpiece of the annual St. Pat's celebration. In the early 1980s, a mineral engineering building (named after prominent alumnus V.H. McNutt) and an engineering management building opened on the northwest corner of the campus. Castleman Hall, which included Leach Theatre, a performing arts hall, opened in 1992. Later that decade, the campus enlarged and updated Emerson Hall, the electrical engineering building. In the first decade of the 21st century, the campus witnessed a major renovation and expansion of Butler-Carlton Hall for the growing programs in civil, architectural, and environmental engineering, the expansion and renovation of Toomey Hall for the mechanical and aerospace programs, and the opening of the Havener Center, which served as a student center and provided meeting space for campus and the community. In 2014, Bertelsmeyer Hall opened as the new home for the department of chemical and biochemical engineering. The following year, the Miner Alumni Association dedicated Hasselmann Alumni House on Pine Street. Toomey Hall, the Havener Center, Bertelsmeyer Hall and Hasselmann Alumni House were all named in honor of alumni who provided significant support for building construction (John Toomey, Gary Havener, James E. Bertelsmeyer and Karl F. Hasselmann).

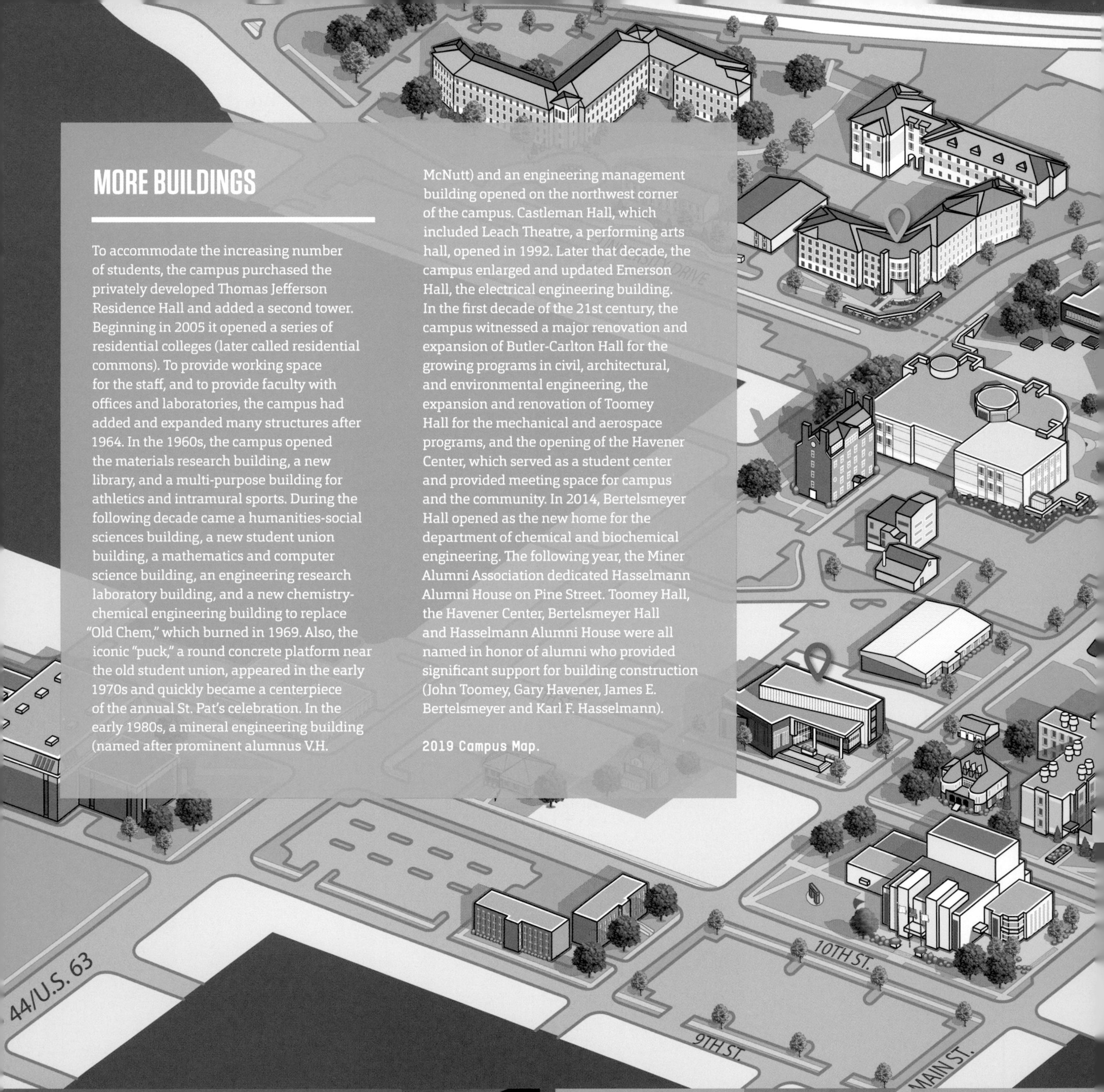

2019 Campus Map.

Bertelsmeyer Hall

Residential Commons

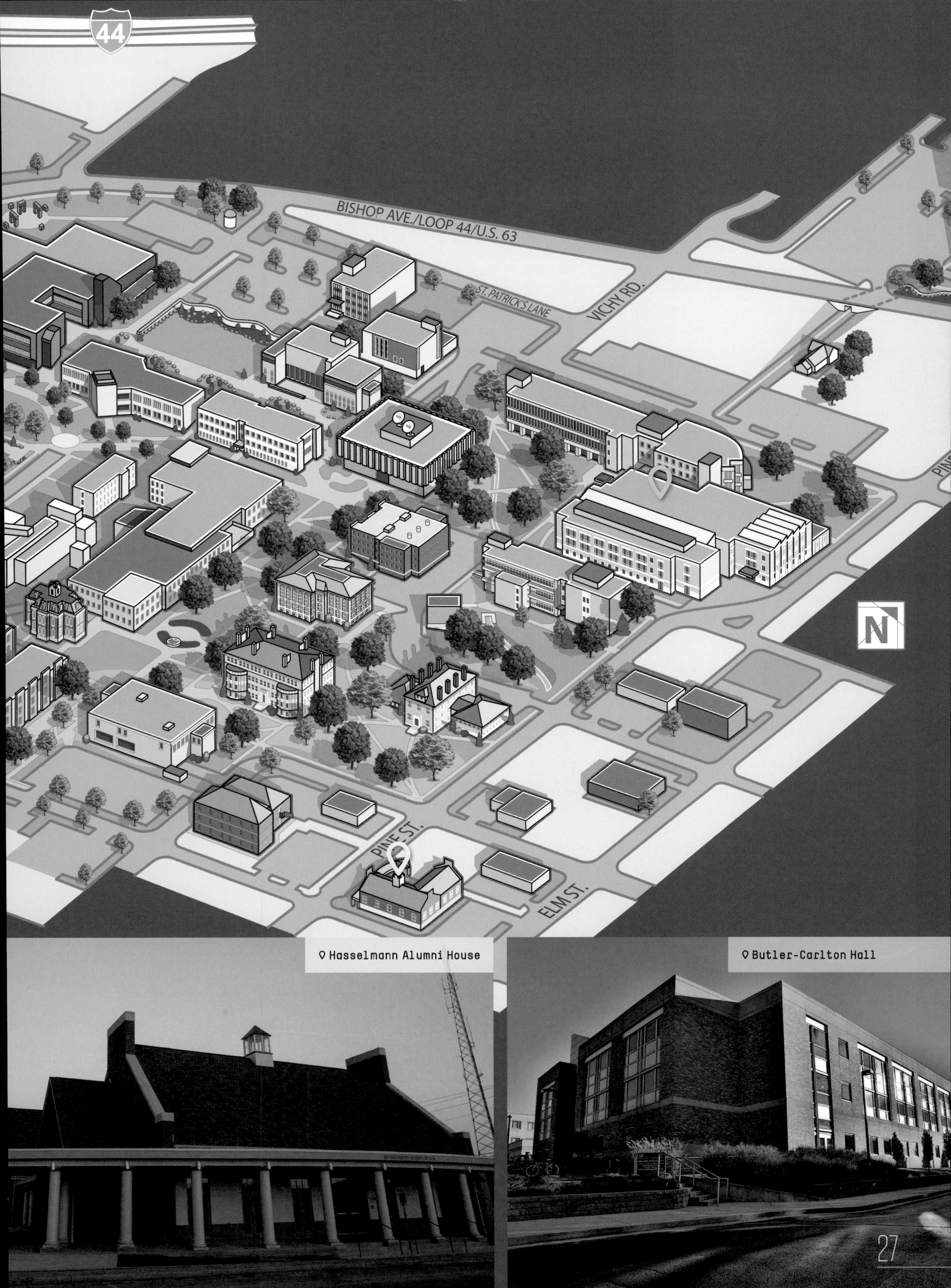

44
BISHOP AVE./LOOP 44/U.S. 63
ST. PATRICK'S LANE
VICHY RD.
PINE ST.
ELM ST.
N
Hasselmann Alumni House
Butler-Carlton Hall

Rolla faculty wants top posts eliminated

By Debbie Buell
Missourian staff writer

ROLLA — Faculty members of the University of Missouri-Rolla have called for the elimination of the offices of the vice chancellor and associate and assistant dean and for salary adjustments between the administration and faculty.

The calls were made in a series of resolutions presented Thursday to UMR Chancellor Raymond L. Bisplinghoff. Three members of a faculty steering committee presented the resolutions, which were "cordially received" by the chancellor, said Earl Foster, professor of engineering mechanics.

Foster, representing the steering committee, and the chancellor set Tuesday for a special faculty meeting to consider the resolutions.

At an off-campus faculty meeting held March 25, 77 out of the approximately 320 Rolla faculty members "generally approved" the resolutions that the steering committee refined before presentation Thursday, Foster said.

At the Tuesday meeting, Foster expects "the resolutions may be modified but should be overwhelmingly received and passed" by the entire faculty.

The decision for action by the faculty stems in part from a study conducted by the UMR Society of Professors on the campus' merit salary system for 1972-75, Foster said. The study indicated widening discrepancies between administration and faculty salaries.

"There's just a general feeling by the faculty that there are too many positions of dubious responsibility in the administration," Foster said "Administrators are paid excessively in relation to faculty salaries.

"It came on us all of a sudden. There's a general feeling of unrest across the campus. We've long suspected the situation but it just never had been brought to light before."

Foster said the study indicated that "anybody with any contact with the administration has received a nice boost (in salary) . . . and quickly."

Foster said the main differences between the protest of the Rolla faculty and the Columbia faculty over administration is that "there's not much we can do about the central administration. The Columbia faculty directs itself more toward the University-wide administration."

The resolutions cover two areas, Foster said: the administration of UMR and the economic status of faculty and administration.

The resolutions concerning the administration of UMR are:

—All faculty with administrative titles must teach at least three credit hours per academic year in the department of their academic appointment.

—All positions of associate and assistant dean shall be abolished effective 1976-77.

—The position of vice chancellor shall be abolished effective 1976-77.

—The duties, responsibilities and lines of authority relevant to each administrative office shall be defined and published Each administrative officer shall be evaluated annually by the appropriate faculty effective 1976-77.

—No faculty member with an administrative title shall receive additional compensation for administrative duties

The resolutions concerning the economic status of faculty and administration are:

—"To compensate for the recent loss in the purchasing power of the faculty, we call for a line item in the next budget for a 12 per cent cost of living adjustment

—"We call for the establishment of minimum salaries for the year 1976-77 as instructor, $12,500; assistant professor, $15,000; associate professor, $17,500; professor, $20,000.

—"In view of the increasing discrepancy between the salaries of administrators as compared to the faculty that has developed in recent years, this salary gap between administrators and the faculty shall be closed or, preferably, inverted "

A final resolution asked for written response to each resolution prior to the regular faculty meeting on April 22, Foster said

"We have been protesting slowly and subtly for the last couple of years over the increase of administrative positions while our student population and number of departments has remained static," Foster said "What was brought to light was the tremendous salary gap between the administrators and the faculty."

The budget crunch is also a contributing factor to the faculty unrest, Foster said "Our teaching loads have gone up. We're not able to replace people who leave but we still see continued administrative appointments."

FACULTY'S ROLE IN GOVERNANCE

From its earliest years the Miner campus saw faculty playing a role in governance. For a century, faculty gathered monthly, sometimes weekly, to develop or change campus policies with a focus on curriculum and student discipline. In 1971, given the large size of the faculty, UMR established an academic council (renamed the faculty senate in 2008) to provide the faculty with a "legislative and policy-making body."

Most years, faculty leaders and senior administrators worked collaboratively. However, faculty members were quite willing to challenge their directors, deans, and chancellors. In 1933, for example, in a report to the board of curators, an alumni committee revealed that "a considerable part of the present faculty" had "lost confidence" in Director Charles Fulton, which had made it "difficult to secure a harmonious faculty action on any issues of prominence." A few outspoken faculty members led an outright rebellion against both Dean Curtis Laws Wilson and President Frederick Middlebush, a campaign that led to the removal of the faculty critics from the campus in 1948.

According to a 1967 report to University of Missouri System President John C. Weaver (1966–70), there was much "unrest" on the Rolla campus, which was "due in part to the feeling on the part of many teachers that the faculty does not have enough voice in determining the policies of the University." That dissatisfaction led some faculty members to form a chapter of the American Association of University Professors. At times, frustration with senior leaders led to discussions of calling no-confidence votes.

Faculty insurgency occasionally caught the attention of members of the campus board of trustees, an advisory board whose members saw campus governance challenges from a much different perspective. For example, according to an article in a 2005 issue of the *MSM-UMR Alumnus* magazine, Robert Brackbill, a 1942 mining engineering graduate, "went on record with the observation that, for too long, the faculty had been in control of the campus instead of the chancellor." Some chancellors, like Gary Thomas (2000–05), were equally dismissive of faculty challenges. In 2005, he noted, "I basically ignored the opposition," and he did not try "to know who has what opinion."

Above: 1976 article discussing faculty steering committee members presenting Chancellor Raymond Bisplinghoff with resolutions condemning the widening salary gap between administrators and faculty.

Left: Chancellor Gary Thomas (2000–05) "basically ignored the opposition" from faculty critics.

COMMUNITY AND POLITICAL RELATIONS

Top: U.S. Senator Christopher Bond (1987–2011) was a strong supporter of the campus. Here Bond (third from left) is on campus in 2009 visiting with civil engineering professor John Myers (left) and two students.

Bottom: Ashok Midha, professor and former chair of mechanical and aerospace engineering, hosts U.S. Representative Joann Emerson (right) in April 2010.

The "town and gown" relationship between local residents and the Miner campus was strong in most eras. The residents understood the economic and cultural benefits of having a college in their small community. Many on the faculty and in the administration became civic leaders, and frequently spouses of faculty members became teachers in the Rolla schools. Student service organizations were a visible presence in Rolla with fundraisers and involvement in community service projects. It was a mutually beneficial relationship, as Rolla High School remained the leading "feeder" school for freshman classes at MSM, UMR, and S&T for many generations. To be sure, when Miner students got too rowdy, particularly during the annual St. Patrick's Day celebrations or party weekends, residents complained to city and campus leaders, and students sometimes complained about the cost of off-campus housing. Nonetheless, for 150 years the Miners and Rolla residents understood, as Lawrence Christensen and Jack Ridley explained, that they shared an important "interdependence" because they needed each other to thrive.

All public colleges and universities need strong supporters in the state legislature, and the Miner campus had many from the early 20th century. Representative Frank Farris and Senator Carter Buford were critical in the passage of the important 1915 law named after the latter that enabled the campus to broaden its curriculum. Senator Emery Allison and Representatives John J. Daily and Booker H. Rucker were steadfast in the 1940s in seeking ways for MSM to have more control over its destiny. They pushed bills to enable the dean of the campus to report directly to the board of curators rather than to the university president. Al Nilges from nearby Bourbon, who chaired the House of Representatives budget committee for many years in the 1980s, and Senators Mike Lybyer and Dan Brown, who chaired the Senate appropriations committee in the 1990s and in 2017–18, respectively, were staunch supporters of funding for UMR and S&T. Jerry McBride, long-time representative from Edgar Springs, and Sarah Steelman, who was in the state senate between 1998 and 2004 and later taught economics at S&T, were also strong supporters. One of the key tasks for these legislators was to explain to colleagues that the Miner campus had needs distinct from those at the larger Columbia campus. Several statewide and federal office holders also were influential supporters of UMR in the late 20th and early 21st century. They included U.S. Senator Christopher Bond, Governor Mel Carnahan, and Secretary of State James C. Kirkpatrick. Finally, local businessman John Powell, who did not hold office, but who chaired the Missouri State Republican Committee between 1980 and 1983, was an influential friend of the campus.

As it reached its 150th birthday, Missouri S&T was one of a select few technological research universities in America. It had a well-deserved reputation for providing outstanding undergraduate instruction and was becoming ever-better known for its research prowess. Members of the board of curators often acknowledged the Rolla campus was the "jewel" of the university system, a campus with a clear STEM focus. Continuing to thrive in an era of diminishing resources and making the campus more welcoming to a diverse population were its chief challenges as the S&T community celebrated their university's many achievements during its sesquicentennial year.

Charles E. Wait

William H. Echols

Elmo G. Harris

Walter B. Richards

DIRECTORS, DEANS, AND CHANCELLORS

Charles Penrose Williams, 1871–77

A.B and A.M., chemistry, Polytechnic College of Pennsylvania, 1859

He had been a geologist and metallurgist in several western states before joining the faculty at Delaware State College. He also served as state chemist in Delaware. He had published more than a dozen technical papers before 1871, including a study of tin in Missouri.

Charles Edmund Wait, 1877–88

B.S., mathematics; professional degrees in civil and mining engineering, University of Virginia, 1872

He taught at St. John's College in Arkansas and worked in the Geological Survey of Alabama, a refinery in California, and an antimony company in Arkansas prior to accepting the offer to become the second director at MSM.

William Holding Echols, 1888–91

B.S., mathematics; civil engineering, University of Virginia, 1882

He managed a mining company and was a resident engineer for a railroad line before accepting the position of professor of engineering and graphics at MSM in 1887. He began his three-year tenure as director the following year.

Elmo Golightly Harris, 1891–93

B.S., civil engineering, University of Virginia, 1882

A classmate of Echols, Harris worked as an engineer for a railway line and as a city engineer prior to becoming the fourth director at MSM. Because Harris was a collegiate and professional friend, Echols had recommended him to succeed him as director.

Walter "Buck" Richards, 1893–97

M.A., University of Virginia, 1882

Richards taught at preparatory schools and at McCabe's University School in Petersburg, Virginia, before accepting a position to teach mathematics at MSM in 1888.

George E. Ladd, 1897–1907

Ph.D., geology, Harvard University, 1894

Besides teaching at Harvard, Ladd had worked for the geological surveys in both Texas and Missouri as well as the U.S. Geological Survey. At the time that he accepted the director's position, Ladd was serving as chemist and assistant geologist for the Georgia Geological Survey in Atlanta.

Lewis E. Young

Leon E. Garrett

Durward Copeland

Austin Lee McRae

Lewis Emmanuel Young, 1907–13

B.S., mining engineering, Pennsylvania State College; engineer of mines, Iowa State College, 1904

After working briefly with a coal company in Pittsburgh, Young served as assistant geologist at the Iowa Geological Survey before teaching first at Iowa State College and then at the Colorado School of Mines.

Leon Ellis Garrett, 1913–15

B.S., science, MSM, 1901

Two years after graduating, he joined the faculty as an instructor of mathematics, but he had become an associate professor at the time of his appointment as acting director. He also briefly served as acting director after his successor resigned after serving only a few months.

Durward Copeland, 1915

S.B., metallurgy, Massachusetts Institute of Technology, 1903

After teaching three years at the Michigan School of Mines, Copeland became professor of metallurgy and ore dressing at MSM. During the 1913–14 academic year Copeland was on a research leave in South America. He resigned in the wake of the controversy over the Buford Act and left Rolla.

Austin Lee McRae, 1915–20

B.S., science, University of Georgia, 1881; D.Sc., Harvard University, 1886

He worked for the U.S. Signal Corps and then accepted a position at the University of Missouri to teach physics before accepting a similar position at MSM in 1891. Three years later he took a position at the University of Texas, but returned to Rolla in 1899.

Charles Herman Fulton, 1920–37

Engineer of Mines, Columbia University, 1897

After working for mining firms, Fulton became a professor of mining and metallurgy at the South Dakota School of Mines and the school's president for six years. In 1911, he became head of the department of metallurgy at the Case School of Applied Science in Cleveland. He succeeded Austin Lee McRae when the latter had to resign due to illness.

William Ruel Chedsey, 1937–41

Engineer of Mines, Colorado School of Mines, 1908

He taught for three years at the University of Idaho School of Mines before becoming an engineer for companies in Central America and Alaska. He returned to higher education, teaching three years at the Colorado School of Mines and two decades at Pennsylvania State College.

Curtis Laws Wilson, 1941–63

Ph.D., University of Goettingen, Germany, 1939

Wilson had worked for a year at Anaconda Copper before joining the faculty of the Montana School of Mines where he became head of the metallurgy department.

Merl Baker, 1963–73

Ph.D., mechanical engineering, Purdue University, 1952

He was a mechanical engineer on the faculty of the University of Kentucky. For a decade, he served as executive director of the Kentucky Research Foundation, and coordinated the university's overseas cooperative program with the U.S. Agency for International Development. Baker became the campus's first chancellor in 1964.

Joseph M. Marchello

John T. Park

Martin C. Jischke

Dudley Thompson, 1973–74

Ph.D., chemical engineering, Virginia Polytechnic Institute, 1950

He came to MSM as chair of chemistry and chemical engineering in 1956. He became director of the school of engineering and dean of faculties before being appointed acting chancellor.

Raymond L. Bisplinghoff, 1974–76

Sc.D., Swiss Federal Institute of Technology, 1957

An aerospace engineer, he had been dean of the school of engineering at Massachusetts Institute of Technology and deputy director of the National Science Foundation.

Jim C. Pogue, 1977–78

Ph.D., English, University of Missouri, 1964

He had headed the humanities department and served as provost before becoming interim chancellor.

Joseph M. Marchello, 1978–85

Ph.D., chemical engineering, Carnegie Mellon University, 1959

He had taught chemical engineering at Oklahoma State University before joining the faculty at the University of Maryland. There he became the chair of the chemical engineering department and the provost of mathematics, physical sciences, and engineering.

John T. Park, 1985–86, 1991–92, and 1992–2000

Ph.D., physics, University of Nebraska, 1963

He served as department chair of physics and vice chancellor for academic affairs before serving twice as interim chancellor prior to becoming chancellor in 1992.

Martin C. Jischke, 1986–91

Ph.D., aeronautics and astronautics, Massachusetts Institute of Technology, 1968

He taught at the University of Oklahoma where he became the director of the school of aerospace, mechanical, and nuclear engineering and dean of the college of engineering.

Gary Thomas, 2000–05

Ph.D., electrical engineering and computer science, University of California at Berkeley, 1967

He taught at the State University of New York-Stony Brook and New Jersey Institute of Technology where he became provost and senior vice president for academic affairs.

John F. Carney III, 2005–11

Ph.D., civil engineering, Northwestern University, 1966

He taught at the University of Connecticut and served as head of civil engineering at Auburn University, associate dean for research and graduate affairs at Vanderbilt University, and provost and vice president of academic affairs at Worcester Polytechnic Institute.

John F. Carney III

Warren K. Wray

Mohammad Dehghani

Cheryl B. Schrader

Christopher G. Maples

Warren "Kent" Wray, 2011–12

Ph.D., civil engineering, Texas A&M University, 1978

He served as chair of civil engineering at Texas Tech University, dean of engineering at Ohio University, and provost at Michigan Technological University before becoming provost and executive vice chancellor at UMR in 2006. He served as interim chancellor in 2011–12.

Cheryl B. Schrader, 2012–17

Ph.D., electrical engineering, Notre Dame University, 1991

She served as associate dean of sciences and engineering at the University of Texas at San Antonio, and dean of the college of engineering and associate vice president for strategic research initiatives at Boise State University.

Christopher G. Maples, 2017–19

Ph.D., geology, Indiana University, 1989

He worked at the Kansas Geological Survey, held program director positions at the National Science Foundation, served as vice president for research at the Desert Research Institute in Nevada, and was president at Oregon Institute of Technology before becoming interim chancellor at S&T.

Mohammad Dehghani, 2019–

Ph.D., mechanical engineering, Louisiana State University, 1987

After teaching at Ohio University, he was new technologies division leader at Lawrence Livermore National Laboratories and director of Johns Hopkins University Systems Institute before becoming vice provost for research, innovation, and entrepreneurship at Stevens Institute of Technology.

University of Missouri Presidents, 1870–2020

Daniel Read, 1866–76

Samuel Spahr Laws, 1876–89

Richard Henry Jesse, 1891–1908

Albert Ross Hill, 1908–21

John Carlton Jones, 1922–23

Stratton Brooks, 1923–30

Walter Williams, 1931–35

Frederick Middlebush, 1935–54

Elmer Ellis, 1955–66

John C. Weaver, 1966–70

C. Brice Ratchford, 1971–76

James Olson, 1977–84

Mel George, 1984–85 (interim)

C. Peter Magrath, 1985–91

George A. Russell, 1991–96

Mel George, 1996–97 (interim)

Manuel T. Pacheco, 1997–2002

Elson S. Floyd, 2003–07

Gary D. Forsee, 2008–11

Stephen J. Owens, 2011–12 (interim)

Timothy M. Wolfe, 2012–15

Michael A. Middleton, 2015–17 (interim)

Mun Y. Choi, 2017–

CHAPTER 2

MINER STUDENTS

In 1948, Enoch R. Needles, famed alumnus of the civil engineering program at MSM, delivered the homecoming convocation address in the Parker Hall auditorium. During his talk, Needles sought to explain the "one big thing which makes a college, which gives it life and vitality, character and individuality."

"With all due respect," Needles said, "it is not the faculty. Nor is it the administration. It is not the campus or the buildings. These things have all a part. But they all shrink to very modest stature in the light of what the students and graduates mean."

While the campus has attracted an increasing number of out-of-state and international students, most who attended MSM, UMR, and S&T during its first 150 years were Missourians of modest means, and they were the young people who U.S. Representative Justin S. Morrill of Vermont had in mind when he fervently promoted the Land Grant College Act of 1862. Morrill was a passionate advocate of "universal education," specifically in the realms of "agriculture and the mechanic arts." The milestone legislation that bears his name helped make higher education available to all social classes by providing land grants for participating states to help them improve access to higher education. In commemorating the centennial of the passage of the law, Harvard historian W.K. Jordan claimed "it was responsible for the democratization of education."

In 19th-century Missouri, those who sought instruction in agriculture headed to the Columbia campus of the University of Missouri, and those interested in mining, metallurgy, and civil engineering headed to Rolla. Missouri residents have dominated the Miner student body from the campus's earliest days. Almost all in the first class of students were from Rolla and the surrounding counties. In 1880, 95 percent were from Missouri, a figure that slipped in 1920 to 58 percent of the freshman class. However, from 1941 on, between 70 and 84 percent of students in freshman classes were from Missouri. Roughly two-thirds of these in-state students hailed from St. Louis and its suburbs, but the campus continued to attract students from small towns and rural areas throughout the state. Over time, the campus attracted students from most states and an increasing number of international students, particularly graduate students from other nations.

1

1: Enoch R. Needles, prominent civil engineering alumnus.

2: Surveying class (1911-12).

3: Students head to their next class on campus in the fall of 1972.

4: Maigha, a Ph.D. student in electrical engineering, receives her hood from Marisea Crow during the 2018 spring commencement.

"... it is not the faculty. Nor is it the administration. It is not the campus or the buildings. These things have all a part. But they all shrink to very modest stature in the light of what the students and graduates mean."

2

3

4

Daniel C. Jackling (second from the right) in an 1891 surveying class at MSM. He ultimately became one of the world's premier mining engineers.

FULFILLING THE LAND GRANT MISSION

Among the thousands of students from Missouri who have attended, the experiences of five dramatically illustrate how the campus has met Morrill's expectations. Gustavus Duncan, Daniel C. Jackling, Harry Kessler, Lelia Thompson Flagg, and Sam Mahaney, all of whom came from modest backgrounds, saw MSM or UMR as an institution that would help them fulfill their hopes for a successful life.

Gustavus Duncan

Born in 1850, Duncan moved with his family from Newark, New Jersey, to Arlington, just west of Rolla, after the Civil War. In 1871, unsure about what kind of job to pursue, Duncan had decided he would try moving to St. Louis to work for a hardware company. On the way, he stopped off in Rolla and attended the "dedication exercises" for the new college. Impressed by the oratory of the day, he met with Director Charles P. Williams, who persuaded him to change his "plan of life," and Duncan became "the first to matriculate as a student in the Missouri School of Mines and Metallurgy." Graduating three years later with a degree in civil engineering, Duncan spent the next half century in the American West as a successful miner and consultant in several states from Minnesota to Nevada. "A pioneer in the development of filtration methods in working with the slime problem in gold cyanide mill practice," Duncan secured five patents during his career.

Daniel C. Jackling

Daniel C. Jackling was born near Appleton City, Missouri, in 1869. Orphaned at age two, he lived with his aunt who farmed in Missouri, Arkansas, and Illinois. He went to school when he could, ending up in the Sedalia public schools, but worked every summer on farms and as a teamster. He attended the State Normal School in Warrensburg, hoping to teach a few years and earn enough to have his own 100-acre tract of land, believing that this was his way to "agricultural independence." However, while working with the city engineer in

Sedalia, Jackling became interested in engineering and transferred to MSM in 1889. He earned a bachelor's degree in metallurgy in three years while working as a student assistant with chemistry professor Cuthbert Conrad. He remained on the faculty one year before departing for the West where he had an extraordinary career as one of the great men of mining in American history. Applying the principles of mass production to mining low-grade copper ore, Jackling was the key force in developing the massive Bingham Canyon open-pit mine in Utah, which enabled him to become one of the richest men in America.

Harry Kessler

Harry Kessler remembered growing up in "a tough section of St. Louis, populated largely by lower, middle-class working families of Irish and German descent." Born in 1901, Kessler had seven siblings, and even though his father owned a wholesale fruit and produce business, the family was poor. Yet, in his late teens Kessler heard "fabulous stories of mining adventures in far-flung corners of the work world" from one of his sister's boyfriends who was a student at MSM, and Kessler decided that he had to enroll there. While his mother was able to give him "a small sheaf of $5 bills" upon his departure for MSM in fall 1920, Kessler worked his way through college in part by gaining employment as a student assistant in both the athletic department and for a mechanical drawing professor. A boxer in high school, Kessler started the boxing program at MSM and became a referee after graduation with a degree in metallurgy. The co-inventor of an improved process in metal casting, Kessler became a consultant for nearly 50 foundries around the country, and, according to a 1955 article in *The New York Times*, he emerged as "the No. 1 foundry trouble-shooter in the nation." Indeed, the paper dubbed him "one of America's top industrialists." Kessler gained even greater fame as a referee on the nationally televised "Friday Night Fights" from New York's Madison Square Garden. Among his more than 150 televised boxing matches, Kessler refereed 15 world title bouts, including two of Muhammed Ali's.

Top: Gustavus Duncan, the first student to register at MSM.

Bottom: Harry Kessler.

Right: Harry Kessler refereeing Muhammad Ali's 1966 heavyweight title boxing match with Cleveland Williams.

1

Lelia Thompson Flagg

Lelia Thompson Flagg graduated from Sumner High School in St. Louis in January 1956 and attended Harris Teachers College for a semester. During her semester there, a professor recommended that she transfer to MSM because of her strong math skills. One of the first African-American students at MSM, Flagg faced a host of challenges in the largely segregated Rolla community. Most significant was a lack of financial assistance. She had a scholarship from Alpha Kappa Alpha Sorority, but little else. Her parents were unable to help her, so for spending money, Flagg played piano for weddings and funerals, an effort that provided her about $10 a month. Moreover, she almost never saw another female student or African-American student during her years (1956–60) at MSM. Fortunately, white students did not treat her badly, and only one professor "picked" on her. Most important, Flagg found great support in her home department of civil engineering, where all the professors treated her well. Professor J. Kent Roberts, her advisor, who also asked her to be his lab assistant, was particularly important to her success. With Roberts' backing Flagg graduated in four years, and her MSM degree led to jobs with the Bureau of Sanitary Engineering in Berkeley, California, the California Department of Water Resources, the Illinois Division of Highways, and admission to the graduate program at the University of California, Berkeley. With a master's

2

3

1: Lelia Thompson Flagg (far right) was one of the female students who established a chapter of the Society of Women Engineers at MSM in 1960.

2: Lelia Thompson Flagg was the first African-American female student to graduate at MSM.

3: Civil engineering professor J. Kent Roberts not only served as Lelia Thompson Flagg's academic advisor, but also asked her to be his lab assistant.

4: Sam Mahaney, a history major at UMR, had a storied military career, rising to the rank of a two-star general.

degree in hand, Flagg also taught at the UMR Engineering Education Center at the University of Missouri-St. Louis, and eventually served as an assistant director of admissions at UMR.

Sam Mahaney

Born in Poplar Bluff, Missouri, in 1962, Sam Mahaney lived for a few years in St. Charles but his family moved to St. James when he was 14. His father, who drove over-the-road trucks, had a small farm between St. James and Cuba. Before going to college, Mahaney worked on the farm "bucking hay bales." He first attended Benedictine College in Atchison, Kansas, before transferring in 1981 to UMR, where he became a history major. To help pay his way through college Mahaney joined the Air Force ROTC. Following graduation in 1985, he led a storied life in the Air Force. His path from electronic warfare navigator to two-star general included earning a master's degree in public administration and working five years for a law degree from Saint Louis University. He became a Georgetown University Capitol Hill Fellow in Washington in 2004 and then a Legislative Fellow of the chairman of the House of Representatives Defense Appropriations Committee. In 2007–08, he became a National Security Fellow at Harvard University. He even spent some time as an adjunct professor at Georgetown University Law Center. By 2018, Mahaney had become chief of staff for Air Mobility Command at Scott Air Force Base in Illinois. During a talk to his Harvard class, a three-star general informed his classmates that Mahaney was a "genius" because he had graduated from the "Harvard of the Midwest," an institution that had given him a substantial leg up in his successful quest for a rewarding career.

4

WHAT MAKES A MINER?

Most who described the students attracted to the Rolla campus found them to be first-generation college students like Duncan, Jackling, Kessler, Flagg, and Mahaney: ambitious, hard-working young people intent upon getting a good job after graduation. The staff of the 1939 *Rollamo* yearbook described a "typical" day for Miners of that era that would also apply to most other eras. "The average student arises sometime between seven and half-past each morning in order that he may thus have enough time to prepare rather leisurely for his eight o'clock class. The routine of class attendance is quite similar for each of the four years — lecture classes each hour from eight till noon." After a lunch break, laboratory classes lasted until 4 p.m., and then it was time to study, and "engineering students have plenty of it."

There was good reason for all the work. Regardless of their choice of major, most generations of Miner students encountered degree programs with a challenging curriculum, and a large number of credit hours. Between 1918 and 1922, when the campus was on a trimester plan, students had to complete between 185 and 197 credit hours, depending upon the degree program. Over time that number dwindled. In 1922, engineering degrees required 172 hours, and the general science program required 130 hours. In 1969, all the engineering degree programs reduced the number of required hours to 132. Fifty years later, degree programs ranged from 129 hours in the humanities and social sciences to 131 hours in chemical engineering.

Even with the diminished number of credit hours, the school from its earliest years had made it clear that it was "no place for *idlers*." MSM did not want "those who do not propose to give their *whole time* to the work allotted to them by the faculty." Freshmen discovered that attitude during their orientation, when administrators were given to telling the new crop of students, as Dean Curtis Laws Wilson did in 1947, "Fifty percent of you will not be here for your sophomore year." As Harry Kessler explained, MSM "was a hard school in the sense that it took its purpose very seriously as did I." While there would always be exceptions, the vast majority of the thousands of Miner students agreed with Kessler. Walter Remmers, who was at MSM with Kessler, recalled believing that he did not have to work too hard because he had been fortunate to have a good high school education. Initially, he did not make much of an effort until one of his professors called him "the laziest man in school." That got him started working, and he never stopped.

Later graduates similarly remembered what was required to handle the demanding curriculum and heavy workload. Douglas Christensen, who entered MSM in 1940, remembered "a very lot of hard studying" with "all eight o'clock classes plus every day laboratories including Saturday mornings." Kenneth Cole, who graduated in 1954, recalled that "we only got long hours and hard work." Richard L. Brake, a 1961 graduate, noted, "I studied, went to class, and then studied some more." Everett E. Adam Jr., a 1963 graduate, agreed: "Most of my time was spent in class, labs and studying." Adam's classmate James R. Knox wistfully recalled "taking breaks from studying to walk around town at night with a friend, seeing 'normal' people in their living rooms relaxing and enjoying life, with no worries about homework problems or exams."

Below: Once called the "laziest man in school" by a professor, Walter Remmers earned two degrees at MSM in the 1920s. He and his wife Miriam (left) provided funding for the Remmers Special Artist/Lecture Series. Here, they are with 1985 Remmers Lecture speaker Jeane Kirkpatrick, former U.S. Ambassador to the United Nations.

Opposite: Geology professor Tom Beveridge was a keen observer of the "typical" Miner undergraduate.

ROUGH SHOD, ROUGH MANNERED

Hard-working they certainly were, but Miners were not particularly sophisticated. In 1915, a state legislator argued that Miners were unlike the students at the University of Missouri campus, who he claimed wore "pigeon-toed shoes and high collars." Rather, MSM students "wore brogans and flannel shirts and were close to the people." Walter Remmers remembered that his fellow students in the 1920s were "unschooled in the social graces." Mining, metallurgy, and engineering seemed to attract only those seeking a rough and rugged vocation. English Professor Jim Pogue, who joined the faculty 40 years later, recalled his students as "macho, rough shod, rough mannered, and roughly dressed," although they tended to be polite at least when they were around faculty members.

In the mid-1970s, geology professor Tom Beveridge offered a "composite" picture of typical Miner undergraduates, a description that expands upon the Remmers and Pogue descriptions. He agreed that they could be "slightly raunchy"; however, they were "tolerably clean." More important, you would not find "a social snob" among them, as they come "from a middle class background." Beveridge believed that they tended to accept "fellow students for what they are regardless of their background." Because they were "democratic," Miners were "informal" and given to addressing their professors as "Hey Prof." Yet, they were also "somewhat conservative," and rarely fell "prey" to political "extremists."

Indeed, Miner students were generally indifferent to national politics. In the depths of the Great Depression, for example, only 4 percent participated in a poll on the presidential election of 1932. Yet, even with that small sample, the "somewhat conservative" nature of Miners noted by Beveridge was evident. Fourteen favored Republican incumbent Herbert Hoover, seven favored Democratic challenger Franklin Roosevelt, one favored Socialist Norman Thomas, and another favored Communist William Z. Foster.

1926 *Missouri Miner* editorial on Prohibition.

PAGE SIX. THE MISSOURI MINER.

THE MISSOURI MINER.

The Official Publication of the M. S. M. Alumni Association.

Published by the ... the Alumni, Students, and Faculty of the Missouri School of Mines and Metallurgy, Rolla, Mo.

Entered as second class matter April 2, 1915, at the Post Office at Rolla, Missouri, under the Act of March 3, 1879.

STAFF.

Harold S. Thomas......Editor
C. F. Luckfield......Business Manager

News Department.

Paul L. Hopper......Associate Editor
Prof. C. Y. Clayton......Alumni
E. R. Cushing......Sports
Howard Histed......Assistant
M E. Suhre......Assistant
J. H. Reid......Assistant

Features Department.

E. C. Miller......Associate Editor
W. C. Keniston......Columnist
R. S. Reich......Exchanges
J. E. McCauley......Assistant
J. H. Brickner......Assistant

Business Management.

R.A. McReynolds Asst. Business Mgr.
R. P. Baumgartner Advertising Mgr.
K. R. Neal......Asst. Advertising Mgr.
H. B. Moreland......Circulation Mgr.
C. W. Ambler Asst. Circulation Mgr.
M. B. Layne....Asst. Circulation Mgr.

Dr. J. W. Barley......Faculty Advisor

Subscription price: Domestic, $1.50 per year; Foreign, $2.00. Single Copy, 8 cents.

Issued Every Monday.

LIQUOR-DRINKING AT M. S. M.

The much-discussed question of whether prohibition is a success or a failure comes to mind when we view St. Pats in retrospect. It would of course be out of the question to endeavor to draw comprehensive conclusions from observations made on our recent festival. Judging by the St. Pats celebration and by other social events over a period of some months, however, we feel safe in saying that drinking is decidedly on the decline among the students at M. S. M. Comments have been heard from visitors, faculty members, and townspeople on the absence of liquor from the house parties and dances during St. Pats, and the students are to be commended on this. Colleges and universities have at times received much unfavorable publicity due to drinking bouts and parties, and although students as a class are not the chief violators of the Eighteenth Amendment, the colleges stand in the full glare of the limelight and receive the unsavory notoriety due to liquor parties and the scandals in which they often end.

We do not intend to create a false impression or to intimate that drinking has ever been a great evil among the students at M. S. M. It has never been necessary for the faculty to take drastic action against drinking here. The average student has a definite purpose in attending M. S. M. and is here for business. The fact that the Eighteenth Amendment means something at M. S. M. and the creditable manner in which the big celebration was staged is worthy of comment. We take pride in the fact that our school is a leader in the field of Engineering. We might also take pride in the fact that no faculty coercion is necessary to prevent the promiscuous use of liquor in our campus activities.

However, because many Miners have liked to drink, they were attracted to the politics surrounding the 18th Amendment to the Constitution that banned the manufacture, distribution, and sale of alcohol in 1919. Two polls taken by the *Missouri Miner* illustrate how the students felt. In March 1926, the editor argued "that drinking is decidedly on the decline among the students at MSM" Yet, three weeks later, only a few favored retaining Prohibition. Thirty-nine percent favored repeal, and 58 percent supported a modification of the Volstead Act (which provided for the enforcement of the 18th Amendment) "to permit the sale of wines and beer." Three years later, 44 percent favored repeal, and 36 percent favored a modification. Yet, as Beveridge's comment illustrated, their views were more moderate than those at other schools. As a journalist for the *Missouri Miner* pointed out in April 1930, "recent articles in the larger papers show us that Dartmouth, Purdue, and many larger schools have polled a much heavier wet vote than did MSM."

In the early 21st century, the campus conducted surveys of the political views of entering freshmen, and the results demonstrate the enduring conservatism of the student body. In 2007, for example, nearly half defined themselves as "middle-of-the-road," a third defined themselves as "conservative," and only 16 percent defined themselves as "liberal." On the major issues of that year, they were liberal on a few issues — 75 percent believed "the federal government is not doing enough to control environmental pollution," 60 percent believed "a national health care plan is needed to cover everybody's medical costs," and 55 percent believed "the federal government should do more to control the sale of handguns." However, they were conservative on most other issues. Seventy-eight percent did not want the death penalty abolished, 77 percent "believed that marijuana should not be legalized," 64 percent believed "undocumented immigrants should be denied access to public education," 58 percent believed that abortions should not be legal, 54 percent believed that affirmative action in college admissions should be abolished, and 53 percent believed that same-sex couples should not be permitted to marry.

The Vietnam War was a particular challenge for the conservative campus. In the 1968 presidential campaign, one that featured a nation deeply divided over the war in Southeast Asia, Miner students again displayed their conservatism. In national polls taken in spring 1968, most college students across the nation expressed a preference for liberal Democrat Eugene McCarthy, but Miner students favored conservative Republican Richard Nixon. Similarly, while only 21 percent of students nationally favored "an all-out" effort to win the war, nearly a third of Miner students did.

The growing anti-war movement came to the UMR campus in fall 1969 with a "teach-in." Students filled the Mechanical Engineering Auditorium as philosophy professor Bob Oakes led a discussion in support of a nationwide movement to have a moratorium on the war, and the College Young Democrats presented a petition to Senator Thomas Eagleton "calling for immediate withdrawal from Viet Nam [sic]." *Missouri Miner* editor Tim Corbett pointed out, however, that the moratorium "was largely ignored by the students." Two weeks later, students had an opportunity to sign petitions in support of withdrawing from Vietnam or in support of President Nixon's policies. More than half supported the president.

In March 1970, over 200 Miner students drove to Fort Leonard Wood to donate blood "to show support for the men and forces fighting in Vietnam." Two months later, following the shooting of four students at Kent State University by Ohio national guardsmen, about 150 anti-war students gathered in front of the Wilson Library. They were opposed by about 50 others, many of whom were ROTC cadets there to

protest the demonstration. The diminishing anti-war sentiment among students was clear in April 1971 when David Dellinger, a leading anti-war activist, attracted only a small crowd, one a critic characterized as "peaceniks, long-hairs, whoopies, and other interested students."

A few other national and international events attracted students' attention. In 1979, several hundred demonstrated to protest the Iranian seizure of the U.S. Embassy in Tehran. Four years later, members of the Korean Student Association, Chinese Student Association, Thai Student Association and Vietnamese Student Association held a demonstration in response to the Soviet Union's downing of a South Korean airliner, an act that killed 269 people. In 1985, several students took part in a day of protest against apartheid in South Africa. On September 13, 2001, several hundred UMR students, faculty, staff, and administrators gathered near the "Hockey Puck" to pay tribute to the thousands of Americans killed in the 9/11 attacks on the Twin Towers in New York and the Pentagon in Washington. Nearly 400 of them also donated blood as a symbolic gesture of support for all the injured who survived.

On rare occasions, students protested conditions on campus. In 1949, following the posting of mid-semester grades for physics classes, disgruntled students held a demonstration. According to the *Missouri Miner* account, angry students "gathered at Harris Hall" and walked along State Street, "carrying torches" and dummies representing three of the physics professors. They walked downtown to Pine Street and then back to campus. "On the lawn in front of the physics office in Norwood Hall the group applied torches to the dummies accompanied by chants of 'Down with Physics.'"

The Missouri

MINER

UNIVERSITY OF MISSOURI - ROLLA

VOL. 56 WEDNESDAY, MAY 13, 1970 ROLLA, MISSOURI NO. 25

A UMR First

Students Take Lunch-Break To Demonstrate

By Jim Wrobleski

Last Friday, a few UMR students and faculty members closed their books and laid down their slide rules to express their feelings about conditions in the U. S. and in Indochina. Tempers [illegible]

and began milling around. The crowds remained until the twelve thirty bell rang. After that time a small gathering remained around the base of the flagpole and students could be seen under the shade trees working physics problems and talking together.

There were a few interesting events though. The first came about as a result of a desire by the people in charge of the gathering to lower the U. S. flag to half-mast in mourning for the loss of lives in Indochina and at Kent University. Some students protested and a tight knot of them, with teeth showing, pressed around the flagpole, formed a defensive wall and held firm. A petition was passed around to request lowering of the flag, and by twelve thirty, had gained more than two hundred signatures. The defenders still held their position and cried out that any flag-lowering would have to take place through proper channels. So, as soon as was decided what were proper channels, the matter was brought up to the Student Council where it apparently died for lack of nourishment. A delegation was sent to Dr. Baker to gain his opinion. But, ...

By one thirty Old Glory was still waving at the height of the pole, the sprinklers were going, the light poles down the quadrangle were on. A small, but diligent gathering of students stood by the flag pole, occasionally tugging at the lines to make sure the flag was still up. Talk of peace and war and Viet Nam was replaced by talk of Statics and girls and cars. Administration officials walked by and smiled.

But wait, what about the demonstration? One student said; "Well, if you take X and then square it, you . . . ."

Students Protect Flag

Above: Bob Oakes, who in 1969 moderated a campus open forum on a possible moratorium on the Vietnam War, was a professor of philosophy at UMR.

Right: May 1970 *Missouri Miner* article on the campus anti-war demonstration in support of the students killed at Kent State University.

1: The Newman Club, an organization for Catholic students, held registration on campus for new members.

2: House of Mercier Club in 1928.

3: January 20, 2012, marked the opening of the Islamic Center of Rolla. Members of the center provided tours of the new building for S&T students and the community.

4: Jewish Student Community, Hillel, walked in the 2015 Celebration of Nations parade in Rolla.

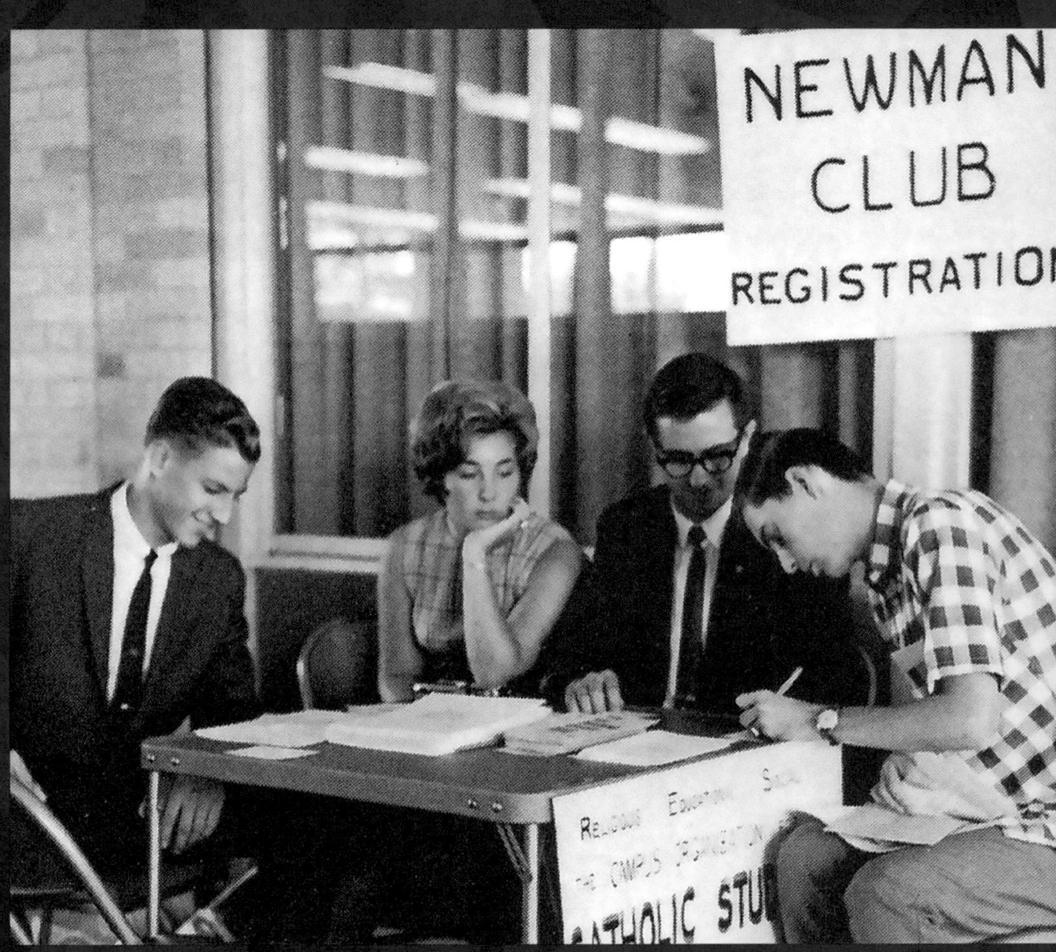

RELIGIOUS AFFILIATIONS

Over time, ever-fewer college students nationally identify with a religious affiliation, but the opposite has been true with Miner students. In 1922, 32 percent of students at MSM had no religious affiliation, a percentage that dropped to 12 in 1949. That trend continued into the 21st century, with only 8 percent of entering freshmen in 2007 having no religious affiliation. Most were Methodists, Presbyterians, Catholics, or Baptists in the early 1920s, but by 2007, over a quarter of Miner students were Catholic, 12 percent were Baptists, and 9 percent were Lutherans. Most not only had a religious affiliation, but also were more likely to attend religious services than college students nationally. In 1925, the first religious organization on campus was established. The Mercier Club, formed by the local parish priest Father S.P. Stocking, initially had 17 members and developed into a short-lived fraternity. Other religious organizations developed rapidly on campus after World War II, including Gamma Delta, the Wesley Foundation, and the Baptist Student Union. By 1961, there were nine religious organizations, with the Newman Club and its nearly 200 members emerging as the largest. In 2019, there were 16 religiously affiliated groups, and with a Muslim Student Association and Hillel they reflected a more diverse student body.

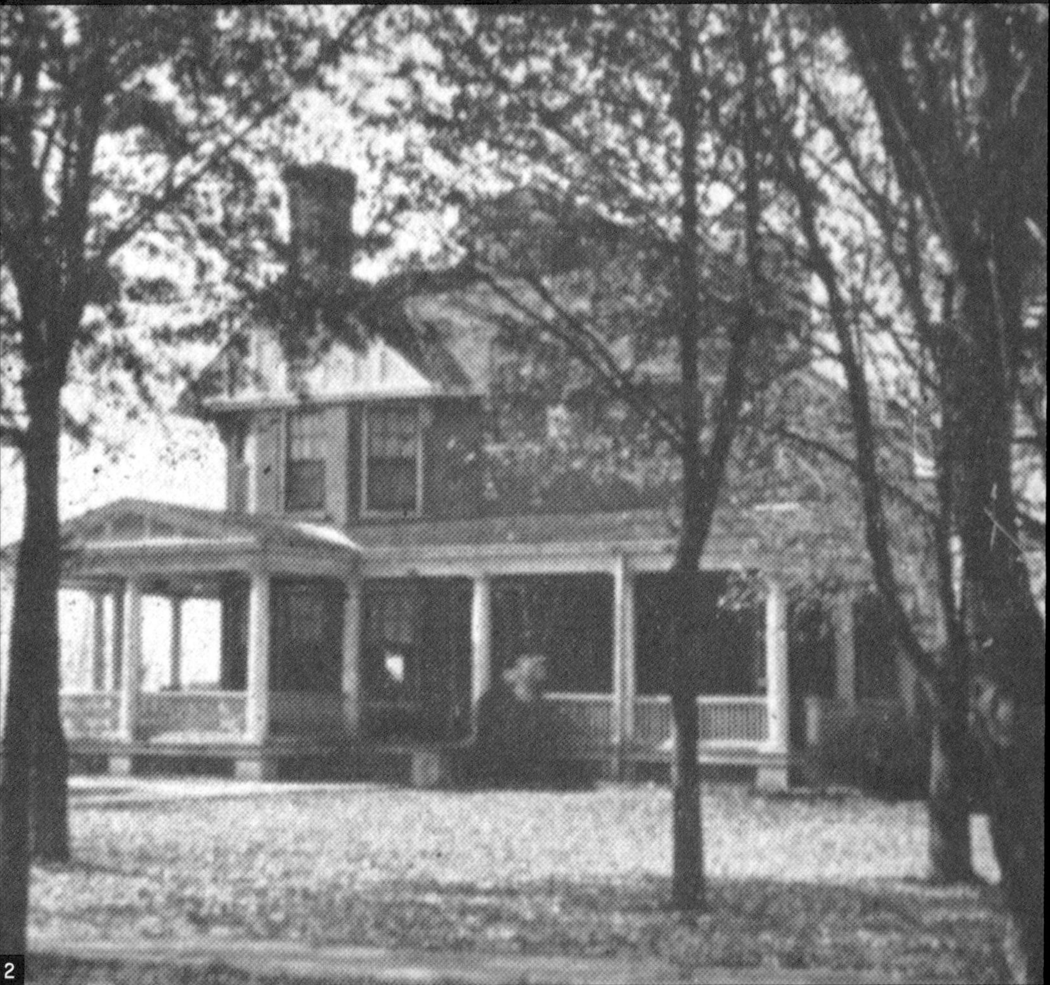
2

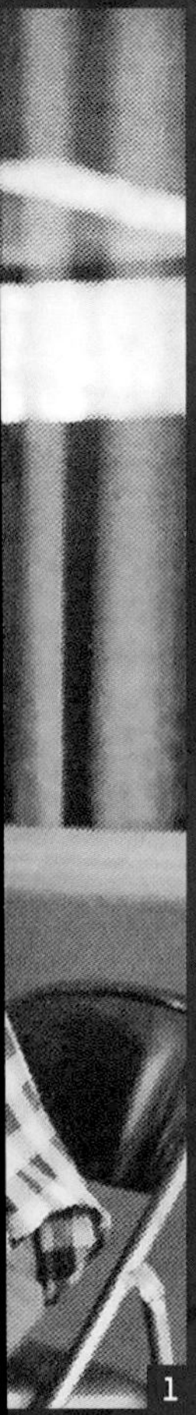

1

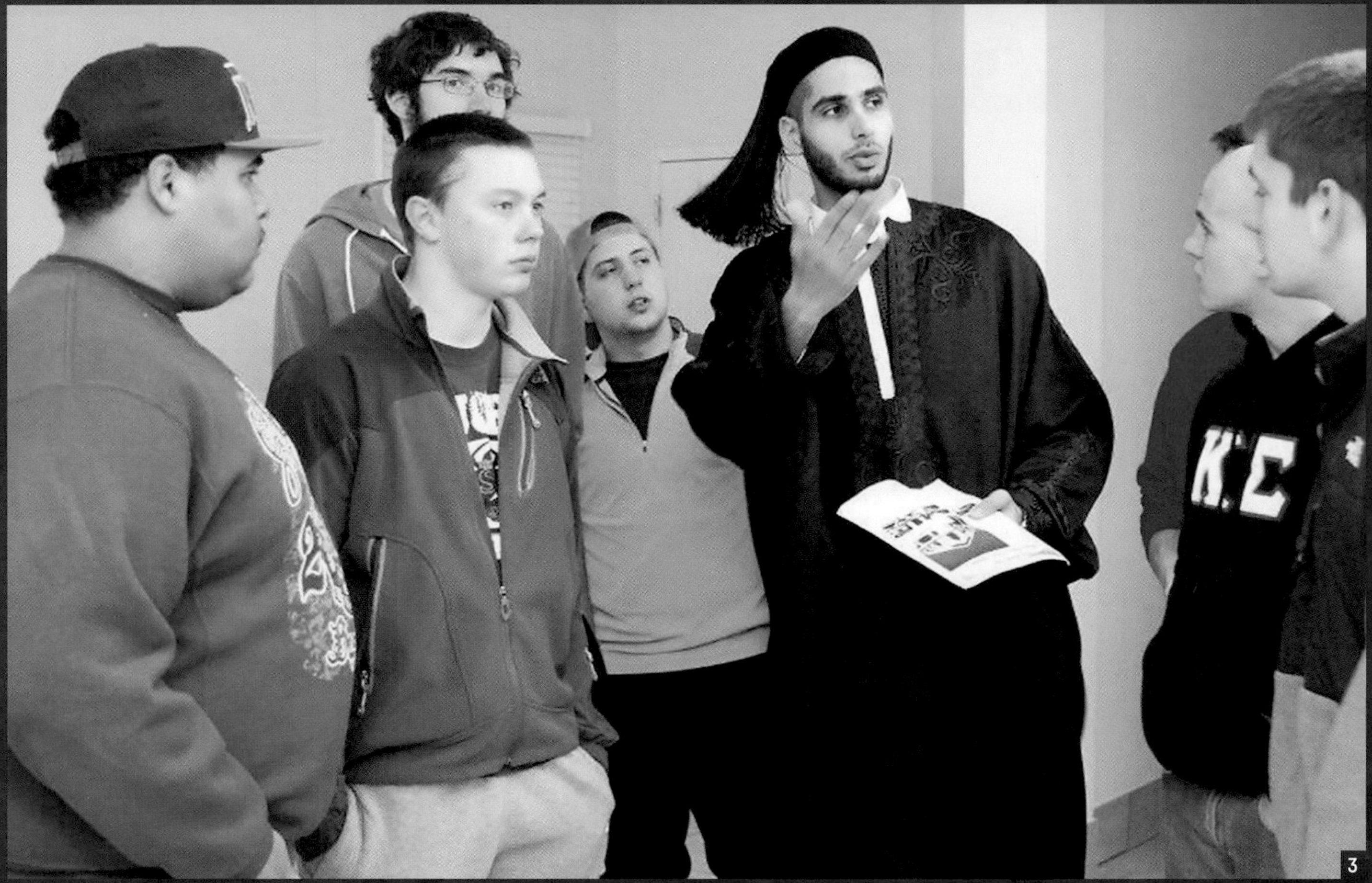

3

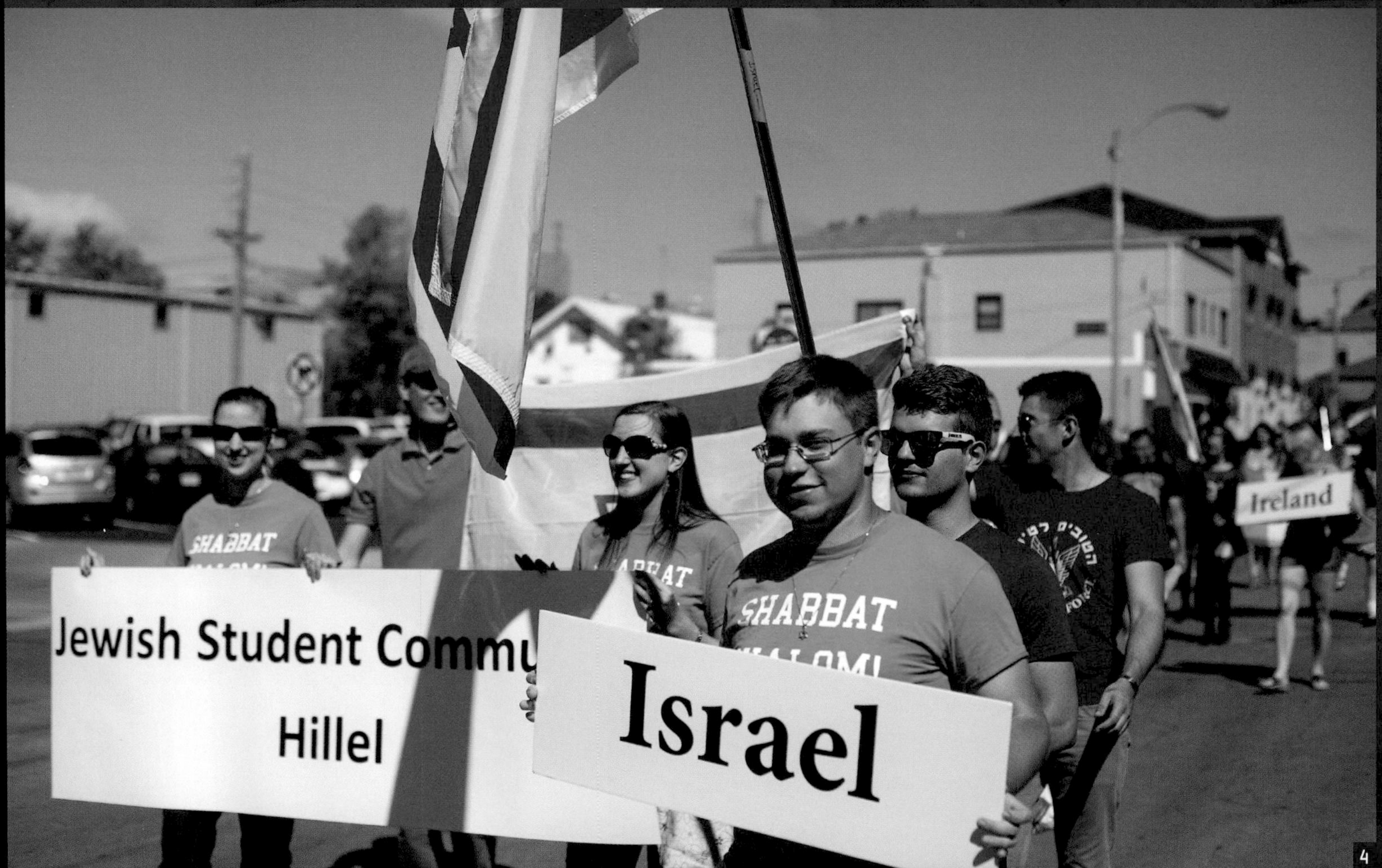

4

FINANCIAL ASSISTANCE

Because there was no financial assistance available, it was fortunate for students in the early decades at MSM that the cost of attendance was modest. For example, for the 1888–89 academic year, the estimated cost of tuition, laboratory fees, books, and renting a room was roughly $200. Three decades later, the total had only risen to about $300. To pay their way some early 20th-century Miners found employment as student workers in academic departments, the library, the gymnasium, or in administrative offices. In 1929, for example, the 35 student assistants made 35 cents an hour for their labors.

Offered in 1917, the first scholarship — from the Woman's Auxiliary of the American Institute of Mining and Metallurgical Engineers — provided $750 a year for four years. In the 1920s, the A.P. Green Fire Brick Co. of Mexico, Missouri, began offering scholarships and loans to students majoring in ceramic engineering. While it took several years for other scholarships to emerge, Daniel C. Jackling established an important loan fund through a 1909 gift of $1,000; he periodically added to that figure until he had contributed $20,000 three decades later. The amount of money available increased annually as students repaid their loans at 4 percent interest. In 1951, the *MSM Alumnus* reported that the Jackling Fund had assisted 1,400 students in 40 years. Others followed Jackling's lead, and by mid-century 300 students were receiving a total of over $23,000 a year. Passage of the National Defense Education Act in 1958 led to loans of about $600 annually for students with financial need and who had graduated in the top 25 percent of their high school class. In 1950, the board of curators made available 125 "Curators Scholarships" to cover incidental fees. The following decade, Amy McNutt established two foundations: one for her husband, MSM alumnus Vachel H. McNutt, and the other for her second husband Robert Emmett Dye, also an MSM alumnus, to provide scholarships for students majoring in geology and mining engineering.

Eventually the campus began investing money from general operating funds in financial aid. For the 1962–63 academic year, 278 students received scholarships, and another 366 received loans. To administer that assistance, UMR established the position of director of student financial aid in the mid-1960s. Ray Pendergrass was the first to hold this position critical to providing access to higher education. The campus commitment to provide meaningful financial assistance continued to grow. By 1978, nearly a third of students received either grants, scholarships, or loans from the campus as well as from federal and state grants. Twenty years later, over three-quarters of undergraduate students received financial aid; from 2007, the proportion increased to between 80 percent and 94 percent every year.

Above: Amy McNutt established foundations in honor of her first husband Vachel H. McNutt and her second husband Robert Emmett Dye.

Above right: Ray Pendergrass, director of student aids and awards.

ACCOMMODATIONS

In 1871, the campus had only one building, and so it could offer no accommodations for students. Most of the first students lived at home in Rolla. Others had to rent rooms from residents or above businesses. Gustavus Duncan and five friends were pioneers in this regard. They rented rooms above the Morris Hardware Store downtown. Their bedroom was a large room with a fireplace, the front room was a study, and they had a kitchen, all for $12 a month including meals. In 1880, almost 60 percent of the students still lived at home while the rest boarded in private residences except for two who stayed at the Crandall House Hotel on Eighth Street near the railroad tracks downtown. The state legislature did appropriate funds for a dormitory that opened in 1889. Known as the Club House, it could accommodate more than two dozen students who paid $12 a month for room and board. It lasted little more than a decade, with only four students living there in 1900. Eventually, it became the residence for the director. Well into the early 1960s, many students still rented rooms in private residences for $15 to $30 a month.

1: Arthur Terrell and H.P. Rogers in their 1890s room off campus.

2: Many students rented rooms in boarding houses in the early 1910s.

3: The Club House, which functioned as MSM's first dormitory, opened in 1889. It later served as the residence for the directors, deans, and chancellors of the campus.

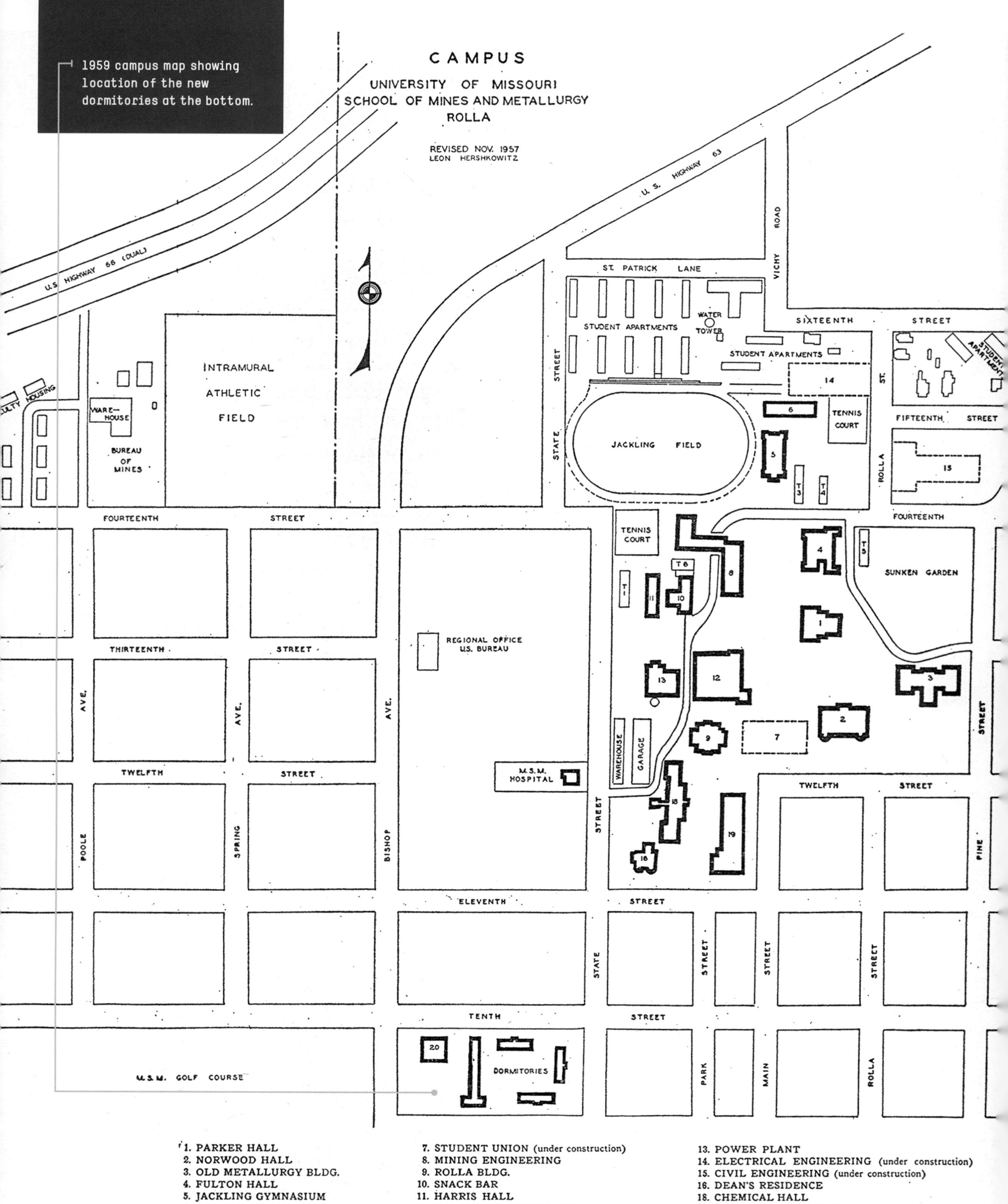
CAMPUS
UNIVERSITY OF MISSOURI
SCHOOL OF MINES AND METALLURGY
ROLLA
REVISED NOV. 1957
LEON HERSHKOWITZ
U.S. HIGHWAY 66 (DUAL)
U.S. HIGHWAY 63
INTRAMURAL ATHLETIC FIELD
WARE-HOUSE
BUREAU OF MINES
ST. PATRICK LANE
VICHY ROAD
STUDENT APARTMENTS
WATER TOWER
SIXTEENTH STREET
FIFTEENTH STREET
FOURTEENTH STREET
THIRTEENTH STREET
TWELFTH STREET
ELEVENTH STREET
TENTH STREET
JACKLING FIELD
TENNIS COURT
SUNKEN GARDEN
REGIONAL OFFICE U.S. BUREAU
M.S.M. HOSPITAL
WAREHOUSE
GARAGE
STATE STREET
ROLLA ST.
POOLE AVE.
SPRING AVE.
BISHOP AVE.
PINE STREET
PARK STREET
MAIN STREET
ROLLA STREET
DORMITORIES
M.S.M. GOLF COURSE
1. PARKER HALL
2. NORWOOD HALL
3. OLD METALLURGY BLDG.
4. FULTON HALL
5. JACKLING GYMNASIUM
6. MILITARY BLDG.
7. STUDENT UNION (under construction)
8. MINING ENGINEERING
9. ROLLA BLDG.
10. SNACK BAR
11. HARRIS HALL
12. MECHANICAL ENGINEERING
13. POWER PLANT
14. ELECTRICAL ENGINEERING (under construction)
15. CIVIL ENGINEERING (under construction)
16. DEAN'S RESIDENCE
18. CHEMICAL HALL
19. CHEMICAL ENGINEERING
20. NEW CAFETERIA

1959 campus map showing location of the new dormitories at the bottom.

Wooden barracks purchased from the military served as temporary structures needed for post-World War II veterans attending MSM on the GI Bill.

Nagogami Terrace opened in 1960 and consisted of a group of two-story apartments built by the university for use of married students and their families. All units included a living room, kitchen, bath, and one or two bedrooms.

The post-World War II flood of GIs who came to campus put enormous pressure on the administration to find suitable housing. Dean Curtis Laws Wilson was able to purchase over 20 wooden barracks from the Army Airport at nearby Vichy and from the military base at Fort Leonard Wood. He located them on the block between Jackling Field and St. Patrick's Church and on an empty lot one block east of Jackling Gymnasium. The latter buildings served as accommodations for married students. Some opted to live in mobile homes in various locations including the Huffman Trailer Court in east Rolla. By 1960, married students could opt to live in the Nagogami Terrace apartments just two blocks west of Jackling Field. For two decades after World War II, some athletes, commonly called "Jackling Jocks," lived in Jackling Gymnasium in cramped rooms around the basketball court and indoor swimming pool. Although Dean Wilson initially deemed that option "undesirable" and "abolished" that policy, he permitted its renewal in the wake of the school's enormous housing needs of the late 1940s.

"It allowed me to get through college without starving to death."

Many students purchased meal plans at eating clubs scattered around the perimeter of the campus. With the first one established in 1902, they remained a critical meal option for students for over 70 years. By 1916, the Grubstakers, Muckers, Prospectors, Corsair Club, Bonanza Club, and Beanery provided meals for nearly half of the campus's 265 students. In addition to the campus eating clubs, which students managed, there were also women in Rolla who operated eating houses. In the post-World War II years, students could get good, home-cooked meals at the eating clubs for about $30 a month. These arrangements were vital for many. As 1960 alumnus Harold Bennett recalled, "It allowed me to get through college without starving to death." As late as 1960 there were still five with several hundred members: Engineers' Club, Fifty-Niners Club, Prospectors' Club, Shamrock Club, and Tech Club.

A few of the eating clubs also provided rooms for students and some reorganized as fraternities. Beginning with Sigma Nu, social fraternities came to MSM in 1903 and eventually provided an important housing option for students. Within four years there were four more fraternities. Sigma Nu, Kappa Alpha, and Kappa Sigma had houses for their members. The number of fraternities steadily grew, joined by Pi Delta Chi, the first sorority, in 1940. By 1978, fraternities housed about 1,100, and two sororities housed about 70. Two decades later there were 20 Greek houses still accommodating the same total number of students.

1

2

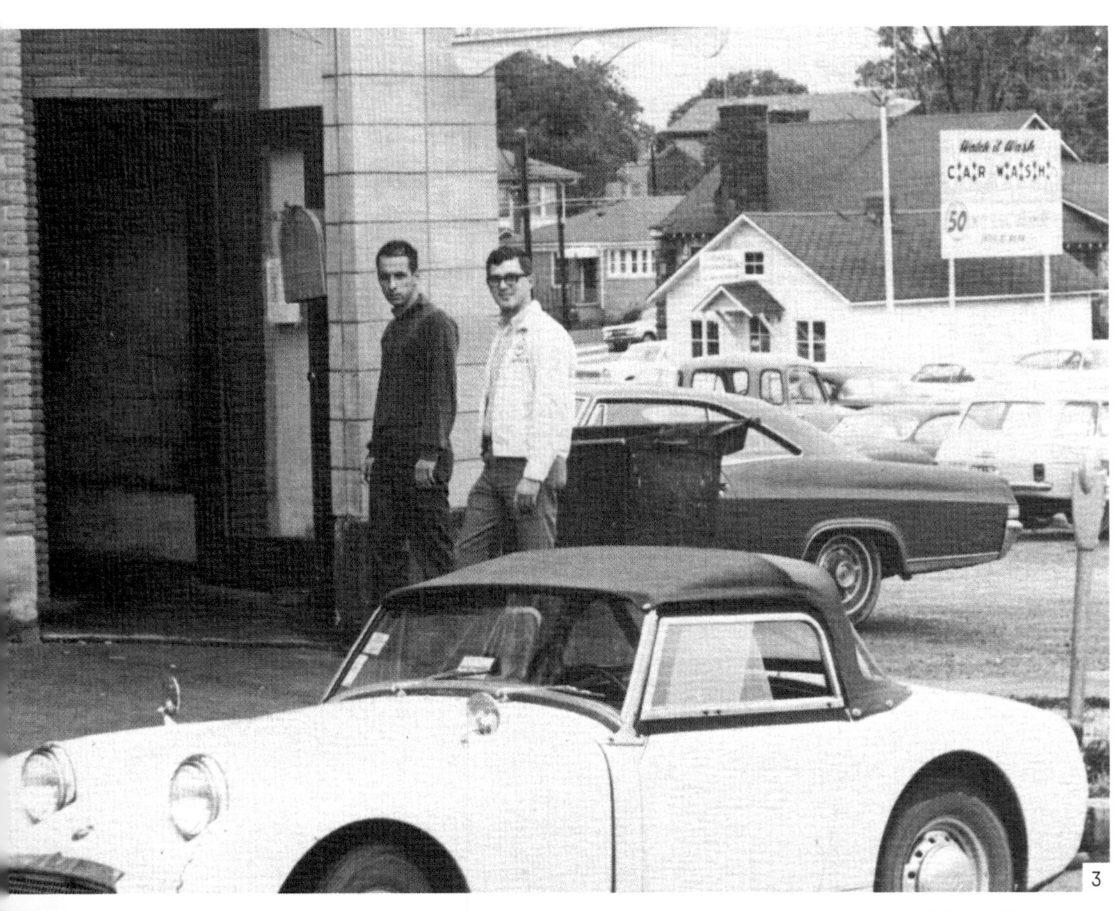

3

1: The Prospector's Club was one of the many eating clubs that provided meal plans for students.

2: Sigma Nu was the first social fraternity to come to MSM in 1903.

3: Like many eating clubs, the Fifty-Niners Club provided students with nutritious meals at reasonable rates. Students cleaned up after meals in exchange for their board.

4: Kappa Delta, one of two sororities in the late 1970s, provided additional housing and social options for female students.

4

UNIVERSITY OF MISSOURI-ROLLA
THOMAS JEFFERSON
RESIDENCE HALL
1

INTER STATE
MOTEL
NEW
2

3

4

1: Members of Thomas Jefferson Residence Hall's 1979 Executive Council are pictured in front of the single-tower building. The university purchased the building in 1976 to provide housing for over 500 students.

2: Before completing the second tower of Thomas Jefferson Residential Hall in 1982, the university leased several area motels, including the Interstate Motel, to accommodate an influx of new students.

3: University Commons residential complex in 2019.

4: Miner Village residential complex in 2017.

Eventually, dormitories, later called residence halls or residential commons, became the most important option for students. After the aborted attempt of establishing a dormitory with the 1890s Club House, MSM did not have a dormitory until 1950. Eight years later it had four, all named for MSM alumni killed in World War II: Thomas Wallace Kelly, John Milroy McAnerney, William Altman, and Willard Farrar. Along with a cafeteria named for alumnus John Rayl, the complex was between 9th and 10th Streets along State Street. Nearly a decade later the campus added a fifth dormitory named for Orvid Holtman, another MSM alumnus killed in World War II. In 1962, MSM bought a house on State Street to provide a dormitory for the slowly growing number of female students. Fourteen years later, UMR purchased the Thomas Jefferson Residential Hall. It had struggled as a private dormitory, but with its capacity to accommodate over 500 students, TJ helped to meet the university's need to address a rapidly increasing enrollment. In the late 1970s and early 1980s, before a second tower could be completed for TJ in 1982, the crush of new students forced the campus to lease off-campus private housing, including several motels.

A far cry from the beginning of the century, by the end of the 20th century, UMR provided accommodations for over half its students through residence halls, Greek housing, and apartment complexes. More changes were on the horizon as the campus opened Residential Commons 1 and 2 and University Commons between 2005 and 2017 with their suite- and apartment-style accommodations, as well as apartments in Miner Village and Rolla Suites. Including TJ, the university had rooms for over 2,200 students in 2018.

Popular mathematics professor George Dean was critical of MSM's low entrance and graduation requirements in the late 19th century.

STUDENT SUCCESS

In the early decades of MSM most of the students were not ready to tackle collegiate-level work. Gustavus Duncan, the first student to register, wrote, "I presume that rarely in our Country was there assembled for technical collegiate education a class so unprepared as the one then confronting the teachers of that school. I think none of us had completed the common school courses of that time." He and his fellow students were not unusual. Outside St. Louis and Kansas City, high schools were not widespread in Missouri in the early 1870s. Because Rolla was one of those communities without a high school, several residents asked Director Charles Williams to begin a program of preparatory studies at MSM, focusing upon "advanced arithmetic and elementary algebra." It was not an unusual request. The University of Missouri had had a preparatory program from the early 1840s. Over the first two decades of MSM's existence, preparatory students made up a sizeable portion, if not an outright majority, of enrolled students. The faculty enhanced the program, adding spelling, English grammar, civil government, U.S. history, and astronomy. In addition, the campus offered "optional" courses in bookkeeping, Latin, Greek, German, French, Spanish, and drawing. The purpose of the program was to prepare students for the technical degree programs in mining engineering, metallurgy, and civil engineering. However, many students used the program to gain certification in bookkeeping and teaching.

Walter "Buck" Richards, who became director of MSM in 1893, was appalled by all of this. MSM in the 1880s, he claimed, "seemed to have sunk the instruction to meet the abilities, the preparation, and the disposition of the actual applicants. Everyone who wished to enter was admitted, and was taught whatever he might elect to study or might be capable of learning." George Dean, who began his studies at MSM in 1888 and later became one of its most popular professors, was even more uncharitable. Much given to hyperbole, Dean wrote, "In the old days, when a student had nerve enough and thought he had enough credits for graduation, he used to get a club in one hand and a gun in the other, and go around and hold up the faculty."

The state legislature ended the preparatory program in 1894, forcing the Rolla community to develop its own high school. More important for MSM, under Richards' leadership, the campus required entrance examinations in mathematics, English, science, and languages for students who had not attended a growing list of accredited high schools in Missouri. George Ladd, Richards' successor, claimed that the new "entrance requirements of the school are as high or higher than are those of the Michigan and Colorado School of Mines." Yet, in 1915, in a letter to A. Ross Hill, the president of the University of Missouri, an official with the Carnegie Foundation wrote about MSM, "it is clear that the standards of admission at that institution are, and have been, exceedingly low, with little or no regard to the conditions laid down in the catalogue."

In the early 1920s, the campus began to administer both a "technical test" and a "test for quickness of thinking" to entering freshmen and discovered that MSM students performed below the average of their peers at 43 engineering colleges and universities on both tests. Fortunately, as high schools spread throughout the state most of them offered the courses in algebra, plane geometry, and solid geometry that MSM expected of entering freshmen. Yet, as students became better prepared for the rigors of college mathematics, their preparation lagged in other areas. In the early 1950s, for example, faculty complaints about the reading and writing skills of their students led the humanities department to offer a special once-a-week class in reading to address that deficiency.

By the mid-1960s, the caliber of entering freshman classes had markedly improved, with nearly a third of them ranking in the top 10 percent of their high school graduating class, and virtually every new freshman class was stronger academically. By the late 1970s, fully 40 percent were in the top 10 percent of their high school class, and over the next four decades that percentage remained between 42 percent and 51 percent. Another measure of the ever-stronger freshman classes was in their average composite ACT score. In 1977 it was 24.6 and rose to 26.3 in 1990. From

1994 it remained in the range of 27 to 28. In 2018, as a consequence of the progressively stronger freshman classes, Missouri S&T became only the second university in Missouri, joining Truman State University, to gain the designation of "highly selective" in its admissions criteria. This meant that students with a score of 27 or higher on the ACT were automatically admitted.

Predictably, as freshman ACT scores improved, so did grade point averages. In the early years, the campus used a 10.0 grade scale. Among the first 22 students, the highest average was 9.68 and the lowest 3.25. In 1926, the campus adopted a 3.0 grade scale, which it maintained for three decades. That year, the freshmen had a miserable .49 grade point average and the seniors a 1.34. In 1957, the campus adopted its current 4.0 grade point system. The overall grade point average for the campus was 2.39 in 1966. The overall grade point average increased subsequently over the next half century, reaching 3.09 in 2018.

Retention rates likewise improved dramatically. Almost 40 percent of the 1907 freshman class did not return for a second year. The author of the 1908 sophomore class history in the *Rollamo* noted that "many of our dear class mates [sic] have departed for scenes of lesser strife." Worse, the author of the 1914 junior class history noted a woeful retention rate: "Of the original thirty five men who entered in 1911, scarcely a full dozen remain." Retention rates for first-to-second-year students remained in the low to mid-60 percent range through mid-century. Yet better prepared entering freshmen and more campus attention to the retention of students led to dramatically improved rates. By 1987 the retention rate reached 76 percent, and through the 21st century it remained between 81 percent and 88 percent. By the late 20th-century, six-year graduation rates had become an important measure of student success. In 1988, only about half of students who began as freshmen in 1982 had graduated, but the six-year rate had improved to almost two-thirds in 2009.

Missouri S&T welcomed its smartest entering class in at least the last decade in 2019, as determined by grade point average and test scores.

1

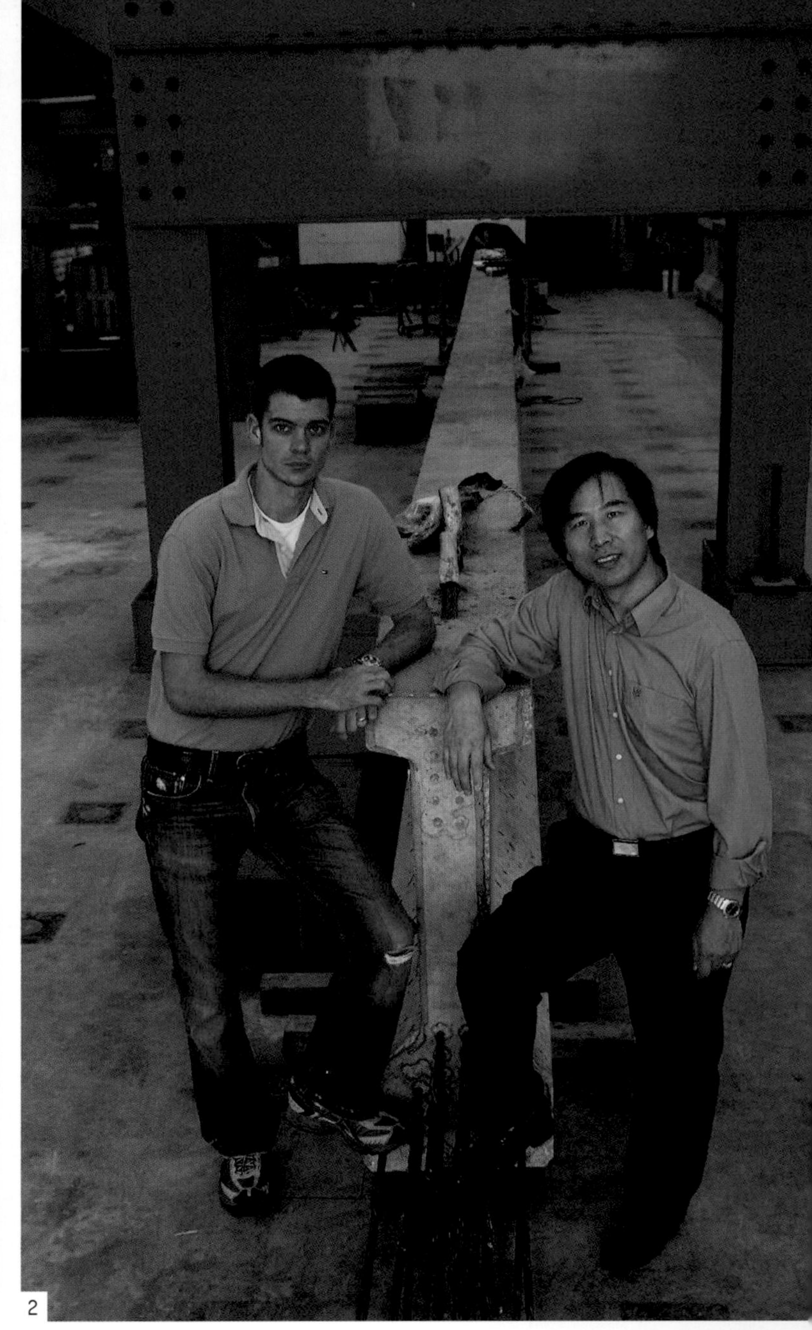

2

GRADUATE STUDENTS

For most of the institution's history, the focus remained upon undergraduate education. The first graduate student enrolled in 1891. The number grew slowly, averaging fewer than 10 a year in the first decade of the 20th century. Through 1941, the number of graduate students on campus never surpassed 27, a number achieved in the 1914–15 and 1934–35 academic years. The campus awarded its first master of science degree in 1900, and over the next 37 years, granted fewer than 150 overall. The MSM experience fit the national pattern. In 1921, for example, there were fewer than 370 engineering students pursuing graduate degrees in the entire country.

The number of graduate students remained low until the campus adopted a more aggressive research agenda, which led to more external funding and more graduate students to help with the research. There were 25 graduate students just after World War II, a figure that grew to 364 in 1964. By that time, UMR established a graduate school. Growth continued each decade, with almost 700 graduate students in 1994 with an increasing emphasis upon recruiting Ph.D. students to enhance the research productivity of the faculty. By 2017, there were 654 on-campus Ph.D. students, and 900 on-campus and distance master's students.

3

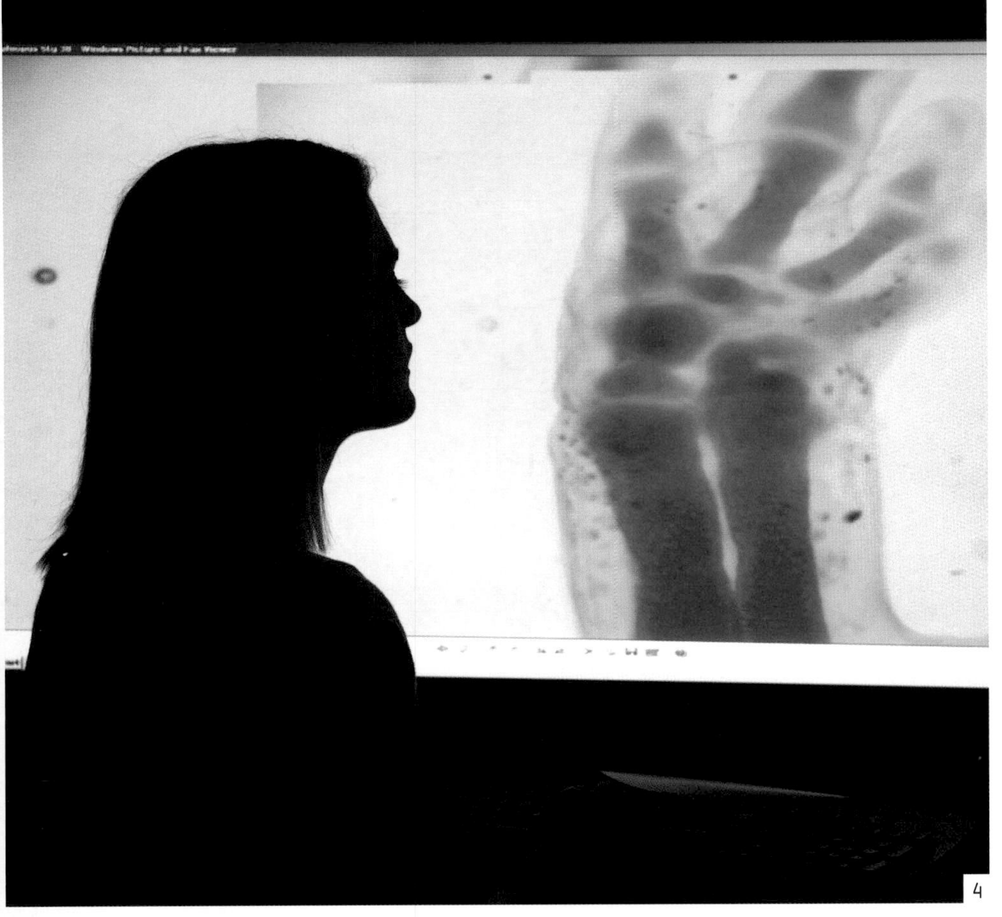

4

1: A four-story unit operations lab in Schrenk Hall provided chemical engineering graduate students with the equipment to apply the theory of process engineering in 1967.

2: Graduate student Brian Wood and civil engineering professor Genda Chen studied how to retrofit bridges in Butler-Carlton's high-bay lab in 2007.

3: Under the direction of Venkata Allada, engineering management graduate students in 2005 study ways to design products to reduce waste.

4: In the early 2000s, S&T biologists and computer scientists joined forces to create an online tool to better understand why amphibian populations are on the decline.

5: Graduate student Brandon Ludwig conducts additive manufacturing research in 2016.

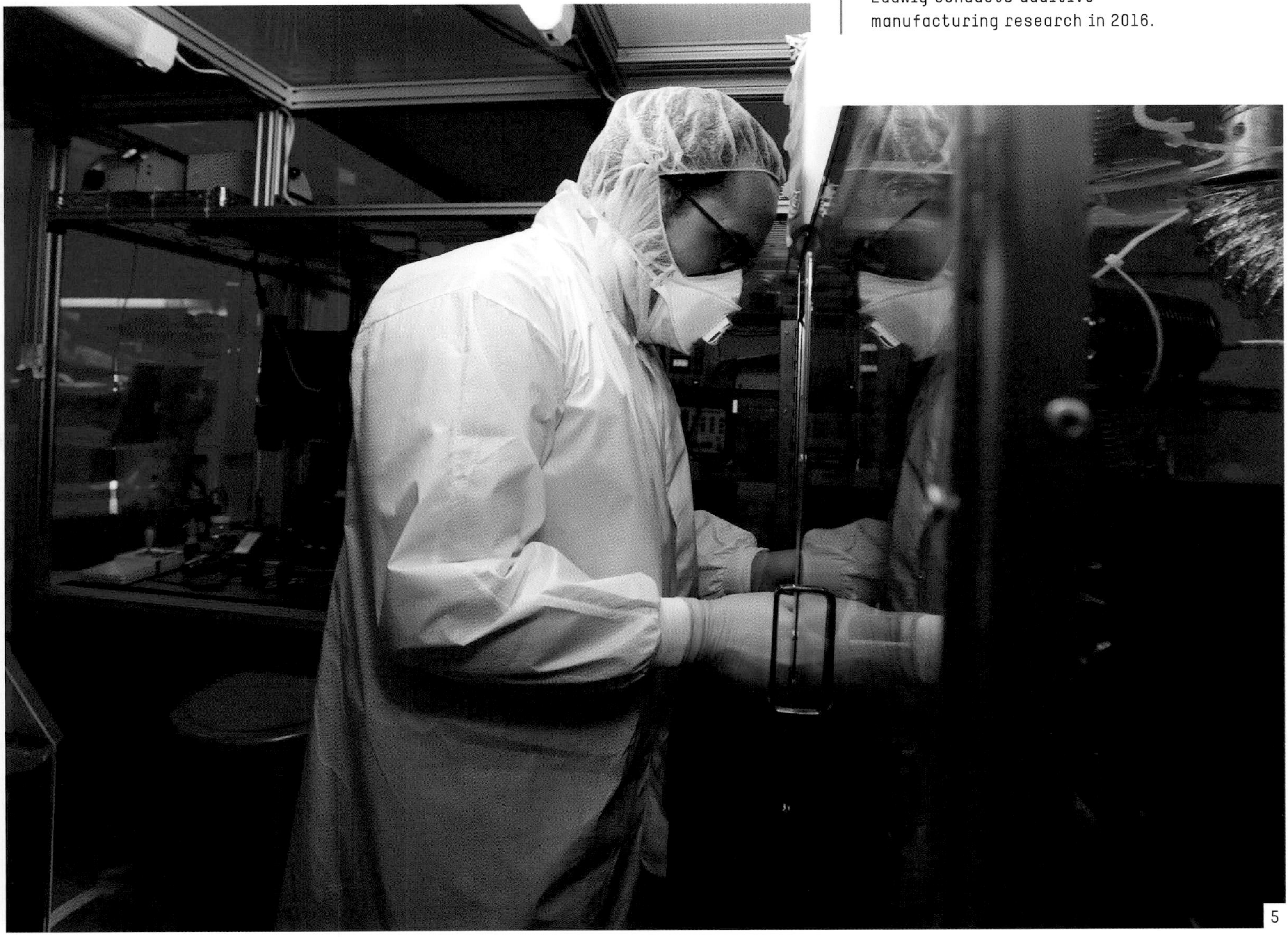

5

CAREER PLACEMENT

For the campus's first half century, graduating seniors, with some help from their professors and alumni, were responsible for securing a job by writing letters to potential employers. Most years the students were successful. In 1916, for example, the *St. Louis Republic* reported, "Dr. Austin Lee McRae, director of the school and professor of physics, says that he expects to find an immediate opening in the mining profession for every one of the 50 young men of this year's class."

When Noel Hubbard became the assistant registrar in 1923, one of his tasks was to develop an effective placement program for MSM students. In the spring semesters Hubbard sent the names of graduating seniors to the companies that had previously hired MSM students, "asking those interested to communicate with us." He also sent personal letters on behalf of graduating seniors to some employers. Under Professor George Dean's leadership as secretary, the alumni association also assisted. As Dean explained in a letter to alumni in 1924, "we have done all we could towards finding employment for MSM men. When we have had news of positions open we have notified the men, who, we thought, would be interested in the matter" and "a regular canvass of employers is put on in the spring about a month before commencement." Both Dean and Hubbard claimed great success with their approaches. Dean reported in 1924 that "in 95 percent of the cases," he had helped land a job for graduating seniors. Four years later, Hubbard said that he had placed all but two of graduating seniors in jobs, and for mining engineers he "could have placed perhaps fifty percent more students than we had." Hubbard continued to have success in placing MSM seniors in most years, but in the depths of the Great Depression, as Director Charles Fulton explained in spring 1934, only 44 percent of seniors had found positions. Fortunately, there was a good rebound by 1937 when 83 percent of seniors had jobs before completing their studies.

In 1946, Professor Rex Z. Williams became assistant dean and director of placement. During his six years in that role, Williams took a more aggressive approach, inviting "vast numbers of potential employers" to campus to interview MSM seniors. "Accommodations for the interviews," however, "were rather crude." Employers used rooms in the basement of Parker Hall or in any available rooms in academic departments. The problem worsened each year, with the number of on-campus interviews exceeding 600 by the late 1950s. In his 1949 report Williams noted what employers were looking for when interviewing MSM seniors: "Men with good scholastic standing, and men with outstanding personality are quickly employed. It seems that exceptional scholarship will compensate for below average personality in the opinion of the employer just as exceptional personality will compensate for below average scholarship."

In 1956, Aaron J. Miles, chair of the mechanical engineering department, took the initiative to develop a cooperative education program to further enhance students' job prospects. In the 1920s, MSM had begun requiring students to do what many had been doing for a generation on their own. They had to have at least three months of work in their chosen field. This they normally did during the summers. In the 1956–57 academic year, Miles and a committee of seven faculty members, along with Registrar Noel Hubbard, developed a program that offered students who had completed their freshman year to "obtain professional industrial experience while pursuing their academic programs" and have an additional income by working for

Above: One of Assistant Registrar Noel Hubbard's tasks in the 1920s was to develop a placement program for graduates.

Right: Rex Z. Williams, assistant dean and director of placement (1946–52).

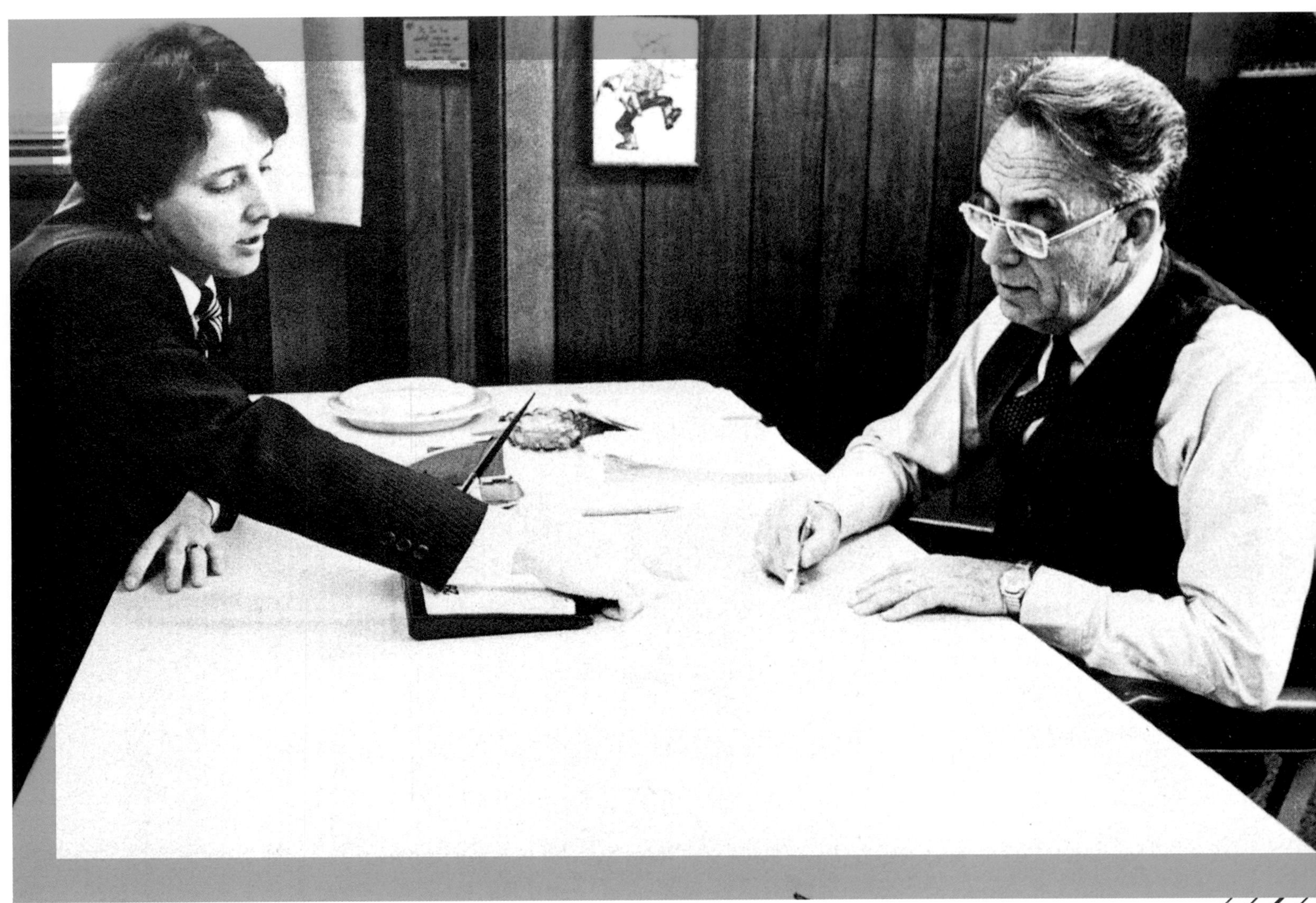

Charles "Chuck" Remington (right) became director of placement in 1982.

a semester with an employer. In the first year, 11 employers, led by the Missouri State Highway Commission, hired 65 students. By 1978, nearly 350 students were involved, and the total peaked in 1997 with 608 co-op students. Similarly, the number of employers dramatically increased to over 180 by 2014. Increasingly, students also pursued internships during which they worked for employers during the summer. By 2017, over 500 students had secured internships with 182 different employers.

By the mid-1960s, placement services had moved to the Buehler Building downtown at Ninth and Rolla Streets, but would eventually move to the third floor of Norwood Hall on campus. Both locations provided a recruiter's lounge and many interview rooms. When Professor Charles "Chuck" Remington replaced Larry Nuss, the retiring director of placement, in 1982, the placement office merged with the cooperative training program to form the Career Development Office. Eventually, this office gained the title of Career Opportunities and Employer Relations, and it added fall and spring career fairs, which by the second decade of the 21st century regularly attracted over 300 employers.

The overwhelming majority of Miners who completed degree requirements graduated with jobs in hand at average starting salaries higher than the national average for college graduates. In 1949, for example, the average annual starting salary for an MSM graduate was nearly $3,200 and rose to over $7,500 in 1965. Harley Hickenbotham, a 1967 graduate in chemical engineering, recalled "employers were swarming the campus BEGGING for grads to interview ... What a windfall! High salary offers and multiple offers to consider!" By 2019, the average starting salary for an S&T graduate had reached just over $60,000. For master's graduates, the average was nearly $80,000. For generations, employers have seen great value in Miner graduates. They had always been pleased to have "career-ready" miners and engineers in their employ. By the late 20th century they also were hiring Miners with degrees in a much wider range of majors like economics, biology, English, history, business, psychology, and technical communication. Regardless of a student's degree program, surveys of employers between 2015 and 2019 found that *all* employers of Miners were satisfied with the students they had hired.

ALUMNI SATISFACTION

Alumni satisfaction with their Rolla education generally has paralleled that of their employers. Virtually all alumni, regardless of their degree program, have noted how demanding their course work had been, yet they concluded that the effort had been worth it. Those who participated in the annual campus Golden Alumni events, celebrating the 50th anniversary of their graduation, usually completed questionnaires about their time in Rolla and about their careers. From the hundreds of questionnaires, several themes emerge.

Alumni affirm that their experiences in Rolla were life changing, or as 1963 graduate George R. Schillinger noted, it represented a critical rite of passage. Beyond the considerable knowledge they gained, there were invaluable tools the Rolla experience had given alumni. Their professors had helped them to think logically, and they became solid problem solvers, but to complete their degree programs, they had to develop a solid work ethic, set priorities, and become disciplined. In other words, they realized they had to become accountable for their own success. As 1966 graduate Robert L. Heider explained, his time in Rolla taught him "how to learn." Many would have agreed with 1964 graduate David Blume's conclusion about his four years at MSM, where he "transitioned from a naïve, immature person to a more confident and self-assured person," or with 1967 graduate Harley Hickenbotham, who said UMR instilled in him "the will to strive toward things greater than myself." They also noted the many friendships that developed while on campus, particularly those who had lived in fraternities and sororities. Those ties did not end with their college years; they became life-long friendships.

Once in the work world, alumni realized the "sterling reputation" of their alma mater. As 1962 graduate Gary J. Buckrod put it, "If you graduated from 'Rolla' people know you were well qualified." "After a lifetime of relating to graduates of the finest engineering schools," 1962 graduate John P. McKeone reflected, "I can honestly attest that not one of them received a better undergraduate education than was provided by MSM/UMR/Missouri S&T." Perhaps James McDuff, a 1964 graduate who served in Vietnam and Thailand, best captured the essence of what the Miner experience provided its students: "In every unit I served in the Army there were fellow MSM graduates and I quickly discovered the MSM guys were the first to handle the toughest jobs, were very successful and highly respected." Satisfaction with their experience at UMR and S&T continued into the 21st century. A 2014 survey of alumni, for example, revealed that over 90 percent were proud to be Miner graduates.

Above: Missouri Industry Day in 1984 had 52 companies in attendance for students to meet with for future employment and internships.

Right: Missouri S&T's February 2019 Career Fair drew hundreds of employers.

COLTON'S
ACAR
HOPPERS PUB
PAPA JOHNS
LEE'S
PRICE CHOPPER
EXTREME
REALTY EXECUTIVES
MiTek
YASKAWA
FlightSafety
CLAYCO
Cerner
Become a woman of steel.
ArDOT
THE ROAD TO YOUR CAREER STARTS HERE
STREETSCAPES
PEDESTRIAN BRIDGES
TRAFFIC
TRAILS & SIDEWALKS
CLEAN WATER
GARMIN
AUTO | SPORTS | OUTDOOR | MARINE | AVIATION
GARMIN
careers.garmin.com
Aviation | Marine | Fitness | Outdoor | Auto
Help the world thrive
GARMIN

FIRST GRADUATING CLASS AT
MISSOURI SCHOOL OF MINES
1874.
John H. Gill

MSM ALUMNUS

Alumni Association, School of Mines and Metallurgy, Rolla, Missouri

Vol. 1. September 15, 1926. No. 1.

HOME-COMING OCTOBER 14-15-16

REGISTRATION AND NEW FACULTY MEMBERS.

The registration this fall was the largest in the history of the school for any one semester. A total of 411 have registered. These are classified as follows:

Freshmen	147
Sophomores	103
Juniors	71
Seniors	64
Graduates	8
[illegible]	6
[illegible]	12

[illegible] will register [illegible] second semester, the total registration for the year will [illegible] of 150, showing a [illegible] over last year [illegible] for the year. [illegible] and 7 foreign countries were represented in the registration. The alumni, as in past years, did good service in connection with new students. Many of them mention- [illegible]mni as their source of inspira- [illegible] coming to M. S. M. Harry [illegible] '23, came downduring registration to get another [illegible]

at Manhattan up until he came here.

F. C. Farnham has been appointed instructor in physics. Mr. Farnham came from New York University where he was also instructor in physics. He graduated from Nebraska Wesleyan.

M. H. Griffitts has been appointed instructor in German, taking the place of Prof. O. A. Henning, who is away on leave for one year doing graduate work. Mr. Griffitts came here from the University of Michigan, where he graduated and where he was also instructor in German.

A. V. Kilpatrick, new instructor in mechanical engineering, came here from Ames, Iowa, where he had been graduate assistant in mechanical engineering. Mr. Kilpatrick graduated from South Dakota College.

I. L. Hebel, a graduate of the University of Colorado, has been appointed instructor in mathematics. Mr. Hebel was instructor in mathematics at the University of Colorado during the past year.

OLD GRADUATES SEND THEIR SONS TO M. S. M.

More and more the [illegible]

FOOTBALL PROSPECTS GOOD.

First game, Miners 41, McKendree 13.

The presence of nine letter-men from last year's successful eleven points toward a strong '26 team for the Missouri School of Mines football contingent. Coach McCollum possesses a brilliant back-field quartet in Captain Lee, Ledford, Lemon, Thomas. Also Berry, a '24 letter-man, is out for a position in the back-field. Young, R. Johnson, G. Johnson, Allebach and Bolon are the line men of ability who earned varsity positions in '25 and will form the nucleus for the development of a stalwart line. The forward wall will be the object of much attention in order to enable the Miners' fast-stepping back-field to function properly. Scrimmage is already being practiced daily as Coach McCollum drills his charges for the McKendree College game to be followed by the Miners' annual game with the Washington U. Bears in St. Louis.

In all about sixty men are out for football, and among [illegible]

Above: The first three graduates of MSM: John W. Pack, John H. Gill, and Gustavus Duncan, 1874.

Right: The first issue of the *MSM Alumnus* was published on September 15, 1926.

Pictured in front of Norwood Hall, nearly half of the members of the Class of 1939 returned for their golden anniversary reunion.

ALUMNI ASSOCIATION

In the end, alumni were grateful for their fulfilling careers and the financial support they could provide for their families. As a result of their education in Rolla they had enjoyed upward mobility and comfortable lives, and because of that many sought to retain their ties to the campus.

There were several attempts to begin an alumni association in MSM's first 50 years. In 1874, John W. Pack, Gustavus Duncan, and John Holt Gill, the first three graduates, all found jobs at a smelter near Boulder, Colorado. One night, after a 12-hour day of work, the three were relaxing, and Pack called the trio "to order in 'The First Meeting of the Alumni of the Missouri School of Mines and Metallurgy.'" Eight years after that light-hearted effort, during the American Institute of Mining Engineers meeting in Denver, about a dozen alumni gathered for a celebratory dinner. However, the first formal effort in establishing an association took place in 1896. The MSM catalog noted "an Association of Alumni of the School of Mines has been formed" with the intention of meeting at each Commencement, but the organization foundered.

Between 1915 and 1917, several alumni took the initiative to organize alumni associations in Kansas City, Joplin and St. Louis in Missouri, as well as Tulsa, Oklahoma; and Platteville, Wisconsin. For a time, some of the St. Louis alumni had a weekly luncheon at the American Hotel to discuss "old friends" and "old times." Meanwhile, according to the *Missouri Miner*, in 1915, "a number of the Alumni" had been talking to Director Austin Lee McRae "about organizing a general Missouri School of Mines Alumni Association, to represent the entire alumni."

Finally, in 1921, to commemorate the 50th anniversary of the opening of the campus, Arthur Terrell of the class of 1898 became president of what became the permanent Alumni Association. Within two years, there were over 300 members and mathematics professor George Dean, who had taken the

1

4

2

3

lead in establishing the association, became its secretary. Dean usually spent two to four hours a day, beyond his teaching and research duties, promoting "good-fellowship and ... loyalty to MSM." When he stepped down in 1925, Dean recommended that the association publish a magazine to update alumni on campus developments and better build membership rolls. The association leadership agreed, and the following year published the first issue of the *MSM Alumnus*. Assistant Registrar Noel Hubbard not only edited the magazine, but also took over Dean's task as alumni recorder. The publication, which in the 21st century became *Missouri S&T Magazine*, remained an indispensable way for the campus to keep in touch with alumni. Due to budget cuts resulting from the COVID-19 pandemic, publication of the alumni magazine was suspended in summer 2020.

Incorporated in 1946, the association established an office on campus, and by 1949 had helped establish alumni sections in 13 cities from coast to coast. Four years later, Francis "Ike" Edwards, the association's first full-time professional, became executive secretary. Edwards and his successors became familiar names and faces to thousands of alumni. Frank Mackaman became Edwards' field secretary in 1968 and became Director of Alumni Activities in 1972. Chancellor Joseph Marchello designated Mackaman to head a combined alumni and development office in 1978. Donald Brackhahn, Lindsay Bagnall, Marianne Ward, and Darlene Ramsay (both she and Lindsay Bagnall were alumnae) succeeded Mackaman as director and executive vice president of an organization, now called the Miner Alumni Association. Today, the organization serves nearly 60,000 graduates living all over the world.

CONTINUING THE LAND GRANT MISSION

The continuing support of an active Alumni Association, whose membership included a multitude of first-generation college graduates, illustrated the campus's long-term commitment to the mission of the land grant college concept of providing a university education to those with the ability and motivation to benefit from such access. In the 21st century, however, Missouri S&T began exhibiting some of the traits of an elite institution. By 2018, with only 20 percent of its undergraduates being first-generation college students and its highly selective admissions designation, S&T seemed to scarcely resemble the "blue collar" MSM of the earlier generations. However, in its strategic planning, the campus remained committed to providing access and scholarship support to qualified first-generation, low-income, and underrepresented minority students. In that regard S&T truly was keeping faith with the vision of Justin Morrill. The campus's purpose remained, as Clark Kerr, the president of the University of California System explained the land grant college mission in 1963, "to serve less the perpetuation of an elite class and more the creation of a relatively classless society, with the doors of opportunity open to all through education."

"... a relatively classless society, with the doors of opportunity open to all through education."

Opposite: (1) Donald Brackhahn, (2) Lindsay Bagnall, (3) Marianne Ward and (4) Darlene Ramsay served as either director of alumni and constituent relations or assistant vice chancellor for alumni relations and advancement services between 1985 and 2020.

Below: Students sign thank-you cards and make photographs at Hasselmann Alumni House in 2016. Scholarship recipients participate in this annual event to show their appreciation for donor generosity.

CHAPTER 3

MINER FACULTY AND STAFF

History Professor Jack Ridley was one of the campus's first Curators' Distinguished Teaching Professors.

The best professors at MSM/UMR/S&T shared fundamental perspectives on their roles at the university. In 1972, historian Jack Ridley, the most honored teaching professor in the second half of the institution's history, believed that professors carried a substantial obligation for student success, explaining that a professor "should inspire, stimulate and direct student intellectual energies" and be "imaginative enough to adapt both to the needs of the individual student and to the collective personality of each class." Professor James Grimm, who taught in the electrical engineering department between 1948 and 1973, added another critical responsibility. A successful professor, he argued, must establish a "personal contact with each individual student" because they needed that meaningful connection in the campus's challenging learning environment.

Just as important, most professors asserted that it was their duty to make students understand that they were also accountable for their success or failure. Alumnus Walter Remmers recalled that his professors in the early 1920s were "demanding." Indeed, they wanted all their students "to do more than what was required." One of Remmers' professors, mathematician George Dean, was legendary for throwing tantrums and erasers at the students who dared enter his classroom unprepared, and many alumni remembered his "Damns" and "Goshes" as his students flailed away at the chalkboard. Geology Professor Charles Laurence Dake, who joined the MSM faculty in 1913, "had very little tolerance for the student who loafed on the job." Generations later, students taking classes in metallurgical engineering from Professor David Van Aken understood that he was always considerate of students who came to class prepared, but that he would "rain death and destruction on all who enter the class unprepared."

For over 90 years, the faculty believed that their primary mission was to offer excellent undergraduate programs. They defined themselves first and foremost as teachers, most of whom sought to improve their craft. For example, in a 1929 survey of their research activity, most MSM faculty members noted that in the limited time that they had for research they focused upon exploring ways to improve "class instruction" or "testing." For example, chemical engineering professor Walter Schrenk explained, "It is our aim to give the student the best instruction possible. This can only be accomplished by varying the instruction to meet the different personalities of the students. This type of instruction necessitates conference and personal contact. We are continually striving for better methods of imparting subject matter to the student as well as of evaluating his grasp of the subject." Schrenk assuredly was not alone. Professors who joined the faculty through the 1960s understood this commitment to undergraduate student success. Dudley Thompson later explained that he accepted the position of chair of chemistry and chemical engineering at MSM in 1955 when he discovered from conversations with the faculty that they wanted to continue their focus upon teaching, which reflected his preference. Similarly, Ken Robertson found a campus still largely devoted to undergraduate teaching when he joined the chemistry department a decade later.

"We are continually striving for better methods of imparting subject matter to the student as well as of evaluating his grasp of the subject."

Above: Chemical engineering Professor Walter T. Schrenk.

1: Metallurgical engineering Professor David Van Aken was a Curators' Distinguished Teaching Professor.

2: Electrical engineering Professor James Grimm was legendary for his commitment to student success.

3: While he developed an enviable research record, geology Professor Charles L. Dake had high expectations for his students.

Left: Charles Fulton served as director of the campus from 1920 to 1937.

Below: 1920 *Rollamo* illustration representing the faculty by Joe M. Wilson.

FACULTY BACKGROUNDS

During the MSM years, few of the faculty or campus leaders had a Ph.D. and almost all faculty who had a doctorate were not in the disciplines of mining, metallurgy, or engineering. The campus was fortunate in attracting faculty members who had earned a Ph.D. from premier graduate programs. Late 19th century chemist Chase Palmer had a Ph.D. from Johns Hopkins University, and early 20th century chemist Louis Agassiz Test had a Ph.D. from the University of Chicago. Charles L. Dake received a Ph.D. in geology from Columbia University. Leon Woodman had a Ph.D. in physics from Columbia University. W. Scott Boyce came to MSM in 1921 with a Ph.D. in economics from Columbia University and William Randel, who had a Ph.D. in English from Columbia University, was on the faculty in the 1940s. Yet, in 1924, only 13 percent of the faculty had a doctorate, a percentage that increased to 27 percent two decades later and remained at that level into the early 1960s.

For most of the early decades, the campus largely relied upon metallurgists and engineers who had a bachelor's degree or master's degree and some experience in their fields. In 1920, for example, Director Charles Fulton reported to the campus executive committee that he had hired four new faculty members, three of whom had both teaching and "practical" experience and a fourth who had no teaching experience, but who had worked for several years at mines in Utah and Chile. All of them had degrees from either Pennsylvania State College, the University of Colorado, or Columbia University. The campus also hired some of its brightest graduates to remain in Rolla on the faculty. This approach to hiring produced a pedagogy, as described by alumni as "hands on," not "theoretical" science, an approach that for generations led to a well-deserved claim that MSM produced "street-ready" miners and engineers.

With notable exceptions, these were not "ivory tower" faculty members. During World War I, for example, Director Austin McRae also served as the chairman of the Phelps County Council of Defense. In that

Prof. Geo. Emerson With Students
At School of Mines
About 1880

Civil engineering professor and Civil War veteran George Emerson.

role, McRae was responsible for identifying outstanding speakers to give patriotic talks to the public. In September 1917, McRae had to report to the secretary of the State Council, "I regret that we haven't a single orator in our faculty" and he worried that crowds "would be disappointed" if he dispatched any of them to give a speech.

They were a rough and tumble lot who worked hard and enjoyed hunting and fishing in south central Missouri, a good billiards game, a few drinks, mixing it up with the students in intramurals, and spending the summers working in the mines or for an engineering firm. Indeed, one alumnus from the early 1920s claimed that his professors were not particularly cultivated. He remembered one "professor who attended a black-tie affair in all the proper attire — except for his shoes. He had on a pair of the yellowest bricklayer's boots you'd ever seen."

A few, however, aspired to develop a more intellectual milieu in Rolla. In 1921, seven faculty members and Director Charles Fulton established the Highbrow Discussion Club. They met twice a month in a member's home for dinner and hours of discussion on a variety of subjects ranging from Margaret Sanger and birth control, the Scopes Trial, and psychic phenomena to whether psychology will become the foremost science in the future, how ill-prepared students were for the rigor of MSM, and whether franker sexual relations led to a healthier life. Initially, they added a few members from the community, but for 16 years, the members were almost all faculty members.

Language professor and Civil War veteran Robert W. Douthat.

STUDENT PERCEPTIONS OF FACULTY

Students were gratified to discover that most of their professors were committed to their success, even the ones who had the highest expectations of them. Gustavus Duncan fondly remembered Charles P. Williams, MSM's first professor and director, because of his "constant interest in our advancement." George Emerson, who was one of Williams' first faculty hires, became the most beloved of the professors in the campus's first two decades. A bachelor, Emerson arrived in 1873 and lived for a time in a log cabin just a short walk from campus. He loved to sit with his feet on the desk as he lectured in a "somewhat falsetto voice" while puffing away on his pipe. When students asked why he could smoke in the building while they could not, he would always jovially respond, "Well, now, you must consider who I am." Besides teaching civil engineering, the popular Emerson took students on field trips to caves and to examine railroads and bridges, and he established a community book discussion group called the Emersonian Club. One of his students decades later recalled that Emerson, who remained at MSM for 14 years, "lived to teach" and "would do anything in the world to make you know what he was trying to do."

There were other student favorites. Robert William Douthat, a Civil War veteran who had participated in General George Pickett's famous charge at the Battle of Gettysburg, was a contemporary of Emerson's. A professor of languages, Douthat was a large but energetic man with a strong voice who talked, as one student explained, like "hill-billies," always dropping the letter "g" on words. He would say "Readin'" and "Writin'." Students in the early 20th century liked to call Guy Henry Cox, a professor of geology and mineralogy, "Baldy" for obvious reasons. Still, they respected him as a good teacher despite "his sternness" in the classroom.

Yet, through the early 1930s, Professor George Dean was the commanding presence and influence for most students, a man they frequently just referred to as "Old Prof." Dean's colleagues saw him as a mathematical genius, occupying an intellectual plane higher than the rest of them. At a time when few MSM professors were engaged in research, Dean published in a range of journals from the *American Mathematical Monthly* to the *Physical Review* and he occasionally spent the summer months working in the General Electric Laboratory in New York. A revealing story about Dean involved his offering a series of seven lectures for faculty and students on his research. After the third lecture Dean announced that it would be the last because it was clear to him "you are all too damn dumb" to understand. Indeed, near the end of his career, he concluded he had had only four truly strong students of mathematics, one of whom was Aaron Miles, who became the chair of mechanical engineering and the first dean of the college of engineering at MSM.

The *Rollamo* staff dedicated the 1931 yearbook to Professor George Dean.

Right: Cantankerous but popular mathematics Professor George Dean.

DEDICATION

To an alumnus and professor of The Missouri School of Mines: to one who has worked with the interests of his students at heart, and who has engendered liking and respect in the hearts of those who know him: to one who has shown us the way to a broader view of life, and who has shown us the true engineering spirit: to GEORGE REINALD DEAN, we, the 1931 Rollamo Board, dedicate this book.

In Director George Ladd's view, the irascible Dean "was a teaching genius, but had an erratic and unstable temperament." "Old Prof" constantly railed against all the unprepared students who enrolled in math classes. As he wrote in 1927, "We spend at least half our time, not all at once but as it seems necessary, some of it outside the regularly scheduled hours, trying to teach what students are supposed to have learned in the public schools." While the *Rollamo* staffs might admit they had "sat in calculus in a cold sweat while he informed us in his original manner that we 'didn't know nuthin,'" they still respected "the Wizard of Integrals, Unknowns, and Calculus" whose "chief aversion" was "feeding Mathematics with a spoon."

Several times the *Rollamo* staff dedicated their volumes to Dean. When he died in 1937 his colleagues on the faculty approved a memorial resolution noting that Dean's "interest in the individual student was as keen as his interest" in research and that "he was always in demand at alumni gatherings, and to his colleagues it was a common thing to hear his old students reminisce of days spent in his classes."

Professors like Dean, Williams, and Emerson set the bar high for others in the eyes of the students who were not shy to criticize the professors who failed to meet their expectations. For example, in both 1912 and 1913, students in civil engineering called upon Director Lewis Young to replace Professor Elmo G. Harris, who they claimed was incompetent. Harris marshalled a successful defense to University President A. Ross Hill and the board of curators despite Director Young's recommendation that he seek "another position." In 1930, the *Missouri Miner* staff sent a questionnaire to fraternities, eating clubs, and independents. On a three-point scale, they asked students to rate professors on intelligence, personality, ability to teach, character, interest in subject, impartiality, and "All in all how does he rate with you?" They also had the audacity to publish all the results in their March 20 issue, where the reader could learn that civil engineering professor Clarence E. Bardsley had the highest evaluation and English professor Sterling Bradley had the lowest. The faculty called upon campus leaders to stop the publication of student ratings, arguing that it could lead to some professors resigning, but the student evaluation of faculty remained a part of campus culture for the next 90 years.

POST-WORLD WAR II FACULTY

As the enrollment at MSM increased from just 314 in 1945 to over 4,300 20 years later, the campus hired hundreds of new faculty members. The vast majority of these arrivals on campus embraced the institution's commitment to providing a quality education for undergraduate students. Alumni from this era remember several of them as particularly driven to offer rigorous courses, but also that they were willing to help students achieve success. Albert Schlecten and Robert Wolf in metallurgical engineering, Harold Q. Fuller in physics, Chuck Remington in mechanical engineering, Dewey Allgood in athletics, Sylvester Pagano and Richard Kerr in mathematics, Theodore Planje in ceramic engineering, James Grimm in electrical engineering, and seemingly all the faculty members in civil engineering — William Andrews, Jerry Bayless, John Best, Vernon Gevecker, John Heagler, Paul Munger, and J. Kent Roberts — were the most memorable. Students appreciated them because they were outgoing, friendly, or humorous. They were known as superb lecturers or as extraordinarily well organized in their labs, or as professors with a remarkable work ethic. Some were deeply involved with student organizations. What they shared was a willingness to make time for their students' questions about class problems, scheduling, career options, or personal challenges. In essence, what they demonstrated was that they cared about their students.

When Professor Grimm retired, a colleague revealed that the electrical engineering professor had developed into the quintessential example of this collective belief about a faculty member's most essential job. Grimm could "always be counted upon to be in your corner when the chips are down, the kind of guy who would pat you on the back or kick you in the pants depending on what you needed at the time." He was "freshman advisor and ... coordinator of the entire department advising program." He had "come to know each of the electrical engineering students personally and professionally. He knows their home of origin, and in most cases he has met and had numerous exchanges with parents, the wives, and even the brothers and sisters of most of our students." Grimm had also "initiated the freshman orientation program and the senior seminar series."

Above: Civil engineering Professor Elmo G. Harris struggled to meet student expectations in the classroom.

Below: Civil engineering Professor Clarence Bardsley had the highest student evaluations in 1930.

Ida A. Bengtson was the first woman to be hired as a bacteriologist in the U.S. Public Health Service, now known as the National Institutes of Health.

Above: Director Charles P. Williams was an active researcher before becoming first director of MSM.

Right: Ida Bengtson taught bacteriology at MSM in the 1920s and conducted extensive research on trachoma at MSM as the first female scientist at the U.S. Public Health Service.

RESEARCH EMPHASIS

In 1967, a letter to the editor of the *Missouri Miner* revealed a new reality. "The old fashioned concept of teach is rapidly being replaced with research, status, and glory for the fatherland (UMR)." While the bitter student had overstated the case, UMR truly had entered a new phase in its long development, one focused upon research.

Despite their teaching obligations, there had always been a few researchers of note on the faculty. Charles P. Williams, before becoming MSM's first director in 1871, had published a number of technical reports. A self-styled analytical chemist, Williams had completed analyses of many types of ores in Michigan, California, Nevada, and Mexico and he continued his research while in Rolla. In the late 19th and early 20th centuries there were others beyond the gifted George Dean who were scholars publishing research findings. Civil engineer Elmo G. Harris published over 20 articles and reports on road construction, hydraulics, centrifugal pumps, and a widely used text on compressed air. Geologist Charles L. Dake became a nationally known scholar for his many publications, notably his 1918 study titled *The Sand and Gravel Resources of Missouri* with a focus upon the state's Saint Peter Sandstone sedimentary rock formation. A few of the professors in the humanities were also active scholars. English professor William Randal, for example, revised his dissertation into a well-received book on 19th century author Edward Eggleston titled *Edward Eggleston: Author of the Hoosier School-Master.*

Ida Bengtson emerged as the most consequential of the early researchers at MSM. She arrived in 1924 with a Ph.D. in bacteriology from the University of Chicago. The first female scientist in the U.S. Public Health Service (now the National Institutes of Health), Bengtson had been dispatched to Rolla to research trachoma, which is a bacterial infection of the eyes spread by contact, usually on hands, towels, and clothing. Rolla's hospital on 13th street was the site of one of only four trachoma hospitals in the country. Delighted to have an "expert Bacteriologist" in the community, Director Charles Fulton not only provided a small lab space for her research in the basement of Parker Hall, but also hired her as a lecturer in bacteriology. In Rolla through 1931, Bengtson worked, according to a report in the *Kansas City Star*, "with

student assistants and volunteer helpers from the hospital staff" using a "menagerie" of guinea pigs, rabbits, monkeys, and a horse in her experiments. Over 1,500 patients treated at the Rolla hospital benefited from her research, and she shared the results of her important work at a meeting of the Saint Louis Ophthalmic Society before moving on to work in the typhus unit of the National Institutes of Health, where she helped develop a vaccine for typhus and discovered the complement fixation text, which is still used to diagnose some diseases, including typhus and Rocky Mountain spotted fever, prior to retiring in 1946.

Interest in research grew slowly, but steadily. Between 1937 and 1947, faculty members published over 80 articles and books, and between 1951 and 1953, the faculty had 93 publications. Still, Dean Curtis Laws Wilson referred to MSM as a "research desert" when hiring a new faculty member in 1953.

Two researchers — Martin Straumanis and William James — emerged as the leading scholars on campus in the 1950s. Born in Lithuania in 1898, Straumanis had been a fellow of the Rockefeller Foundation in Germany at the University of Goettingen in the late 1920s, where he had met Curtis Laws Wilson. Following the dislocations of World War II, Wilson persuaded University of Missouri President Frederick Middlebush to let him hire Straumanis as a research professor in metallurgical engineering in 1947. Straumanis had already published over 100 books and papers, primarily in the field of "lattice controls of metal

Martin Straumanis (left) professor of metallurgical engineering, and chemist William James were the leading researchers at MSM in the 1950s.

alloys." When chemist William James arrived in 1953, Straumanis took him on as a research partner. Between 1956 and 1962 they obtained grants totaling about $100,000 from the Atomic Energy Commission and the National Science Foundation for equipment and funding for graduate students for their research on X-ray crystallography, corrosion of nuclear metals, and crystal growth. They also both were named Fulbright Research Fellows, Straumanis in Austria and James in France. Working with Otto Hill and Gordon Lewis, the two other senior staff members of the new Materials Research Center, Straumanis and James secured funding for a new building, completed in 1967.

However, it was the charge that President Elmer Ellis gave to new Chancellor Merl Baker in 1963 that triggered an emphasis upon research, an initiative that sought to increase the acquisition of external grants and a rapid expansion of Ph.D. programs. Baker encouraged departments to hire faculty with doctorates and, according to historians Lawrence Christensen and Jack Ridley, he "instituted a policy of encouraging those on campus without doctorates to earn them." Moreover, he provided research grants and funds for purchase of needed equipment.

Grants from the Atomic Energy Commission, National Science Foundation, the National Institutes of Health, and the U.S. Office of Education funded some initiatives. The most significant was in 1967 when the NSF awarded the physics department $550,000, one of only four such awards nationally (and the largest) to "improve the quality of science and engineering research and education." It enabled the department to hire more faculty and laboratory technicians, purchase research equipment, and support more graduate students.

Baker also supported the establishment of several research centers: the Rock Mechanics and Explosives Research Center (1964), the Environmental Research Center (1965), the Graduate Center for Cloud Physics Research (1966), and the Transportation Institute (1967) to promote research teams. During Baker's decade of leadership, the campus also saw the number of Ph.D. degrees offered more than double to 16 and the establishment of a graduate school and a graduate dean. All of these developments led to a dramatic increase in the number of graduate degrees conferred, 55 doctorates and over 300 master's degrees by 1973. When Baker stepped down as chancellor, 83 percent of the faculty had a Ph.D., sponsored research exceeded $2 million (up from $75,000 13 years earlier), and the faculty published over 500 articles and a dozen books in a single year.

To maintain this momentum, the campus continued to add research centers and devoted more funding to support research professors. Between 1979 and 2019, for example, beginning with chemist Stig E. Friberg, the campus selected over 20 faculty members as Curators' Distinguished Professors, appointments that came with a salary stipend and financial support for research activities. Curators' Professors pursued wide-ranging research agendas. In the 1980s, mining engineering professor David Summers focused upon the development of water jet technology to improve rock drilling effectiveness and civil engineering professor Franklin Cheng worked to improve reinforced concrete structures. Thirty years later, aerospace engineer S.N. Balakrishnan was researching missile guidance and control systems while historian John McManus was emerging as one of the nation's leading chroniclers of Americans in combat. Through substantial external funding by donors and companies, the campus also had established 20 named research professorships by 2011. With about three-quarters of the 21st century faculty engaged in research activities, the amount of external funding continued to rise, reaching almost $15 million in 1998 and nearly $40 million 20 years later.

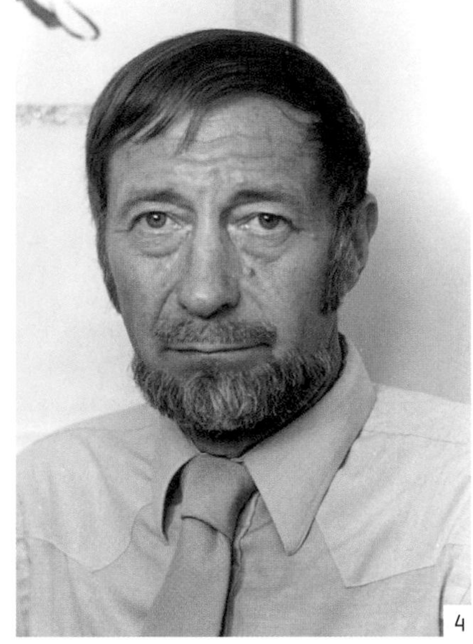

1: Mechanical engineering Professor S.N. Balakrishnan researched missile guidance and control systems.

2: Mining engineering Professor David Summers gained renown for his development of water jet technology.

3: Civil engineering Professor Franklin Cheng published extensively in his field of reinforced concrete structures.

4: Chemist Stig E. Friberg was UMR's first Curators' Distinguished Professor.

5: History Professor John McManus, the first Curators' Distinguished Professor in the humanities at S&T, is one of the nation's leading military historians.

EMERGENCE OF TEACHING-SCHOLARS

This increased emphasis upon research did not come without consequences. Stories proliferated among students that they could not find their professors during their posted office hours because the latter were in their labs or somewhere else writing journal articles. Some secretaries acknowledged that a few professors even hid from their students. Such developments led to a stinging editorial in the *Missouri Miner* in 1971, arguing that too many professors "place such a heavy emphasis on research and graduate work that the undergraduates suffer." "Basically, the beef against the faculty," the editor wrote, "is that quite a few instructors do only what the regulations call for and very little else. Indeed, a good instructor should care about his pupils."

Above: Metallurgical engineering Professor Donald Askeland was the first Curators' Distinguished Teaching Professor.

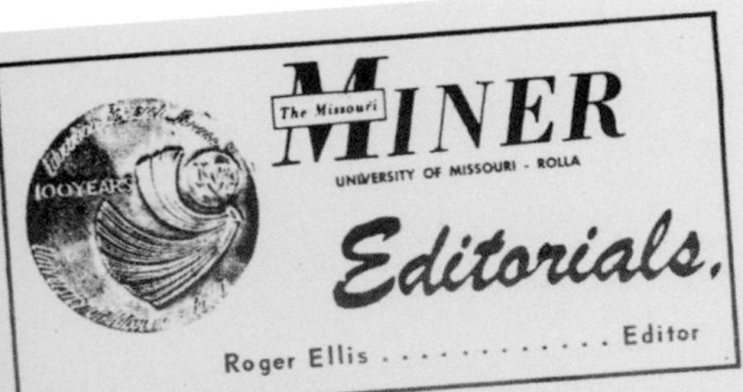

The Missouri MINER
UNIVERSITY OF MISSOURI - ROLLA
Editorials
Roger Ellis . . . . Editor

Our Inept Faculty

As stated in the last issue of the Missouri Miner, the objective of this and editorials to come in the pursuance of faculty evaluation. Thus far, the official requirements of the faculty have been printed in hopes that both the faculty and students realize and know what is officially expected from the faculty.

Perhaps the best way to approach this problem of faculty evaluation is to air the views and complaints of a smattering of students, and wait for a response from both faculty and students. Then, an official poll drafted from ideas presented by both the faculty and student body can be employed to help determine a solution to the problem everyone at UMR can no longer ignore.

One problem already discussed in a previous editorial is the fact that many professors and departments place such a heavy emphasis on research and graduate work that the undergraduates suffer, and they constitute a vast majority.

Another problem is that many instructors do not have any previous teaching experience or education courses, so though they themselves know the material, they cannot present it to the students.

Many instructors have low curves with averages below forty, and is it reasonable that if the average student has learned less than forty percent of the material that the course is valid???

Many students do not get the benefit of the doubt, commonly known as the "shaft."

Many instructors fail a considerable percentage of their classes semester after semester.

Many instructors do not care whether their students pass or fail, and maintain this completely impersonal, apthetic attitude throughout the years.

Many instructors do not offer help sessions when the students desire them.

Many instructors are complete failures in their role of advisors.

Basically, the beef against the faculty is that quite a few instructors do only what the regulations call for and very little else. Indeed, a good instructor should care about his pupils, what he teaches and what is learned. Those who don't should be evaluated and discarded if they do not meet certain "intangible" standards.

Left: 1971 *Missouri Miner* editorial critical of the campus emphasis upon research and graduate studies.

Partly in response to these complaints, but also conscious of the need to be dutiful in helping professors become better instructors, the campus leadership, even as it aggressively pushed sponsored research, provided pedagogical training for new faculty. As early as 1951 MSM had a "Committee on Improvement of Teaching" and for three years a "Young Engineering Teachers" unit. However, they did little more than bring in guest speakers on teaching. In the early 1960s, however, campus leaders established an Effective Teaching Seminar. Meeting each week during the fall semester, the seminar offered guidance on establishing course objectives, testing, and planning. By 1965, 15 assistant professors, 18 instructors, and over 50 graduate assistants participated.

Sporadic efforts continued through the 1970s and 1980s and in 1994, a campus curriculum task force provided funding for 10 faculty members to incorporate computer assisted methods to improve their teaching. In 2003, Harvest Collier, the vice provost of graduate and undergraduate studies, established a center for educational research and teaching to promote improvement in teaching effectiveness and four years later staff from within instructional technology formed an educational technology group to assist faculty members who wanted to more effectively incorporate technology in the classroom. Provost

Robert Marley's establishment of the center for advancing faculty excellence in 2017 to help faculty from "hire to retire" develop as more effective teachers and researchers represented the culmination of these two developments.

Beyond promoting more effective instruction, the campus leadership since the 1960s believed that it was essential to acknowledge and honor outstanding teachers and advisors. For several years, the campus honored a "faculty advisor of the year" at a banquet for faculty advisors across campus. Student organizations nominated award winners like Paul Munger, Robert Wolf, David Oakley, and Joel Kramme for extraordinary service beyond their classroom obligations. Either drawing exclusively upon student evaluations of teaching or a combination of student and faculty votes, for over 50 years the campus honored excellence in the classroom and laboratory with awards going to approximately 10 percent of the faculty each year. Between 1991 and 2018, beginning with the appointments of metallurgical engineer Donald Askeland, historian Jack Ridley, and petroleum engineer Leonard Koederitz, the campus selected nearly 20 Curators' Distinguished Teaching Professors. These appointments, comparable to Curators' Distinguished Professorships in research, reflected the campus leaders' determination to demonstrate a continued commitment to outstanding teaching. By the second decade of the 21st century, the campus had implemented an annual awards banquet to honor faculty for excellent records in teaching, research, and service, a recognition of all the responsibilities of faculty.

To be sure, their ranks needed to be supplemented by adjunct teachers to deal with immediate instructional needs, something the campus had done from its earliest years. However, in the 21st century, the campus established a growing cadre of non-tenure-track professors whose responsibilities were either exclusively to teach or do research. Yet, what had emerged was a recognition that tenure-track professors could best serve as teaching-scholars, faculty members committed both to quality instruction and outstanding research. Even Curators' Distinguished Professors like Martin Bohner, William Fahrenholtz, Greg Hilmas, and John McManus retained a passion for undergraduate teaching in part because they cared about student success, but also because they saw an essential connection between their research and what they could share with their students.

In fact, there was a widely shared belief on campus that the research work of teaching-scholars constantly enhanced their instruction. As biology professor Ron Frank explained in 2012, "If I was at a university where I was only asked to teach, I don't think I would be as enthusiastic in the classroom." Similarly, Reza Zoughi, former Schlumberger Distinguished Professor of electrical engineering, explained, "The best part of my day, the most gratifying part, is the hours I spend in the classroom."

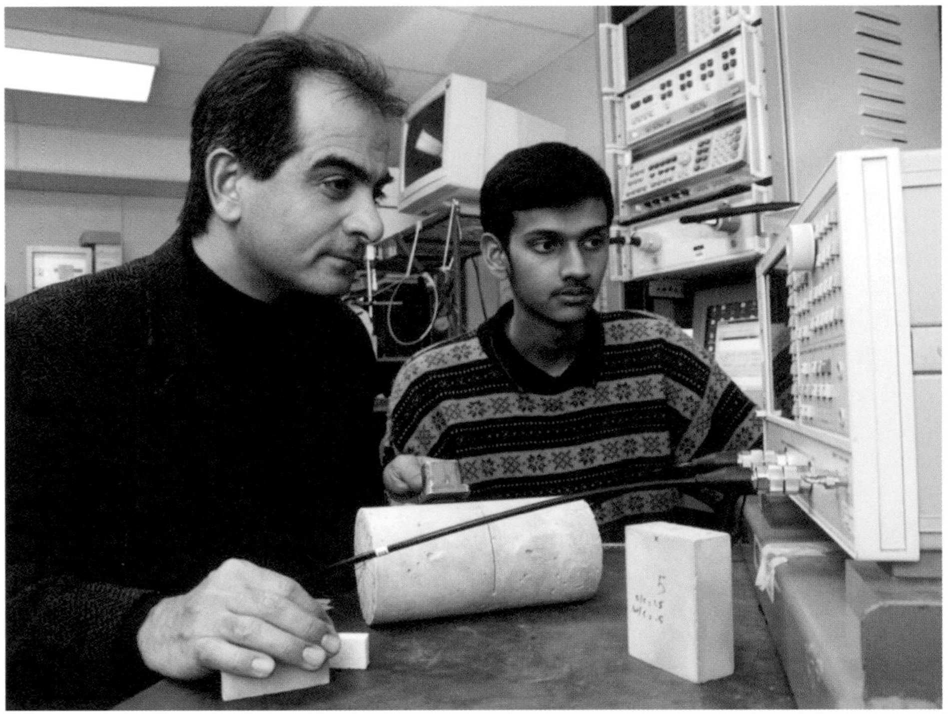

Top: Petroleum engineering Professor Leonard Koederitz (left), a Curators' Distinguished Teaching Professor, with Chancellor Martin C. Jischke.

Bottom: Reza Zoughi (left), former Schlumberger Distinguished Professor of electrical engineering, working with a student.

Above: As a student and faculty member, ceramic engineer Delbert Day was a part of the campus for over six decades.

Right: Philosophy Professor Carol Ann Smith, a passionate advocate of shared governance, was known to challenge campus administrators.

FAMILIAR FACES

After World War II, a few faculty members became true fixtures of the campus. Chemist William James, who joined the faculty in 1953, became one of its most celebrated researchers, a scholar who maintained office hours even at age 96. The University of Missouri System bestowed upon him its most prestigious honor in 1989 with the Thomas Jefferson Award for his civic engagement and civil liberties activism in addition to his outstanding teaching and research record. Ceramic engineer Delbert Day, one of James' colleagues in research at the Materials Research Center, started as a student at MSM in 1953 and, excluding his time at Pennsylvania State University working on a Ph.D. and an 18-month stint in the Army, was a faculty member from 1963. He developed a research record in specialty glasses that ultimately earned him membership in the National Academy of Engineering and also led to him being named a National Academy of Inventors Fellow.

Civil engineer Jerry Bayless, who enrolled at MSM two years after Delbert Day, stayed at the institution, except for a few months with the Missouri Highway Department, from 1959 until his retirement in 2017 as a professor of civil engineering. An outstanding teacher of thousands of students and advisor to hundreds, the campus came to know him best for his incredible commitment to service as advisor to multiple student organizations, as an assistant chair of his department, and as an associate dean of engineering. In the years leading to his retirement, most around campus simply knew him as "Mr. S&T," the most beloved of Miner professors after World War II.

A few other faculty members like geology Professor Richard Hagni, professor of foreign languages and etymology Gerald Cohen, mechanical engineer Al Crosby, and chemist Gary Long were also on the faculty for over a half century. Professor Cohen and his colleague philosophy Professor Carol Ann Smith became familiar faces at academic council and faculty senate sessions, where they developed reputations as champions of faculty rights always willing to challenge campus leaders to honor the concept of shared governance.

Other professors were familiar faces through their media outreach. Beginning in 1978, history professor Wayne Bledsoe began bluegrass music programming on KUMR (later KMST), the campus public radio station, and, after his retirement from teaching, Bledsoe became the general manager of the station. James Bogan, Curators' Distinguished Teaching Professor of art history and film, who was an author of award-winning prose and poetry, made outstanding films available to his classes and the Rolla community through his campus film series. Bogan, one of the last true characters in the faculty, gained quite a reputation for his "Bogantics," which involved his wacky improvisations while introducing many of the over 800 films screened in the series.

Chemist Harvest Collier, who served as chair of the chemistry department, and as associate dean, and was a fifth-degree black belt in taekwondo, was best known as the most important face among the

1: Language Professor Gerald Cohen was on the faculty for over 50 years and was widely known as an advocate for faculty rights.

2: Chemistry Professor Harvest Collier was the leading champion of undergraduate student success in the 1990s and early 21st century.

3: Civil engineer Jerry Bayless graduated from MSM in 1959 and was on the faculty until his retirement in 2017. This beloved professor was known as "Mr. S&T."

4: History Professor Wayne Bledsoe not only was a success at programming bluegrass music on public radio KUMR (later KMST), but also the station manager following his retirement.

5: Curators' Distinguished Teaching Professor James Bogan was known for his "Bogantics" while he introduced movies in the campus film series.

1: English Professor Elizabeth Cummins was on the faculty for over 30 years, was the first woman to chair an academic department, and was the first recipient of the campus Woman of the Year award.

2: Electrical engineering Professor Mariesa Crow, beyond being a successful researcher, served as dean of the School of Materials, Energy, and Earth Resources, and as vice provost for research.

3: Biology Professor Paula Lutz served as an associate dean, chair of the biological sciences department, and dean of the College of Arts and Sciences during her two decades at UMR.

faculty for student support. After joining the chemistry department in 1982, Collier moved up the ranks, becoming vice provost for undergraduate and graduate studies in 2001 and vice provost for undergraduate studies six years later. He became a committed champion of student success with a particular focus on first-year students. As vice provost, Collier implemented several programs involving collaborative and experiential learning. His efforts contributed to an increase in the campus first-to-second year retention and his accomplishments led to his being named an Outstanding First-Year Student Advocate by the National Resource Center for the First-Year Experience.

Amid the sea of familiar male faces, a few female faculty members had sustained careers as well. Physicist Barbara Hale came to UMR as a visiting professor of mathematics in 1969. She joined the physics department four years later and remained until her retirement in 2018. An active researcher and award-winning teacher, Hale was also the personal advisor for Chi Omega sorority for over 30 years and was a frequent participant in deliberations in the academic council and faculty senate. For nearly 40 years Dee Haemmerlie Montgomery was a member of the psychology department and besides teaching over 6,000 students, researched gender differences in academic performance and social anxiety. In 1994, she became the first female faculty member at UMR to be named a Curators' Distinguished Teaching Professor. Mariesa Crow was in the electrical engineering department for almost 30 years. One of the campus's leading researchers with over $21 million in sponsored research and over 200 publications, Crow was also an award-winning teacher. She held a number of important administrative positions including dean of the School of Materials, Energy, and Earth Resources and vice provost for research. In 1976, Paula Lutz earned a bachelor's degree in chemistry with a biology preference at UMR and then a Ph.D. in microbiology and immunology from Duke University. She returned to UMR as a faculty member in the biological sciences department. In her two decades on campus, Lutz was awarded several National Institutes of Health grants, and won several teaching and faculty excellence awards. She also served as associate dean for graduate affairs in the College of Arts and Sciences, chair of the biology department, and dean of the College of Arts and Sciences before moving on to hold similar administrative posts at Montana State University and the University of Wyoming.

Professors Hale, Montgomery, Crow, and Lutz all received the campus Woman of the Year award, but Elizabeth Cummins was the first recipient of that honor. She joined the humanities department in 1967 after teaching five years at the University of Missouri-Columbia. Beyond her teaching and scholarly accomplishments, including three faculty excellence awards, Cummins was one of the driving forces in the campus's establishment of a writing center and she co-directed, with Professor Catherine Riordan, an award-winning "Women at Work" series at UMR. Most notably, in 1990, she became the first female to chair an academic department, leading the English department for almost a decade.

Above: Physics Professor Barbara Hale was on the faculty for nearly 50 years. An award-winning teaching-scholar, Hale was also advisor for Chi Omega for over three decades.

Left: Psychology Professor Dee Haemmerlie Montgomery was on the faculty for nearly 40 years and became the first woman at UMR to be named a Curators' Distinguished Teaching Professor.

Lynn Martin (right) meets with students in the testing and counseling center.

Robert Barefield headed the testing and counseling center for a decade, starting in 1971.

MINER STAFF

As the campus grew so did the need for staff. In 1892, with only 83 students, seven faculty members, and two academic buildings, MSM required only a librarian, a secretary, one janitor, and a treasurer. Three decades later, with 363 students, 28 faculty members, seven academic buildings, and a gymnasium, there was a need for a greater variety of staff including a librarian and assistant librarian, a secretary to the director, a superintendent of buildings and grounds, an experiment station mechanic, a machinist, a custodian of instruments, three supply clerks, an auto mechanic, an engineer, a carpenter, an electrician, a plumber, a painter, six stenographers, seven janitors, three firemen, and a night watchman.

As the campus became an ever-more complex business operation and one committed to greater student support, the staff size increased rapidly. In the 1960s, the campus saw the expansion of both the dean of students' office staff and the student health department and the establishment of a counseling and testing center and a student financial aid office. By 1963, the number of support staff on campus exceeded 800 and in 2017 there were just over 1,000.

Many of the staff became familiar faces to students. Robert Barefield, who succeeded Lynn Martin in 1971, headed the testing and counseling center for a decade. Lou Moss, who joined the counseling center in the 1960s, remained a fixture on campus working with international students for over three decades. Bob Whites, who became director of financial aid in 1982, remained in that vital position for over three decades. Students who became ill got to know Dr. James Myers, who served first as a staff physician for 21 years and then as director of the student health service from 1968 to 1983, and Melba Read, who became head nurse in 1981 and then director of the service.

Above: In over 30 years at UMR, Lou Moss worked in the counseling center and with international students.

Top left: Moss (standing) pictured with assistant director of student personnel, Joe Ward.

Bottom: Bob Whites was the director of financial aid for over three decades.

Top: Rex Z. Williams was named assistant dean in 1946 by Dean Curtis Laws Wilson.

Bottom: Paul Ponder served nearly two decades as assistant dean in charge of student affairs.

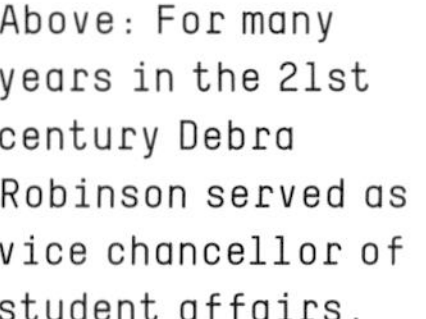

Above: For many years in the 21st century Debra Robinson served as vice chancellor of student affairs.

Right: Chemistry Professor B. Ken Robertson served seven years as dean of students.

Henry H. Armsby served both as student advisor and as campus registrar.

There was a long evolution to the establishment of the dean of students position. In 1921, Director Charles Fulton named Henry H. Armsby as student advisor, a position he retained even after becoming campus registrar two years later. Under Dean Curtis Laws Wilson, however, the role of student advisor became one of the duties of a new position that he created. Wilson named Professor Rex Z. Williams as assistant dean in 1946. Between 1952 and 1960 there were four other assistant deans. That year Wilson appointed Paul E. Ponder, who filled the position for almost two decades, eventually having the title of dean of student affairs. During his successor chemistry professor B. Ken Robertson's seven years as dean of students, the office was in charge of the counseling and testing service, financial aid, student activities, and programs in minority engineering and women in engineering. In 1986, the campus established a division of student affairs headed by a vice chancellor. By 2019, that division, headed by Vice Chancellor Debra Robinson, had grown to include athletics and recreation, career opportunities and employer relations, counseling services, Leach Theatre, the office of dean of students, Miner wellness, parent and family relations, residential life, student affairs services, student disability services, student health services, student involvement, and the testing center.

Above: Wilbert Burton, better known as "Bear Tracks," was a familiar face on campus in the 1960s and 1970s delivering mail.

Right: Most people called Louise Tucker "Dean Tucker" because for over 20 years she was responsible for ensuring that all graduating seniors had met graduation requirements.

MEMORABLE STAFF

The stories of a few of the thousands of Miner staff that have served the campus so well over the past 150 years reveal the importance they played in the life of the institution. Fred H. Lane, who many simply called "Po Po," was a laboratory technician in the chemistry department between 1902 and 1946. Initially, everybody had called him "Pop," but when an international student always pronounced his nickname with a long "O," fellow students began calling him "Po Po." When he retired, his fellow workers agreed that "Po Po" not only had "ruled the chemistry department stock room," but also had interacted "with almost all who have matriculated at the school." Similarly, Sam Williams was the stock room clerk in the metallurgical engineering department for four decades beginning in 1909. Prior to that Williams had been a janitor and had worked on the campus maintenance crew. Once he joined the department, everyone agreed that he became "an indispensable assistant to the professors and students of the department." At his retirement in 1949, Williams was the "Oldest MSM Employee."

When Louise Tucker retired in 1973, everyone called her "Dean" Tucker. For over 20 years she had worked as an assistant in the registrar's office with the responsibility of checking all the credits of graduating seniors. James Collins, who graduated in 1964, later recalled "the scariest time" for him at MSM was making an appointment with Tucker "to find out if I had taken all the courses I needed to graduate." Actually, most students called her the "senior's friend" because she helped make sure that they had fulfilled all the graduation requirements for their degree. In all, Tucker advised over 14,000 students. She also played a critical role in preparing commencement programs, proofreading all the names, degrees, and dissertation titles.

Patty Frisbee was the director of new student programs at S&T for over a decade beginning in 2003 and in that role emerged as one of the most critical people new students would encounter. Supervising over 140 staff, student leaders, student mentors, and student volunteers, Frisbee coordinated and implemented the campus's registration and orientation for incoming freshmen and their families as well as an opening week orientation for freshmen and transfer students. The latter activities,

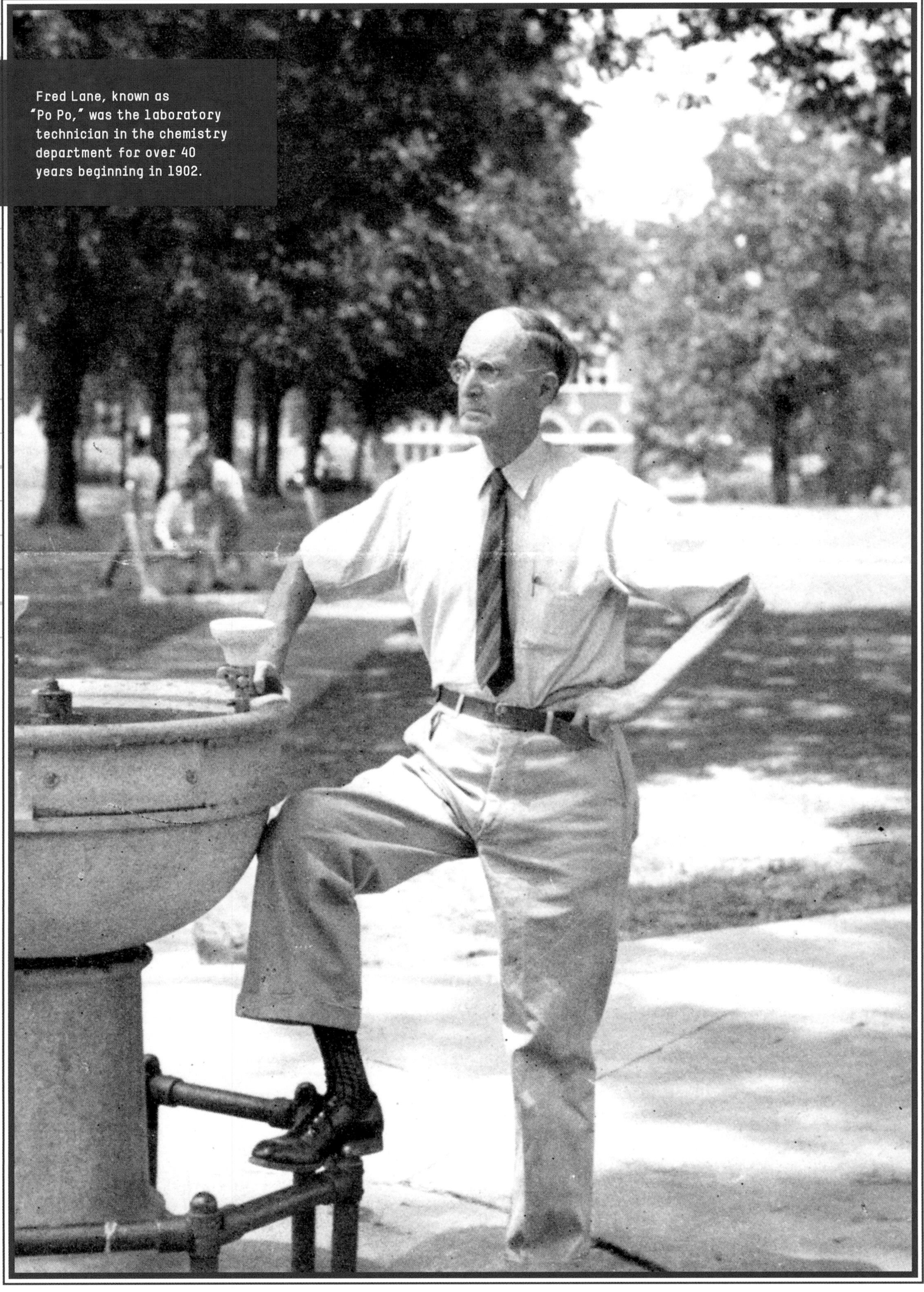

Fred Lane, known as "Po Po," was the laboratory technician in the chemistry department for over 40 years beginning in 1902.

Left: Beginning with Chancellor Merl Baker, Juanita Waters was the cook in the Chancellor's Residence for over 30 years, serving meals to over 2,000 guests annually including speakers in the Remmers Special Artist/Lecturer Series. Here she is with her favorite Remmers speaker, Colin Powell, former chairman of the Joint Chiefs of Staff and former U.S. Secretary of State.

Above: Juanita Waters prepares dinner for Chancellor Joe Marchello, his wife Louise and dinner guest President Gerald Ford in 1979.

a combination of specialized workshops and interactive programs, provided a vital introduction for students to mentor groups and the campus culture. The week's activities culminated in a team project to design a vehicle to compete in a race to demonstrate campus values and teamwork.

Between 1965 and 1979, most faculty, staff, and students got accustomed to seeing Wilbert "Bear Tracks" Burton walking from building to building. The 6'4" Burton, who had worked at a shoe company, bowling alley, and the Top Hat Lounge in Rolla before starting work at UMR, along with three co-workers, was responsible for two mail deliveries each day on campus. They first had to sort all the mail and packages from the U.S. mail and the inter-campus courier system in preparation for two rounds of mail delivery, one starting at 8:30 in the morning and the other starting at 1:30 in the afternoon.

Juanita Waters, who had worked for Chancellor Merl Baker and his wife when he was at the University of Kentucky, came with the Bakers in 1963 when he began his decade-long tenure. A gifted cook, Waters annually served gourmet meals to approximately 2,000 visitors to the Chancellor's Residence for over three decades. Those visitors included many noted public figures like former President Gerald Ford, former British Prime Minister Margaret Thatcher, and former Secretary of State Henry Kissinger, who gave talks in the Remmers Special Artist/Lecture Series. Waters' particular favorite was former Chairman of the Joint Chiefs of Staff Colin Powell, who she recalled as "very patient and very kind." Just as important Waters helped "raise" the children of Chancellors Baker, Joseph Marchello, and Martin Jischke.

Chancellors also had substantial support at the office. Connie Goodridge and Linda Bramel were sources of continuity amid the many changes in leadership in Parker Hall. Goodridge joined the university in 1979, and, after working in the purchasing department, the office of public information,

university relations and affirmative action, and the chancellor's office, she was away from the university between 1992 and 1995. She returned in 1996 to work in the chancellor's office where she remained first as a secretary and eventually as executive assistant. She took dictation, helped plan Remmers Special Artist/Lecture Series events and other events, handled accounts for the chancellor's office, as well as correspondence, and worked on special reports, all the while having to learn how to work with the changing personalities of the various chancellors. Linda Bramel began work at UMR in 1983 at the engineering research laboratory and then in electrical engineering and the English department before joining the chancellor's staff in 1992. She remained until 2014 with speech writing and creating PowerPoint slides as her primary duty. As was the case with Goodridge, Bramel had to learn to adjust to the different ways that chancellors wanted their messages presented.

The best of the staff and faculty always knew why they were at MSM, UMR, and S&T. While they might work in an academic department, in the administration, student affairs, or in physical facilities, their jobs were to help students be successful. They not only understood, but embraced that mandate.

1: Connie Goodridge, executive assistant in the chancellor's office, joined the university in 1979.

2: Linda Bramel and Goodridge were fixtures in the chancellor's office from the 1990s through the second decade of the 21st century.

3: Patty Frisbee directed New Student Programs for over a decade in the 21st century.

CHAPTER 4

MAKING THE MINER CAMPUS MORE WELCOMING

In a 1991 message to the campus, Chancellor Martin Jischke affirmed UMR's commitment that every "student, visitor, faculty or staff member" would "feel not just welcome, but valued." He had issued his statement in response to news that someone had put a Ku Klux Klan sign on the door to the affirmative action office. The reality that prompted Jischke's swift reaction reflects the long struggle for many groups to feel truly welcomed and valued as Miners.

The prejudices many underrepresented groups faced on campus mirrored the challenges they faced across the country. This chapter focuses on five groups whose experiences are representative of the difficulties underrepresented groups encountered: African-Americans, women, the LGBTQ (lesbian, gay, bisexual, transgender, and queer or questioning) community, international students, and Japanese-American students during World War II.

Right: The *St. Louis Globe-Democrat* covered the efforts of MSM's first African-American students, Elmer Bell Jr. and George E. Horne, to gain admission.

Below: A poll in 1950 revealed that 78 percent of students were in favor of admitting African-Americans to MSM but many of the white students weren't welcoming once Bell and Horne arrived on campus.

MAY 18 1950

M. U. Seeks Delay on Negroes' Suit

COLUMBIA, MO., May 17.—The University of Missouri wants a court action here delayed until a broader decision covering the same points is returned in another suit.

The request came in an answer filed by the university to action brought by Elmer Bell Jr. and George Everett Horne, St. Louis Negroes, to gain admission to the School of Mines and Metallurgy at Rolla. The suit is before the Boone County Circuit Court.

Since the two filed suit, however, the university has brought a declaratory judgment action in Cole County asking for a broader interpretation of state and federal laws applying to segregated educational facilities. The Cole County decision when it is obtained, will cover the action brought by Bell and Horne.

FEB 7 - 1950

10A St. Louis Globe-Dem

2 Negroes Sue to Enter Rolla School

Two young St. Louis Negroes sought yesterday to force the University of Missouri School of Mines and Metallurgy at Rolla to admit them as students.

A suit was filed in Boone County Circuit Court at Columbia in behalf of Elmer Bell Jr., 18, 4726A Vernon ave., and George Everett Horne, 17, of 4217 Finney ave. They are graduates of Sumner High School.

A writ of mandamus directing the university's Board of Curators and Noel Hubbard, registrar of the Rolla school, to issue permits to enroll was demanded in the suit.

THE AFRICAN-AMERICAN EXPERIENCE

MSM was segregated until 1950, and the campus culture well into the 20th century reflected the broader American culture of bigotry and intolerance. At a Red Cross fundraiser during World War I, MSM Director Austin McRae permitted the exhibit of a painting of his son Austin Lee "blacked up like a little darky, and eating a big piece of watermelon … as a picture of supreme happiness." Minstrel shows, with some students appearing in blackface, were a regular feature of campus social life through the 1950s. Indeed, as late as 1975 there were performers in a student show who appeared in blackface. The *Rollamo* account of a 1909 minstrel show characterized one student in blackface as a "catchy coon." During a freshman smoker in 1910 one student sang "darkey songs," and 15 years later in the joke section of the *Rollamo* one character named Rastus called another character the N-word. That same issue featured another joke about the Ku Klux Klan.

Campus leaders resisted integration through the middle of the 20th century. In 1938, following the U.S. Supreme Court decision ordering the University of Missouri to admit Lloyd Gaines to its law school or to establish a separate law school for Black students, MSM English Professor Eugene Johnson wrote a letter that Director William Chedsey sent to President Frederick Middlebush. Chedsey explained to Middlebush that Johnson was from Georgia and thus "has had considerable familiarity with the handling of the negro problem." Chedsey noted that he agreed with Johnson's argument that "the South" and, by implication, Missouri "will not want negroes in schools with its white students. The attempt will work for ill will between the two races." In 1946, a transfer student from Virginia wrote a letter to Middlebush thanking him for maintaining segregation at MSM. He was delighted to attend a university "free of any undesirable contact and association with Negroes." More important than the student's letter was MSM Dean Curtis Laws Wilson's reaction to it. He told Middlebush, "I shall look forward with pleasure to talking" to the student.

The Rolla community likewise was segregated in 1950. There were only 42 Black residents, a figure that included their children who went to the segregated one-room Lincoln schoolhouse on the south side of town for grades one through six. Students in grades seven through high school traveled, at state expense, to Jefferson City for their education. Black residents worshipped at the Elkins Methodist Church, located just a block from the Lincoln school. Hotels and motels were segregated in Rolla, and the only option for Black residents wishing to dine out was one reserved table at the bus depot. As one local resident explained, "Missouri is a border state" and merchants "would go broke in thirty days" if they were to "cater to negroes." Purchasing a home was difficult. Housing covenants in some Rolla neighborhoods prohibited property owners from selling their homes to minority groups, and the expectation was that Black families would live in the blocks surrounding Lincoln schoolhouse and the Elkins Church.

Such was the situation facing George E. Horne and Elmer Bell Jr. when MSM admitted them as the campus's first Black students. Although he had won his suit against the University of Missouri, Lloyd Gaines never attended as he disappeared soon after the Supreme Court's decision. Other students had sought admission to the University of Missouri and MSM to no avail. For example, in summer 1948, MSM Registrar Noel Hubbard, citing Missouri law stipulating that Black residents had to attend Lincoln University, rejected an application from Charles Brantley, a graduate of Sumner High School in St. Louis and a student at Stowe Teachers College (now known as Harris-Stowe State University) in St. Louis.

LINCOLN SCHOOL BUILDING.

Top: In the 1950s African-American residents attended the Elkins Methodist Church just a block from the Lincoln School.

Bottom: African-American children in Rolla attended the segregated Lincoln School on the south side of town until 1954.

With the assistance of NAACP lawyers Sidney Redmond, Henry Espy, and Robert Witherspoon, Horne and Bell, both students at Sumner High School, sought admission to MSM to study engineering. After Hubbard rejected their applications, the lawyers filed suit on their behalf in Boone County Circuit Court. The University of Missouri board of curators had hoped that state legislators in 1949 would pass a law admitting Black students. Because that had not happened, with Redmond's approval, curators, through their attorneys, sought and received a declaratory judgment from Cole County Circuit Court Judge Sam Blair in summer 1950 requiring that MSM admit Horne and Bell and that the University of Missouri admit Gus Ridgel to the graduate program in economics. This was not a complete victory for Black students. The judgment affected only students seeking admission to programs of study not offered at Lincoln University. All barriers dropped following the U.S. Supreme court ruling in the 1954 *Brown v. Topeka Board of Education* decision, which declared racial segregation in public schools unconstitutional.

Horne and Bell arrived in Rolla in time for freshman orientation week and found accommodations in the campus's first dormitory. However, the cafeteria was not open that week, and when they tried to get a meal downtown, they encountered Rolla's segregation practices. Not only were they not admitted into the restaurant, but also they learned that the restaurant owner called Dean Curtis Laws Wilson to instruct him to keep the Black students away from his business. Horne and Bell had to buy food at a local grocery store for that first week. Because the dormitory

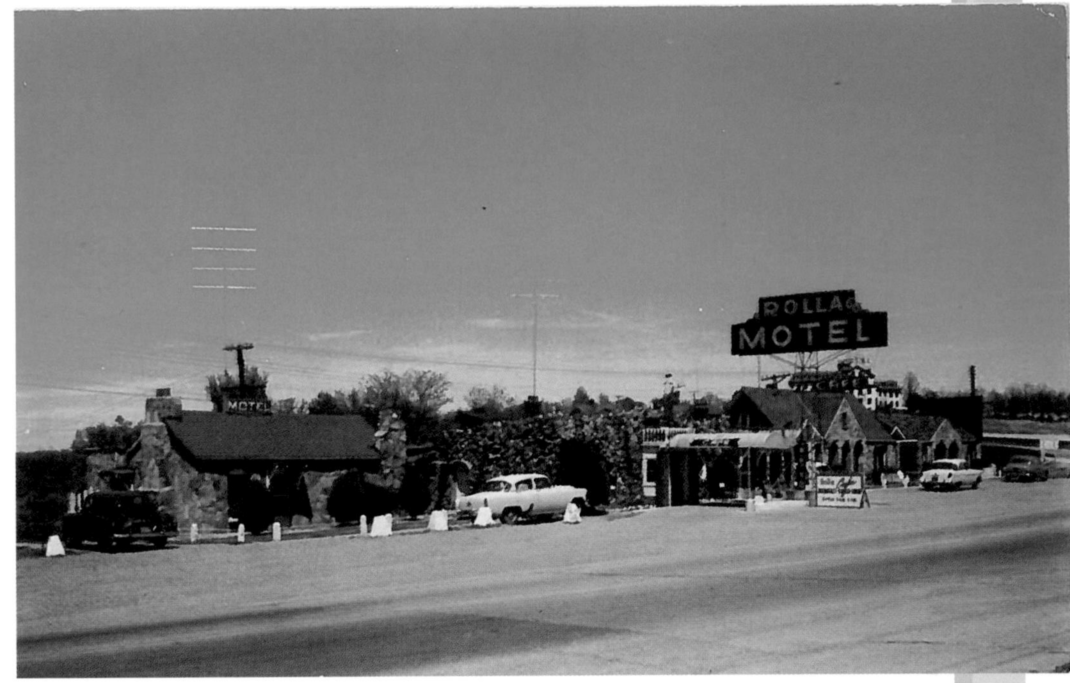

Top: Downtown Rolla in the 1950s where MSM's first African-American students, Elmer Bell Jr. and George E. Horne, faced discrimination when they tried to get a meal at a local restaurant.

Bottom: 1955 postcard of the Rolla 66 Motel and Cafe located along Route 66.

Top: Silas Garrett, a physics major, became the first African-American student to receive a degree at MSM in 1956.

Bottom: George E. Horne, along with Elmer Bell Jr., were the first two African-American students at MSM.

had no air conditioning, Horne and Bell left their door open and had to endure, as Horne recalled, "cat calls and the N-word" from white students. In March 1950, a poll among MSM students revealed that 78 percent "voted in favor of admitting Negroes to MSM," but clearly it was another matter for MSM's white students to accept living in a dormitory with Black students.

When Horne and Bell expressed an interest in playing football at MSM, Coach Gale Bullman told them to "come on out." Bell and Horne were both on the junior varsity football team, and Horne was on the basketball team, becoming the first Black students to play in intercollegiate sports for a public college or university in Missouri.

While they had no difficulties with their professors, Horne and Bell grew weary of the stifling bigotry they encountered in the community and decided to transfer to the University of Missouri campus, knowing that there was a larger Black community in Columbia. They remained in school there until drafted during the Korean War.

The admission of Horne and Bell did not lead to a rapid increase in the number of Black students at MSM. In the 1950s, never more than six enrolled, and it was not until 1956 when the first Black student, physics major Silas Garrett, earned a degree at MSM. Lelia Thompson Flagg, who attended MSM between 1956 and 1960, recalled that she might not see another Black student during an entire week of classes. By 1978, the number of African-American students at UMR had reached 175, but that still represented under 4 percent of the student body. Because of their low numbers, African-Americans were often the only Black students in a class or lab, which led many to feel nearly as isolated as Flagg had felt two decades earlier. The absence of Black faculty members as late as 1980 exacerbated the students' sense of exclusion. Interactions with white faculty members further complicated their lives. While they encountered exceptions, Black students, through the 1980s, believed that most professors had low expectations for their performance in classes and that few faculty seemed willing to help with course challenges.

While there were few examples of overt racism on campus, there were still occasional ugly reminders of bigotry. In the 1984 "April Fool's" issue of the *Missouri Miner*, the staff included a parody of Black History Month with a story titled "Honkeys Celebrate." It noted a "White Culture Month," which would have lectures on topics like "Ice Hockey — the White Sportsman's Final Frontier," and a "Wasp Ball." Three years later, a student wrote a letter to the editor of the *Missouri Miner* ridiculing the idea of the Martin Luther King Jr. holiday and the celebration of Black History Month. He suggested a "Christie Brinkley Birthday and KKK Day." In 1993, someone hung a noose over a Black faculty member's home front

Lelia Thompson Flagg, a civil engineering major, became the first African-American female to graduate from MSM in 1960. Here she is pictured with all the white male members of Chi Epsilon, the civil engineering honor society.

CHI EPSILON

First Row, Left to Right: Carlton, Rizer, Carver, Tharp, Halbrook, Woods, Weddle, Fisher, Thompson, Corbin, Patterson. *Second Row*: Swier, Dickens, Lovelace, Blevins, Bell, Fulton, Roberts, Fink, Stevenson, Ponzer. *Third Row*: Craig, Cain, Love, Owsley, Odendahl, Gilbert, Lortz, Wolf, Davis, Lynch. *Fourth Row*: Wisdom, Taylor, Popp, Brunkhart, Hyatt, Derx, Kern, Whelan, Blalock. *Fifth Row*: Bannister, Boston, Sidwell, Baumgartner, Adams, Logsdon, Hooper.

Chi Epsilon, National Honorary Fraternity of Civil Engineering, was founded at the University of Illinois in 1922. A charter was awarded the M.S.M. Chapter in 1950.

The keystones of Chi Epsilon are scholarship, character, practicality and sociability. The activities of this organization are designed to develop these characteristics in the prospective engineer.

Chi Epsilon chooses its members from the upper one third of the junior and senior classes.

OFFICERS

First Row, Left to Right: Thompson, Cain, Rizer. *Second Row*: Baumgartner, Bannister. *Third Row*: Fisher.

African-American students established a chapter of Alpha Phi Alpha fraternity at UMR in 1965.

ALPHA PHI ALPHA—FRONT ROW: Marsh; Price, Corresponding Secretary; Jackson, President; Manning, Vice President; Abram, Treasurer; Harvey, Recording Secretary; Jackson. ROW 2: Brown, Davis, Middleton, Denton, Coleman, Reed, Brown, Bester. ROW 3: Robinson, Hill, Barnett, Flowers, Rowland.

door. Twice a Black faculty member had his name plate removed from his office door. In the second instance, someone epoxied then screwed the name plate into a brick wall.

The challenge for Black students — as well as the faculty, staff, and administration — was how best to make the campus a more welcoming place, one that valued Black students and employees, a place where they could be successful. Change began with individual students. A determination to succeed and a sense that they had to perform at a higher level than the rest of the class, drove many. As electrical engineering major Ron Porter explained in 1994, "Every day, when I get up and go to class, I feel like I'm representing the entire race. I feel like I've got something to prove to white students at UMR."

Developing a group identity was also critical. In 1965, 18 Black students established a chapter of Alpha Phi Alpha, the oldest Black fraternity in America. The fraternity helped freshmen get acclimated to the campus and community and provided students an opportunity to develop leadership skills as well as a place to discuss racial issues. Having a campus-sanctioned organization gave Black students access to student government and intramurals. The fraternity also successfully lobbied for a change in campus policy regarding off-campus housing. Landlords had to agree not to discriminate against students on the basis of race, religion, or national origin if they wanted to list their property with the university. In 1981, Alpha Kappa Alpha sorority established a chapter at UMR, giving Black female students a comparable organization.

In 1969, about 30 male and female students, led by Frank Winfield and Gregory McClain, established the Association of Black Students, which initially called on the campus to hire Black professors and offer courses in Black history and literature. It also established a Martin Luther King Jr. Memorial Scholarship fund, sponsored a Black Culture Week, and brought prominent speakers to campus. Most importantly, in 1973, working with some faculty members, the association initiated a plan to call upon companies that hired UMR graduates to provide scholarship support to attract more minority students to campus. As a result, in 1974 the university established the Minority Engineering Program (MEP). Primarily under the leadership of Floyd Harris, who began as a peer counselor in that first year and then directed the program for 26 years, MEP provided scholarship support, a program of study in the summer before the freshman year, and the help of peer counselors and tutors for students from underrepresented groups.

Faculty members also played an important role in making the campus more welcoming for Black students. Jacques "Jack" Zakin, professor of chemical engineering, not only served as the first faculty advisor of Alpha Phi Alpha, but also on the Rolla Advisory Committee on Race Relations and as the first director of the Minority Engineering Program. History Professor Lawrence Christensen served as a faculty advisor for the student chapter of the National Society of Black Engineers, and, drawing upon the research he had completed for his dissertation, developed a course in Black history. Black students came to know other professors like Charles Remington in mechanical engineering and J. Kent Roberts in civil engineering as faculty members committed to their success.

To one degree or another, all chancellors and provosts, in a marked change from the views of Director Chedsey and Dean Wilson, played a role in making the campus more welcoming. For example, while serving as interim chancellor in 1985 and 1986, John Park established the Chancellor's Advisory Committee on African-American Recruitment and Retention. For over three decades, the committee, composed of alumni and current students, assisted campus leaders in promoting educational opportunities for Black students. Between 1986 and 1991, Chancellor Martin Jischke sent consistent messages on the campus's

BLACK STUDENT ASSOCIATION—FRONT ROW: Karam, R., Advisor; Compton, N., Secretary; Winfield, F., President; McClain, G., Vice-President; Brown, B., Treasurer; ROW 2: White, Fred, Wilks, R., Morrison, R., Johnson, B., Nash, Z., Moore, D., ROW 3: Hamilton, J., Newman, R., Curby, R.

Black Student Association

"If the entire American population were properly educated—by properly educated—I mean given a true picture of the history and contributions of the black man—I think many whites would be less racist in their feelings." From this statement were obtained the objectives of the Association of Black Students, an organization for the purpose of uniting and obtaining further representation for black students, and improving the relations among the black students, the white students and the members of the community. Although this organization is one of the newest on the UMR campus, it has successfully completed a

Inter-Varsity Christian Fellowshi

The goal of the Inter-Varsity C at UMR is to spread the good news o and to encourage each member in Chr was done mostly through speakers, gro Bible studies at the weekly meetings. Special events that were sponsored by Inter-Varsity included a free movie entitled "Lost In The Crowd," and a concert by Linda Rich, a folk singer who writes contemporary Christian music. Also a book drive was held for the Missouri State Penitentiary. As far as their activities go it seems that UMR's Inter-Varsity Christian Fellowship placed special

Frank Winfield and Gregory McClain led the formation of the Association of Black Students in 1969.

ALPHA KAPPA ALPHA

Left: African-American students established a chapter of Alpha Kappa Alpha sorority at UMR in 1981.

Below: Floyd Harris directed the Minority Engineering Program for over 25 years.

commitment to a diverse student body, faculty, and staff, particularly following campus incidents involving bigotry. He appointed an Affirmative Action Advisory Committee to investigate and "address the problems of the campus climate for minorities" and sought to diversify the faculty with more hires of minority and female faculty. In 2006, Chancellor John F. Carney III established a Female and Underrepresented Minority Faculty Recruiting and Retention Task Force in a further effort to diversify the faculty.

These efforts collectively produced positive results. In 1992, UMR was one of only 15 universities "to receive above average marks" in the retention of minority engineering students. In addition, from having no Black faculty members in 1980, by 1993 there were seven. The MEP program in its first two decades contributed to the graduation of 500 minority students, and by 2012 over 300 Black undergraduate and graduate students were enrolled. In some years the first- to second-year retention rates of Black students was superior to that of white students.

Yet to sustain the gains, there had to be champions of Black student success. Three individuals were instrumental. In over two decades of leading MEP, Floyd Harris was, in the words of 1979 graduate Robert Henry Jr., "almost like a parental figure. He'd let you know if you weren't studying hard enough or if you were hanging out at the University Center too much. He'd keep us in line." Chemistry Professor Harvest Collier became a mentor for MEP students in the early 1990s and also developed an orientation class for minority students to assist them in their transition to UMR. Lawrence George, who arrived in Rolla in 1960 as a chemist for the U.S. Bureau of Mines, became a critical advisor for Black students for over four decades. He helped secure a building for Alpha Phi Alpha and was its resident advisor. He worked tirelessly to recruit and retain Black students and publicized segregation practices in the community. In the 1990s he joined the staff at UMR as the assistant to the chancellor for affirmative action and equal opportunity, a position he held for 16 years.

While S&T was a much different place than the institution George Horne and Elmer Bell Jr. encountered in 1950, challenges remained. Well into the 21st century, there were few Black faculty and staff, and in a 2017 campus climate survey some of them, along with Black students, indicated that they "had experienced exclusionary, intimidating, offensive, and/or hostile conduct."

Above: Interim Chancellor John Park established the Chancellor's Advisory Committee on African-American Recruitment and Retention. In 2015, past and current members returned to Rolla for a 30th anniversary celebration.

Middle left: From the early 1960s into the 21st century, Lawrence George was an influential champion for African-American students. He also served for 16 years as the assistant to the chancellor for affirmative action and equal opportunity.

Middle right: History professor Lawrence O. Christensen served as faculty advisor for the National Society of Black Engineers.

Bottom: Besides serving as a mentor for students in the Minority Engineering Program, Harvest Collier offered an orientation course for minority students. Here, he addresses the freshmen students at the 2011 opening week convocation.

Rollamo
U.S.
THERE STANDS A MINING ENGINEER;
HE COMES FROM OUT THE WEST.
A GUN IS STRAPPED UPON EACH THIGH;
THERE'S HAIR UPON HIS CHEST.
HE WEARS A PAIR OF BUCKSKIN PANTS.
A FLANNEL SHIRT AS WELL.
OH HE'S NOT SO TOUGH, BUT TOUGH ENOUGH;
– AND THATS AS TOUGH AS HELL.
1929
Page One Hundred Fifty-eight

Left: 1929 *Rollamo* cartoon focused upon the masculinity of mining engineers.

Opposite: Eva Endurance Hirdler was the only female student at MSM in 1909. Although she completed all the requirements for a degree in mining engineering, MSM awarded her a general science degree.

Below: Eva Endurance Hirdler kowtows before St. Patrick during a knighting ceremony.

THE CHALLENGE FOR WOMEN

"Throughout the nineteenth century and most of the twentieth," historian Amy Bix writes, "American observers treated the professional study of technology as men's territory. For decades, women who studied or worked in engineering were popularly perceived as oddities at best and outcasts at worst." The experiences of student Eva Endurance Hirdler and faculty member Elizabeth Cummins illustrate the many challenges that women faced in Rolla — challenges that mirrored those experienced by women nationally on engineering campuses.

A native of St. Louis, Hirdler, after working several years as a stenographer and secretary, enrolled at Washington University in 1907 hoping to become a chemical engineer. Two years later, she learned that the faculty had no intention of awarding engineering degrees to female students, so she transferred to MSM to major in mining engineering.

Initially, Hirdler was a curiosity, the only female student at MSM. She later recalled that as she approached Norwood Hall to enroll she could see young men at all the

EVA ENDURANCE HIRDLER,
St. Louis, Mo.
She needs no eulogy, she speaks for herself.
Washington University, '08, '09
Missouri Mining Association.
"Little Eva," according to the St. Louis newspapers, is the only female mining engineer in the world. Has been with us two years and says she is sorry that it has not been four. Puts great dependence in her unlimited amount of nerve, and expects to operate a gold mine in California.

IVORY SMA
San An
Society is no co
Mass. I
Athletic
Student
After tr
M. S. M. was
here is caused

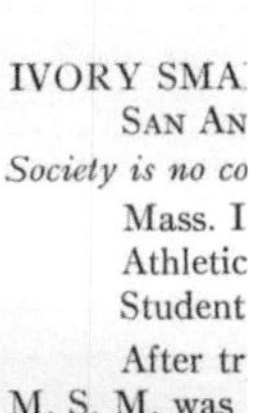

JACOB ADO
St. Lou
I pray thee, cea
As profitless as
Grubsta
Athletic
Basebal
Basketb
Basketb
Y. M. C
How he
cine advertiser
the faculty lik

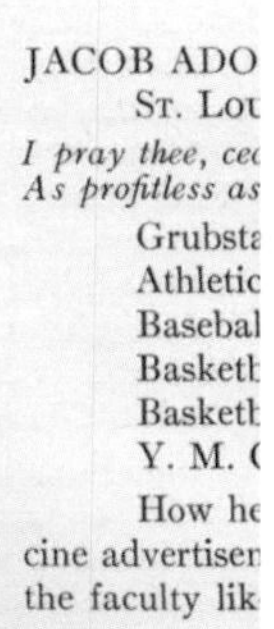

SAM PAUL I
Libert
I would rather
William
R. Way
M. S. M
Athletic
Paul co
blame him for
lar with the y
the bass viol.

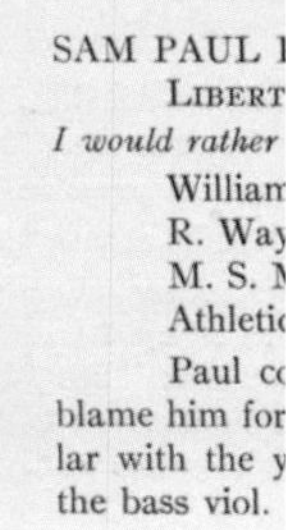

windows hoping to see what "'the Co-Ed' looked like." She tried her best to fit in. For example, realizing that virtually everyone smoked, Hirdler always had some "Bull Durham" tobacco and cigarette papers for those who bummed a cigarette.

However, she soon encountered "considerable objection" to her presence on campus from "particular groups of men." Hirdler persisted, doing well in her classes, serving as treasurer of the senior class, and becoming a St. Pat's knight and a member of the Missouri Mining Association. Moreover, some professors served as her "guardian angels," men who stood on the "sidelines ready to cheer me on when I needed some encouragement." Still, after Hirdler completed all the requirements for a degree in mining engineering, the faculty voted that she should get a bachelor's degree in science instead. For the rest of her life, she believed "that the faculty's refusal to grant her the engineering degree for which she had worked, was because she was attempting to break into what was then an all-male profession."

Six decades after Hirdler's disappointment, English Professor Elizabeth Cummins (her name at the time was Elizabeth Cogell) raised a question about facilities that triggered a debate on campus about equity for women. In the spring 1971 semester, Cummins taught a course in the Mechanical Engineering Building. When she unsuccessfully attempted to use a restroom restricted to female staff, Cummins protested to Thomas Faucett, the chair of the mechanical and aerospace engineering department. After Faucett explained that he was only following the architect's recommendation that there should be limited access to the restroom because it did not meet code requirements, Cummins sent memos to campus administrators, including Chancellor Merl Baker. He referred the matter to Harold Q. Fuller, the dean of arts and sciences. Along the way, Jim Pogue, the chair of the humanities department, and William James, the director of the Graduate Center for Materials Research, got into the fray and the entire "Privy Affair" became a topic at social events.

The outcome meant much less than the larger challenge that it raised. "At the heart of this entire issue," Pogue wrote, is "the feelings of the minority group and their attempts to seek equal and just treatment from the majority." Those who had the power to address those feelings did little and were dismissive. Baker did not even respond to Cummins' memo, and Faucett, in one of his memos, referred to "the principle of equality for women (whatever that means)."

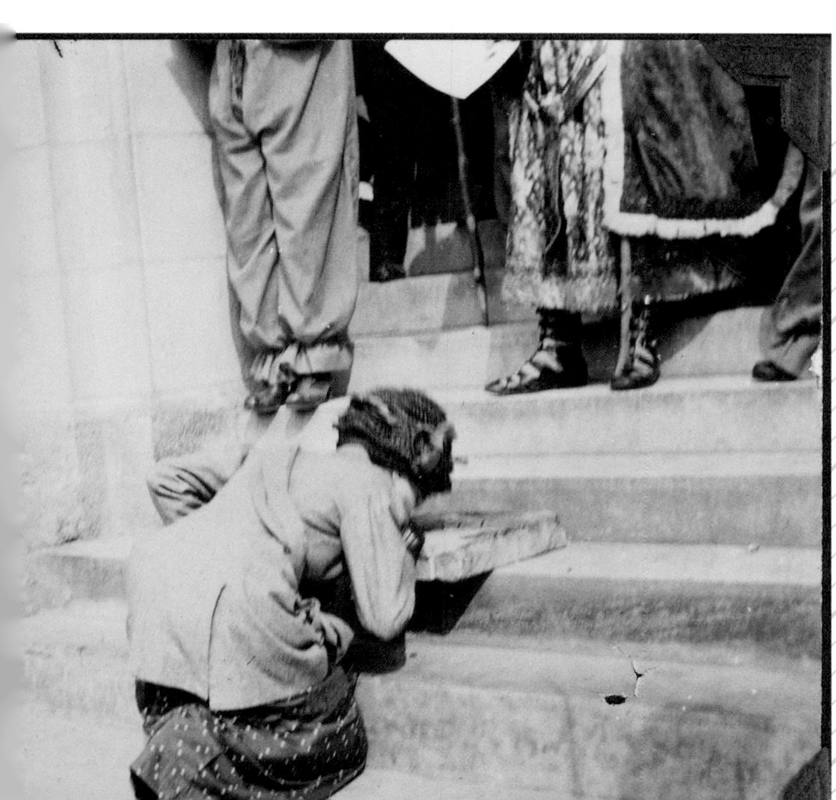

1: 1928 photo of eight female students at MSM. While the editors of the *Rollamo* wished for more female students they wondered "just the why and how of a co-ed engineer."

2: English professor Elizabeth Cummins' 1971 request to use a restroom in the mechanical engineering building designated for female staff set off a campus controversy over equity for women.

3: Jim Pogue, chair of the humanities department, supported Professor Cummins' request for equal treatment.

The Rollamo

Co-Eds

And here are those among us who change the whole trend of our school; everyone feels their influence, even Prof. Garrett, and we wish there were more to help make M. S. M. co-ed in fact as well as in name. But even at that we wonder just the why and how of a co-ed engineer.

1928

Page One Hundred Ten

1

2

3

MSM accepted female students from its earliest years; it needed them to bolster low enrollments. Between 1875 and 1895 the average number of female students was 19, which was more than a quarter of the students in most of those years. They were not at MSM to pursue degrees in mining, metallurgy, or engineering. Instead, most were "preparatory" students taking essentially a course of study comparable to the last two years of high school, or "special" students who could take any courses they chose. At a time when Rolla did not have a high school, this was their opportunity to complete their pre-collegiate education. In the process, several earned certification to teach in the public schools, and some took training in bookkeeping. There was, between 1878 and 1883, even a "girl's course in arts."

When the state legislature abolished the preparatory program of study in 1894, the number of female students dropped rapidly until there were none in 1905. Two years later, Director George Ladd reported to the board of curators executive committee that "there are no young women in the School," which pleased him because he saw that as a result of "its elevation to a true technical institution." Across the nation professors of and students in engineering believed that the "mental inferiority" of women made them incapable of studying the rigorous curriculum associated with mining, metallurgy, and engineering. Moreover, they saw engineering as a "male" calling, a career characterized by a rough and tumble, "hands-on" work life that women could not handle.

In a story sent over the press wire services in 1926, a reporter discovered that MSM students had a "pre-conceived idea of an engineer" as a "two-fisted individual, rather hard, and not inclined toward pink-tea affairs." They also were "strongly opposed to attending a co-educational school." Veteran mathematics Professor George Dean agreed because he believed that the male students would be distracted by "pretty ankles" if there were female students in the classroom, particularly in "these days of modern dress." The "boys wouldn't be thinking about Calculus," he said. In 1928, the *Rollamo* included a photo of eight female students. In the caption, the editors wrote that they wished there were more women enrolled, "but even at that we wonder just the why and how of a co-ed engineer."

Such dismissive commentary continued for decades. In a 1938 article in the *Missouri Miner*, a reporter noted the "feminine menace" of the slowly growing number of female students posed to "Rolla's traditional masculine stronghold. The rustle of skirts can be heard in every classroom. The feminine aroma of perfume is all over the campus."

Some believed that the women on campus really were not interested in a career in engineering. Rather, as a 1963 *Missouri Miner* article pointed out, many of the male students believed the women enrolled at MSM only to find a husband. One of the humanities professors agreed. He had three female students in one of his classes and wondered "whether they were actually here to study or merely hunting a husband."

There clearly were similar sentiments at the other 112 colleges and universities that granted engineering degrees to female students at the time. In 1892, Elmina Wilson became the first woman to earn a degree in engineering while she attended Iowa State College. Over the next six decades only 1,254 other women earned a bachelor's degree in engineering. Purdue led with 104 degrees, and MSM was tied for 25th with 15. While MSM was relatively high in granting engineering degrees, the female students on campus still were invisible to many. In 1952, for example, when the campus reported having nine female students, Dean Curtis Laws Wilson, in a letter to President Frederick Middlebush, noted that MSM "has no girl students."

The number of females attending MSM and other engineering schools grew slowly. Yet, as historian Amy Bix has shown, wherever the number of women enrolled increased, "a casual sexism" emerged with a focus upon "women's beauty and

In 1959, Barbara Lay had the highest grade point average in the freshman class.

Professor's Daughter Chosen Outstanding MSM Freshman

Russell Cochran, president of the MSM Chapter of Tau Beta Pi and one of the first freshmen to receive the MSM Alumni Association's Scholarships in 1955-56 and 1956-57, presented the Outstanding Freshman Award to Miss Barbara Lay, daughter of Professor O. K. Lay '32, and Mrs. Lay.

Barbara was chosen the Outstanding Freshman out of 763 freshmen enrolling in September 1957. She is majoring in Science-Chemistry, and has a grade point average of 3.85 out of a possible 4.00.

Russell's other achievements have been: Curators Award 1955-56; Sigma Pi Sigma Outstanding Physics Student Award; President, MSM Chapter, Sigma Pi Sigma; Phi Kappa Phi; Who's Who in American Colleges and Universities; Phi Kappa Phi Book Plate Award (all semesters); Phi Kappa Phi Gold Key Awards; Dean's Honor List (all semesters). Five of his grades have been "S." The remainder of his grades have been "E's," with a grade point average of 3.91.

JEAN LLOYD FIRST WOMAN EE GRAD

Miss Jean Lloyd, daughter of Prof. and Mrs. S. H. Lloyd, was MSM's first woman graduate in Electrical Engineering, receiving her degree in January, 1944.

Jean was an outstanding student ranking tenth in a class of 77. She was graduated with second honors and was made an honorary member of Tau Beta Pi, the honorary membership being due to the fact that only male engineering students are eligible for full membership.

Numerous offers of employment were made to Jean before graduation but she finally decided to join the WAVES and specialize in electronics. She is now taking her basic training at Smith College after which she will take further training in Radar and Electronic subjects at M.I.T.

JEAN LLOYD*

Above: Jean Lloyd, like many other female students, demonstrated that women could handle the rigorous MSM curriculum by ranking second in her freshman class.

Opposite: The wives of male students formed the University Dames in 1941.

bodies rather than brains." Magazines "frequently objectified women," and at many engineering schools the males portrayed "women students as sex objects."

Such was the case at UMR. In 1968, with more than 200 female students on campus, the *Rollamo* focused on their appearance: "All in all the changing look is one of beauty," and in 1973, the *Alumnus* magazine published an article that asked, "Can Engineers Be Pretty?" Female students through the 1970s reported being asked by their male counterparts, "What's a pretty girl like you doing in a place like this?" A 1965 issue of the *Missouri Miner* featured a cartoon showing a couple ready to leave for the military ball and the woman had a topless gown. The caption reads: "Of course, I still love you! I just don't think MSM's Military Ball is ready for a topless evening gown." Over the next four years many issues featured photos of attractive young women in alluring poses or in bikinis with captions like "Spring is Busting out All Over."

The September 28, 1988, issue of the *Missouri Miner* featured an article on those nominated to be homecoming queen that included a silhouette of one woman in a bikini and another one in the nude. In response, the following issue included a letter to the editor from 21 female students and one university employee. They wrote that they felt "gratuitously insulted and exploited." They also demanded an apology. The Student Union Board did so on the same page, acknowledging that the graphics were "very inappropriate and should not have been used."

Despite these attitudes, female students not only came to campus, but also persisted. One of the most important reasons was their success in exploding the myth of the "mental inferiority" of women. In 1941, Jean Lloyd, who became the first woman to earn a degree in electrical engineering, "ranked second scholastically in the freshman class." Eighteen years later, Tau Beta Pi, the engineering honor society, named Barbara Lay the "Outstanding Freshman" because she had the highest grade point average among all freshmen. Lloyd and Lay were not outliers. Virtually every year, when the registrar reported the campus's grade point averages, women were more successful than men.

Some of the female students in the early 20th century were the daughters of faculty members, and many took a few courses and then transferred to another college. When UMR began offering a bachelor of arts degree in 1967, students, like the first two — Dixie Finley in psychology and Glenda Dickman in history — seized the opportunity to pursue studies other than engineering or the sciences. However, engineering appealed to most because of their interest in science in high school and their belief that they would have better opportunities for well-paying jobs and interesting careers.

In the 1960s and 1970s, as historians Lawrence Christensen and Jack Ridley have explained, "Spurred by the women's rights movement that urged them to be anything they wanted to be, young women enrolled in engineering and science curricula." There was also an increased demand for engineers as companies across the country looked to meet affirmative action goals. As a consequence, the number of women enrolled at the university increased from 57 in 1964 to 469 a decade later.

University Dames

The National Association of University Dames was founded at the University of Chicago in 1921. The M.S.M. chapter was established in 1941. It is an organization composed of students' wives, and was organized to promote a spirit of friendliness, furnish a means of entertainment, and stimulate general culture among its members. It is sponsored by a board of faculty wives headed by the wife of the dean.

In order to give its members a greater variety of activities, the University Dames organized groups to study dramatics, singing, handicraft, cards and many types of outdoor sports. In addition to the entertainment at monthly meetings they have many social events.

Because of the enthusiasm of the officers and the members, the enrollment has been considerably increased. In the future the organization of the University Dames hopes to become even more popular and interesting.

Sadie Mueller............Pres.
Mary Gerlach............V. Pres.
Verda Minton............Sec.
Wanda Allmon............Treas.
Rose Carnahan............Asst. Treas.
Betty Johnson............Corr. Sec.
Marilyn Blackstun............Corr. Sec.

FIRST ROW: Rucknah, Edwards, Carrell, Allmon, Johnson, Gerlach, Carnahan, Blacksteen, Walker, Reed, Fowler, Bates, Schanbacher. SECOND ROW: Kalin, McClane, Trippe, Unnerstall, Hinds, Harbaugh, Mackey, Matthews, Coonce, Spratt, Gunther, Ford, Andreas, Penn. THIRD ROW: Macalady, Matias, Cassmeyer, Cooksey, Ledbetter, Marlow, Camper, Hollandsworth, Gregory, Jenkins, Sapp, Marsh, Heagler. FOURTH ROW: Minton, Geil, Morrison, Hadler, Spittler, Cox, Walker, Williams, Micka, Henninger, Link. FIFTH ROW: Gender, McCulley, Bramon, Lickteig, Speidel, Abbott, Mallow, Welch, Bramon, Arnstrong, Wehi.

Right: Florence Whiting (far left) at a faculty picnic 1880

Below: English professor Nadine Sease was the first female faculty member to have a long tenure at MSM (1928–44).

Nadine M. Sease, B. S., M. S.,
Assistant Instructor in English

John Herman Dougherty, A. B.,
Librarian and Associate Professor of Library Science

Over time, a network of support developed on campus for female students. In 1931, Director Charles Fulton appointed Mrs. B.H. Rucker as the first "Dean of Women." Alberta Schrenk, the wife of faculty member Walter T. Schrenk, followed her in that role. A succession of organizations began with the Rollamo Co-Eds in 1939, with Alberta Schrenk as advisor. It evolved into Pi Delta Chi sorority the following year. Students established a chapter of the Society of Women Engineers in 1960, and within five years it was the second largest in the nation. That chapter has remained strong on campus, and in 2019, the national organization named a Missouri S&T graduate, Natalie Vanderspiegel, as its director of diversity and inclusion. In 1963, an organization called Women Students at MSM was established, and 12 years later, the campus established a Women in Engineering scholarship program. That program evolved into Women in Science and Engineering in 2004 and in the same year, the Women's Leadership Institute emerged.

Another type of women's organization emerged at MSM in 1941. The University Dames, whose members were male students' wives, promoted entertainment and "general culture" for its members. By 1957, the group had nearly 200 members and a highlight of its annual activities was a "graduation." As the *Rollamo* explained in 1960, "while the husbands receive a degree, their wives are presented a degree in 'Putting Hubby Thru School.'"

Beginning in 1962, following the initiative of the Society of Women Engineers, the campus opened a series of dormitories for women. First a house on State Street, then a converted apartment building, then Thomas Jefferson Hall, and finally, McAnerney Hall, previously a men's dormitory, provided accommodations for women between 1962 and 1972. More housing became available when Kappa Delta became the campus's first national sorority in 1972, followed by Zeta Tau Alpha, Chi Omega, and Alpha Kappa Alpha over the next nine years.

Increased accommodations were essential as the enrollment of female students rose rapidly. With increases in virtually every academic year, there were 2,009 undergraduate and graduate female students on campus by 2016, a figure that represented almost 23 percent of the student body.

The campus rarely had a female faculty member prior to 1965. Between 1878 and 1883 Florence Whiting taught mathematics in the preparatory program, and Virginia

Conkling taught the subject in the 1884–85 academic year. Ida Bengtson taught an occasional lecture course and directed some graduate work in bacteriology between 1924 and 1931. Nadine Sease, who held bachelor's and master's degrees from MSM, taught English from 1928 through 1944.

University of Missouri President Elmer Ellis chided Dean Wilson in 1962 for MSM's "old tradition of employing only men." This made no sense, Ellis argued, particularly in the humanities fields where the Rolla campus had a reputation for mediocre professors. Apparently in response to Ellis' pressure, the campus employed seven female faculty three years later. Five taught English, while the others were in the ceramic engineering and mathematics departments.

Overall, the number of female faculty grew slowly. In 1997, there were only 24 tenure-track female faculty members. Women who joined the faculty through the 1990s often found themselves to be the only female in their department, and they commonly encountered dismissive male colleagues. Having a network of mentors was critical to help acclimate them to the campus's culture. Moreover, two policy changes made the campus more welcoming for female faculty members. One, adopted in the mid-1970s, permitted the hiring of spouses within a department. The second was the campus implementation of the federal Family and Medical Leave Act in 1997. This provided paid maternity leaves as well as leaves for women or men to care for ill children or aging parents. Nonetheless, there was a continuing problem of retention of female faculty hires. Chancellor John F. Carney III sought to address these challenges with the creation of the Female and Underrepresented Minority Faculty Recruiting and Retention Task Force.

Top: Connie Eggert, named as vice chancellor for university advancement in 2002, was one of the first women named to a major administrative post at UMR.

Bottom: In 2012, Cheryl Schrader became S&T's first female chancellor. Here she is speaking at a 2016 board of curators meeting.

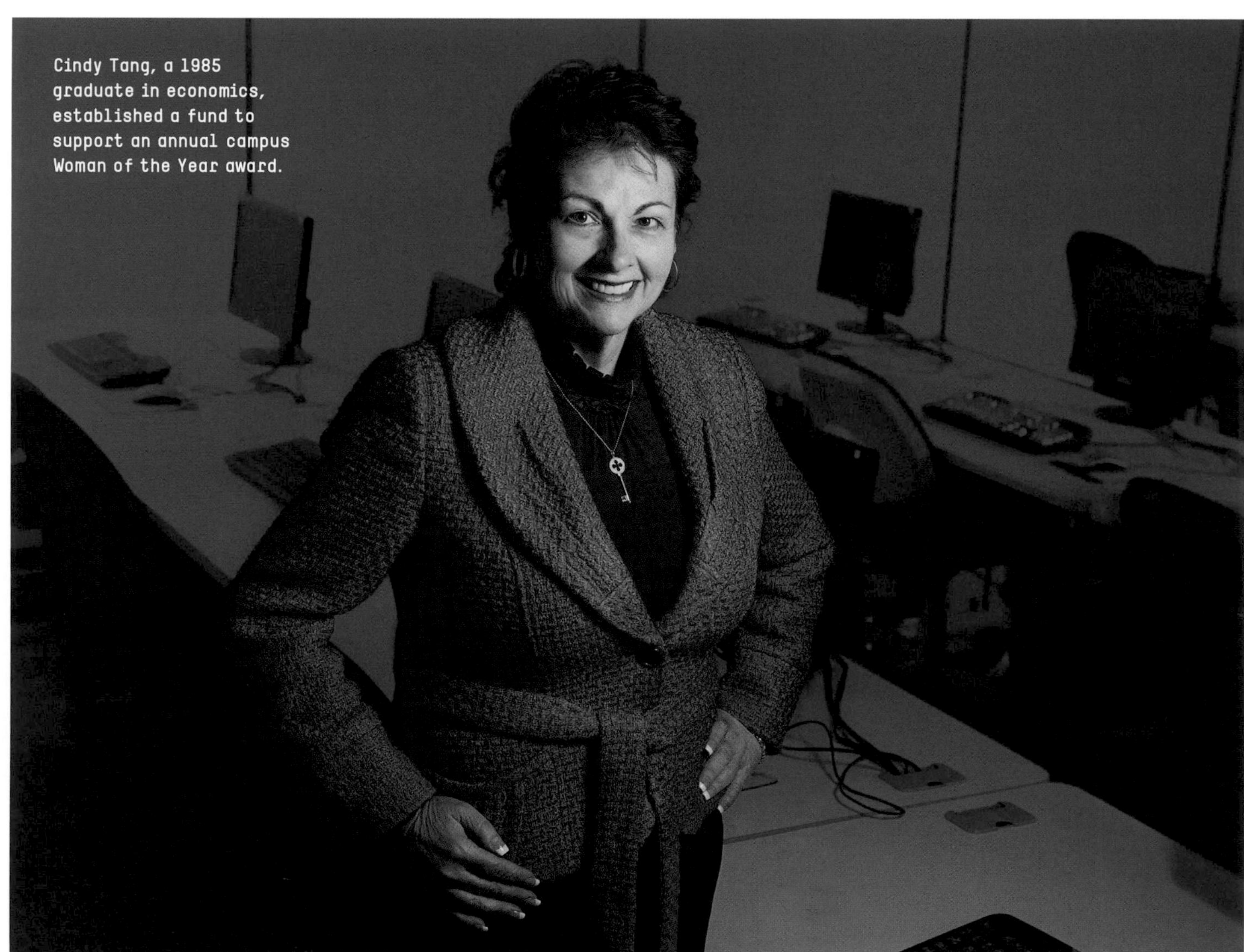

Cindy Tang, a 1985 graduate in economics, established a fund to support an annual campus Woman of the Year award.

As more females moved through the ranks reaching full professor status, the campus leadership began selecting them to fill administrative posts. In the 21st century, several women became named professors and served as department chairs, associate deans and deans of colleges, vice provosts, and vice chancellors. In 2002, Chancellor Gary Thomas named Connie Eggert as the first female vice chancellor for university advancement. In 2020, Melissa Ringhausen became the first female athletic director, and in 2012, Cheryl Schrader broke the ultimate glass ceiling on campus, when University of Missouri President Timothy Wolfe appointed her chancellor. The campus also established the Woman of the Year award in 1997 through funding provided by Cindy Tang, a 1985 graduate in economics, to recognize female faculty members who are "dedicated to student education and committed to diversity." Appropriately, the first recipient of this honor was Elizabeth Cummins, who served as the campus's first female department chair.

THE EXPERIENCES OF THE LGBTQ COMMUNITY

Gay activism on college campuses began at Columbia University and Cornell University in the late 1960s. In 1971, a group called Gay Lib sought recognition on the University of Missouri campus. Following rejections by the dean of student affairs, chancellor, and university president, the group, joined by the Gay People's Union at the University of Missouri-Kansas City, appealed to the board of curators. After a lengthy hearing, in late 1973, the board backed President Brice Ratchford's decision to reject the request and concluded that "homosexuality is an illness and should and can be treated as such and is clearly abnormal behavior." In 1978, after a series of legal challenges, Gay Lib gained a victory when the Eighth Circuit Court of Appeals overturned the university's decision.

At UMR, there was no activism until the late 1980s. In March 1988 the gay social community placed an ad in the *Missouri Miner*. That prompted a series of obscene telephone calls to the *Miner* staff. In a lengthy letter to the editor on April 20, the GSC (gay social community) explained that it was critical "to form a gay and lesbian organization" primarily to provide a "support group" for "anyone trying to come to terms with their homosexuality." Moreover, "a gay/lesbian group ... would provide a setting in which people could find an escape from the stifling and oppressive elements" of Rolla.

Between 1991 and 1993 the *Missouri Miner* became the focal point for a series of articles, editorials, and letters to the editor on homosexuality with titles like "High Moral Values vs. Homosexuality," "The Truth About Homosexuals and Their Lifestyles," "Some Hard Facts on Homosexuality," and "Do We Really Know the Facts About Homosexuality?" In October 1993, 19 faculty members signed a letter to the editor expressing their "alarm at the increasing levels of ignorance, fear, and hatred toward homosexuals on the UMR campus." "We are disturbed," the letter continued, "that for the past several years there has been a continuing diatribe against homosexuals in the form of letters, columns, and crude cartoons in the campus newspaper." In the end, the letter called upon "the campus community to maintain open dialogue between diverse groups in order to foster a climate of tolerance and understanding that should be maintained at a great University."

Despite this plea for tolerance, according to a report to the chancellor, there was a "series of sexual harassment incidents directed to the Gay and Lesbian/Bisexual community" in 1994. In this volatile context, students formed the Da Vinci Society "to provide a network for discussion and support for students with lifestyles that are alternative to heterosexuality." Because of the toxic atmosphere on campus, only the four officers were willing to be identified. Indeed, for several years, members maintained their anonymity. The Da Vinci Society remained a viable organization for many years, then evolved into Spectrum,

Below: In 1993, nearly 20 faculty members sent a letter to the editor of the *Missouri Miner* calling for "a climate of tolerance" on campus following years of vitriolic letters about homosexuality to the campus newspaper.

Wednesday, October 13 1993 Missouri Miner Page 3

Opinions

Faculty Respond to Homosexual Debate

Jeff Lacovich, Editor in Chief
Missouri Miner
Rolla, MO

Dear Editor:

As faculty members of the University of Missouri-Rolla we wish to express our alarm at the increasing levels of ignorance, fear, and hatred toward homosexuals on the UMR campus. These conditions led to the cancellation of a University sanctioned social activity for gay and lesbian students last August 27, in order to avoid confrontation, and possible violence, between gay students and a cadre of students who were protesting the event. The protesters' stated reason for opposing the gay social function was that student activities money was inappropriately expended for this activity. Whether this is true or not, one suspects, based on published interviews in the local newspaper, that the protesting students were driven to their actions less by a concern for fiscal responsibility than by an intolerance for anyone leading a different lifestyle.

We are disturbed that for the past several years there has been a continuing diatribe against homosexuals in the form of letters, columns, and crude cartoons in the campus newspaper. The polemics have gone largely unanswered. A point now apparently has been reached when extremists feel that they can use "strong arm" tactics to force their opinions on the rest of the university community. If the present conditions are not diffused it seems likely that violence to homosexuals or suspected homosexuals will follow.

A university should be a place where diversity is not only tolerated but expected and encouraged. It is a place where a multitude of cultures and lifestyles should coexist without fear of molestation by others. Additionally, the freedom of an individual to maintain a lifestyle that may differ from the majority is protected by the traditions upon which this republic was founded.

We therefore encourage students to treat all people with respect, regardless of their race, religion, or personal lifestyle. We call on the campus newspaper to exercise journalistic responsibility when inflammatory and degrading articles and cartoons are submitted. We ask that the newspaper strive for reasonable and balanced coverage. Finally we encourage the campus community to maintain open dialogue between diverse groups in order to foster a climate of tolerance and understanding that should be maintained at a great University.

Signed by

Jay M. Gregg
Larry Vonalt
Jack Morgan
Larry Gragg
Linda Manning
Gregg Keller
Catherine Riordan
Chris Ramsay
Richard Hall
Leo Soisson
J. Scott Saults
David Hentzel
Elizabeth Cummins
Cary L. McConnell
Paula Lutz
James Bogan
Richard Boyart
Juana Sanchez
Carol Ann Smith

1 and 3: Spectrum members discuss their organization during recent MineRama events on campus.

2 and 4: A poster encourages students, faculty and staff to "come out as an ally" to the LGBTQ community.

which maintained in 2019 that it existed "to create and maintain an inclusive, safe, and accepting environment on our campus and in our community for people of all sexual orientations and gender identities."

Despite the presence of these organizations, most students, faculty, and staff who identified as LGBTQ largely remained anonymous because they worried about discrimination and harassment for their orientation. In a campus climate survey released in 2017, for example, they "reported experiencing exclusionary, intimidating, offensive and hostile conduct" because of their orientation.

The year 2013 saw one positive development for LGBTQ employees. After years of campaigning by advocates, in 2012, the S&T Faculty Senate, by a vote of 21 to 4, joined the other University of Missouri System campus faculty senates in recommending that same-sex domestic partners of university employees "be allowed the same rights, privileges, and benefits to which opposite-sex spouses currently are entitled." A year later the board of curators voted to expand health-care benefits to same-sex partners.

INTERNATIONAL STUDENTS

From the late 1870s international students have been Miners. Between 1879 and 1909, students from 14 different nations found their way to Rolla. During the 1909–10 academic year, 19 of the 254 students were from foreign lands. In an era when the campus had a minimal recruitment budget, these students largely came to Rolla because of the influence of alumni who had found employment in many nations.

While they came from Japan, China, India, and even the British colony of Barbados in the West Indies during the first several decades of Miner history, most often they came from Mexico, Peru, and Chile, lands of numerous copper, lead, iron, coal, silver, and

Top: Boris Daniloff, an international student from Russia, earned a graduate fellowship at Carnegie Institute of Technology after graduating in 1929.

Bottom: Hector Boza, a 1911 graduate at MSM in mining engineering, returned to his home country of Peru where he later held many significant positions in government, including serving as his nation's ambassador to the United Nations.

gold mines. By the mid-20th century, most of the students were coming from Turkey, China, and India, but in the 1960s and 1970s they were joined by large contingents from Middle Eastern nations and Venezuela eager to study petroleum engineering. By the early 21st century, recruitment of international students became ever more important for the campus. In 2016, S&T had over 1,000 international students from 59 nations. Most were graduate students from China, India, and Saudi Arabia.

Among the thousands of international students were some intriguing figures. Boris Daniloff was a Russian who had fought in the anti-Bolshevik White Army following the communist-led Russian Revolution in 1917. Following the defeat of the White Army in 1920, Daniloff fled to China, where he worked for a couple of years before sailing to San Francisco. Daniloff wanted to study mining and return to his native Siberia. He heard about the Missouri School of Mines and after securing financial support from the Russian Student Fund, he came to Rolla. Even though Daniloff struggled with English, he had the top grade point average in his freshman class and graduated with honors. Following graduation in 1929, Daniloff secured a graduate fellowship at Carnegie Institute of Technology in Pittsburgh and then spent over 30 years as a metallurgist for the U.S. government.

Born in Peru in 1888, Hector Boza attended MSM from 1907 to 1911, earning a degree in mining engineering. After graduate work at the University of Wisconsin, Boza returned to Peru and developed a successful mining company. Active in public service, Boza served as Peru's ambassador to Columbia and the United Nations and led his nation's delegation to London for the coronation of Queen Elizabeth. Boza also served several terms in the Peruvian Senate, eventually becoming president of that legislative body. In 1937, Boza learned that Oscar Benavides, son of Peru's president, was interested in transferring to a university in the United States to continue his studies in mining engineering, and Boza urged him to enroll at MSM. Benavides did so, graduating in 1940 with a degree in mining engineering.

Hoping to foster "a closer relation among foreign students and those interested in foreign students," 11 international students established a chapter of the Cosmopolitan Club in 1909. It was short-lived, as was the Latin-American Club established in 1913. However, by mid-century, with several dozen international students on campus, over 50 established the International Fellowship "to promote friendship and understanding among all of the nations and with the American students." Over the next three decades a plethora of international student organizations emerged — including the India Association, Chinese Students and Scholars Association, Korean Student Association, Iranian Student Association, Federation of Latin American Students, Organization of Arab Students, Muslim Student Association, Venezuelan Student Association, Hong Kong Club, and Turkish Student Association.

These organizations offered international students a sense of reassurance in a place culturally different from their home country. "There's a feeling of security that comes along when one joins an organization; a sense of belonging," one of them explained in 1985. Another noted, "It's a nice, familiar feeling when someone speaks the same language, eats the same food and follows the same customs that you do."

Notably, it provided a refuge in a community that could be both welcoming and hostile. In the early 1900s, *The Rolla Herald* told readers that there were going to be students from Mexico, Japan, and China at MSM, and "although they are not of our race and our habits not quite the same, the boys should extend them the glad hand and make them at home with us." Editors of early editions of the *Rollamo* treated international students with the same ridicule it extended to all other students. In 1909, for example, they wrote that Aaron M. Shah, who was from

The Cosmopolitan Club

Russia, a nation plagued by anarchism, "once tried to be an Anarchist and still has hopes of succeeding. Studies the chemistry of explosives very assiduously, and one day intends to go back to Russia and show them how." In 1938, Oscar Benavides had done most of his high school work in England and France, where fellow students treated him as "just a foreigner." However, at MSM, he felt accepted, just "one of the boys."

On the other hand, as their numbers grew on campus some domestic students began to complain about their presence. As one domestic student explained in a letter to the *Missouri Miner* in 1963, foreign students insisted "upon going everywhere and doing everything in their own group, speaking their own language." Farouk El Baz, a native of Egypt and president of the Organization of Arab Students at MSM in the early 1960s, complained about "the lack of hospitality shown the foreign students on campus." Indeed, while he did not mention it, El Baz likely was also responding to the increasingly common epithet "camel jockeys" many MSM students used to describe students from Middle Eastern countries.

In 1975, a more serious challenge emerged for international students. That year an ad hoc faculty committee recommended a limitation on admission of international students. "The most critical limiting factor on the number of International students that can be enrolled by UMR," they wrote, "is the Rolla community. Adequate housing on or off campus is difficult to obtain and the community would like to see a reasonable balance between American and international students in the city of Rolla." As far as the campus was concerned, these faculty members wanted "to keep a reasonable balance between American and international students ... in order to assure a quality academic program for American students." Consequently, the committee recommended "No more than 10 percent of the total UMR student body shall be composed of international students." The campus did not adopt their proposal.

International events often made international students uneasy. After Iranian students seized the American embassy in Tehran in 1979, terrorists attacked the United States on September 11, 2001, and President Donald Trump's bellicose language about immigrants shortly after his 2017 inauguration, international students worried about potential harassment and reprisals on campus and in Rolla.

In part to combat these negative responses to their presence, international students began staging events with exhibits, shows featuring traditional dance and music, and traditional food. The culmination of that effort was the establishment of the Celebration of Nations event each fall in the second decade of the 21st century. The day-long event featured a parade of nations, dozens of booths with crafts and foods of various nations, and traditional music.

Above: The Cosmopolitan Club, established in 1909, was the first campus organization for international students.

Below: Farouk El Baz, who later gained fame for his work with NASA, served as president of the Organization of Arab Students in 1964.

In the second decade of the 21st century, Celebration of Nations became a showcase of the multitude of cultures represented by the many international students at S&T.

Seniors Jack Nomi (left) and Carney Fesler (right) served as vice-president and secretary-treasurer on the student government.

THE EXPERIENCE OF JAPANESE-AMERICAN STUDENTS

Two months after the December 7, 1941, Japanese attack on Pearl Harbor, Hawaii, President Franklin Roosevelt signed an executive order that led to the interning of people of Japanese descent in relocation centers in the interior of the country. The order prompted the removal of over 100,000 people, most of whom were U.S. citizens. The federal government permitted over 4,000 of those interned, after being screened by an agency called the National Student Relocation Council and passing an FBI background check on their loyalty, to attend college. By the 1945–46 academic year, they were attending 451 institutions, and 15 percent of them were studying engineering.

Six of those students attended MSM. On the surface, Jack Nomi, Kay Ikeuye, Yasuyuki Kuwamoto, Makoto Kawaguchi, Jack K. Ozawa, and Kor Uyetake, like most of the Japanese-American students, did not find themselves in an enviable position. They were in a small community where virtually all the people they encountered were Caucasian. Registrar Noel Hubbard explained that "none of us are burning with enthusiasm over the prospect" of having Japanese-American students. Indeed, he told Woodson Canada, his counterpart at the Columbia campus, "we don't think that we should take very many boys of this status here." Moreover, the portrayal of the Japanese military in popular culture was one of an uncivilized, incredibly cruel, and brutal fighting machine with absolutely ruthless soldiers.

Rather than hostility, however, all the available evidence indicates that the six students found a welcoming campus, and they all were successful. All but Ozawa were transfer students. They all did well in their classes, all made the honor list, and four served as officers in student organizations. Some participated in intramural sports. Jack Ozawa, for example, was selected as the best quarterback in intramural football. They became, as did many other Japanese-Americans, "ambassadors of good will" during the war, and this surely helped them gain the acceptance of the campus and Rolla community.

While all six had a positive impact on the campus, Jack Nomi was a whirlwind of success. A freshman in engineering at Oregon State University when Roosevelt signed his executive order, he was first sent by the federal government to an "assembly center" in Portland, Oregon, before being transferred to the Minidoka internment camp in Idaho in fall 1942. As he awaited a review by the National Student Relocation Council and his FBI clearance, Nomi picked

After coming to Rolla from a World War II internment camp in Idaho, Jack Nomi was successful in student government and on the football field.

Iron Greats

Gene Kennedy, Freshman. Gene held the end slot n conjunction with Rother and he brought down end uns consistently.

Jack Rother, Sophomore. Jack was one of the ends that gave a good account of himself during every game.

Carney Fesler, Senior. One of the few men who layed the game for the game itself. He played full me nearly every game.

Jack Nomi, Senior. The small quarter-back who kept the Miners driving during every moment of the game.

Charles Ecklund, Sophomore. Ecklund was a hard tting back who was hard to stop once he got started.

Joe Hepp, Freshman. A powerful little guard who was always in there fighting with everything he had.

Kennedy	Rother
Fesler	Nomi
Ecklund	Hepp

"We Want a Touchdown"

Page Fifty-one

sugar beets and potatoes for area farmers. In their assessment of Nomi, the Relocation Council staff described him as "poised" as well as "friendly and attractive," a young man who was "persistent and dependable, and an active leader in church, YMCA, school, and athletic affairs." He arrived in Rolla in early 1943 as an electrical engineering major. Over the next three years he realized the potential that the National Council saw in him. He became business manager of the *Rollamo*, chair of the student chapter of the American Institute of Electrical Engineers, vice president of the senior class, president of the student council, and the starting quarterback on the MSM football team, all while achieving good grades.

The campus has yet to fully reach the ideal of a place where all feel "not just welcomed, but valued," but over time it has become more accepting of people who were not white straight males born in the United States. While the percentage of female students has remained consistently at 23 percent since the 1990s, and the percentage of African-American and international students has declined in recent years, the number of minority students hit a record of 1,200 in 2019. That same year, S&T enrolled record numbers of Hispanic-American students at 341 and Asian-American students at 318. Most Miners in the 21st century understood that accepting diversity was in the best interests of the institution because it enabled S&T to draw upon all people who could contribute to building a stronger university. That acceptance also provided an opportunity for students to learn in a more diverse environment, which helped prepare them for a work place where they encountered people who were unlike them.

CHAPTER 5

MINER SOCIAL LIFE

The campus's rigorous curriculum left precious little time for relaxation, reflection, and recreation, but, regardless of the era, Miner students created a world of social and Greek organizations, department clubs, and intramural sports that afforded breaks from their studies, however brief. Freshmen, at least in the early decades of MSM, also encountered hazing, which most students surprisingly accepted as part of their initiation into the life of the campus. In every era students got into disciplinary trouble, particularly in their proclivity to drink too much alcohol. Beginning in 1908 celebrating St. Patrick, the patron saint of engineers, became the signature social event of the academic year. By the mid-20th century students also incorporated altruistic activities into their social life.

Eating clubs like the Shamrock Club, pictured here in 1940, provided students with nutritious meals at reasonable rates.

SHAMROCK CLUB

Above: Quo Vadis was a popular social club that celebrated the "hobo" lifestyle of students.

Below: The YMCA was a thriving organization on the MSM campus well into the 1920s.

SOCIAL LIFE IN THE EARLY YEARS

Alumnus Walter Remmers accurately captured what the social world was like for most students at MSM in the early 1920s. He described the campus as "a 'cloistered' place, a closely-knit, isolated community of men. Students had little communication with the world beyond Rolla. Radios were rare; cars were even rarer. 'You got off the train at Rolla in August and you didn't go home until Christmas.'" When the campus opened in 1871, there were just over 1,300 people in Rolla, a community with four churches, a bookstore, four restaurants, and six saloons. Fifty years later, the population was still under 2,100. So, it largely fell to the students to develop their own opportunities for a social life. By the time Remmers had graduated, students had established several social, technical, and Greek organizations, and had begun to enjoy intramural sports.

In 1876, the faculty approved the creation of the "Mutual Social Club." Its members could play billiards as long as they stopped by 10 p.m., did not play at all on Sundays, and drank no alcohol. Through the mid-1890s students participated in dramatic and debating societies. In 1874, for example, the faculty approved the establishment of a "literary debating and dramatic society" that presented many plays, including *The Merchant of Venice*. The plays usually involved community residents in some of the roles. In the early 1890s, the Philo Literary Society offered programs of readings, music, and debate to students, faculty, and the Rolla community. In December 1891, for example, they had a debate on whether civil engineers were "more useful to mankind" than mining engineers; the judges ruled that the team arguing the affirmative won. Over the next few years, members conducted debates on subjects ranging from capital punishment and prohibition to granting women the right to vote and government ownership of the railroads. Students also established a few technical societies such as the Mining Club, which became the Mining Association; an Electrical Club; an Engineer's Club; a Metallurgical Society; and a Journal Club for chemistry students.

As enrollment more than doubled in the first two decades of the 20th century to over 400 by 1921, students eagerly established more social organizations. The Satyrs, the Argonauts, and the Pipe and Bowl all lasted for a few years. Ten Masonic students, along with 10 faculty members and three alumni, organized the Trowel Club in 1914.

Quo Vadis was the most unusual of the organizations. Established at the University of Missouri in 1906, chapters opened at four other colleges in Missouri and at the University of Oklahoma and the University of Arkansas. In 1917, the MSM chapter had 16 members, including two faculty members. They celebrated the carefree life of the hobo and to become a member, one had to have ridden a prescribed number of miles on the railroad without paying. The organization claimed that only "men who have been prominent in some college activity" could join. Members wore a pin shaped like a tin can with the lid peeled back; their motto was "Please Mum."

For over a decade the Young Men's Christian Association may have been the most important organization, as it assisted new students in making the transition to campus life. Established in 1904, the MSM chapter slowly built its membership, which only cost one dollar a year, to over half the student body a dozen years later.

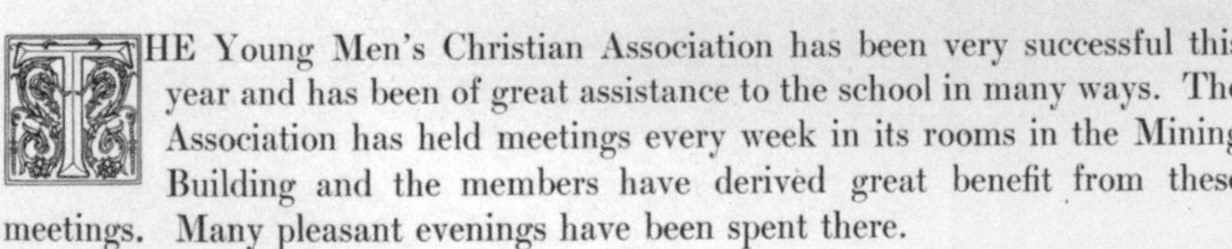

THE Young Men's Christian Association has been very successful this year and has been of great assistance to the school in many ways. The Association has held meetings every week in its rooms in the Mining Building and the members have derived great benefit from these meetings. Many pleasant evenings have been spent there.

The Lyceum Course, given under the auspices of the Young Men's Christian Association, has proved a greater success than ever before. The course consisted of the best talent obtainable, enough of variety being introduced to make it more popular. Every number was well attended, and all who came were well pleased with the course. As good a course is promised for next year, presenting the best talent obtainable in more numbers than ever before.

During the first week of school the Young Men's Christian Association rendered valuable assistance to the new students in placing them in desirable quarters and helping them to get acquainted with their surroundings and associates.

The Association has enjoyed a very successful year, and expects to continue to gain in strength and helpfulness to the School in the coming year as it has during the year just passed.

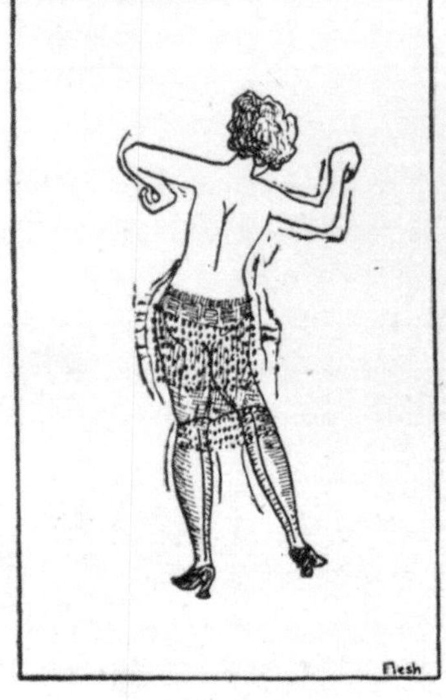

Freshman Smoker

AFTER the burning of the green caps at Thanksgiving holiday, the Freshmen took on an entirely different attitude. Boots and John B's. became quite the prevailing garm with them. In fact, a Freshman began to be treated like "white folks." He was recognized on the street and respected more among the upper classmen. In appreciation of this change in affairs, the Freshman class gave an entertainment in the form of a "Smoker." This wonderful fete was staged on January the fourteenth, and the attendance lacked very little of being 100%. On such an occasion as this no self-respecting Freshman class could depend on local talent for entertainment. They needed real professional entertainers, and they sure enough had them. Before we come to this stage of the game we must bring in some minor points that went to make up the program.

The party opened promptly at nine o'clock. A large circle of chairs was made around the boxing ring. This did not begin to accommodate the spectators, however, so some of them were persuaded to take back seats in another circle of chairs. The customary method of passing the pipe of peace was not attended to, but each man was presented with a handsome meerschaum pipe—made in Missouri. Then the peace smoke was started with no hesitancy as to the "biting" of a new cob pipe and "Old Hillside" combined. No drinks were served by the class. The first address was made by Professor Armsby: "Boys, the Sky is the Limit." After that the first bout was staged by two welter weight "dingies." This was not a hot scrap and up to the present time we have been unable to find out the kinship of the two negroes, but from the way they fought, one of them must have been depending upon the other for a livelihood and did not want to disable him. The next bout was of a more exciting nature. The opponents were Richardson and Stogsdill, who fought to a draw. Enthusiasm had reached its height, but we want to tell you that the entertainment had just begun. Mr. Abie Goldstein was introduced and his repertoire consisted of a bunch of good jokes. Every one brought down the house. The lady entertainers were then brought in to bring about the evening's grand finale. Miss Fawnette was a beautiful blonde, who appeared dressed in a very scanty costume of pink chinensis. Miss Phyllis Savonarola wa[illegible] type. She was a brunette of much heavier stature and was garb[illegible] creation of red satin. These two renowned actors were encor[illegible] account of their wonderful ability in their song and dance numb[illegible] nature and friendliness with their sudience were probably their [illegible] make their act a success. In all entertainments of this kind t[illegible]

The campus had many "smokers" during the 1910s and 1920s. These events provided opportunities for entertainment and collegiality.

Sigma Nu Swimming Team
Pounds, Eaton, Dean, Webster,
Kusa, Borrow, Thieker.

The administration provided space for members, including two rooms in the new Parker Hall in 1913. The YMCA published a student handbook, which new students received when they arrived at the Frisco depot downtown at the beginning of the fall semester. YMCA members helped students find rooms, held regular meetings and a Bible study class, and provided a reading room and lounge. Their purpose, according to the 1913 handbook, was "to promote the growth of the character of the men, to develop genuine good-fellowship, school spirit, and aggressive Christian work by and for students."

By the second decade of the 20th century several organizations had dances. For those who felt challenged by the prospect of hitting the dance floor, "two young ladies of Rolla ... conducted a dancing school during the winter months" between 1911 and 1913. Smokers, sponsored by the freshman and sophomore classes, the faculty, and the YMCA, became common throughout the year. A 1907 smoker featured pipe smoking, a pillow fight, a boxing match, a pie-eating contest, a fencing match, a wrestling match, and a "stag dance." The following year, the freshmen staged a smoker in the chemistry building with "a large array of corncob pipes and tobacco for the bowl" and "a bar which typified frontier conditions." By the 1920s, smokers featured troupes of "cabaret dancers" from St. Louis, women who prompted "fervent sighs" with their performances. The campus had smokers for several more decades, but their heyday was in the 1920s.

As early as the 1870s, students participated in baseball games, and in 1892 the campus had a graded athletic field north of the Rolla building. In 1906, four fraternities organized a Pan Hellenic Baseball League. Four years later, the independents and the faculty also fielded teams. By 1915, cross country and basketball were added to the developing intramural program. Thirty years later, under legendary athletic director Gale Bullman, the intramurals program had added football, wrestling, boxing, volleyball, swimming, and cross country. By the 1970s, women could also participate in intramural sports such as basketball, volleyball, golf, and swimming. Intramurals always attracted many students. Over 2,000 students participated in the early 1980s, and a quarter century later, the campus boasted more than 250 intramural teams with over 3,000 participants.

INTRAMURAL

SWIMMING

The Sigma Nu's turned out the superior swimming team this year in winning the intramural swimming meet. The victors took five firsts in the eight events of the meet, Pounds winning the 120 yard free style and the 60 yard individual medley. George Eaton won first place in the diving match and also in the 60 yard free style. Sigma Nu came out on top in the 160 yard relay also.

Triangle was the closest competitor to Sigma Nu with 18 points or 12 less than the winning score. Kortjohn took two firsts, one in the 120 yard medley relay and another in the 60 yard back stroke. Theta Kappa Phi nosed out the Frosh to take third place. Markway and Christman were the mainstays of that organization, bringing home 7 points. The Freshmen and Lambda Chi Alpha tied for fourth with 5 points each. The Engineers Club slipped by Kappa Sigma in taking seventh honors.

HANDBALL

Among the many sports in intramural competition, and one about which little is heard, is handball. Handball is a sport well-liked by many, athletes and business men alike. Here at MSM we, too, have handball. The courts, of which there are two, are located on the third floor of Jackling Gym.

The intramural handball tournament is held in the fall of every year, each organization entering a singles and a doubles team. Winners this year were Thorwegan of Theta Kappa Phi who defeated Dawlforth of Pi Kappa Alpha in the singles. Fink and Seltzer of Triangle defeated the Engineer's Club to take first place in the doubles.

Triangle and Theta Kappa Phi tied for first in the tournament, followed by Pi Kappa Alpha in third place, Engineer's Club and Sigma Nu in fourth, with Kappa Alpha and Kappa Sigma tied for sixth, followed by Lambda Chi in eighth, Sophs, ninth, Sigma Pi, tenth, and the Frosh taking eleventh and last place.

CROSS-COUNTRY

During the half-time of the football game between the Miners and Maryville, held here on October 19, 1946, the annual intramural cross-country race was held. Each organization was allowed to enter two men. At the crack [illegible] the men ran one lap around the track, [illegible] to Campus

Above: Swimming was one of many sports in MSM's increasingly popular intramural program.

Left: Intramural swimming story from the 1947 *Rollamo*.

MINER MEDIA AND PERFORMANCE OPPORTUNITIES

From its early decades, the campus had a newspaper. The first was *The Notebook*, published in the 1880s. Rolla newspapers occasionally published a student column, and in 1912 and 1913 there were a few issues of "a little sheet" called the *Missouri Miner* printed and distributed by a student named Augustus Gleason. In January 1915, the long-running *Missouri Miner* began publication. Editor James Head explained that the staff had a straight-forward hope for their paper: "If in the end it draws some of the old men back to us; helps some students to formulate a desire to do things for the old school; or to entertain and amuse any of you, we shall feel repaid for our efforts." For over a century the *Missouri Miner* remained an important chronicle of Miner social life, as did the *Rollamo*, the yearbook that began publication in 1907. In the early volumes, the editors provided histories of each class and narratives about campus life, usually ending with a joke section.

In the mid-20th century, students often criticized the programming on Rolla radio station KTTR. In 1951, for example, the station replaced "Turn Table Time," the one program MSM students liked, with "Strike out the Band" and "Organ Portraits," which the editor of the *Missouri Miner* advised would drive fellow students "to the books." There had been a Radio Club from the 1930s, and in 1952, the electrical engineering department sponsored WOEEE, a 1,000-watt station. After a few students experimented with radio broadcasting in the dormitories in the early 1960s, the campus approved the establishment of FM radio station KMSM. It began broadcasting in 1964 with the aim "to provide quality programming in both the music and educational broadcast fields." In the early years, the music featured a combination of light classical, easy listening, and jazz, but over the decades, after becoming KMNR, it became a "free format station" featuring funk and progressive metal. While the station had a faculty advisor, students ran it. In 1973, public radio station KUMR went on the air. It remained area listeners' source for popular National Public Radio shows like "Morning Edition" and "All Things Considered." KUMR also featured local programming. For over three decades history professor Wayne Bledsoe hosted popular bluegrass music shows and also published a magazine called *Bluegrass Now*. In 2017, St. Louis Public Radio took over operation of KMST, which became the call letters of the station after the campus changed its name to Missouri University of Science and Technology in 2008.

Besides the movie theaters in the community, students could see films on campus as early as 1913 in the Parker Hall auditorium. In 1953, the International Fellowship and General Lectures Committee opened a foreign film series to the campus with the acclaimed "The Bicycle Thief." Beginning in 1975 and continuing for over four decades, students, faculty, and the community enjoyed the UMR/S&T free film festival, which screened classic and critically-acclaimed films.

FIRST ROW, LEFT TO RIGHT: Manning, Marshall, Station Manager; O'Bryant, Business Manager; Mueller, Huckabee, Musical Director; Kettler, Educational Program Director, Smith. SECOND ROW: Strain; Engineer-in-Charge, Lytle Whites; Wheeling, Bowles.

Above: Cover of the first issue of the *Rollamo*.

Below: First staff of KMSM-FM radio in 1964.

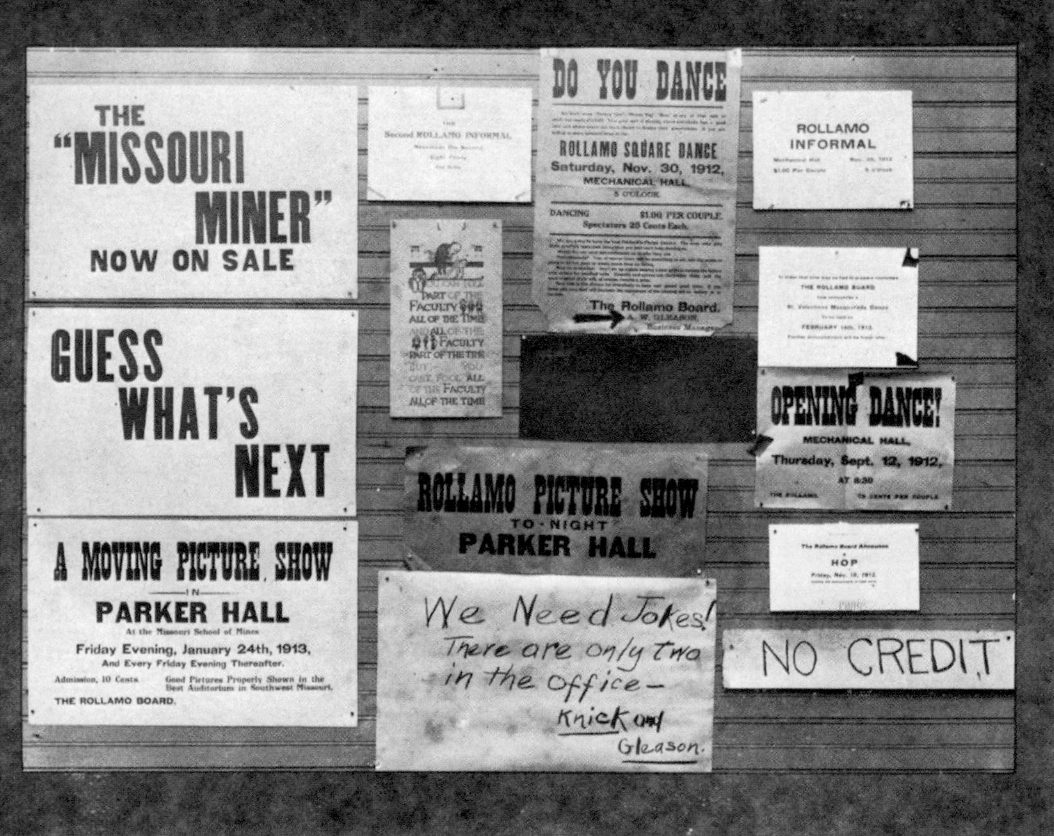

As early as 1906 MSM had an orchestra, usually with faculty joining students, and a glee club was established in 1921. For most of its history the campus had a band, but the MSM ROTC band was the oldest continuous unit. The man responsible was John W. Scott. He had attended MSM in the late 1880s and owned a drug store downtown where he also sold school supplies and textbooks, along with musical instruments. Scott's Drug Store became a popular hangout for many generations of students. Scott directed the Rolla symphonic orchestra at MSM commencements, campus concerts, and benefit performances to raise money for the campus athletic association. In 1926, Scott established the ROTC band, which he directed for two decades at no charge to the university. Scott was a legendary figure on campus, as was David Oakley, one of his successors. For over 30 years after his appointment in 1960, Oakley was a professor of music, as well as the director of orchestras and bands on campus, with a focus upon his beloved bagpipe band. Beginning with the Star and Garter Club in 1921 and the MSM Players a year later, students, often with Rolla residents joining the casts, continued the long tradition of theater productions begun by the Irving Literary Society a half century earlier. Under the guidance of theater directors Margie Boston, John Woodfin and Jeanne Stanley, the campus and community became accustomed to several musical and drama productions each year by the early 21st century. The performing arts had become so popular that students could minor in music and theater or join the Perfect 10 Improv student group.

STUDENT ORGANIZATIONS

The number of student organizations grew even more rapidly than the student population. In 1970 there were over 80 recognized student organizations, a number that jumped to 285 in 2019. By that year there were faith-based, governmental, intercultural, recreational, and media organizations with interests limited only by the imagination. Students could join groups as different as the Aerial Swing Dance Club, Geeks for God Club, Free Thinkers Society, Longboarders Club, or the Underwater Robotics Design Team.

Above left: Bulletin board advertising a movie in Parker Hall in 1913. It also notes the current issue of the *Missouri Miner,* which did not begin regular publication until 1915.

Below: The Underwater Robotics Design Team, pictured here in 2018, develops underwater remotely operated vehicles (ROVs) to ensure the health and safety of the world's port cities.

JOHN W. SCOTT & COMPANY

DRUGGISTS AND BOOKSELLERS

TWENTY-TWO YEARS IN THE BUSINESS

WE CARRY ALL THE

TEXT BOOKS, DRAWING MATERIALS, STATIONERY

AND SUPPLIES OF EVERY DESCRIPTION
NEEDED IN SCHOOL WORK

ALSO A FULL LINE OF

Photo Supplies, Magazines, Sporting
Goods and Musical Instruments

We want your trade. Our prices are right and we give you the best that money can buy. Call on us often and remember we are always at your service. Pharmaceutically yours,

JOHN W. SCOTT & COMPANY

Eighth and Pine Streets, ROLLA, MO.

Top: The MSM Players became part of the campus social life in 1922.

Left: John Scott, who attended MSM, owned a drug store that was a popular hangout for students downtown. He also conducted the community orchestra and established the ROTC band.

Above: David Oakley, professor of music.

Gamma Xi of Sigma Nu
INSTALLED JANUARY 23, 1903

COLORS:
White, Gold and Black

FLOWER:
White Rose

YELL:

Hi rickety hoop de doo
What's the matter with Sigma Nu?
Hullabaloo
Terragahoo
Ausgeseichnet
Sigma Nu

Above: Sigma Nu was MSM's first fraternity, established in 1903.

Right: 1966 Greek Week featured parties, carnivals, and competitions.

GREEK LIFE

In January 1903, 12 students established the Gamma Xi Chapter of Sigma Nu, the first fraternity at MSM. Before year's end there were two more fraternities — Kappa Alpha and Kappa Sigma. In December 1905 Pi Kappa Alpha joined them. With the addition of Lambda Chi Alpha, MSM had five fraternities by 1918, and three years later saw the establishment of a Pan-Hellenic Association "organized for the purpose of establishing a better spirit of co-operation between the fraternity and non-fraternity men." A century later there were 22 fraternities. Pi Delta Chi was the first campus sorority, with a chapter established in 1940, and by 2018 there were six. In that year over 20 percent of students were members of a fraternity or sorority.

In her study of undergraduate student social life titled *Campus Life: Undergraduate Culture from the End of the Eighteenth Century to the Present,* Helen Lefkowitz learned that Greek life had many appeals for students across the country. Some enjoyed the hedonistic aspect of Greek life, seeing fraternities as "a private club unencumbered by restrictions." Others liked the access to back files of tests and lab reports. Increasingly, students and their parents sought to tap the "useful connections" alumni offered to fraternity brothers and sorority sisters as they pursued successful careers. While there was an ebb and flow to these appeals over time, the constant attraction was the opportunity for service and leadership. Much of what Lefkowitz learned about the appeal of Greek life nationally also applied to Miner students.

According to the editors of the 1909 *Rollamo,* fraternities in their early years on campus provided "a large source of social enjoyment," with parties, dances, and even "moonlight sleigh rides." Over time, this social aspect of Greek life became well organized. By the 1950s, the Interfraternity

Right: Members of Pi Delta Chi, MSM's first sorority, established in 1940.

Below: Interior shot of the Kappa Alpha fraternity house in 1910.

Pi Delta Chi Sorority

Council had begun sponsoring a Greek Day after spring break to provide a respite before final examinations. Eventually, it became a Greek Week, with parties, dances, carnivals, and competitions. In 1975, for example, there was a keg toss, limbo contest, tug-of-war, and chariot race. Proceeds generated by the carnivals went to local charities. With widespread participation, Greek Week became, in the minds of some, "undoubtedly the most enjoyed party weekend of the year."

In 1922, in discussing the growth of fraternities, the editors of the *Missouri Miner* reported, "It is generally known throughout school that there is bitter feeling between the Fraternity and non-Fraternity men." As a consequence student advisor Henry Armsby had to meet with representatives from fraternities, clubs, and independents to deal with the strife. Yet, that was unusual, according to historians Lawrence Christensen and Jack Ridley, who wrote, "Little animosity existed between fraternity members and independents" most years. "They joined together in campus organizations and refused to divide politically along membership lines." In 1935, several students nonetheless formed the Independent Students of MSM to provide social activities comparable to those of fraternities, to gain access to student government, and to participate in intramural sports. By the early 1970s, there were about 1,000 GDI, as they liked to be called, and they enjoyed party weekends and an Independents Weekend event comparable to Greek Week.

Parties truly were important to campus life. Douglas Christensen, who was a member of Pi Kappa Alpha in the early 1940s, explained that parties were an essential way to deal with the stress of all the challenging academic work. "Saturday night," he recalled, "was the night for us to howl, and there were dances, fraternity and college, beer busts, tea parties, hay rides, canoeing, two movie houses, and lots of intramural sports."

Above: The Independent Students of MSM, shown here in 1957, grew in popularity over time.

Right: This 1909 cartoon illustrates that, at times, relations between Greeks and Independents were not cordial at MSM.

Below: Description of Independents from the 1957 *Rollamo*.

ninger, Schwegal, Vetter, Nauert, Segelhorst, Lange, Croddy, Nodge. SIXTH ROW: Deboard, Hayes, Wegener, Crist, West, Fiedler, Wright, Baskin, Jones, Gammon, O'Neal, Beasley, Stole.

Independents

The Independents were recognized as a campus organization in 1935 to represent all men not affiliated with a social fraternity in student government and student affairs. The purpose of the founding of the organization was to provide a common meeting place for all independent students where they might exchange ideas and interests and also develop a certain amount of fellowship. The organization also provides a means whereby the athletic talents of the independent students might be combined to enter as competition in the intramural tournaments with the fraternities. All non-fraternity men are considered Independents and are thereby eligible to join the Independent organization and have a voice in campus activities.

The Student Council and St. Pat's Board are among these activities and the Independent student representatives are elected from the Independent organization.

The pity of it!

At times, Greek social functions got out of hand and led to sanctions by the faculty or administration. Most of the problems dealt with alcohol consumption. Fraternity members often faced punishment for violating campus and university bans on drinking on campus. Administrators sought to address this by having chaperones, usually faculty members, at dances. Yet, as English Professor Joseph Barley explained in 1933 at a faculty meeting, "a chaperon must either wink at drinking" at the dances or "quit." In early 1953, a frustrated Curtis Laws Wilson decided to order fraternities "to remove the bars" from their houses after struggling with this problem, one which having married chaperones at parties did not solve.

Winona Roberts wrote about the other side of Greek life in a 1972 article for the *MSM Alumnus* magazine. Roberts explained that most fraternities stressed academic success, and that fraternity members were responsible for running their houses in consultation with faculty advisors. Other than six or seven designated "party weekends," most weeknights and weekends were relatively quiet. Fraternities and sororities were also quite civic minded. They raised money for the Muscular Dystrophy Association, the Cerebral Palsy Foundation, Easter Seals, and the local United Fund.

Regardless of the era they attended, alumni contended that the most lasting element of Greek life was the opportunity to make lifelong friends and to develop leadership skills in running a large organization.

ROLLAMO

PAN HELLENIC COUNCIL

Top: Missouri S&T students participated in the Greek Day of Service in September 2013.

Bottom: 1921 Pan Hellenic Council.

Above: A blanket toss of freshmen was a common feature in hazing the new arrivals to campus (1919).

Above right: The fate of a freshman who wore corduroy pants in 1919.

Below: For over four decades, the "Freshman Fight" was the most raucous part of the campus hazing ritual.

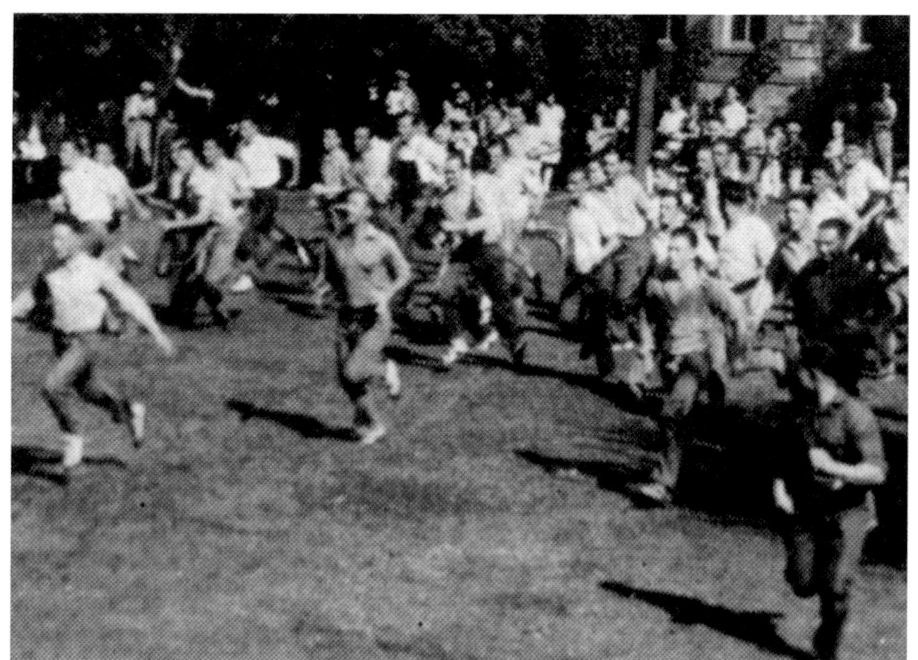

HAZING

Students at MSM, like those at most universities around the country, engaged in hazing. There was widespread agreement in the early 20th-century student body that this was useful not only in initiating freshmen, but also in demonstrating to them the importance of campus traditions as a way to boost campus spirit. As one upperclassman noted in late September 1904, the sophomores had "done little in making the incoming class submissive," which was an essential step in helping them understand "the routine of their new world." Through the 1920s, freshmen arriving on campus might well be met at the Frisco depot by members of the YMCA who offered a helping hand. Also, they likely encountered sophomores who taunted them as they left the depot, a signal of what was to come for the next few weeks.

Freshmen faced being marched downtown to perform humiliating tasks like using their noses to roll peanuts across the street, or being captured and then tossed in the air on a blanket, or being thrown into the nearby Frisco Pond. They also encountered rules of behavior. The 1908 freshmen, for example, could not wear ties or corduroy pants, could not step off the sidewalk onto the grass, and had to tip their hats to upperclassmen they encountered. After a "fight" with the sophomores, freshmen had to wear green caps, and by the 1920s, they had to wear green suspenders, too.

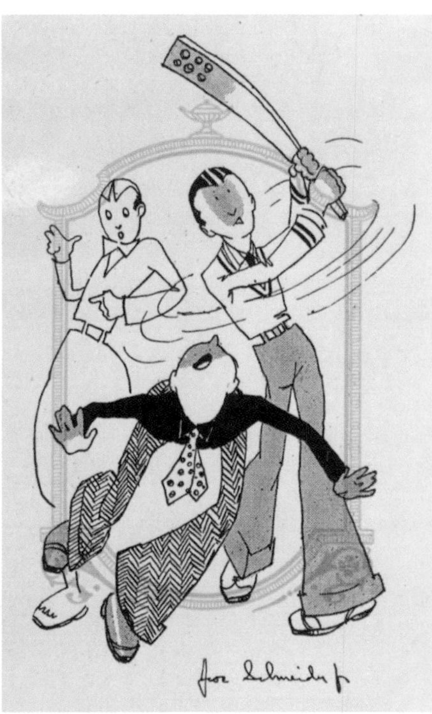

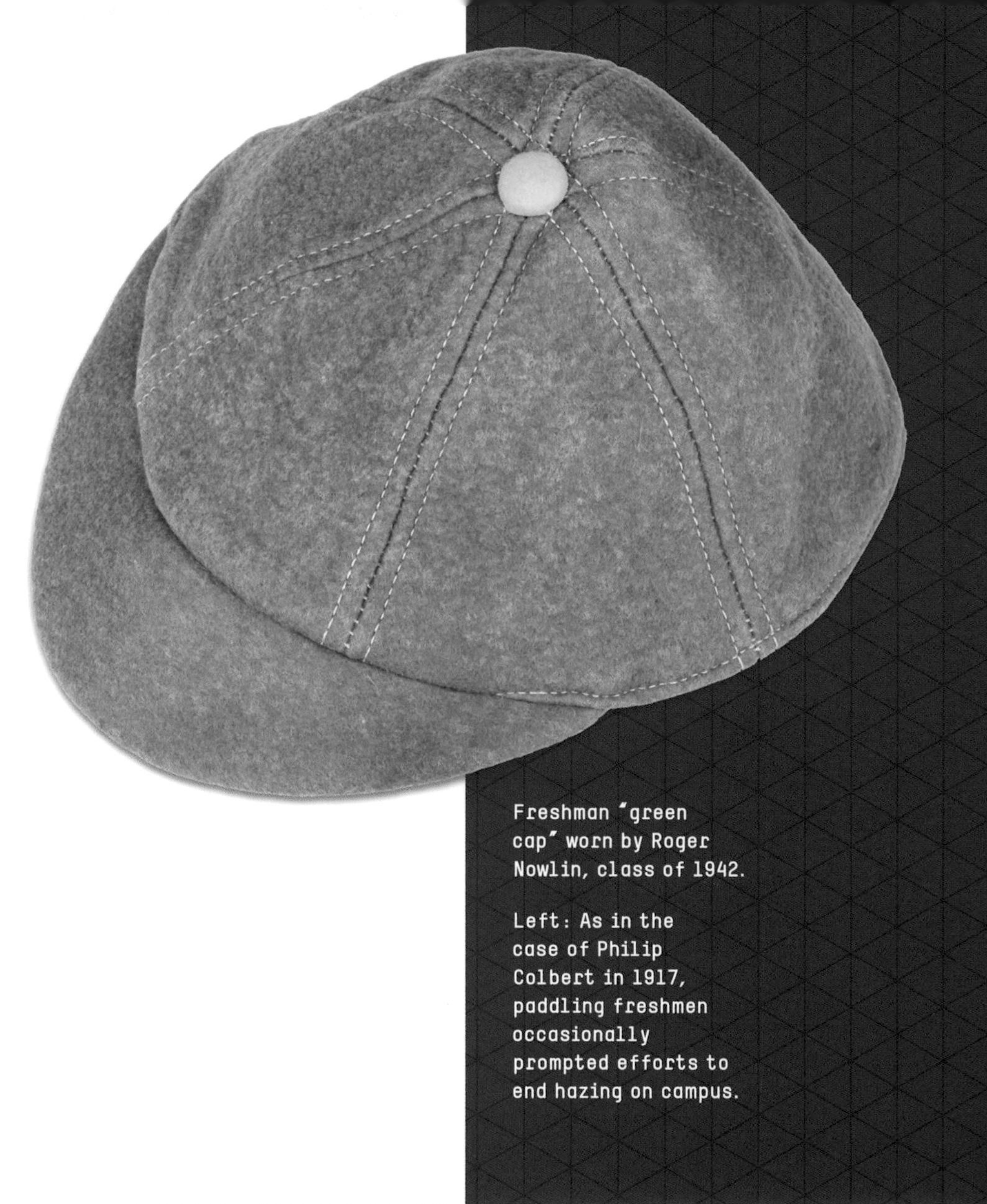

Freshman "green cap" worn by Roger Nowlin, class of 1942.

Left: As in the case of Philip Colbert in 1917, paddling freshmen occasionally prompted efforts to end hazing on campus.

Green Cap Day, usually in late September, was the occasion of the fabled "Freshman Fight," when everyone expected the sophomores to defeat the new students in a brawl in the middle of campus. The event drew faculty, staff, and often Rolla residents as spectators. In the days leading up to the fight, both classes posted proclamations around campus condemning their opponents as, for example, "damnable, driftwood, spineless belly-ticks and scum of the Ozarks." The object of the sophomores was not only to defeat the freshmen, but also to humiliate them by painting their faces green, shampooing their hair with molasses, "pantsing" them, and tying them all up and marching them downtown to be exhibited to the broader public.

Not surprisingly, there were often excesses in the treatment of freshmen. The most egregious case involved a freshman named Philip Colbert. On September 20, 1917, George Colbert wrote to Director Austin McRae and the faculty claiming that his son Philip had been "brutally and inhumanly treated." In response, a faculty committee of three investigated the "alleged hazing" of the freshman. They learned that a group of seven sophomores had caught Colbert pasting anti-sophomore posters on campus. They made him remove those posters and replace them with posters ridiculing the freshmen all the while paddling him. They then took Colbert to the Frisco Pond, stripped him, put a poster on his back, and made him return to campus, climb a light post, and then run a gauntlet of paddle-wielding sophomores. The paddling truly was severe, leaving his buttocks black and blue. He was in "considerable pain" for several days.

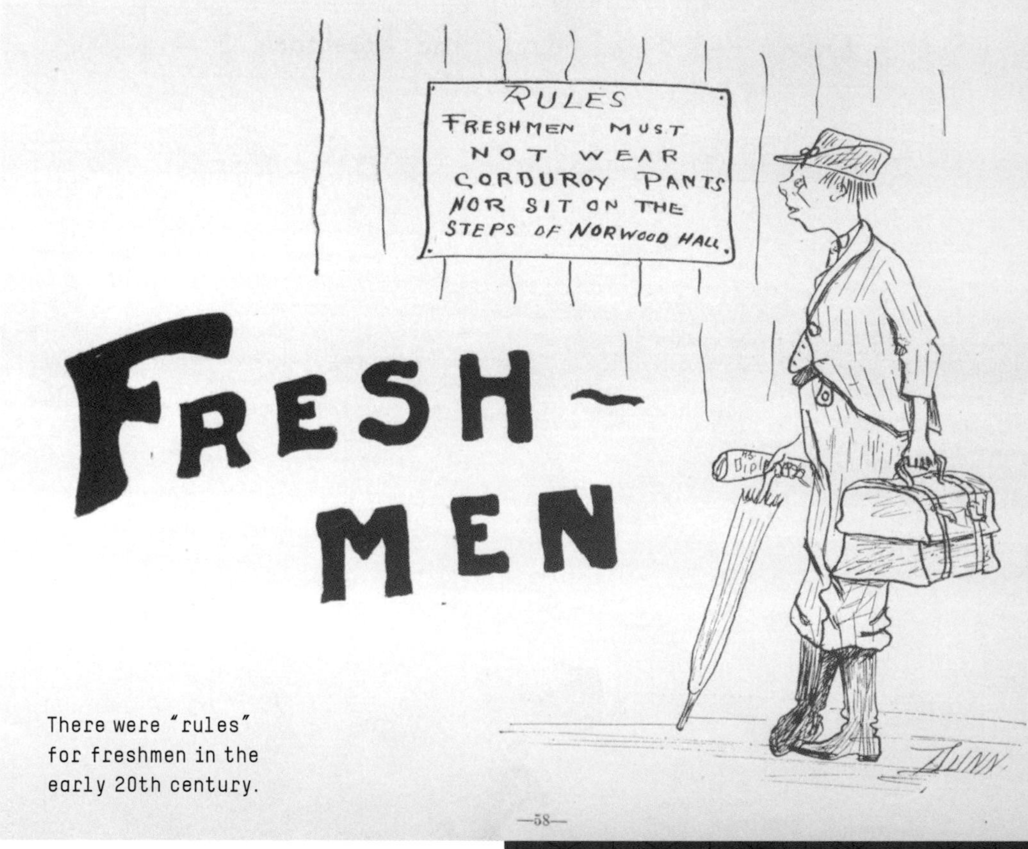

There were "rules" for freshmen in the early 20th century.

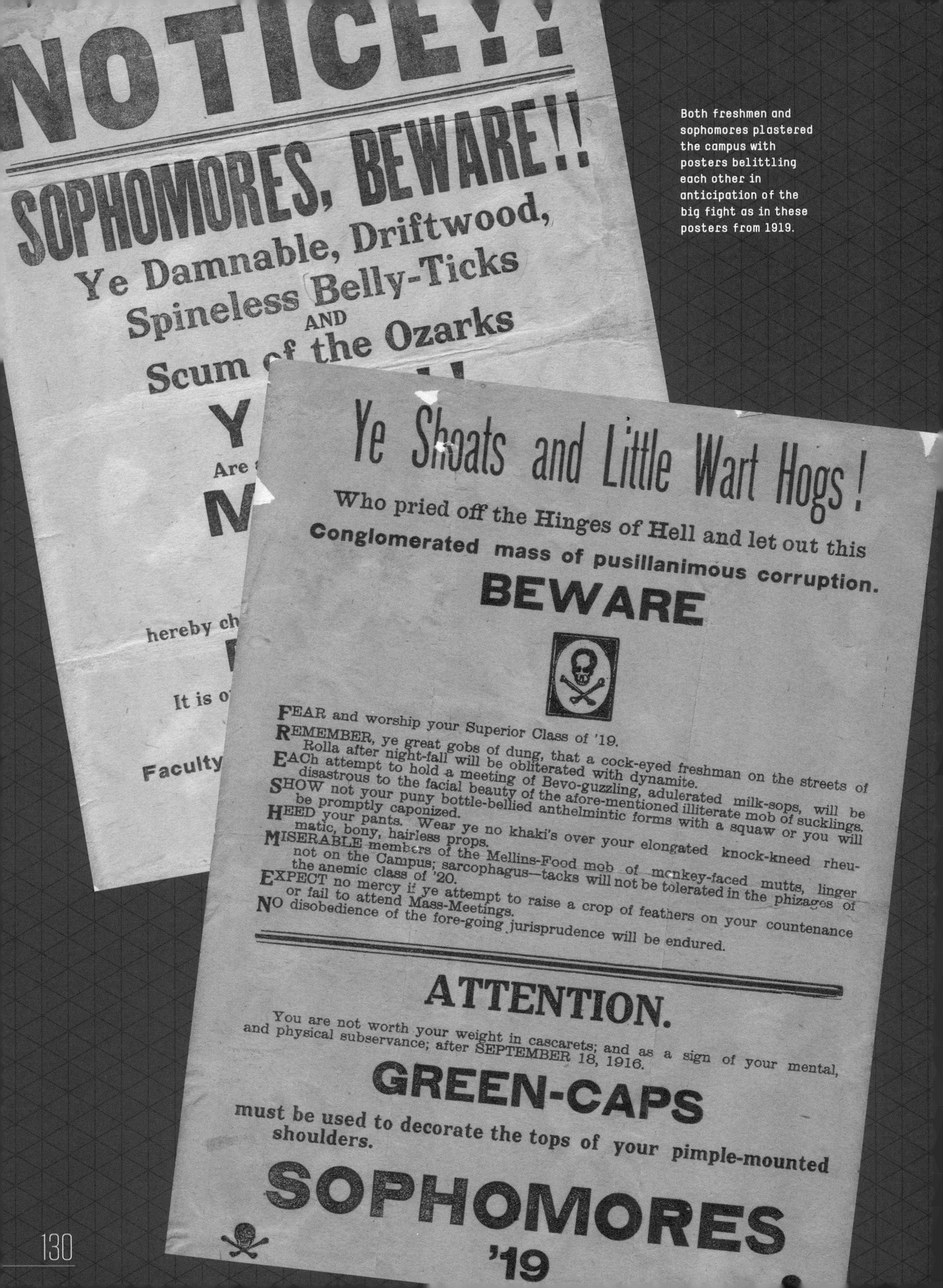

Both freshmen and sophomores plastered the campus with posters belittling each other in anticipation of the big fight as in these posters from 1919.

NOTICE!!

SOPHOMORES, BEWARE!!

Ye Damnable, Driftwood,
Spineless Belly-Ticks
AND
Scum of the Ozarks

Y

Are

M

hereby ch

It is o

Faculty

Ye Shoats and Little Wart Hogs!

Who pried off the Hinges of Hell and let out this **Conglomerated mass of pusillanimous corruption.**

BEWARE

FEAR and worship your Superior Class of '19.

REMEMBER, ye great gobs of dung, that a cock-eyed freshman on the streets of Rolla after night-fall will be obliterated with dynamite.

EACh attempt to hold a meeting of Bevo-guzzling, adulerated milk-sops, will be disastrous to the facial beauty of the afore-mentioned illiterate mob of sucklings.

SHOW not your puny bottle-bellied anthelmintic forms with a squaw or you will be promptly caponized.

HEED your pants. Wear ye no khaki's over your elongated knock-kneed rheumatic, bony, hairless props.

MISERABLE members of the Mellins-Food mob of monkey-faced mutts, linger not on the Campus; sarcophagus—tacks will not be tolerated in the phizages of the anemic class of '20.

EXPECT no mercy if ye attempt to raise a crop of feathers on your countenance or fail to attend Mass-Meetings.

NO disobedience of the fore-going jurisprudence will be endured.

ATTENTION.

You are not worth your weight in cascarets; and as a sign of your mental, and physical subservance; after SEPTEMBER 18, 1916.

GREEN-CAPS

must be used to decorate the tops of your pimple-mounted shoulders.

SOPHOMORES
'19

After hearing from witnesses and the students involved, the faculty made a curious decision. Rather than hold the students accountable for their treatment of Colbert, they concluded that "the trouble was caused by the hazing custom and practices and not by willful maliciousness on the part of the participants." Thus, rather than punish the students involved, the faculty voted "to abolish all hazing" and "made expulsion the penalty for violation of this rule." Yet, they made a notable exception: "This does not apply to the class contests on Green Cap Day." This was only one attempt from the 1910s by the faculty, administration, student council, and board of curators to limit, if not eliminate, all these hazing activities. All to no avail.

This reluctance to eliminate hazing was a product of an embrace of its humiliations by most students. As the editors of the 1908 *Rollamo* explained, participating in hazing activities "typify the 'hang together' spirit which goes to make college memories dear in after years." In the following decade, the editors of the *Missouri Miner* were more expansive on hazing's place at MSM. They told the freshmen that, although sometimes hazing "does go too far," it actually was a good way to make friends. If they took "all hazing in a good spirit," the upperclassmen would admire their stoicism. In the end, the editors promised, "You will laugh, you will be glad that you went thru the whole ordeal, for the friendship of others who are real men is a prize worth striving for."

While there were changes over time, Green Cap Day continued into the 1940s. With the end of World War II, however, the ritualistic humiliation of freshmen ceased. As historians Lawrence Christensen and Jack Ridley have pointed out, "Veterans of Corregidor, North Africa, or Normandy were not inclined to tolerate dress codes, green beanies, or the freshman fight."

Still, hazing did not disappear. Rather, it became part of the initiation into living groups. Fraternities, sororities, eating clubs, and dormitories developed hazing rituals. Fraternities had long subjected pledges to weekend duties. As Douglas Christensen explained, Saturday duties including "painting, cleaning windows, yard work, etc., all on top of studies." Then, there was "hell week" which involved "a loss of sleep over three days with some outlandish duties to perform." Professor Michael Patrick wrote in 1987 that those rituals remained: "Greek groups have 'midnight kitchen' for pledges, who work from midnight on cleaning. The Frisco Pond is still used for some rites of baptism. Some groups have study halls for their initiates."

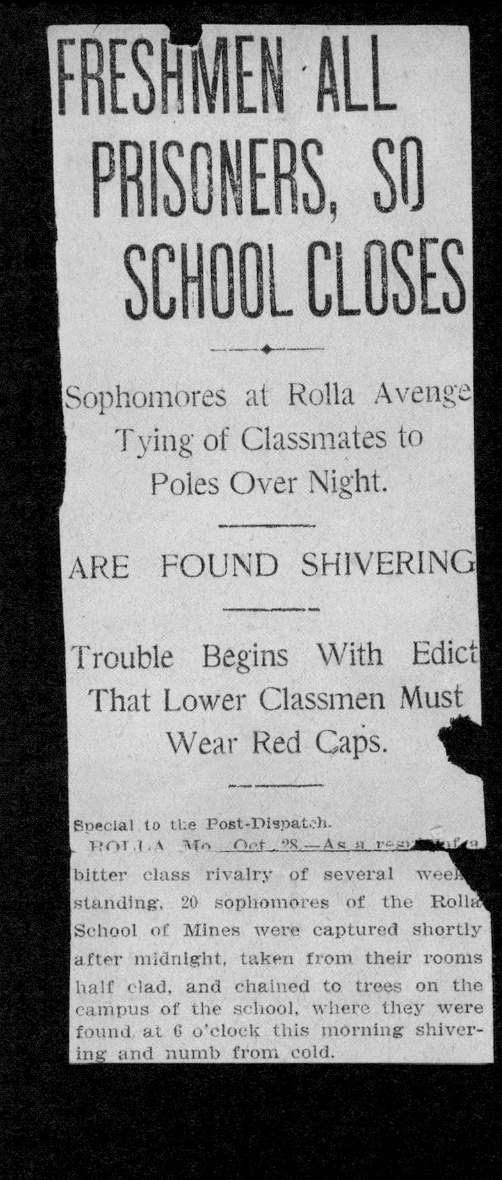

FRESHMEN ALL PRISONERS, SO SCHOOL CLOSES

Sophomores at Rolla Avenge Tying of Classmates to Poles Over Night.

ARE FOUND SHIVERING

Trouble Begins With Edict That Lower Classmen Must Wear Red Caps.

Special to the Post-Dispatch.

ROLLA, Mo., Oct. 28.—As a result of a bitter class rivalry of several weeks standing, 20 sophomores of the Rolla School of Mines were captured shortly after midnight, taken from their rooms half clad, and chained to trees on the campus of the school, where they were found at 6 o'clock this morning shivering and numb from cold.

After they were released the sophomores organized and took 75 freshmen prisoners, tied them together with ropes and chains, and marched them to the Postoffice to the music of the school band. The sophomores refused to release their rivals until they wrested an agreement from them to adhere to a set of rules mapped out by the sophomores.

There was not a pupil in the school building this morning at the hour of opening, and L. E. Young, director of the institution, ordered a half-day suspension. Prof. Young appealed to the sophomores to release their prisoners, agreeing to take them all back without punishment if they complied promptly. He also offered them the forenoon as a half holiday, but they refused to agree to any arrangement which precluded a complete surrender on the part of the freshmen.

Demanded Wearing of Caps.

The trouble arose principally over the demand of the sophomores that the freshmen appear at the school in green caps with yellow buttons. The rule as to the caps was to become effective today. The sophomores ordered 100 of the caps, and they insist that the freshmen must wear them.

Late yesterday, by soms means, the freshmen learned of the intention of the sophomores and set about at midnight to forestall them. Most of the sophomores were in bed and they were not given time to dress completely. One sophomore known as "Red" Barrett, resisted and, after a desperate struggle, put 20 freshmen to flight.

Last week the sophomores issued a pamphlet attacking the freshmen and applying uncomplimentary names. This was partially the cause of the trouble.

Director Young said today that the sophomores would be conceded the right to demand that the freshmen wear caps, but that they should neither designate the color nor select them.

Above: 1907 *St. Louis Post-Dispatch* article describing the bitter class rivalry between freshmen and sophomores. Note the headline should read "Trouble Begins With Edict That Lower Classmen Must Wear *Green* Caps."

STUDENT DISCIPLINE: HOW DID MINERS GET INTO TROUBLE?

From MSM's earliest years, the faculty had great concern that students be focused upon their studies rather than develop a fascinating social life. In 1878, they imposed demerits on several students for being tardy to or absent from classes. Two years later, they punished eight students, five of them female, for "negligence of studies" and they required them to sign pledges "to devote ourselves more diligently to our studies." In 1892, the faculty punished two female students who violated "regulations requiring young ladies to be either in recitation or in the library when upon school premises." Faculty also punished students for carrying a concealed weapon in 1873, for entering a billiard hall in 1891, and for assault in 1910.

LUMNUS

' Mines and Metallurgy
LLA, MO.

TER, 1943 NUMBER 4

ROLLA, AS I FIRST SAW IT

by

*F. E. DENNIE

Under my agreement with the College, and at that time I thought I was going to the University of Missouri, I was due in Rolla on September 1, 1909. I left Boston at 10:00 p.m. on what was then the fastest Big-4 train to St. Louis and arrived at the Union Station in St. Louis the morning of September 1, after two nights and a day on the train.

Country boy that I was and not knowing how far it was to Rolla nor the price of a ticket, I stepped up to the ticket agent in Union Station and laid down a twenty dollar bill and asked for a ticket to Rolla. I got the ticket and eighteen silver dollars — more silver dollars than I knew existed. I asked the ticket agent if he supplied a boy to carry that small amount of change and he kindly offered to give me the eighteen dollars in paper money which I gladly accepted.

There was a train which left St. Louis at 9:00 a.m. for Rolla and as we whizzed along at something like forty miles per hour I enjoyed looking at the countryside, noticing the widely scattered homes in contrast to the closely settled New England from which I had come. Every now and then we would pass what looked to me like a box car alongside the tracks, with sometimes a man standing in the door waving. Upon inquiry, I was told that those were depots, indicating that there was a town there, although, in some cases the town must have been hidden by the *box car*.

Coming from Massachusetts, where a trip to Boston, twenty miles distant, was an event in my young life, I thought a trip of one hundred miles from St. Louis to Rolla warranted my purchase of a pullman seat, for which I paid the sum of fifty cents, which included the Porter as a tourist guide who answered all my questions.

As the train slowed down for Rolla, I stood on the car platform observing the property along the tracks. Of course, the worst view of a city or a town a visitor gets is generally along the tracks as the train pulls in. First I saw the Frisco Pond which didn't look inviting as a swimming pool, or for moonlight boating. We pulled into the Rolla Station, a magnificent, dilapidated shanty, painted a Sears-Roebuck red. The platform was so old and worn that it didn't look as if it could bear all of my 150 pounds. Everything looked dirty and uninviting. I was in doubt as to the wisdom I had shown in coming. I stood on the lower step of the Pullman debating with myself whether to get off or go back to my seat and continue further West, when a man about six feet six inches tall, in company of another man walked up, and introduced himself as Dr. Young, Director of the School of Mines. As I accepted Dr. Young's extended hand in greeting, I was forced to step to the station platform and was rather perturbed to have the train pull out without me while Dr. Young introduced his companion, Professor Copeland, then Professor of Metallurgy. Professor Copeland was from Sommerville, Mass. and a graduate of Boston Tech, so we had quite a bit in common, mostly our peculiar New England pronunciations.

After introductions, we proceeded to walk toward Eighth street, which was the only paved street that Rolla could and did boast of. Eighth street was paved with bricks from the tracks to the east side of Pine street. As we proceeded up Eighth street, there was the Baltimore Hotel with Fred Strobach's Saloon occupying the lower floor, and the usual saloon smells occupying the outside air spaces. Then, in order, came McCassel's, Oscar Strobach's and Gilmore's Saloons with now and then a lunch room or a store between. I thought at the time that this must be a town of hard drinkers but soon found that all the drink emporiums were huddled on the north side of Eighth street.

As it was [illegible] Young and Professor Copeland took me to the Grant House (now the Heller Apartments) to dinner. I had [illegible] main thoroughfare of the town was a [illegible] from the east to the west side of the street on flag stones and over several chug holes. A canopy, as part of th[illegible] sidewalk along Pine street and under [illegible] tilted back against the building wall were some of the influential citizens of Rolla enjoying a noon siesta after dinner. Also along that side of Pine street was the old hitching ra[illegible] townspeople to tie their teams to. On the south side of Eighth street I noticed a series of small stores [illegible] the National Bank of Rolla—Capital $25,000. R[illegible] letters on windows so dirty one could see inside with difficulty.

After a [illegible] I was extremely hungry—we headed up Pine [illegible] the College. At the north end of the Grant House the Opera House was the entrance which I later found [illegible] of the dances, the moving pictures and prize fights which were popular at that time. Just north of the hotel was a vacant lot where, in later years, Fred "Hookem" Smith had hist first outdoor picture shows. Where the Post Office now stands was Hawkins' Livery Stable where they rented teams and saddle horses to students.

As we approached the campus it was noticeable that the best walks of the town were on the campus. The Metallurgy Building was then a one story affair with only the west wing. It rather looked like a building growing out of the ground.

Norwood Hall, then quite new, contained the Executive

Frank "Spike" Dennie offered a vivid description of the taverns in downtown Rolla in recalling his 1909 arrival.

Above right: William Jennings Bryan, three-time nominee for president, drew an enormous crowd to campus for a speech in 1902.

Big Crowd at Scho
Urges the Elect
Congress.

In 1899, the faculty faced a different challenge. They expelled Frank Beyer for his relations with "lewd and notorious women." Yet, Beyer was defiant, claiming that he could name 30 other students who were similarly guilty. Moreover, he asserted that "intimacy with lewd and notorious women was right, that he practiced it, and believed that it ought not be objected to, if he were not too public about it, or if it did not interfere with his studies."

For the first 40 years of MSM history, the biggest faculty concern was with students who fell to the temptations offered by the many saloons along Eighth Street in Rolla, only four blocks from the campus. Between 1872 and 1904, the two blocks between the Frisco depot and Pine Street had at least six and sometimes eight saloons. Many contemporaries called it "Whiskey Row." The local newspapers bemoaned the fact that "most every day" residents had to witness the "shameful conduct" of "drunken men." One alumnus who arrived in 1875 to begin classes recalled walking along Eighth Street with his father and seeing "a great many drunk men lying in the gutters."

Things changed little over the next three decades. When football coach Frank "Spike" Dennie arrived in 1909, Director Lewis Young met him at the Frisco depot, and they walked up Eighth Street where Dennie saw "the Baltimore Hotel with Fred Strobach's Saloon occupying the lower floor, and the usual saloon smells occupying the outside air spaces. Then, in order, came McCassel's, Oscar Strobach's and Gilmore's Saloons with now and then a lunch room or a store between. I thought at the time that this must be a town of hard drinkers but soon found that all the drink emporiums were huddled on the north side of Eighth Street." There had been an active temperance movement from the 1870s to eliminate the saloons, but the leaders of the movement always failed when they pushed public votes on the issue.

The faculty and the administration were vigilant in dealing with students who went to these saloons. In 1875, the faculty charged 19 with drinking, and those students could remain in school only if they signed a pledge "not to enter any saloon" for the rest of their time at MSM. When Director George Ladd arrived in 1897, he sought to address the problem of students frequenting saloons by backing the opening of a billiard room near campus. The proprietor did not serve alcohol, "no swearing was permitted, and signs notified students that they should not play billiards there during school hours." However, Ladd's reform backfired. After learning that Ladd dropped by to play a little pool himself, some local residents and his political opponents charged that "the director habitually frequents a public billiard hall in the city of Rolla, sometimes during school hours and plays pool in the presence of students of the School of Mines, and he gave his approval to the playing of billiards and pool therein by the students of the institution." While not the only factor, this controversy contributed to Ladd's resignation in 1907.

From 1914, the concern shifted from too many students going into the saloons to excessive drinking at school functions such as senior picnics, fraternity parties, or at MSM football games, even during Prohibition. Indeed, the faculty expelled one student in 1930 for "drunkenness," "promiscuity," and "bootlegging." The biggest challenge, however, was controlling drinking at the annual St. Pat's celebration.

In 1933, the responsibility for handling student discipline cases shifted from the faculty to the student advisor and the director of the campus. Over the next nine years, sometimes working with a faculty committee, they handled 66 cases. Theft, destroying public property, threatening people with a gun, cheating, and riding a horse across campus were in the mix, but the vast majority of cases dealt with drinking, typically at St. Pat's knighting ceremonies or at campus dances.

Dean Curtis Laws Wilson, who arrived on campus in fall 1941, decided to have a faculty committee and the registrar join him to handle discipline cases, but in the 1950s he decided that it was best to once again have a faculty committee in charge. Eventually, the dean of students took over, and, by the 1990s, a judicial affairs office was responsible. In the 21st century, the vice provost for undergraduate studies handled incidents of cheating, and the office of student affairs handled all other indiscretions. The nature of discipline cases changed over time. In the 1950s, the primary concern of the faculty discipline committee was scholastic deficiency. For a time in the late 1960s and early 1970s, the era of the counterculture, some students not surprisingly faced criminal charges for possession of hallucinogenic drugs and marijuana.

Indeed, in 1970, Zane White, Phelps County's crusading prosecuting attorney, reported that "undercover work" done by his office had persuaded him that there were people on the campus "who receive funds from communist subversive groups for purposes of supplying drugs and supporting anti-American activities." He went further, contending that there were professors on campus working in collaboration with that effort to distribute drugs to students. White identified physicist James Paul Wesley as the chief culprit. The charges against Wesley were eventually dropped because of insufficient evidence, but three years later he became the first tenured professor at UMR to be dismissed. The faculty tenure committee recommended and the campus leaders agreed that he be dismissed on charges of moral turpitude.

In the early 1990s students faced punishment for a variety of charges, from forgery and assault to the theft of university property, disorderly conduct, and possession of alcohol on the campus. The larger concern in the second decade of the 21st century was evidence of students violating campus expectations of academic integrity. In 2018 over 70 students faced punishment for assignment or exam misconduct and plagiarism.

INER
CHOOL OF MINES AND METALLURGY

ROLLA, MO., WEDNESDAY, OCTOBER 17, 1934

HIP CUP IS
ED AT MEETING

ndents held their fir-
uesday, Oct. 9 at 7p.
emistry Building.
l, president, present-
rship cup, which is a
phy awarded by Tau
he campus organiza-
he highest scholastic
each semester. The
was held by Sigma

g was attended by a
including two re-
from Pi Kappa Al-
eral from the Sigma
hich was voted into
on last year.
was made that Pi
also be voted in. The

SCHEDULE OF MINER
1934 FOOTBALL GAMES

Pittsburg Kansas Teachers 18; Miners, 6 at Pittsburg at Rolla.
Arkansas Tech, 6; Miners, 0
Oct. 5—Kirksville Teachers, 19; Miners 0 at Kirksville.
Oct 13—McKendree 20; Miners 6, at Rolla.
Oct. 20—Open date.
Oct. 27—Arkansas University at Fayetteville.
Nov. 2—St. Louis University at St. Louis.
Nov. 10—Open date.
Nov. 16—Springfield Teachers at Springfield.
Nov. 23– Maryville Teachers at Rolla.

TO SPEAK HERE FRIDAY

AMELIA EARHART

13 PLEDGES
PHI K. PHI

Organization Announces New Membership at Friday Mass Meeting

At the mass meeting held last Friday morning, thirteen men were pledged to the Phi Kappa Psi Fraternity.

Those pledged are as follows: A. J. Boles, W. H. Coddington, W. D. Danforth, D. W. Dutton, M. M. Fisher, A. T. Frank, L. H. Green, E. D. Hoffman, J. W. Mashek, W.

AVIATRI
TO S

Miss Amelia Earha
Flyer to Give
tures Address H

Declaring that th
danger in flying an
that her experiences
ventures, Miss Ear
foremost aviatrix wi
Oct. 19, under the a
General Lecture Se
Committee.

Miss Earhart says
for fun and she cal
"Flying for Fun." I
Miss Earhart won t
being the first wom
non-stop flight acros
can Continent, she a
record to the many
held.

In 1928 she crosse
on the famous "Frie
the first woman to f
ic. On the fifth a
Lindbergh's pioneer
flew the Atlantic alo
foundland to Irelan
only woman to have
lantic solo. Only o
son has done this,
Lindbergh.

Since 1920 Miss E
private life is Mrs. G
Putnam, wife of t
publisher, explorer
has been flying and
are so many that a
them here might
reading.

Previous to her
Miss Earhart was a
settlement work. S

Amelia Earhart, who appeared twice at MSM, was one of the most popular of the many guest lecturers.

NOTABLE SPEAKERS

From the early 20th century the students, faculty, and staff, along with the Rolla community, had remarkable opportunities to hear notable speakers, people who enriched the social life of the campus. The first notable figure was William Jennings Bryan, who spoke at MSM in 1902. He had carried the state of Missouri in his failed run for the presidency two years earlier and was making a campaign swing through Rolla to help Democratic candidates running for office. He arrived Sunday night, September 21. The next morning Director George Ladd led him on a tour of MSM prior to a reception for Bryan downtown where he shook hands with hundreds. After lunch at the Grant Hotel a parade brought Bryan back to campus for a speech. According to the local newspapers, word had spread quickly about Bryan's appearance and "the stout yeomanry from Crawford, Dent, Texas, Pulaski and Maries" counties had come to town where they joined the campus and Rolla residents to hear the greatest political orator of the era. About 5,000 had gathered to hear Bryan's two-hour oration, which *The Rolla Herald-Democrat* claimed was "the finest ever delivered in this part of the country and time and again he was given tremendous applause."

In 1924, the campus initiated a general lecture series that lasted for a half century. Amelia Earhart, who spoke in the Parker Hall auditorium both in 1924 and 1934, was one of the favorites. In her second talk Earhart regaled a packed house with a tale of her 1932 solo flight across

1: 1936 Olympic star Jesse Owens attracted a large crowd to his lecture in 1969.

2: In 2015, before her talk in the Remmers Special Artist/ Lecture Series, former Secretary of State Condoleezza Rice met with a group of students in a political science class.

3: Prior to his performance in the Remmers Special Artist/Lectures Series in 2017, world renowned cellist Yo Yo Ma, pictured here with Chancellor Cheryl B. Schrader, signed autographs at a reception.

4: Walter E. and Miriam Remmers with pianist Leonard Pennario (right), the second Remmers guest to perform in the series.

Left: Louis Armstrong appeared before MSM students in 1957.

Above: Ike and Tina Turner wowed UMR students in 1965.

the Atlantic Ocean. The account in the *Missouri Miner* described her as "a striking presence on the MSM stage, and with her ready wit and boundless humor was one of the best speakers ever heard here."

There were men of letters such as Nebraska's poet laureate John Neihardt; Vachel Lindsay, the nation's poet laureate; and English novelist J.B. Priestly, all of whom came to campus between 1928 and 1937. Artist Thomas Hart Benton lectured in both 1937 and 1940, and Margaret Bourke-White, famed photographer and war correspondent for the U.S. Army, spoke to students in 1943. Science fiction aficionados got to hear author Arthur C. Clarke in 1967 and Gene Roddenberry, the creator of *Star Trek*, in 1984.

Notable sports figures also appeared. St. Louis Cardinals general manager Branch Rickey appeared in 1931, and Bill Veeck, the former owner of the Cleveland Indians, St. Louis Browns, and Chicago White Sox, spoke in 1966. Three years later both Olympic track star Jesse Owens and Green Bay Packers all-pro running back Paul Hornung were speakers.

Public affairs lecturers were most common. In the 1960s, Wernher von Braun, internationally known for his work on jet propulsion and rocketry; Pulitzer Prize-winning journalist David Halberstam; consumer advocate Ralph Nader; and astronaut Scott Carpenter all gave lectures. In 1979, Walter Remmers, a 1923 alumnus, and his wife Miriam funded a lecture and artist series that brought to campus speakers such as former President Gerald Ford, former Secretaries of State Henry Kissinger and Condoleezza Rice, former Chairman of the Joint Chiefs of Staff Colin Powell, and former British Prime Minister Margaret Thatcher.

PERFORMERS

Over the years, Miners were also able to see some extraordinary performers. The Russian Cossack Chorus was an early favorite, appearing at MSM three times between 1929 and 1950. Jazz and classical solo performers, bands, and orchestras were commonly on the campus calendar. Jazz pianist Hazel Scott, jazz trumpeter Wynton Marsalis, and the New Orleans-based Preservation Hall Jazz Band drew big crowds. The St. Louis Symphony and Kansas City Philharmonic, along with solo performers pianists Jesus Maria Sanroma and Leonard Pennario, violinists Shlomo Mintz and Itzhak Perlman, classical guitarist Julian Bream, and cellist Yo Yo Ma all thrilled audiences. Audiences got a taste of opera as well when the Opera Theatre of Saint Louis performed Jacques Offenbach's "The Tales of Hoffman" in 1970, when lyric soprano Anna Moffo appeared in the Remmers series in 1986 and baritone Sherrill Milnes did so a dozen years later.

Through the 1950s, some of the biggest stars of the Big Band era performed, often for St. Pat's celebrations. Lawrence Welk, Ted Weems, Les Elgart, Duke Ellington, Louis Armstrong, Jimmy Dorsey, and Harry James all brought their bands to Rolla. In the 1960s and 1970s, an array of pop groups and soloists also performed. The Four Freshmen, Kingsmen, Lettermen, New Christy Minstrels, Kenny Rogers and the First Edition, Serendipity Singers, the Fifth Dimension, Nitty Gritty Dirt Band, Neil Sedaka, John Denver, Don McLean, and Harry Chapin were all hits with the students, but no one could match the enthusiasm students had for Ike and Tina Turner, who appeared in Rolla both in 1965 and 1968.

George Menefee was MSM's first student to portray St. Patrick. His surveyor's transit was a whiskey bottle placed on a forked stick.

Above: Escorting St. Pat from the railroad station in 1908.

Left: The "Grand Kowtow," here on the south side of Norwood Hall, was a key element in the St. Patrick's celebration (1908).

Below: The Blarney Stone sits outside Norwood Hall, the site for many St. Pat's activities in 1908.

ST. PAT'S CELEBRATIONS

The celebration of St. Patrick's Day began at the University of Missouri in 1903 and within five years became what the press called "one of the most distinctive features of life at the University of Missouri." The engineering students "never do any work" during the celebration. Instead, in 1908, the Columbia campus saw a parade of 500 students, former Knights of St. Pat's, and a brass band all headed by St. Pat bearing "a surveyor's level." They conveyed the Blarney stone in a carriage. Seniors were in cap and gown, and the freshmen carried shillelaghs. Everyone was in green, and most puffed on "smoky dirty pipes."

Prior to 1908, MSM students had done little more than wear something green to observe St. Patrick's Day. However, everything changed that year. Engineering students on the Columbia campus invited MSM students to send a representative to join in their activities and senior John Bowles made the trip.

Inspired by their Columbia counterparts, MSM students George Easley, Clay Gregory, and David Forrester rapidly planned a similar event in Rolla. They named George Menefee to serve as the campus's first St. Patrick. A transfer student from Georgetown College in his native Kentucky, Menefee was known around campus as the "Kentucky Colonel." The committee called upon fellow students not only to decorate the entrance to Norwood Hall, but also to put up posters around town declaring March 17 a school holiday and calling upon all students to meet at the Frisco depot. About 300 people gathered at the depot where they got green sashes and shillelaghs.

According to *The Rolla Herald-Democrat*, once St. Pat arrived, the enthusiastic crowd "marched over the town headed by the college band" before walking to campus. St. Pat, adorned in "flowing silk robes," led them to Norwood Hall, where he laid off a quadrangle using a surveyor's transit, which actually was a forked stick with a whiskey bottle attached. Students filled the space and dutifully performed a "Grand Kowtow" to St. Pat, who promptly dubbed all the seniors "Worthy Guards and Knights of St. Patrick." He then made Director Lewis Young an honorary knight, and Young offered a few remarks about St. Patrick being a mining engineer.

Students Benjamin Cody and Oscar Randolph then brought forward a Blarney stone that read "Erin Go Bragh." Feeling compelled to give a speech, St. Patrick told the crowd, "Either marry a rich girl, or a poor one with a big appetite; but by no means to marry one with cold feet." As the band played along, the crowd sang a few "college songs," after which they marched

Beer bust after the 1908 St. Pat's knighting.

back downtown, and St. Patrick declared the big day over. However, Menefee and a few of his friends gathered for a "beer bust." to wind down the day.

With a critical assist from Menefee, students Easley, Gregory, and Forrester (who became St. Pat in 1911) had set some precedents for what became the most significant annual social event for Miner students. Every year, with the exception of three years during World War II and the 2020 celebration, which the university canceled because of the COVID-19 global pandemic, the campus experienced a student-led celebration featuring St. Patrick, a parade, a knighting ceremony, and considerable alcohol consumption.

Yet, the celebration evolved considerably from the hastily arranged affair in 1908. In the following year, the junior class became responsible for organizing the event, and they remained in charge until 1930 when the St. Pat's Board, with a faculty advisor, took control. The buying of green apparel by the community began in 1909. As one local newspaper explained, "a number of citizens turned out in en masse as well as in green." From a one-day event, St. Pat's developed into a two-week celebration with an ever-growing number of activities. Between 1912 and 1915, the junior class added snake killing, had St. Pat ride a manure spreader during the parade, and initiated a ceremony to crown a queen of St. Pat's.

Shillelaghs played an important role from the beginning. In 1919, a reporter for the *Missouri Miner* wrote that it had already become a custom "on the Sunday immediately preceding St. Pat's" for freshmen to "make a pilgrimage into the wilderness surrounding Rolla" to secure their shillelaghs. That all changed in the 1970s when Sigma Tau Gamma began replacing shillelaghs with hollowed-out tree trunks called cudgels. The campus quickly got used to seeing young men carrying enormous chunks of wood over their shoulders during the days leading up to the St. Pat's parade.

The knighting ceremony took place at many locations over time, from the steps of Norwood Hall to a masque ball, the student union building, Lions Club Park, and Leach Theatre. Beginning with the spontaneous knighting of campus Director Lewis Young in 1908, the junior class

Above left: Kissing the Blarney Stone, shown here in 1938, has been a tradition since the celebration's early days.

Above right: A prize-winning cudgel in 1986.

1939 photo of students in descriptive geometry class with shillelaghs.

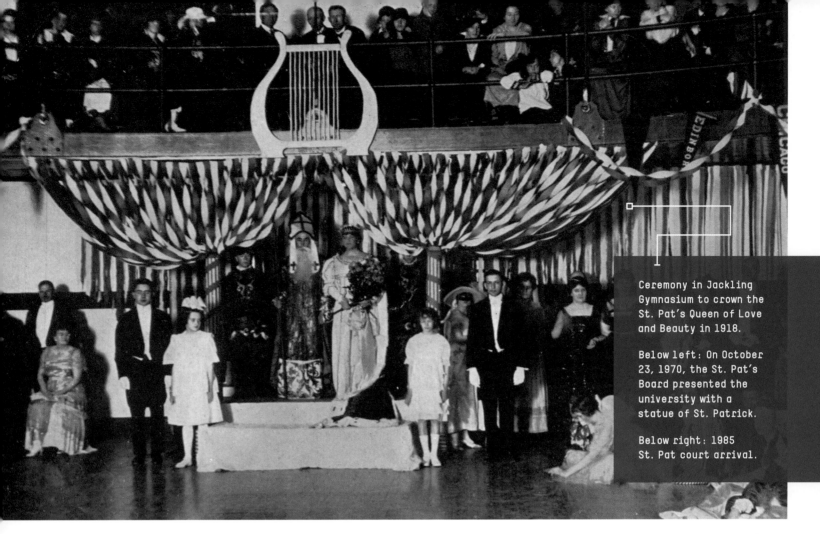

Ceremony in Jackling Gymnasium to crown the St. Pat's Queen of Love and Beauty in 1918.

Below left: On October 23, 1970, the St. Pat's Board presented the university with a statue of St. Patrick.

Below right: 1985 St. Pat court arrival.

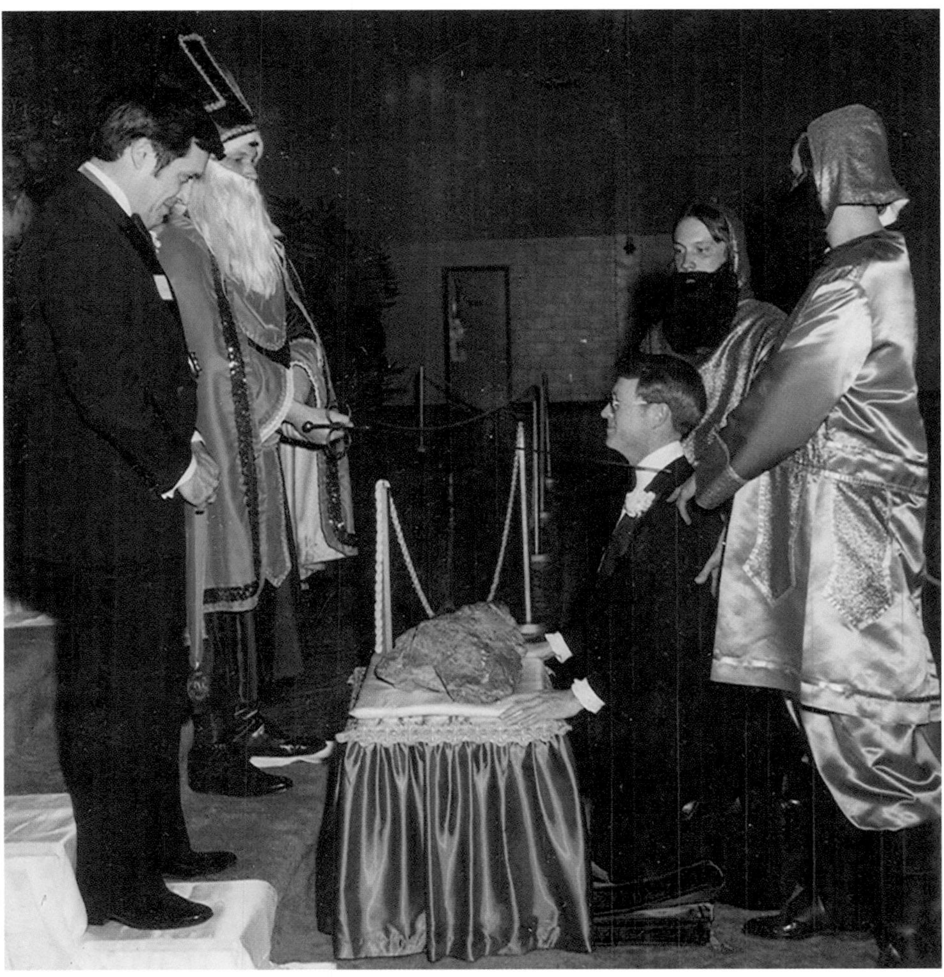

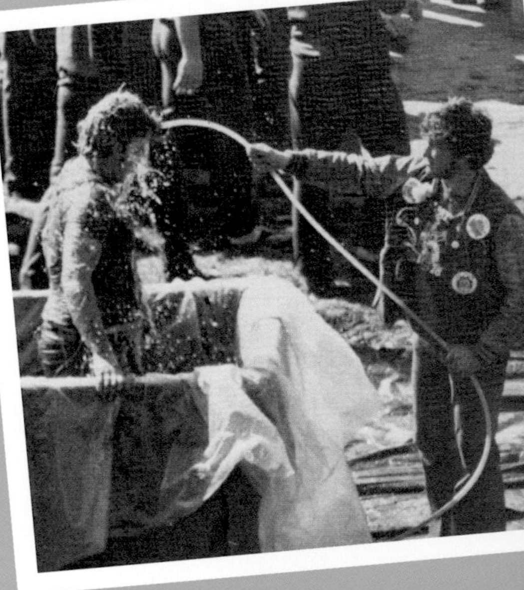

selected honorary knights through the mid-1920s, most of whom were faculty members. However, the practice lapsed for several decades. The St. Pat's Board revived the tradition in the 1960s. For over five decades alumni, notable public figures, faculty, staff, administrators, and friends of the university became honorary knights.

One of the most intriguing St. Pat's traditions involved "Alice." There are many origin stories. One argues that it began in the 1940s with the dunking of the head of each "Knitee" into a bucket of "stuff." Another argues that it began in the 1950s when student knights got dunked into a cattle trough. A third argues that it began in 1961 with a knighting ceremony in the campus's new student union building. Eventually, the initiation of student knights, including female students beginning in 1986, took place in a huge vat at the football field in front of large crowds cheering on the spectacle.

The actual ingredients in the "stuff" also was the subject of legend. Initially, it apparently was drillers' mud, but then became a cocktail of mysterious ingredients, perhaps eating club leftovers and stale beer or dead animals, or whatever one's imagination could conjure. There was even some debate about the origin of the name "Alice" for the gross gooey concoction. Some have argued that students took the name of Lewis Young's secretary, who in 1908 alerted the students planning the first St. Pat's celebration that they would have to deal with faculty members angry about the planning committee's proclaiming March 17 as a holiday from classes. Most, however, accept the explanation offered in the St. Pat's Board Baby Rep Manual, which attributed "Alice" to the name of the former girlfriend of board president Richard Dumay who graduated in 1971.

Most years the annual St. Pat's celebration attracted positive attention in the statewide media. For example, in 1916, one St. Louis reporter claimed that the event surrounding the St. Pat's activities made Rolla "a town you ought to see before you go to Paris and die.'" However, the excessive drinking associated with St. Pat's occasionally caused problems for the administration.

In 1910, the faculty dismissed Robert Mackey for a year because a local court found him guilty of distributing "liquor to students on St. Patrick's day." In 1936, they punished four students for being drunk at the knighting ceremony. The situation truly got out of hand in the early 1980s. For the 75th St. Pat's in 1983, the

Above left: Chemistry Professor B. Ken Robertson kneels before Chancellor Joseph Marchello (left) and St. Pat Brian L. Wagner (right) during the knighting ceremony in 1980.

Above: The infamous "Alice" in 1978. Few knew what ingredients went into the mix.

Above: Chancellor Martin Jischke addresses a student forum following the death of Anthony Busalaki.

Right: For two days each year, the Puck serves as home base for the St. Pat's Follies.

board adopted the slogan "Contributing to the Delinquency of Miners for 75 Years," and the following year Lion's Club Park events included several drinking games including a "Hop, Skip, and Puke" contest.

The situation reached a crisis point in 1988 when St. Pat's Board member Anthony Busalaki died of alcohol poisoning at a board event. Chancellor Martin Jischke responded by forbidding alcohol at any St. Pat's Board event. Three years later, Michael W. Nisbet, a St. Pat's "Baby Rep" (initiate), according to a report in the *St. Louis Post-Dispatch*, "died of asphyxiation complicated by intoxication after attending a gathering of board members." During the party Nisbet "was forced to stand in a line of students and take continued drinks from a bottle of tequila as it was passed along. He also drank large quantities of beer." Chancellor John Park responded by disbanding the Board and replacing it with a St. Pat's Celebration Committee of student council. Campus leaders addressed the challenge through a federal grant to offer peer counseling on problem drinking and they abolished "Alice" in 1996.

Despite these setbacks, the annual St. Patrick's celebration remained an event that drew alumni, current students, faculty, staff, and the community together more successfully than any other moment in the academic year.

The most poignant reminder of the meaning of St. Pat's to alumni involves two of the campus's World War II heroes. Gene Boyt and Robert Silhavy, 1941 graduates of MSM and survivors of the horrific Bataan Death March, spent much of the war in a Japanese prisoner-of-war camp. Yet, they resolved to celebrate St. Patrick's Day. Boyt and Silhavy used their daily ration of rice, along with butter and milk from a Red Cross box, to make an "engineer's cake." In addition, as Boyt explained, "We also had put raisins in a jar and by leaving them in the sun a little bit at a time we were able to ferment them. We made a hydrometer out of a vial to check the fermentation — we wanted champagne." Through their determination, even in the worst of conditions, the MSM alumni were able to toast their alma mater and sing "The Mining Engineer" and "St. Patrick Was an Engineer" while eating cake and drinking raisin champagne.

1 and 2: Floats, Clydesdales and even elephants have been part of the annual parade entries.

3: During Follies, students compete in a series of games, including seeing how many official St. Pat's sweatshirts can be put on in one minute.

4: 1963 St. Pat's sweatshirt.

5: Every year at dawn on the parade day, St. Pat's Board alumni paint Pine Street green.

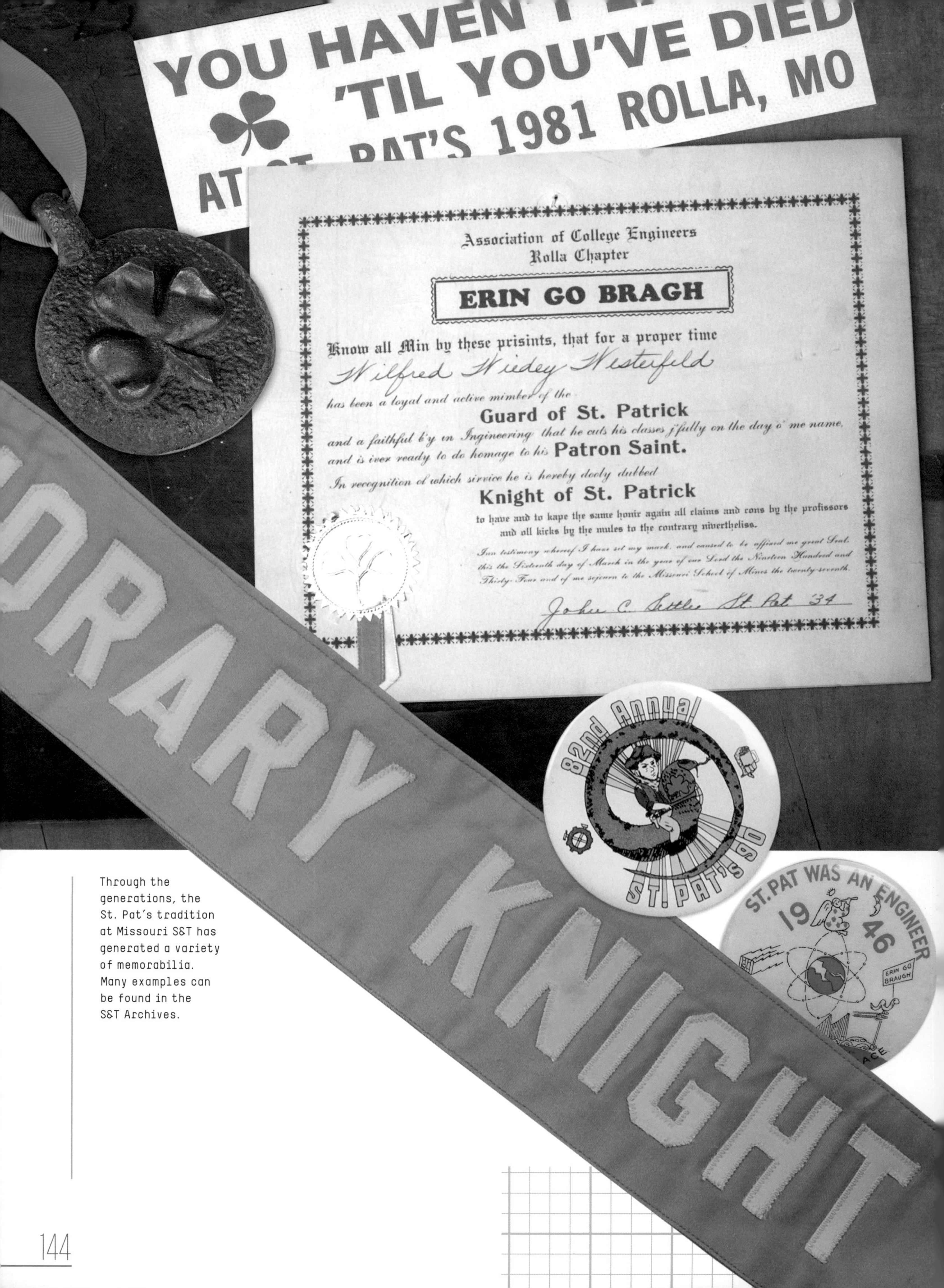

'TIL YOU'VE DIED
1981 ROLLA, MO
Association of College Engineers
Rolla Chapter
ERIN GO BRAGH
Know all Min by these prisints, that for a proper time
Wilfred Wiedey Westerfeld
has been a loyal and active mimber of the
Guard of St. Patrick
and a faithful b'y in Ingineering that he cuts his classes j'fully on the day o' me name,
and is iver ready to do homage to his Patron Saint.
In recognition of which sirvice he is hereby dooly dubbed
Knight of St. Patrick
to have and to kape the same honir again all claims and cons by the professors
and oll kicks by the mules to the contrary nivertheliss.
Inn testimony whereof I have set my mark, and caused to be affixed me great Seal, this the Sixteenth day of March in the year of our Lord the Nineteen Hundred and Thirty-Four and of me sojourn to the Missouri School of Mines the twenty-seventh.
John C. Settle St. Pat '34
KNIGHT
82nd Annual
ST. PAT'S 90
ST. PAT WAS AN ENGINEER
19 46
ERIN GO BRAUGH

Through the generations, the St. Pat's tradition at Missouri S&T has generated a variety of memorabilia. Many examples can be found in the S&T Archives.

At the annual Coronation Ceremony, held the night before the parade, the Queen of Love and Beauty is announced, and student and honorary knights are knighted to officially begin the St. Pat's revelry.

Top: Civil engineering graduate Gary White was one of the first Miner students to travel to Central America on a service activity.

Above: geological engineering professor Curt Elmore developed an International Engineering and Design course.

STUDENT SERVICE AND OUTREACH

Campus social life often featured students exhibiting their altruistic drive. Before World War II, Miners were engaged in service activities. Beginning with the establishment of a chapter of Alpha Phi Omega, the campus saw a growing number of service organizations. By 1970 there were four besides Alpha Phi Omega — Intercollegiate Knights, Circle K, M-Club, and Blue Key. Members were involved in a number of fundraising efforts and blood drives to benefit the campus and community. Faith-based organizations like the Wesley Foundation and Gamma Delta also engaged in service activities, such as visiting patients at the local hospital and repairing inner-city mission churches.

Before graduating in 1985 with a degree in civil engineering, Gary White joined Depauw University students on a trip to Guatemala to build a dormitory for people who came to a small village for medical care. That was a transforming experience for White, who later established Water.org with actor Matt Damon. The non-profit organization is helping millions of people in developing nations get access to safe drinking water. White was the first among many Miner students who chose to draw upon their developing expertise to engage in meaningful service activities far beyond the Rolla community.

Starting in 2002 geological engineering professor and UMR graduate Curt Elmore took students on international trips to improve water quality in developing countries. He developed an International Engineering and Design capstone course for geological engineering majors. In 2005, UMR established a chapter of Engineers Without Borders a year after civil engineering professors Richard Stephenson and Eric Showalter joined Stephenson's brother, a Methodist pastor in Oklahoma, to place a roof on a church in Bolivia. In subsequent years the EWB chapter worked on water quality projects in Bolivia, Guatemala, and Honduras.

Miner students began participating in alternative spring breaks in 2008. These Miner Challenges sent students to places like North Carolina, Louisiana, New Jersey, Mississippi, Michigan, Pennsylvania, Texas, Colorado, Arkansas, and Nicaragua to work on projects like helping Habitat for Humanity build houses, assisting with flood and tornado cleanups, and helping the homeless.

Throughout the campus's history, students have sought a social outlet for the stresses of their academic lives. Clubs, fraternities and sororities, intramural sports, and a few drinks were the most common ways. To be sure, there were excesses, but Miners developed a social life that helped them balance the need to succeed in classes with their desire to have fun.

1: Civil engineering professor Eric Showalter.

2: Civil engineering professor Richard Stephenson.

3: Barbi Wheelden (left) and other Engineers Without Borders members construct a water-holding tank in Bolivia.

4: Luis Pereira (right) collects a water sample in the small village of Santiago, Honduras.

5: EWB members David Longrie, Leah Irwin and Jake Midkiff traveled to Inka Katurapi, Bolivia.

CHAPTER 6

MINERS AT WAR

Beginning with the Civil War in the 1860s, Miners have been involved in all of America's wars. Their legacy of service began with three early faculty members who were veterans of the Civil War: James Abert and George D. Emerson, who fought on the Union side, and Robert W. Douthat, who fought on the Confederate side. An 1842 graduate of West Point, Abert served in the Corps of Topographical Engineers for two decades prior to the war and was part of a railroad reconnaissance survey in Rolla in 1845. During the conflict, Abert was a topographer for Union forces fighting in the Shenandoah Valley and then in the siege of Charleston, South Carolina. Emerson served for three years in a Michigan engineer company. Douthat served four years in the Confederate Army, seeing action in many battles including commanding a company in General George Pickett's ill-fated charge on the last day of the Battle of Gettysburg.

America's increasingly important role in world affairs, particularly when called upon to defend its interests, has had a dramatic impact on the lives of Miners throughout the institution's history. Regardless of the war, Miners, as the examples of Abert and Emerson illustrate, usually served in engineering units, and during most of the conflicts, the campus provided training to help in the war effort. The campus community also usually supported American war efforts, even during the college antiwar protest movement of the Vietnam era. Moreover, since 1920, many Miner students were in the Army or Air Force Reserve Officers' Training Corps (ROTC). Since the end of World War I, thousands of veterans were able to become Miner students because of education benefits provided by the federal government.

Missouri S&T 1930 Reserve Officers' Training Corps (ROTC) Cadet Officers.

THE MISSOURI MINER.

Missouri School of Mines and Metallurgy, Rolla, Mo.

Vol. 3, No. 34. Friday, May 11, 1917. Price 5 C

MANY M. S. M. MEN LEAVE FOR MILITARY CAMPS.

Many students and some professors have left Rolla this week bound for the various military training camps. The great majority joined the military training camp at Ft. Riley, Kansas. Two entered the navy, and two will join the aviation corps. Profs. McCandliss and Forbes, and Coach Dennie will, in all probability, receive commissions in the Engineering Corps. They will leave today for the Kansas fort.

The following men have already left, according to the Miner statistician:

Seniors: C. A. Peterson, J. C. Raible, Jr., M. C. Lucky, Carl Heimberger, T. R. Crawford, R. D. Cooper, E. L. Arnold, T. P. F. Walsh, J. K. Walsh, R. O. Shriver,J. G. Reilly, C. E. Muehlberg, S. S. Leonard,

Juniors: J. W. Pugh, George Burnet, T. L. Dawson, H. P. Lawrence, H. S. Clark, T F. Golick, M. L. Terry, O. E. Stoner, E. N. Murphy, Wesley Mellow, W. G. Hippard, D. C. Beyer.

Sophomores: R. Marston, T. W. Leach, L. M. Tidd, C. C. Wilson, H. F. Shore, C. C. Rice, F. V Moore. W. J. Nolte, L. P. Oakleaf, W. G. Pryor, E. S. Rodenbaugh, D. A. Bash, M. P. Brazill, Phil Bohart.

Freshmen: H. E. Ewing, W. B. Crutcher, K. M. Wright, R. R. Riddlesperger, W. W. Richmond, G. B. Bloom, G. H. Fox.

Friday the following men were called: F. P. Shays, P. F. Pape, B. L. Rinehart, P. G. Foreman, A. C. Gale, C. L. Dorris, Harry Ambler, J. E. Flanders, J. J. Shipley, and Prof. F. H. Frame.

The Miner wishes all the boys God speed.

MILITARY MANUALS.

Several students and faculty members who are planning to attend Army Training Camps have asked the librarian to secure for them the necessary manuals and texts. The Librarian, therefore, has on hand a very limited number of the following manuals, which may be obtained from him at cost price:

Infantry Drill Regulations; Engineer Field Manual; Army Regulations; Field Service Regulations.

Flag Pole Fund Still Growing.

Some big subscriptions to the Flag Pole Fund were received last week. Oscar Lachmund,'87, sent a check for $25, the largest donation received so far. Mr. H. S. Owen, ex-'13, helped the good work along with a $5.00 raise. B. L. Ashdown, last year's Editor of the Miner, also kicked in wtih a substantial check.

We are thankful for all subscriptions, however big or little. They show the right spirit.

The faculty of Columbia University is organized into a general staff, and several special corps for service in the war. A call for service will be issued to each of the present students, the 36,000 graduates, and the 1100 officers of the school, and a woman's committee will deal with the service for women.

A University of Wisconsin Ambulance, recruited by Wisconsin men, will soon be rushing back and forth from battlefields to hospitals in the warring countries, if the present plans are carried out.

God Almighty Hates a Qu

Chicago Tribune.

A college athlete is a h specialized bit of human ma ery. What makes him suc ful as an athlete would mak valuable as a soldier. Fa lied, soft muscled, short w men are of little use as sol They cannot march, much run. If they went over th they would not need a bul stop them. They would st their own accord within a dred feet and either lie dow die or make work for the h al corps.

What the country needs is its lean youth and tough hood. The fat men of sede habit and the lean men o wind and poor hearts may themselves with the th that if the authorities p ted them to get into the they would only make troub army auxiliaries which will quite enough trouble tendi needful cases. The autho will not allow them to ge the scrap, and the autho want the lean youth an tough manhood.

College athletes who no debating whether they ou might keep up intercoll

The staff of the *Missouri Miner* was consistently supportive of the war effort during World War I and most issues in 1917 and 1918 featured articles on the roles of Miners in the global conflict.

the letter Q. A great man will remain in college duri war because they are not cally fit for military work. the athlete is fit for servic

"H" won in 1917 will not for anything honorable

SPANISH-AMERICAN WAR

In support of Cuban insurgents' efforts to gain independence from Spain, the United States declared war on the old colonial power in spring 1898. It was a short conflict with clear American victories in Cuba and the Philippines, which were also colonies of Spain. Because it lasted just a few weeks, only a couple of Miners were involved. One MSM student, Alexis Illinski, left campus in his third year of study to serve with American forces in Cuba. Frank C. Bolles, a former MSM student who had graduated from West Point, served in the Philippines where, according to an article in *The Rolla Herald*, "He commanded a company which participated in the attack and capture of Manila."

WORLD WAR I

On April 2, 1917, in a call to make the world "safe for democracy," President Woodrow Wilson asked a joint session of Congress for a declaration of war against Germany. Within four days both the House of Representatives and the Senate had voted to grant Wilson's request.

Miners responded swiftly and enthusiastically to the president's call to arms. In less than a month, the *Missouri Miner* reported, "Over thirty students of MSM have signed up to take the training at Fort Riley (Kansas), and as many more have sent in their applications to be accepted." The editors of the paper claimed that these young men had "calmly made a decision." They had "not been hasty nor impulsive, nor blindly followed each other as sheep over a precipice." The students' commitment to the war effort never flagged. Over 75 percent of the 273 undergraduate students at MSM in spring 1917 enlisted. Six faculty members and over 300 alumni joined them in what Wilson later called "the war to end all wars." Almost 40 percent served overseas, and nearly 200 became officers, including one who became a brigadier general.

Some were combat heroes. Joseph C. Raible, a member of Kappa Sigma fraternity and a letterman in football, enlisted in the American Air Service in May 1917. After several weeks of training at Kelly Field in Texas, Lieutenant Raible shipped overseas. In July 1918, serving with the 147th Aero Squadron near Chateau-Thierry, France, Raible and three other pilots engaged with eight enemy planes. In a five-minute battle, Raible shot down one of the planes and drove another away. When he returned to Rolla for a visit in spring 1919, the *Missouri Miner* hailed the "genial" Raible as "a real American Ace." For his action, Raible received both the Distinguished Service Cross and the French Croix de Guerre.

Less than a week after Congress declared war on Germany, MSM's athletic director, Frank "Spike" Dennie, told the *Missouri Miner* that he wanted to make sure that "we may not be laggards in this patriotic duty." He led by example in mid-May when he and three other faculty members left for Fort Riley, Kansas, for their basic training. Once overseas, Dennie again led by example. On the last night of the war Dennie "rendered the most important services to his company by skillfully devising and constructing a pontoon raft and successfully transporting a Battalion of Infantry across the Meuse River" in France. Even though Dennie and the men under his command did this under "heavy artillery and machine gun fire," Dennie effected "the landing of the troops without loss." For his heroics, Dennie received a citation for "meritorious action under fire in the Argonne."

Raible and Dennie were not the only men from MSM honored for their service in the war. As the campus celebrated Armistice Day in November 1919, the *Missouri Miner* noted that students, alumni, and faculty had received a plethora of recognitions including seven Citations, six Croix de Guerre, four Distinguished Crosses, two Distinguished Service Medals, and one Legion of Honour. While most Miners were in logistical support units, many were wounded and three were killed in action, one died in an accident, and three more died from influenza. In late October 1918, the faculty approved a resolution "of sympathy and respect" for their sacrifices.

Above: Frank C. Bolles served in the Spanish-American War.

Below: Frank C. Bolles with Arizona the Army mule in 1928.

Regiment Parades for Mule, World War Hero

Miss Ruth Taylor, Colonel Frank C. Bolles and Arizona

On the home front, MSM and the Rolla community consistently supported the war effort. Two weeks after America's entry into the conflict *The Rolla Herald* reported, "The war spirit is rapidly developing around Rolla. Practically every man, woman and child that you meet is in thorough accord with President Wilson." The residents of Rolla were not unusual. As historian Petra DeWitt noted, Congress's declaration of war "produced several spontaneous demonstrations of patriotism throughout the state."

Mobilization in support of the war effort was rapid on campus. From early April, students raised and lowered the American flag every day. Students who did not immediately enlist became part of the "Miner militia" by mid-April. As a notice in the *Missouri Miner* proclaimed, "The least any loyal Miner can do is to drill and learn the movements." In the fall semester this voluntary action became formalized as the administration mandated that "all first and second year men are required to drill from 4 to 5:30 every Monday, Wednesday and Thursday," football players excluded, at least during the football season.

To help maintain support for the war, some faculty members agreed to be Four Minute Men. The idea was the brainchild of George Creel, who Wilson appointed to head a Committee on Public Information. A Missouri journalist, Creel's mandate was to use propaganda to maintain Americans' support of the war, consistently arguing that the nation had a moral obligation to defeat the Germans. Posters and press releases were important, but also an army of speakers was critical. By war's end over 75,000 speakers gave nearly 8 million speeches nationwide. While they gave their speeches in town hall meetings, churches, and lodges, most often the Four Minute Men spoke in movie theaters. It took about four minutes for the projectionist to change reels, thus the speakers had a captive audience for a brief time. From Washington, Creel's committee sent bulletins to the speakers with examples of speeches on topics like purchase of war bonds, the need to ration food, and the importance of all men registering for the draft. Rolla's Four Minute Men included Professors George Dean, William Turner, and Joseph Barley, along with librarian Harold Wheeler.

The state of Missouri also established a Council of Defense, the organization that historian Christopher Gibbs called "the chief agent of mobilization" in the war effort. Governor Frederick Gardner established the council less than a week after Congress declared war and named Frederick Mumford, dean of the College of Agriculture at the University of Missouri, to head it. Besides encouraging increased agricultural production and food rationing, the council supplemented the work of the Creel Committee by creating its own speakers' bureau, which pushed war bond sales. The council also sought to blunt opposition to the war and identify disloyal Missourians.

Each county had a council of defense, and Mumford appointed MSM Director Austin McRae to that post in Phelps County. Despite the challenge of running a campus that was steadily losing enrollment because so many students were enlisting, McRae threw himself wholeheartedly into the effort of leading the county council of defense.

Top: Joseph C. Raible, class of 1917, was a decorated pilot in World War I.

Bottom: Football coach and athletic director Frank "Spike" Dennie earned a citation for "meritorious action" on the last night of conflict.

Right: Missouri journalist George Creel led President Woodrow Wilson's Committee on Public Information during World War I.

Flagpole erected in front of Parker Hall on campus during World War I.

Because the Wilson administration federalized the Missouri National Guard, the state established a Home Guard with over 7,000 volunteers. As historian Petra DeWitt has explained, "those who were too old for the draft or disabled but still wished to join the war effort in a military capacity could join the Home Guard." Director McRae organized the Phelps County Home Guard with about 100 men. He also identified five ministers and three lawyers willing to give patriotic speeches for the state's Patriotic Speakers Bureau and organized rallies for the sale of Liberty Bonds and American Red Cross Humanity Bonds. In October 1917, for example, the residents of Phelps County purchased over $100,000 in Liberty Bonds. Finally, McRae organized a countywide effort that led to nearly 2,100 county residents signing pledges to conserve food during the war. McRae accomplished much in less than a year, but the effort took its toll. In April 1918 he had to resign because his physician ordered him "to give up all work for the present." He relinquished the post to J.A. Spilman, a local businessman who had served as the county food administrator.

There was also a state Woman's Committee, National Council of Defense. By the end of the war all counties but one had a chapter. Luella Dean, wife of Professor George Dean, headed the Phelps County chapter, and Minnie McRae, wife of Director McRae, served as secretary. They organized fundraisers for the Home Guard, promoted food rationing, sponsored patriotic programs, promoted the sale of Liberty Bonds, advocated women's suffrage, and raised money for the YMCA War Work Fund.

The campus also hosted pro-war rallies, notably on March 31, 1918. Following a parade, "led by the famous Rolla band, under the able leadership of Mr. J.W. Scott," from Eighth and Pine streets to Parker Hall, a packed house listened to a rendition of "Onward Christian Soldiers," followed by a speech by guest speaker Dr. Robert Emmet Kane of St. Louis, who discussed the ongoing "struggle for humanity" and "vividly pictured the terrors and atrocities of the Germans" that threatened the world order. He also noted the internal menaces threatening the war effort: "the white flag of pacifism, the red flag of anarchy and I.W.W.ism (a reference to the Industrial Workers of the World, a radical labor union opposed to capitalism) and the yellow flag of the miserable coward and slacker." After Kane's speech the big crowd sang "America" with "great enthusiasm." The event concluded with "a solicitation thru the audience for the purpose of selling Thrift Stamps, which resulted in selling $2,500."

Even the St. Patrick celebration in 1918 had a World War I theme. St. Pat arrived with his court on a hand car and headed a parade, including the Rolla band and numerous floats, from the train station to Parker Hall, "where St. Patrick and his attendants mounted to the throne. St. Pat then gave the command, 'Kowtow,' at which all students fell upon their knees and did homage to the patron saint of all engineers." After a short address, he called for the Blarney Stone. However, sophomore Al Laun claimed "that the Blarney Stone had been stolen by a German spy, but that it now stands as a foot stone at the tomb where the Kaiser's hopes and ambitions are now buried."

A service flag bearing 300 stars representing the contribution of MSM to the service of the nation during World War I, was raised on campus in 1918 with The Stars and Stripes and a green pennant honoring St. Patrick.

In 1918, MSM hosted a unit of men under the auspices of the Federal Board for Vocational Education. The men found housing in Jackling Gymnasium.

MSM alumnus Daniel C. Jackling, who had developed a successful career as a mining engineer, oversaw the construction of two large plants during World War I that produced smokeless explosives.

St. Pat asked, "And where is that?" Laun answered, "Beneath the flag of the U.S.A." St. Pat's attendants raised the American flag and under it was "the service flag of MSM bearing 300 stars, the contribution of MSM to the service of the nation and a green pennant in honor of St. Pat."

In summer 1918, to further the war effort, McRae offered the facilities of the campus for a special school to train soldiers as tradesmen in crafts essential to an American victory. According to a history of technical education in America, the nation faced a critical "shortage of trained workers," a condition that prompted the federal government to establish the Federal Board for Vocational Education. Under its auspices over 100 locations provided training for 62,000 men prior to their induction. MSM was one of those vital training centers. There were four officers and 160 men. They drilled two hours a day and had seven hours of training in Mechanical Hall. Quartered in Jackling Gymnasium, the men slept on the gym floor and dined on the mezzanine floor. There was even a small hospital. McRae also kept the library in Parker Hall open seven days a week, including evenings. According to the *Missouri Miner*, "It is about the only place, on the campus at least, where the men can 'loaf' and read, or write their letters home." The library was packed "every night and on Saturdays and Sundays." After two months of training the men were sent stateside trained as mechanics, carpenters, machinists, electricians, and blacksmiths.

Daniel C. Jackling, MSM's most prominent alumnus, also made a significant home front contribution to the war effort. Hailed in the national press as "one of the most famous mining men of the world" for his development of the massive Bingham Canyon, Utah, copper mine, Jackling, who the *New York Times* described as a "multi-millionaire," agreed in December 1917 to build plants to produce smokeless explosives for a dollar a year. Jackling managed a massive construction project with over 30,000 workers in addition to a staff of 500 architects and engineers to build plants in West Virginia and Tennessee. He moved the construction process along expeditiously and both plants were producing powder in less than a year. President Wilson awarded Jackling the Distinguished Service Medal for his "exceptionally meritorious and distinguished service to the Government of the United States, in a duty of great responsibility during World War I, as Director of United States explosive plants."

The 1919 *Rollamo* noted the short-lived Student Army Training Corps.

MSM cadets outside the Rolla Building in 1877. Note the two sitting outside a third-floor window and the two female students in a second-floor window.

In October 1918, with an expectation that the war in Europe would continue well into 1919, MSM established a Student Army Training Corps. One expectation of the 1862 Morrill Act that established land-grant colleges was that the colleges would include instruction in "military tactics," but it did not specify what those should be nor how they should be taught. MSM did have a company of cadets between 1873 and 1877. At its peak in early 1876 the company had 44 cadets, three commissioned officers, and nine non-commissioned officers as well as an armory on the third floor of the Rolla Building with 99 muskets, 40 Springfield rifles, three flags, two drums, three fifes, and six swords. However, with a rapid drop in enrollment, the faculty voted to eliminate the unit in 1877. When someone suggested three years later that drilling be resumed, the faculty members voted against it because "with only few students, it would be a ridiculous farce." For the next four decades, the campus had no military training, only to be resumed because of the military situation in spring 1917.

The War Department notified college presidents that it intended to begin a program using colleges and universities to train students prior to their induction. The result was the Student Army Training Corps. MSM's SATC unit, established with an impressive ceremony on October 1, 1918, was one of about 500 campus-housed units across the country. Housed in Mechanical Hall, the unit provided students a "special program of studies, chiefly military, and intensive military drill." Although it existed only 10 weeks because of the war's end, 193 of the 440 enrolled were commissioned.

The campus American Legion post was named in honor of Martin Bowles, a major in metallurgy who was killed in action in 1918.

The campus took several actions to honor the service of its students, faculty, and alumni. In September 1919, ex-service men formed an American Legion post on campus and named it in honor of Martin F. Bowles, who had been a senior majoring in metallurgy and was killed in action a year earlier. Mining engineering Professor Carroll Forbes and Athletic Director Frank "Spike" Dennie were among the first members.

Two months later, on November 11, Director McRae canceled classes and most Rolla businesses closed so the campus could observe the first anniversary of the war's end and commemorate its heroes. Prior to the music and speeches, as the 1920 *Rollamo* described the scene, "A large percentage of the old ex-service men appeared in full uniform, some wearing two or three gold chevrons, and many wearing wound chevrons." In addition, "most of the school cadets were ... in uniform when the companies assembled on Jackling Field at 10 a.m. Two companies of cadets and one of ex-service men formed the battalion of which Major H.J. Wild had charge. This battalion was marched to Parker Hall where the morning exercises were held."

Finally, the editors of the 1919 *Rollamo* designated the yearbook as the "Victory Edition" and dedicated the volume to "the Miners who Served Their Country." "You have served," they wrote, "you have done your best, you have proved yourself worthy of the confidence placed in you by our government, and you have made a record of which MSM may well be proud." The *Rollamo* then listed all who had served and published photos of some of them, as well as a history of the Student Army Training Corps.

ROLLAMO

TO THE MINERS WHO SERVED THEIR COUNTRY THIS VICTORY EDITION OF THE ROLLAMO IS RESPECTFULLY DEDICATED

DEDICATION

— 6 —

The editors of the *Rollamo* designated the 1919 yearbook as the "Victory Edition."

Company A of the new MSM Army ROTC unit in 1921.

RESERVE OFFICER TRAINING CORPS

Less than a month after the War Department deactivated the SATC program, MSM had a Reserve Officer Training Corps, organized as an engineer company. By the spring 1920 semester there were enough cadets to have both a basic and an advanced course. Because the campus required that all physically fit freshmen and sophomores be in ROTC, the number of cadets grew with the general student population. Most students took it as a matter of course that they would have to take ROTC, but the initial group was not excited about it. As one early history of the program explained, the students "showed their disfavor by refusal to study or do anything more than attend the required drill and lecture periods." There was also one vocal protest. In 1929, a student wrote a letter to the editor of the *Missouri Miner* denouncing the requirement that students for two years take ROTC. He called it the "farce known as 'Militarism' that is being forced upon the college students throughout the country."

"But seriously, we talk of world peace but force the student to shoulder arms, we talk of disarmament but attempt to teach him to shoot, we boast of personal liberty, but withhold his degree if he is inclined to believe in it," the student wrote.

Discontinued in the last two years of World War II, ROTC at MSM was reinstated in 1946. Within a decade, the MSM engineer regiment had become the largest in the country and remained so until 1964. In 1962, in response to the conflict in Vietnam, ROTC established the "Raiders," a counter-guerrilla unit with a focus on the instruction in counterinsurgency and tactics.

A band organized by students in 1926 became the MSM-ROTC band three years later under the direction of John W. Scott, a local drug store owner who had attended MSM in the late 1880s. With more than two dozen student musicians, the MSM-ROTC

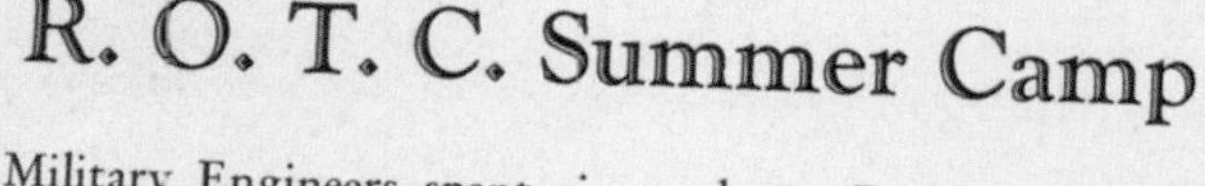

R. O. T. C. Summer Camp

Our Military Engineers spent six weeks at Fort Leavenworth, along with the R. O. T. C. Infantry from Missouri, Kansas, and Arkansas. All the Miners agree that their visit with Uncle Sam was very interesting.

The food was all soldiers food should be (Leavenworth 2 mites). Instruction was given in all engineering work. Trestle, suspension, light pontoon and heavy pontoon bridges were built.

The Reds were beaten back day after day by the latest known tricks used by sneakers and peekers.

Military Band

This year the Miner Band was reorganized by the M.S.M. R.O.T.C. In becoming part of the military organization the band received the government's backing. Instruments and music were furnished. Uncle Sam also reimburses the band members for their time spent in practice and official duties.

A concert was given during the General Lecture Series. The New Military Band is a great asset to the Military Department of the School.

Top: The 1968 UMR-ROTC marching band prepared for football game performances by running drills on campus.

Bottom: 1963 ROTC summer camp.

Right: The ROTC band was directed by local drug store owner John W. Scott in 1929.

Above: Samuel "Bo" Mahaney graduated in 1985 from the Air Force ROTC. In 2019, he achieved the distinguished rank of a two-star general.

Top right: Theresa Laverenz, the first female Army officer commissioned from the UMR ROTC in 1976.

Bottom right: In 2012, S&T's Army ROTC unit had an all-female chain of command: (left to right) Milana Taylor, Kathryn Hendricks and Mandy Grogg.

band played at football games, Armistice Day parades, Parker Hall concerts, and during military drill ceremonies. In the 1930s, rifle marksmanship became an intercollegiate sport, and the MSM team had great success, particularly in the 1950s and 1960s. The 1967 team, guided by Master Sergeant William Meredith, was the best, finishing first in the Fifth Army's Society of Military Engineer's Postal Match Firing Competition. In addition, according to an account in the *Missouri Miner*, "In the National Rifle Association Conventional and Sectional the Miners placed first out of the 55 teams. The Miners also captured first place in the International Intercollegiate NRA Sectionals," and three members — Richard Whelove, Richard Mursch, and Robert Hill — had invitations to "try out for the U.S. Olympic Rifle Team."

In the 1960s and 1970s, ROTC experienced significant change. As historians Lawrence Christensen and Jack Ridley explained, ROTC "became an elective for freshmen and sophomores" in 1965 and "the UMR Army ROTC program was changed to the general military science curriculum in lieu of the corps of engineers course. This made possible the selection of any branch of the Army by the ROTC graduates." In 1971, Air Force ROTC became an option at UMR, and the two programs became open to women in the 1970s. Carmen McCommis was the first female cadet in Air Force ROTC and Lieutenant Theresa Laverenz became the "first woman commissioned from the Reserve Officer Training Corps at UMR." It wasn't until 2013, however, that S&T's Army ROTC program had an all-female chain of command. That year, Milana Taylor, Kathryn Hendricks, and Mandy Grogg were appointed battalion commander, sergeant major, and executive officer, respectively.

With the conclusion of both the war in Vietnam and the draft, fewer students were interested in ROTC. The decline in numbers led to a three-year period ending in 1980 when the Army program was aligned with ROTC on the Columbia campus. A turnaround in enrollment soon led UMR to again become a host unit. By 1982, there were 360 students in the basic and advanced courses. Similarly, interest in Air Force ROTC waned and the UMR detachment was deactivated in 1976, but returned in 1981.

Both Army and Air Force ROTC units continued to thrive in subsequent decades, consistently graduating outstanding first lieutenants. In 1969, for example, Army Chief of Staff General William C. Westmoreland presented UMR graduate First Lieutenant Michael Clayton the Hughes Trophy recognizing Clayton as the nation's "most outstanding commissioned graduate of the Senior Division, ROTC." Similarly, in 2008, First Lieutenant Daniel J. Tabacchi was the highest ranking cadet in the four-state region of Missouri, Arkansas, Illinois, and Oklahoma and ranked 11th in the nation. Samuel "Bo" Mahaney, a 1985 graduate from Air Force ROTC, rose through the ranks to become a two-star general by 2019. Collectively, over 3,000 first lieutenants were commissioned by Army and Air Force ROTC at MSM/UMR/S&T.

WORLD WAR II

A day after the Japanese attack on Pearl Harbor in Hawaii on December 7, 1941, Congress declared war on Japan. Concerned that MSM students would enlist in large numbers as they had done in 1917, Dean Curtis Laws Wilson told students in the *Missouri Miner* on December 10 to stay at MSM during the war, arguing that the nation would "need engineers more than ever before." A month later, the editorial staff echoed Wilson's plea, writing, "Is not an engineering student's most patriotic duty that of completing his education and taking his place in the defense work?"

However, in early January 1942, the *Missouri Miner* reported, "Increasing numbers are informing the registrar's office that they will leave school tomorrow, next week, or next semester to join one of Uncle Sam's fighting units." In part, this rush to enlist derived from a personal loss on campus. Three days after the Pearl Harbor attack, students read in the *Missouri Miner* that George A. Whiteman, who had attended MSM between 1936 and 1938, was the first Missourian killed in action.

Thomas Wallace Kelly (right) shown with British Prime Minister Winston Churchill (left).

1

2

3

4

5

6

In February 1942, the faculty sought to help Dean Wilson by approving an accelerated program of study for students. By attending three summers, students could complete degree requirements in three years, an approach that got a bit easier later in the year when the faculty also voted to reduce by six the number of credit hours required for graduation. Some students enrolled in reserve training programs, but many left despite the admonitions of the dean and the steps by the faculty, and few freshmen enrolled. Enrollment for the 1942–43 academic year was nearly 1,000, but the total plummeted to just 308 two years later.

While it is impossible to determine how many students and alumni served in the conflict, the *MSM Alumnus* magazine staff conducted a survey in 1946 and determined that almost 800 had served. Among them were 568 officers. Twenty-one alumni and 18 current students were either killed in action or listed as missing in action. In the 1950s, the campus honored six of those who died in the war — Thomas Wallace Kelly, John Milroy McAnerney, Willard Farrar, William Altman, Orvid Holtman, and John Rayl — by naming a residence hall or cafeteria after them.

MSM honored the memory of six alumni who died in action by naming a residence hall or cafeteria after them: [1] Thomas Wallace Kelly; [2] John Milroy McAnerney; [3] Willard Farrar; [4] William Altman; [5] Orvid Holtman; [6] John Rayl.

Dedication Ceremonies of Buildings at MSM

Five MSM Buildings Dedicated to Alumni, McAnerney, Altman, Rayl, Farrar, Kelly

Five MSM buildings were dedicated October 25, before a large crowd that was present for the annual observance of Parent's Day.

The life-blood of five World War II heroes was figuratively transfused into the material of the buildings as dedication speakers honored the alumni war dead during the unveiling of plaques bearing their names. Relatives of John Witcig Rayl, Sweet Springs, Mo; John M. McAnerney, Kansas City, Mo; William Altman, Kansas City, Mo; and William Farrar, St. Louis, Mo., unveiled the plaques. The student presidents of Kelly Hall unveiled the name plate of Thomas Wallace Kelly, of Benton, Mo., as Kelly had no known relatives.

Dr. Elmer Ellis, president of the University of Missouri, authorized the dedication in a brief address. Dr. Curtis L. Wilson, Dean of MSM presided and introduced the relatives, then introduced Edward W. Sowers, publisher of the Rolla Daily News, who delivered the dedicatory address. Mr. Sowers reviewed the growth of the School of Mines during the past sixteen years, referring to that period as "The Wilson Era," crediting Dean Wilson with "dynamic leadership" of that growth. He added that President Ellis has distinguished himself in building all the divisions of the University, including the division at Rolla, and suggested the phrase he coined might well be: "Ellis-Wilson Era." He also mentioned

Plaques Adorning the Dedicated Buildings

1958 dedication ceremony of five buildings on campus in honor of alumni who died during World War II.

George A. Whiteman, who attended MSM in the mid-1930s, was the first American airman killed in aerial combat during World War II. He died during the Japanese attack on Pearl Harbor on December 7, 1941.

Lucky, Lucky Me

There were many stories of Miner heroism during the conflict. The aforementioned George A. Whiteman was the first hero. From Sedalia, Missouri, Whiteman attended MSM for a couple of years in the mid-1930s majoring in chemical engineering. He enlisted in the Army because he could not afford to complete his studies. Commissioned as a second lieutenant in the Army Air Corps in November 1940, Whiteman was serving in Hawaii on December 7, 1941. When the Japanese attack began, Whiteman drove 25 miles to Bellows Field, surviving heavy enemy fire. He made it to his P-40B Warhawk and was able to become briefly airborne before being shot down in a fiery crash at the end of the runway. Whiteman became the first American airman killed in aerial combat during the war. For his heroics, Whiteman became the most decorated of MSM men during the conflict, receiving the Purple Heart, the Silver Star, the American Defense Medal, the American Campaign Medal, the Asiatic-Pacific Campaign medal, a Bronze Star, and the World War II Victory Medal. The Air Force honored his memory by re-naming the Sedalia Air Force Base in 1955 as Whiteman Air Force Base.

There were many other stories of Miner heroism during the conflict. Second Lieutenant Robert C. Silhavy, from Overland in St. Louis County, had been a member of Pi Kappa Alpha, and was on the *Rollamo* board as well as the varsity tennis team. He graduated in June 1941 with a degree in ceramic engineering and a commission as a second lieutenant. The Army sent him to Fort Belvoir, Virginia, in July, where he was one of the first to go through the Engineer Officer Candidate School there. In August, the Army ordered him to the Philippines. On the southern end of Luzon, about 200 miles south of Manila, Silhavy trained a detachment in demolition. On December 17, just 10 days after the Japanese attack on Pearl Harbor, his unit had orders to destroy highway and railroad bridges to slow the Japanese advance. Silhavy set a charge on a bridge, but it was not powerful enough to bring down the bridge. Under heavy enemy fire, Silhavy sprinted about 100 yards to set another charge. This one was successful and slowed the enemy advance.

A few months later, Silhavy wrote home to reassure his parents, "Death has come as close as is possible and still missed." In another upbeat letter he wrote, "I am alive and kicking. I can't give any information, but prospects for a long life are still bright." As he was writing that letter on March 5, Silhavy was among American and Filipino troops fighting in defense of the Bataan peninsula. A month later Japanese forces overwhelmed them. The survivors, including Silhavy, endured a 62-mile "Death March" to a prisoner of war camp where he was reunited with MSM buddy Gene Boyt.

The Japanese later moved Silhavy and Boyt to a prisoner of war camp in Japan called Zentsuji. From there Silhavy was able to send a short-wave radio broadcast to his parents, one intercepted by the Federal Communications Commission. Although he and the other officers were existing on rice and soup and losing weight, Silhavy tried to cheer up his parents as he had done with his letters. In hopes that they would hear the broadcast, Silhavy said, "I am getting along fine and my health is good. Keep the old smile working, because I hope to see you all again soon."

Other MSM alumni and students who served heroically included George Munroe Jr., who graduated in 1940 with a degree in metallurgical engineering. Munroe flew on a harrowing bombing mission off Australia in 1942. He was the navigator

1: Robert C. Silhavy, 1941 graduate in ceramic engineering, under heavy fire, destroyed a railroad bridge in the Philippines, slowing the Japanese Army advance. Captured later in the conflict, Silhavy survived the "Bataan Death March" only to spend much of the war in a prisoner of war camp.

2: Gene Boyt, captured by the Japanese during World War II, spent time in a prisoner of war camp with MSM buddy Robert Silhavy.

3: A metallurgical engineer who graduated in 1940, George Munroe Jr. flew over 200 reconnaissance missions in the Pacific theater during World War II.

Top: Robert Miller, a 1941 graduate in electrical engineering, flew on many missions including during the battle of the Coral Sea in 1942.

Bottom: While serving on General George Patton's staff, Dan Kennedy, a 1926 graduate in civil engineering, encountered the horrors of the Holocaust when his unit entered a slave labor camp in Ohrdruf, Germany.

Top right: Civil engineering professor Ernest "Skip" Carlton directed the Engineering, Science, and Management War Training Program at MSM between 1941 and 1943.

Bottom right: Mechanical engineering professor Aaron Miles coordinated the training of over 350 pilots at MSM's Civil Pilot Training Program in 1943.

on a B-17 Flying Fortress, which survived attacks from Japanese Zero fighters and successfully dropped its load on a Japanese transport ship. On return to the crew's home base, the plane ran out of fuel and had to land on an island. Munroe and the rest of the crew spent nine days hacking their way through jungle growth, battling scorpions, spiders, and crocodiles. Aided by natives, the men finally made it to the coast where a U.S. plane rescued them. In addition to that exploit, during the first year of the war in the Pacific, Munroe was on more than 200 reconnaissance missions over enemy-controlled territory and usually encountered heavy anti-aircraft fire. For his service Munroe received the Distinguished Flying Cross.

After graduating in 1941 with a degree in electrical engineering, Lieutenant Robert F. Miller completed flight training at Kelly Field in San Antonio, Texas. He was on many missions including during the battle of the Coral Sea in May 1942. On a mission a month later, according to a United Press account, Miller brought "his plane back to its base although it was riddled with 50 bullet holes, including a 50-calibre cannon shot in the bomb bay."

Miners also saw the worst of the Holocaust. Lieutenant Colonel Dan Kennedy, a 1926 MSM civil engineering graduate who served on General George Patton's staff, encountered the slave labor camp at Ohrdruf, Germany. According to historian John McManus, the camp in March 1945 had almost 10,000 emaciated laborers. Their ration for a twelve-hour work day was bread, "thin soup, and 25 grams of rancid margarine." As were other American troops who entered the camps, Kennedy was horrified. He wrote to his wife, "I never saw such sights. Positively inhuman, and the living skeletons there are pitiful ... I saw twenty-eight poor emaciated prisoners who had been shot through the back of the head."

As students and alumni bravely fought in the European and Pacific theaters, there were big changes on campus during World War II. MSM offered a number of military training programs. From 1941 through 1943, the Engineering, Science, and Management War Training Program, directed by civil engineering Professor E.W. "Skip" Carlton, provided instruction in drafting, radio technician training, machine and tool design, and topographic mapping for 830 students headed into the military or the defense industry. A Civil Pilot Training Program that ended in 1943, coordinated by mechanical engineering professor Aaron Miles, trained over 350 pilots, many of whom served as transport or combat pilots. Two contingents completed the Signal Corps Trainees program conducted by the electrical engineering and mathematics departments. In 1943 and 1944 the campus hosted the Army Specialized Training Program with Mechanical Hall serving as a barracks for 400 trainees. Conducted by commissioned and non-commissioned officers, the program provided both general education courses and advanced courses in surveying, communications, and internal combustion engines. Those completing the latter course went on to officers' candidate school.

Besides a significant drop in enrollment, the campus experienced many disruptions. The *Missouri Miner* had to suspend operations for a time and continued as a weekly special section in the *Rolla New Era* newspaper. The *Rollamo* survived by producing smaller editions during the war years, and one year the Blue Key service fraternity published the yearbook. The athletic department had to suspend varsity sports in 1944, the campus did not see St. Patrick for three years, and hazing ended. In 1944, Dean Wilson reported that the falling enrollment had led to many faculty seeking positions elsewhere. He also expected layoffs among "clerks, stenographers and janitors."

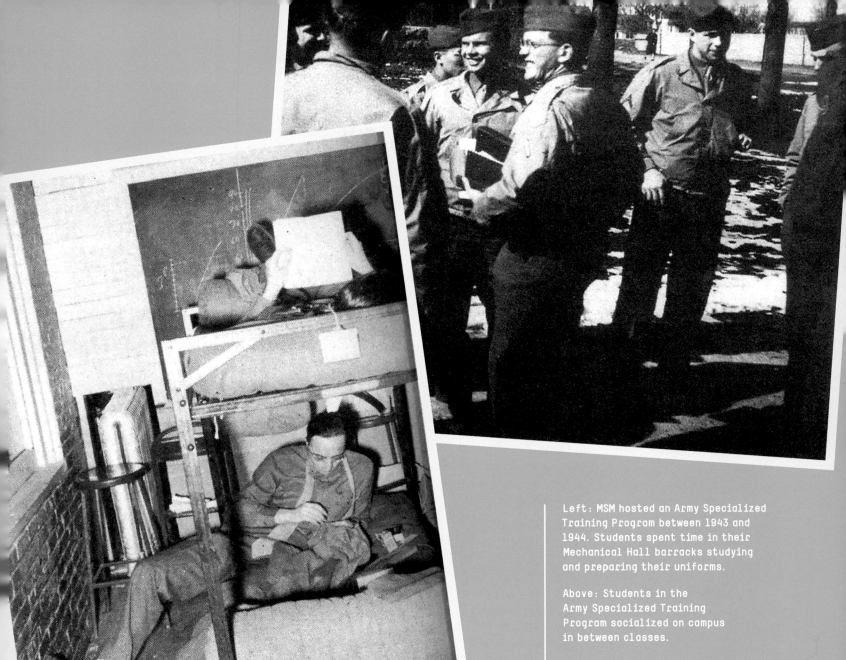

Left: MSM hosted an Army Specialized Training Program between 1943 and 1944. Students spent time in their Mechanical Hall barracks studying and preparing their uniforms.

Above: Students in the Army Specialized Training Program socialized on campus in between classes.

Below: MSM hosted an Army Specialized Training Program in 1943 and 1944.

The Army

Missouri School of Mines welcomed a contingent of about 400 Army men to its campus in August, 1943. The instruction received is deemed necessary by the Army for basic engineering training.

1: Bernard Eck, a 1950 graduate in ceramic engineering, served in the Counter Intelligence Corps during the Korean War.

2: Armin Tucker, a 1940 graduate in mining engineering and World War II veteran, flew several missions during the Korean War.

3: Gerald Rupert, who later joined the MSM faculty, served in the Korean War.

KOREAN WAR

In June 1950, North Korean forces crossed the 38th parallel into South Korea. The United States supported the non-communist South Korean government and President Harry S. Truman quickly gained United Nations Security Council authorization for a "police action" to defend South Korea. U.S. troops engaged in a three-year war with North Korean and Chinese troops before the two sides signed a cease-fire agreement in 1953.

Similar to his approach during World War II, Dean Curtis Laws Wilson encouraged Miners to stay in school. Still, those in the Army Enlisted Reserve Corps were ordered to active duty in fall 1950. As the war developed and U.S. forces needed ever-more personnel, the editor of the *Missouri Miner* expressed concern that the federal government would curtail "occupational deferments" and upon graduation Miners might face induction into the Army, thereby delaying their career pursuits. That happened to Bernard Eck. A 1950 MSM graduate in ceramic engineering, Eck was working for United States Steel in Chicago when the Army ordered him to report for induction. Even though U.S. Steel had requested an occupational deferment, the draft board refused and Eck reported for duty.

Miner alumni like Eck and future Miners alike contributed to the American war effort between 1950 and 1953 in a multitude of ways. Armin Tucker, a 1940 graduate with a degree in mining engineering, had served in World War II, flying missions in the "China-Burma-India Theater with the Air Transport Command," and had won the Distinguished Flying Cross. He was recalled to duty in 1951 and flew several missions in support of American troops in Korea. John Brodhacker, who had graduated in 1944 with a degree in chemical engineering and, like Tucker was a veteran of World War II, served on a destroyer escort in the Navy. Gerald Rupert and Norbert Schmidt, two future faculty members at MSM, also served. Rupert was in the Air Force, and Schmidt was with the 65th Engineers. Schmidt received two Purple Hearts and a Bronze Star for his action in fighting in the Pusan Perimeter early in the war. Eck spent just over a year in Korea, serving in the Counter Intelligence Corps. Stationed near the 38th parallel, usually only a few miles behind the front lines, Eck was assigned to interrogate both North Korean and Chinese soldiers. In 1952, Lieutenant Conrad Wigge, who had attended MSM in 1945, died when his plane crashed into the side of the aircraft carrier *Philippine Sea*. Lieutenant James H. Russell, who attended MSM for two years after serving in World War II, was the commanding officer of an X Corps ration-gas-oil supply point in central Korea.

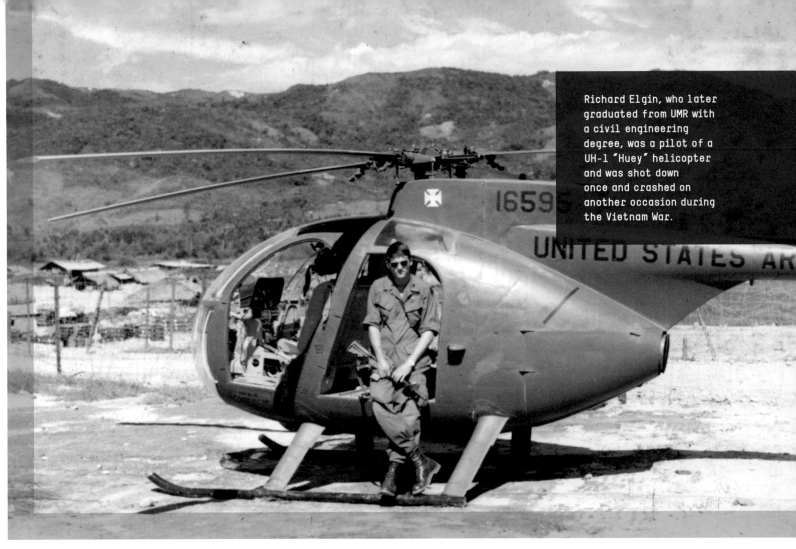

Richard Elgin, who later graduated from UMR with a civil engineering degree, was a pilot of a UH-1 "Huey" helicopter and was shot down once and crashed on another occasion during the Vietnam War.

VIETNAM WAR

America's involvement in the Vietnam War began in the late 1950s. Initially, American personnel served as advisors to the South Vietnamese army in its conflict with North Vietnamese regulars and the Viet Cong, communist guerrillas operating in South Vietnam. Presidents Dwight Eisenhower, John Kennedy, and Lyndon Johnson believed that stopping communist expansion in Vietnam was vital in the American Cold War with the Soviet Union. By 1963, over 16,000 American military advisors were in South Vietnam, and two years later the first combat troops arrived at China Beach to defend the air base at Da Nang. Within three years, there were over 500,000 American troops in South Vietnam. American troops remained in Vietnam through March 1973.

It is not clear how many Miners served in Vietnam, but among the 56 identified by Vietnam War veteran and UMR alumnus Richard Elgin, over half were engineer branch officers and 25 had completed the ROTC program at MSM and UMR. While most were not in the "combat arms" such as infantry, armor, or artillery, several saw considerable action. Wes Scott, a 1968 graduate in mechanical engineering, was a tank commander. Ranney McDonough, a 1966 civil engineering graduate, and Elgin, a 1974 civil engineering graduate, were both pilots of the famed UH-1 "Huey" helicopter. As McDonough explained, his missions were "in support of infantry troops, inserting and extracting infantry soldiers and providing resupply." Elgin was shot down once and crashed on another mission because of a "complete tail rotor failure in a Huey." Dick Baumann, a 1967 mechanical engineering graduate, piloted the iconic McDonnell-Douglas F-4 Phantom fighter-bomber, "flying mostly air support for our guys on the ground."

Top Right: Ranney McDonough, a 1966 civil engineering graduate, piloted a "Huey" helicopter during the Vietnam War.

Right: Dick Baumann, who graduated in 1967 with a degree in mechanical engineering, piloted a McDonnell-Douglas F-4 Phantom fighter-bomber during the Vietnam War.

Right: Wes Scott, a mechanical engineering major who graduated in 1968, was a tank commander during the Vietnam War.

Below: After two tours of duty in Vietnam, Joe Ballard went on to command the U.S. Army Corps of Engineers and retired as a lieutenant general in 2000.

Major Charles T. Stevens, an associate professor of military science, was awarded the "Bronze Star Medal for Valor" in 1967. In June of that year, his 431st Regional Forces Company engaged the Viet Cong. "Although wounded, he tenaciously continued to press the assault, and so inspired the Vietnamese soldiers, that they aggressively swept into the Viet Cong position destroying them in a single powerful attack." In 1966, the *Missouri Miner* reported the death of Captain Sylvan Bradley, a 1961 graduate in civil engineering. According to the article, "enemy ground fire" struck "the helicopter he was piloting" and the "craft crashed and burned." Bradley was the only known Miner killed in action in Vietnam.

Miners like Buddy Barnes, Steve Johnson, Mark Morris, Bryan Stirrat, Richard Waddell, Denny Pendergrass, Joe Ballard, and Wayne Whitehead, all of whom served in engineer battalions or brigades, played critical roles in developing the infrastructure essential to the combat units. They cleared mines from roads and built bunkers, roads, and bridges. After two tours of duty in Vietnam, Ballard went on to command the U.S. Army Corps of Engineers and retired as a lieutenant general in 2000. Morris, who had graduated in 1964 with a degree in physics, was in a battalion that "built infrastructure at Cam Rhan Bay, which was destined to be a major seaport during the war," and later his battalion moved on to Phan Rang "to construct a 10,000-foot runway and facilities for the Air Force."

Morris even wrote a letter to his alma mater to describe the nature of the conflict. He hoped all could "come over here and get a chance at the Viet Cong." He said that he had "finally seen some VC. It was no thrill. They are like everyone else, only they have guns." Yet, his experiences had persuaded him that it would be a long war. "Things are running pretty well as far as battles and operations, but there will be a lot of time involved in completing this war — about six more years unless something unexpected happens." His battalion had not engaged in any battles, "but we've been sniped at and have run over mines." Fortunately, "no one has been killed in our battalion." Notably, Morris reported, "The engineer units over here really have their share of U. of Mo., at Rolla graduates in them. There are eight of us in the 62nd Engineers." Indeed, he reported that most of the engineer units included several Miners.

"Begin the Beguine" ....
"Lonesome Road" ....
"Never Walk Alone" ....
"Halls of Ivy" ....
"For Lovin' Me" ....
"This Is My Country" ....
"Spanish Harlem" ....
Mine Blues Songs ....
("Sixteen Tons," "Ballad of S
"Shenandoah" ....
"Dear Heart" ....
"Come and Go With Me" ....
"Poor Jud Is Dead" ....

Alumnus Dies in Viet Nam

Word has just been received hat Captain Sylvan Bradley, a 961 graduate of the Missouri chool of Mines, was killed in iet Nam on Friday, November 0, 1966, when enemy ground fire it the helicopter he was piloting nd the craft crashed and burned.

Captain Bradley, a civil engieering major, transferred to the Missouri School of Mines in 1957 from Flat River Junior College and immediately became active in the Independents. He became a member of the Prospectors and was elected their treasurer and Student Council alternate in 1959 and their business manager in 1960. He served on the Student Union Board in 1960 as the news service committee chairman and was elected vice president of the Student Council in the same year.

A member of both the American Society of Civil Engineers and the American Society of Mechanical Engineers, Capt. Bradley served as a student assistant in the Civil Engineering Department the fall of 1959.

Captain Bradley was designated a Distinguished Military Student by the Military Department in the fall of 1960 and 1961; and was designated a Distinguished Military Graduate on May 28, 1961.

After graduating, Captain Bradley enrolled in the pilots' training program and after serving his two year tour of duty, he applied for and was accepted into the Regular Army.

A memorial service will be held for Captain Bradley in the Irondale Gymnasium on Sunday, December 10, 1966 at 2:30 p.m. A fund is being established to donate an organ to the Irondale Methodist Church in his memory.

He is survived by his wife and one child.

OLLAMO Schedules roup Pictures uring Semester

This year the Rollamo staff ill be taking group pictures at he end of the first semester intead of waiting until the second emester, as has been done in the ast. This provides more time to ut the book together and may ossibly result in an earlier disribution of the Rollamo next ear.

Pictures will be taken on Deember 14, 15 and January 4, 5.

UMR ROTC Band Recei For Appearance in 'Taler

The UMR ROTC Band recently received a $150 check from the Corinthian Special Production Co., of Houston for its participation in the filming of "Campus Talent '67."

The band and its majorette Miss Myra Jane Wilson were chosen in the fall to be filmed for the program. The show to be presented later in the year, is the second of a series in Missouri sponsored by Southwestern Bell

Captain Sylvan Bradley, 1961 graduate in civil engineering, was the only known Miner alumnus killed in action during the Vietnam War.

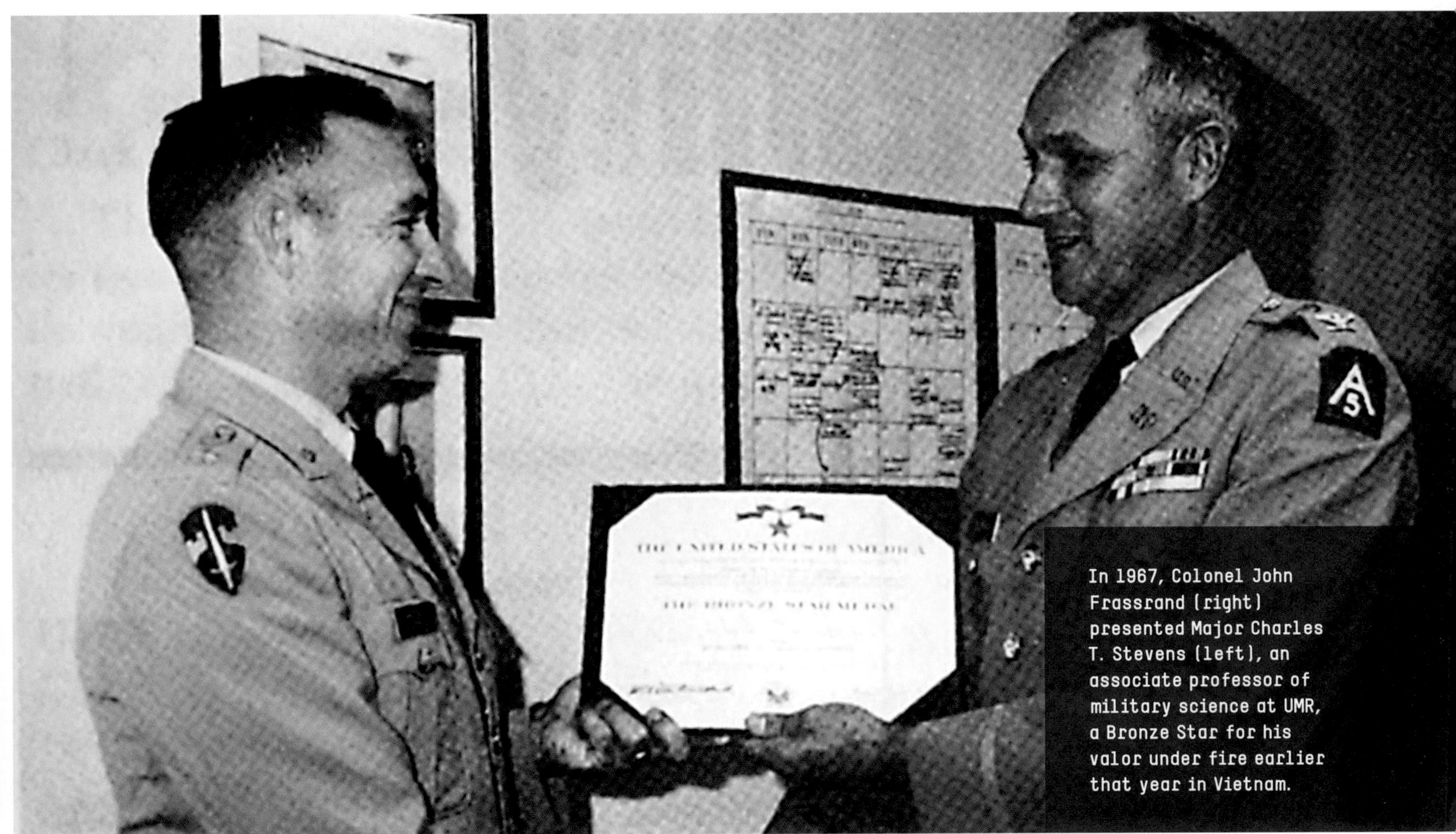

In 1967, Colonel John Frassrand (right) presented Major Charles T. Stevens (left), an associate professor of military science at UMR, a Bronze Star for his valor under fire earlier that year in Vietnam.

Recent Graduate Sends Letter From Vietnam

Following is a letter received from a recent graduate of UMR, presently serving in Viet Nam as a member of the 62nd Engineers Battalion.

Phan Rang, Viet Nam

It's been quite a while since I've written last — I was in Cam Rahn I guess. I hope that you haven't closed school so you all could come over here and get a chance at the Viet Cong — not a chance, huh? I'm glad you haven't because the VC aren't worth it. At the rate the war is going, most of you will have your chance yet. I know it doesn't sound very cool, but I'd say the odds were against you. I don't mean to say the war is going BADLY, It isn't! Things are running pretty well as far as battles and operations, but there will be a lot of time involved in completing this war — about six more years, unless something unexpected happens — and that's a good possibility also.

Well, I've finally seen some VC. It was no thrill. They are like everyone else, only they have guns.

The Phan Rang area is safe so to speak. Outside of the area lots happens. We are not sweating anything, but we are not taking chances either. We haven't had any fights, but we've been sniped at and have run over mines. No one has been killed in our battalion, so you can see we are pretty well off.

Since October of '65, we've been working on an airfield complex, and it should be operating by the end of this month. That will be something — most of the people in the construction battalion have never worked so hard on anything before. Quite an engineering job.

The engineer units over here really have their share of U. of Mo. at Rolla graduates in them. There are eight of us in the 62nd Engineers. Most of the other engineer units have plenty of others, too. Kind of surprising to know so many people on the other side of the world.

I'm a guard duty officer tonight — a pain in the . . ., but quite necessary! The pass-word tonight is "Time-Table" — great combat stuff, huh? I have to stay up all night and walk the perimeter to make sure all the guards are awake (Who's going to keep me awake? I guess they don't worry about that.)

Well, providing Ho Chi Minh doesn't come up with any off-the-wall ideas, I'll see you next Homecoming.

Sincer
Mark

Mark Morris, a 1964 physics graduate of UMR, wrote a letter to the *Missouri Miner* describing the situation in the Vietnam War.

the dual r
Centennial
paign Cha
the plans
which will
solicitation
Enoch R.
honorary
tennial Ch
Repres
Hearnes,
commissi
pledged t
nor to
mended t
forts to c
to suppler
and federa

Office at Ro
Act of March
The subscrip
Missouri Mine
and Faculty c
Editor-in-Chie
70
Business Man
500
Managing Ed
Make Up Edi
Copy Editor .
Secretary ....
Features Edit
Photographer

Under the auspices of the United States Agency for International Development, UMR established an engineering program at the National Technical Center in Saigon during the Vietnam War. At the signing ceremony (left to right) are U.S. Senator Stuart Symington; John Hanna, director of the Agency for International Development; U.S. Representative Richard Ichord, 8th Missouri District; U.S. Senator Thomas F. Eagleton; and UMR Chancellor Merl Baker.

In 1968, UMR began exploring an opportunity to work with the United States Agency for International Development to establish an engineering university in Saigon. Professors Aaron Miles, Robert Carlile, and Lynn Martin made a preliminary visit in 1968 to determine the state of higher education in Vietnam. In December of that year a delegation, led by South Vietnam's minister of education Lee Minh Tri, met with administrators and faculty at UMR. After much negotiation, UMR signed an agreement in 1969 with the federal government "to develop a quality engineering university in Saigon, South Vietnam." Mining engineering professor Ernest Spokes and chemical engineering professor Marshall Findley attended a two-week orientation in Washington, D.C., and then went to Saigon to establish the program at the National Technical Center. Over the next three years, other UMR faculty went to Saigon to help develop courses and faculty in the disciplines of chemical, civil, electrical, and mechanical engineering. Because they were developing this engineering university in a war zone, the faculty were at risk, and family members who accompanied them could not stay in South Vietnam. The dangers were evident after a car bombing that killed Lee Minh Tri just a few weeks after he visited Rolla in late 1968. Still, the UMR faculty persisted through 1973, and in doing so made some progress in meeting a need for the South Vietnamese people. During a 1971 visit, for example, Chancellor Merl Baker found that there were "about 500 Vietnamese studying to be engineers and 500 studying to be technicians."

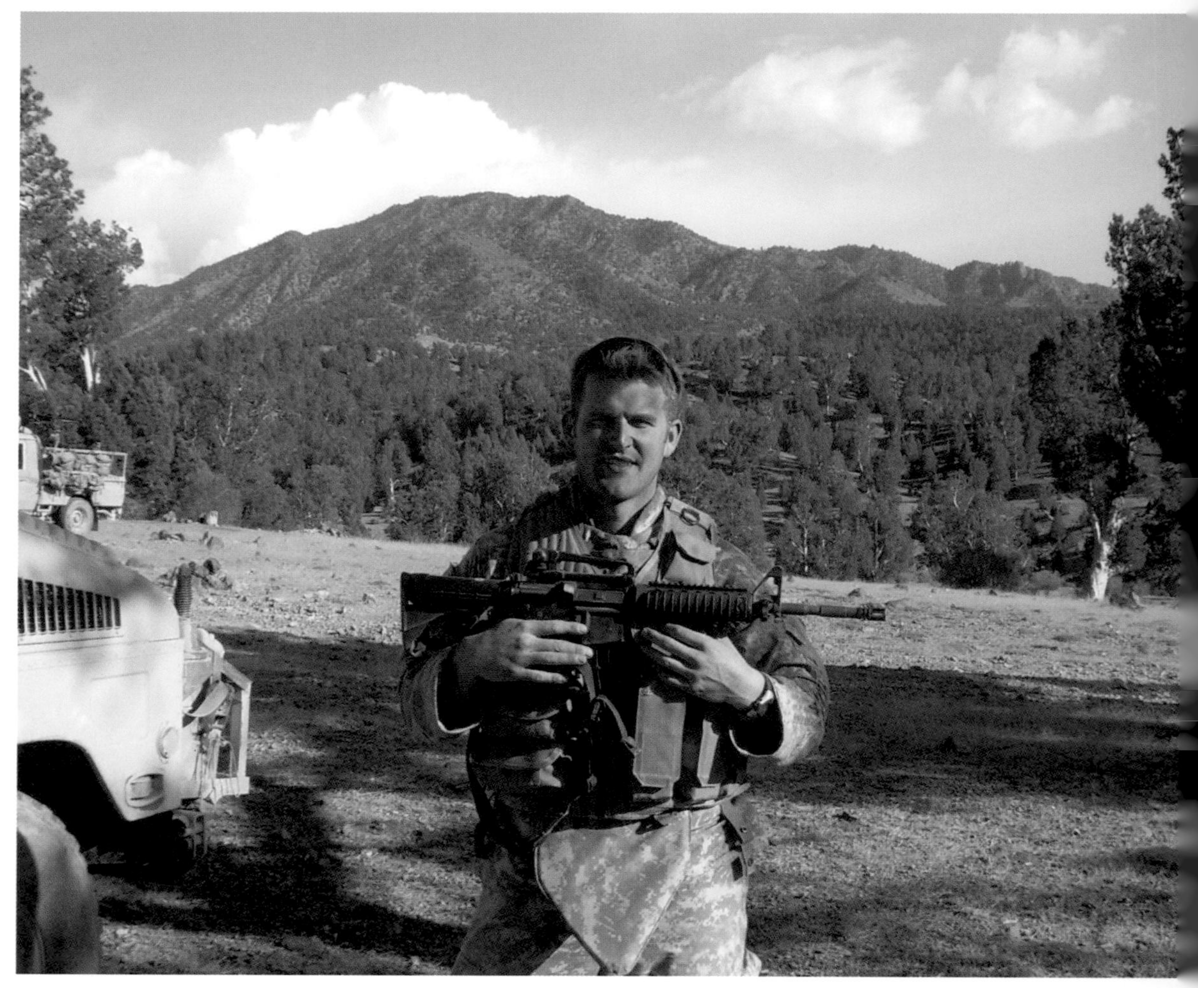

Above: Brigade General Robert Bay (left), commanding general of the 416th Engineer Command, transferring command of the 471st Engineer Company from Captain William A. Stoltz (right), to then Captain Keith Wedge (center).

Right: Courtney Buck, who earned a degree in economics in 2003, served as an explosive ordnance disposal technician in Afghanistan.

POST-VIETNAM CONFLICTS

Although not in the numbers that contributed to the U.S. effort in Vietnam, Miners served in war zones around the world in the late 20th and early 21st centuries from Panama and Somalia to Kuwait, Afghanistan, and Iraq. In January 1991, the United States led a coalition of forces from NATO and Arab nations in a 42-day conflict to remove Iraqi forces that had occupied neighboring Kuwait. In this Persian Gulf War, known as Operation Desert Storm, UMR graduate Keith Wedge was among the 425,000 U.S. forces. Wedge, who held a bachelor's degree (1970), master's degree (1971), and Ph.D. (1974) in geology and geophysics from UMR, was a lieutenant colonel in the U.S. Army Reserve. Assigned to the 416th Engineer Command, Wedge traveled to Kuwait, Saudi Arabia, Bahrain, southern Iraq, and Dhahran, working with senior officials in the Saudi General Directorate of Military Works. According to an article in the *Missouri Geological Survey*, his engineering unit "played a key role in engineering and environmental management before, during, and after the war."

Major Dennis Segrue, brothers Keven and Jeff Schaefer, and Courtney Buck served in Afghanistan. In 2004, Buck, who had graduated a year earlier with a bachelor's degree in economics, enlisted to fight in the Iraq War. Buck served in Afghanistan for several months. An explosive ordnance disposal technician, Buck had the dangerous task of dismantling explosive devices like IEDs and roadside bombs in addition to patrolling the Pakistan border. Army Reserve Major Lisa Peplinski Jaster, who served in both Iraq and Afghanistan, became the third woman and the first Army reserve officer to graduate Army Ranger School in 2015. Another veteran of Afghanistan, Barbara Rutter served in the Marines and after seeing how blast-induced brain trauma affected her fellow soldiers, enrolled at S&T to earn master's and Ph.D. degrees in explosives engineering and to conduct research on traumatic brain injury, a significant concern for the military.

EDUCATING VETERANS

Rutter is one of many veterans who pursued an education from Rolla after active duty. In anticipation of the end of World War I, the federal government passed the Soldier Rehabilitation Act in 1918. It provided federal funding, according to historian Willie V. Bryan, "to provide for the vocational rehabilitation and return to employment of disabled persons discharged from the military." Instruction in mechanical, electrical, and structural engineering began

Top: Keith Wedge, who had three degrees from UMR in geology and geophysics, served in the 416th Engineer Command during the 1991 Persian Gulf War.

Bottom: Army Reserve Major Lisa Peplinski Jaster, who earned a degree in civil engineering in 2004, became the third woman and first Army reserve officer to graduate U.S. Army Ranger School in 2015.

Right: Fort Leonard Wood soldiers attended classes on the S&T campus in July 2010.

bove: Vocational
en on the steps of
rwood Hall.

ght: After World
r I MSM conducted a
cational Training
ogram for veterans of
t conflict. Through
6 the "Vocate" program
matically boosted
pus enrollment.

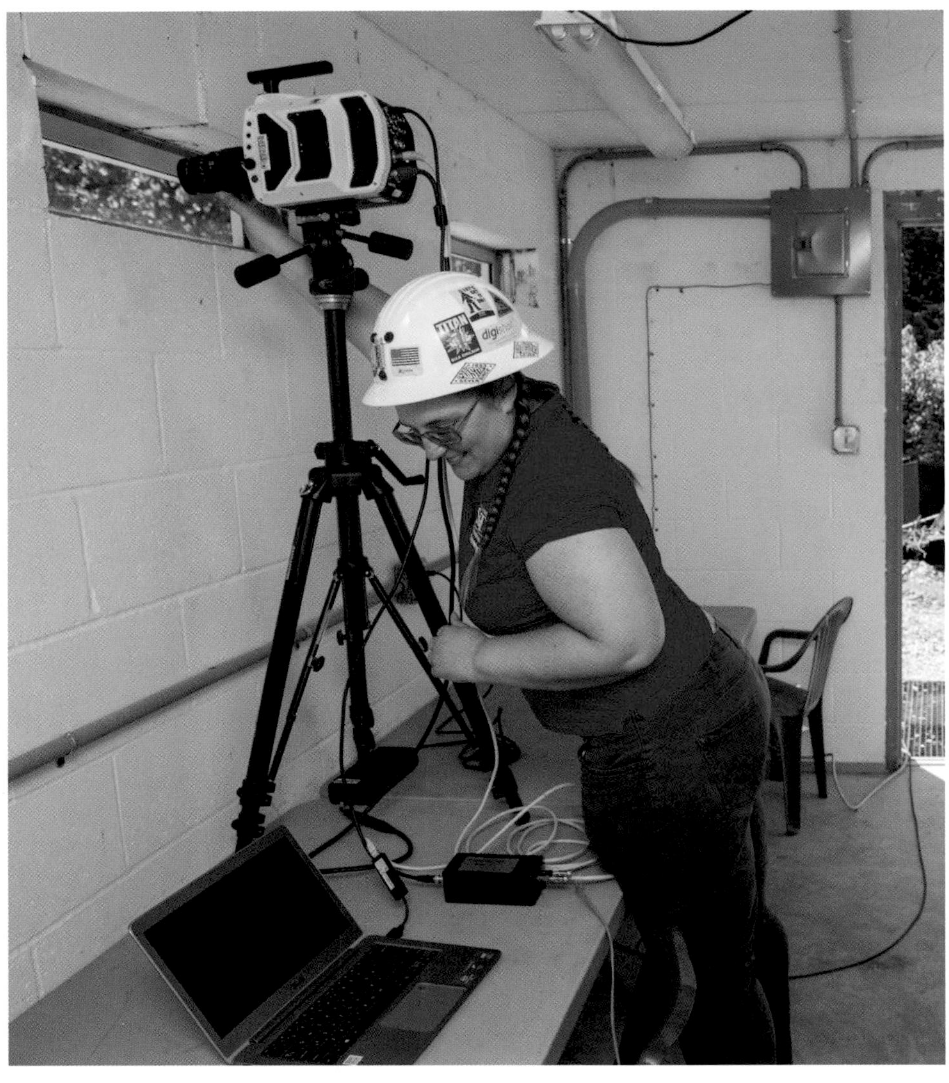

Left: Marine veteran Barbara Rutter, who earned master's and Ph.D. degrees in explosives engineering, conducts research on traumatic brain injury.

Above: Chuck Remington in 1946.

at MSM in 1919 with 50 students. By fall 1920 the focus was on topographical, oil, and highway engineering. Until its end in 1926, the "Vocate" program was critical to campus enrollment. In 1921, for example, 200 of the 562 students at MSM were in the Vocational Training program and the *Missouri Miner* reported that MSM "headed the long list of universities and colleges that gave courses in Vocational Training."

In 1944, Congress passed the Servicemen's Readjustment Act of 1944, better known as the GI Bill. It provided guaranteed loans to veterans for the purchase of a farm, business, or home; an unemployment benefit for a year; and tuition support along with a cost of living stipend for those wanting to attend a college. Across the country nearly half of college admissions in 1947 were veterans. There were subsequent iterations of the GI Bill, including the Montgomery GI Bill passed in 1984, the 2008 Post-9/11 GI Bill, and the 2017 Forever GI Bill, all of which expanded benefits for veterans and, in some cases, active service members.

The GI Bill's impact on MSM after World War II was almost immediate. During the 1946–47 academic year, student enrollment jumped to 2,565 from under 400 the year before, with veterans accounting for over 1,800 of the total. Classes, scheduled from 7 a.m. to 10 p.m. six days a week, were packed. Dean Wilson had to scramble to hire faculty to meet the spike in enrollment, and the campus purchased over 20 temporary structures from the Vichy Airport north of Rolla and Fort Leonard Wood for barracks, most of which were placed north of Jackling Field and a block east of Jackling Gymnasium. As crowded and frustrating as the years between 1946 and 1950 were, alumni from that era credited the GI Bill with giving them the opportunity to attend MSM. For example, Charles "Chuck" Remington, who earned bachelor's and master's degrees in mechanical engineering from MSM and became a faculty member on campus, called the GI Bill "a godsend" because he "received 100 percent" of his education through that support.

The Missouri S&T Army ROTC and Air Force ROTC conduct a wreath-laying ceremony outside of Harris Hall on September 11, 2014.

CONCLUSION

MSM, UMR, and S&T had a good relationship with Fort Leonard Wood from the time that it was built in 1940 just 30 miles from Rolla. In the late 20th and early 21st centuries that relationship became ever stronger. For many years the campus offered coursework at the fort. Master's degree programs in civil engineering, geological engineering, and engineering management were particularly popular with officers, and faculty also engaged in research projects there in part through a research park established at the fort by the University of Missouri System, the efforts of a liaison, and, beginning in 2018, a partnership with Phelps Health and the Army to study traumatic brain injury.

The positive association the campus had with the fort is a good example of how closely connected Miners have been to the American military. In part, it was due to an abiding sense of patriotism shared by most students and alumni, but also because they possessed skills essential to the nation's ability to win wars. Beyond their contributions in combat, during most of the nation's conflicts, students, alumni, and faculty provided essential logistical or combat support service. When America went to war, Miners went along.

Top: The Acute Effects of Neurotrauma Consortium research conclave in 2019 brought together academic institutions and the U.S. military at Fort Leonard Wood, Missouri.

Bottom: Military Appreciation Day on the S&T campus in 2011.

CHAPTER 7

MINER ATHLETICS

The editors of the 1947 *Rollamo* offered some insight into the role of intercollegiate athletics at MSM. "The teaching of engineering," they wrote, "makes it doubly difficult to turn out sensational athletic teams." They praised the coaches who produced successful "teams with a minimum amount of time and with players who played the game for themselves." The following year, the editors agreed with the latter point. "Varsity athletes, like intramural enthusiasts, play the game because they like to." In their assessment of Miner athletics through the early 1960s, historians Lawrence Christensen and Jack Ridley wrote, "With an emphasis on enjoyment and in the absence of athletic scholarships, here was a sports program which stressed academic performance over athletic prowess."

An MSM football helmet from the late 1950s when Gale Bullman was head coach. Football was one of the first sports programs established at MSM.

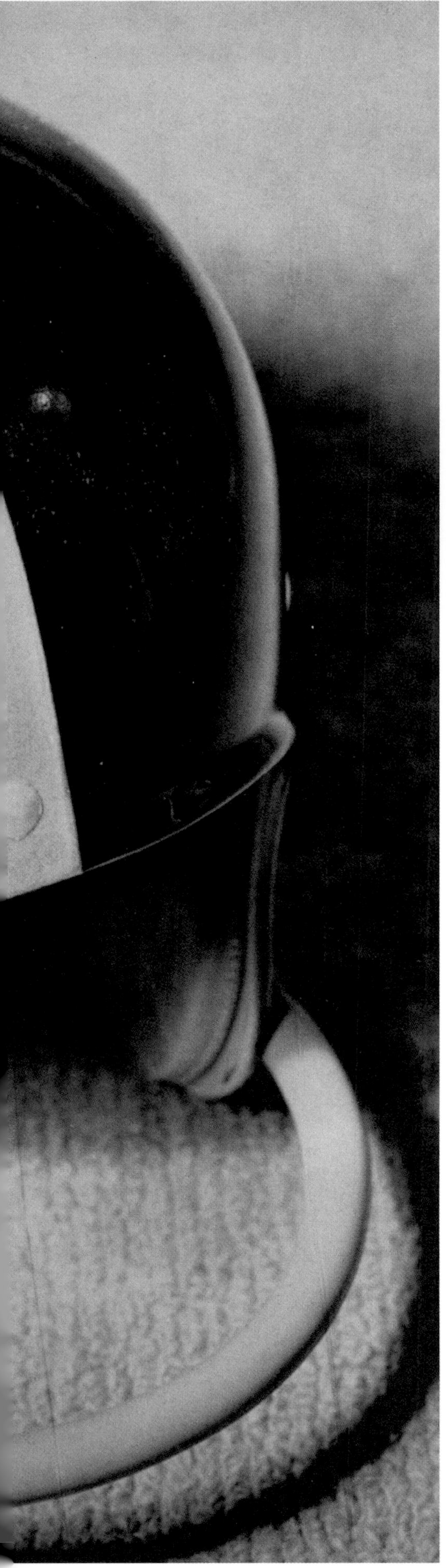

DOCTOR AUSTIN LEE McRAE
Professor of Physics

Physics professor Austin McRae, who had begun the football program at the University of Missouri, started intercollegiate football at MSM in 1893.

All athletes in intercollegiate sports are competitive and ambitious to win contests. Many colleges and universities focus upon winning championships, but from their origins in the 1890s, Miner athletic programs largely served different purposes. They provided an opportunity for students eager to compete in intercollegiate sports to do so, but with an understanding that their academic pursuits took priority.

The Miners began intercollegiate competition with a baseball game against Drury College in 1892. According to a Springfield, Missouri, newspaper account, "the Drury boys defeated" the Miners "by a top-heavy score." Football began the following year under the leadership of physics Professor Austin Lee McRae, who had established the football program at the University of Missouri three years earlier. After only two weeks of practice, the Miners, in orange and white uniforms, lost to Drury 16-0 in a game played in Springfield. In 1907, the editors of the first edition of the *Rollamo* explained that "track and field sports have always held an important place" at MSM, although in that year the Miners had only one meet, narrowly losing to the visiting Washington University squad from St. Louis. The campus struggled to establish a basketball program with a failed effort in 1907 and a limited schedule of games between 1909 and 1914. For example, in 1913, the *Rollamo* reported, "Owing to difficulty in arranging a schedule and an attempt to adjust athletic finances no games were scheduled except one with Drury and one with Springfield Normal" (now Missouri State University). Over the next century, the campus added a wide range of intercollegiate sports for men, including wrestling, boxing, swimming, tennis, golf, cross country, soccer, water polo, and a rifle team and, in the 1970s, added intercollegiate sports for women.

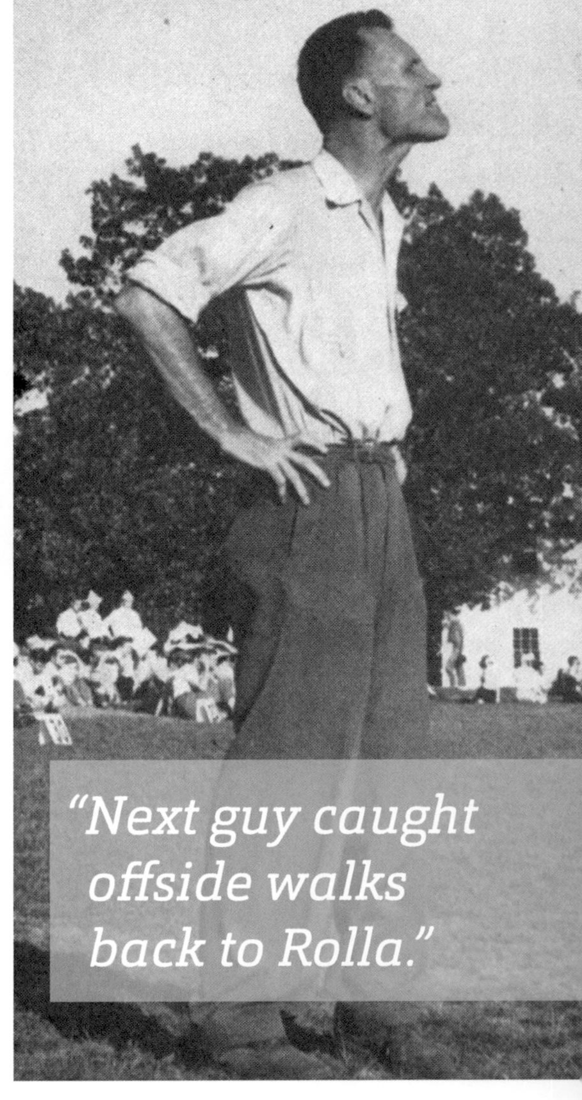

"Next guy caught offside walks back to Rolla."

Above: Frank "Spike" Dennie, who joined the faculty in 1909, became the first athletic director at MSM.

Center: Between 1928 and 1937, Harold Grant served as both head football coach and athletic director at MSM.

Right: Gale Bullman, the coach with the "lantern jaw," came to MSM in 1937 and led the athletic program for three decades.

ATHLETIC DIRECTORS AND THE GROWING NUMBER OF SPORTS

Miner athletics was fortunate to have steady leadership for over a century. Beginning in 1909 with Frank "Spike" Dennie, five men and one woman held the position of athletic director for most of the years through 2020. Dennie had come to MSM from Brown University where he was an All-American and held the distinction of catching the first touchdown pass ever thrown at Brown. He left MSM for three years to coach at Saint Louis University, but returned in 1915. Dennie also served two years in World War I. Upon his return, he remained at MSM for the rest of his career. Although the Miners had winning football teams in 1925 and 1926, they only won two games in 1927, and the basketball team won only three in the latter year. According to the *Kansas City Star*, there was "considerable dissatisfaction on the part of alumni and School of Mines fans regarding the athletic situation at the school." Because of that pressure, Dennie and football coach S.C. McCollum both resigned in early 1928.

Harold Grant, football coach at College of Emporia in Kansas, where he had a record of 34-4-1 and who had been rumored to be in the running to become head coach at the University of Kansas, replaced Dennie in February 1928 to serve as both athletic director and head football coach. Although he had a winning record in his first six years as head football coach, Grant's teams won only four games during his last three years, and he resigned in 1937.

MSM replaced Grant with new head football coach Gale Bullman. He had won 27 letters in football, basketball, and baseball in high school and college. After one year at Marietta College, Bullman played three years at West Virginia Wesleyan. A wide receiver who had 52 receptions one year, Bullman was also an outstanding kicker. His biggest moment at Wesleyan was when he picked up a fumble and ran 94 yards for a touchdown to defeat a heavily favored Syracuse team. He also played one year in the professional ranks for the Columbus Tigers. Bullman served as an assistant coach at Washington University for a decade before coming to Rolla. In that time he earned a law degree as well as a reputation as "Gloomy Gale" because of his somber look.

Top left: Billy Key followed Gale Bullman as athletic director and held the position for over 20 years.

Top right: Mark Mullin, who came to UMR in 1986 to coach the swimming team, was athletic director between 1992 and 2020.

Bottom: Melissa Ringhausen joined S&T in 2020 as athletic director after serving as assistant athletic director and head women's basketball coach at McKendree University.

In his three decades leading the Miners as head coach, the slender, "lantern-jawed" Bullman became legendary, developing a reputation as "wry-humored" and as a "nervous and energetic" coach. Stories abounded about his frequent irritation with players. In a game in Kirksville one year, Bullman got so angry with his players' frequent offside penalties that he yelled, "Next guy caught offside walks back to Rolla." As athletic director, he expanded the intramural program on campus and hired good coaches who produced some successful teams. The 1947–48 academic year was particularly good as the football, golf, tennis, and swimming teams all won conference championships.

Hired as the head basketball coach in 1964, Billy Key became athletic director three years later and held the position through 1990. A successful basketball coach at Nicholls State and Harris Teachers College (now Harris-Stowe State University), Key won a Missouri Intercollegiate Athletics Association (MIAA) championship, the first in the school's history, and took two teams to the NCAA tournament. In all, he won 387 games, and in 1986, the National Association of Basketball Coaches selected Key as its president, succeeding Georgetown University head coach John Thompson. During his long tenure as athletic director, Key added women's sports and expanded the number of men's sports. Most importantly, over 80 percent of student athletes at UMR graduated during the Key years.

Mark Mullin, who served as the head swimming coach for 12 years beginning in 1986, became athletic director in 1992 and continued through 2020. His tenure as athletic director was notable for the most significant upgrade in facilities in the school's history, including artificial turf for Allgood-Bailey Stadium; new flooring, scoreboards, and chair-back seats for Gibson Arena; a student fitness center; and an indoor practice facility. He also promoted a culture among his coaches that emphasized "advancing essential life skills such as leadership, cooperation, and teamwork" as "the cornerstone of Miner Athletics."

In 2020, Melissa Ringhausen became the first woman to hold the athletic director position. She joined S&T from McKendree University in Lebanon, Illinois, where she served as assistant director of athletics and head coach of the women's basketball program.

Pictured here in 1975, Annette Caruso was the first head coach for both women's basketball and volleyball.

For several years MSM sought admission to the MIAA, which had been established in 1912. After a two-decade campaign, the Miners joined the conference in 1935 and remained a member for seven decades. In 2005, UMR left the MIAA — then known as the Midwest Intercollegiate Athletic Association — to join the Great Lakes Valley Conference (GLVC), which had member universities in Wisconsin, Illinois, Indiana, Kentucky, and Missouri.

Women's intercollegiate sports began in 1974 in response to federal legislation. Title IX of the 1972 Education Amendments Act provided that women could not "be subjected to discrimination under any education program or activity receiving federal financial assistance." Under Coach Annette Caruso, UMR began women's athletics with both a basketball team and a volleyball team. In 1974, UMR became a member of the Association of Intercollegiate Athletics for Women, but when that organization suspended operation in 1982, UMR joined the MIAA and the NCAA Division II. In 2005, the women's programs also joined the GLVC. Softball replaced volleyball in 1979, and over the years, the women's athletics program added more sports. In 2019, Missouri S&T had eight men's sports — baseball, basketball, cross country, football, golf, soccer, swimming, and track and field — and seven women's sports — basketball, cross country, golf, soccer, softball, track and field, and volleyball — with just over 350 men and 144 women participating.

THE CRISIS IN COLLEGE FOOTBALL, 1905

In the early 20th century, college football was a brutal sport. Players had little protective gear and, according to journalist David Dayen, games of that era often "resembled a cross between a street fight and the trench warfare of World War I." He explained that "players leaped on downed ball-carriers, and endless pileups featured slugging and eye-gouging. The in-fashion play call was the 'flying wedge,' where players would link arms, form a 'V' ... and careen downfield, running over their rivals."

The Miner football teams in the early 1900s developed a reputation for that rough style of play. In 1904, after his team suffered a 53-0 shellacking by the Miners, the Christian Brothers College coach claimed that "he had never seen such a game and that it was simply a case of eleven prize fighters opposed to a team that was trying to play straight football." Some of his players agreed, arguing that "the miners used everything on them but blasting-powder." There was so much negative coverage of the game in the St. Louis newspapers that Homer T. Fuller, the president of Drury College, traveled to Rolla to attend a faculty meeting and explained that he was concerned that his players would face "a team of rowdies and sluggers." The Miner players said that the charges were false, the MSM faculty convinced Fuller that the charges had been exaggerated, and the Miners were able to play Drury.

Similar charges surfaced against the Miners again in 1905. One fan who saw the Miners play Washington University claimed that he could not determine whether he "saw a fight or a footrace." "I saw a Rolla player swinging his doubled-up fists in several of the musses mighty like a fellow who's doing all the fighting he knows how." That same year, the captain of the Arkansas team claimed that during their game in

Above: Photo taken by George Ladd of the MSM football team from the early 1900s.

Below: MSM director George Ladd (1897-1907) was a strong advocate of reform in college football to limit its "brutality."

Rolla, "from the first kick-off" he and his teammates were "slugged." Moreover, when he complained to the referee, who had graduated from MSM, "I was cursed soundly by him and ordered back to my position."

The excesses of college football caught the attention of President Theodore Roosevelt, who believed "manly" sports like football provided vital life lessons. Writing to a friend in 1903, Roosevelt claimed, "In life, as in a football game, the principle to follow is: Hit the line hard; don't foul and don't shirk, but hit the line hard!" To preserve the game, Roosevelt had a summit at the White House with three prominent college coaches and alumni leaders in October 1905 That meeting was a springboard for several reforms in college football, including legalizing the forward pass, creating a neutral zone between the offensive and defensive lines, and eliminating mass formations like the flying wedge.

MSM Director George Ladd agreed with Roosevelt's stand on football and supported the reforms. In November 1905 he wrote, "It is too good a game to be abolished and too full of evils to run its present course unchecked."

Ladd added, "Full of possibilities for the development of manhood, skill, health, strength and college spirit," college football "is also, under present conditions, not only dangerous, but capable of teaching brutality and underhand practice and of developing unmanly, unscrupulous and unchivalrous character."

"It is too good a game to be abolished and too full of evils to run its present course unchecked."

Miner football star Eddie Bohn died in November 1920 following an injury sustained during a game against Warrensburg Normal.

Within a year of his tragic death, the campus had installed a water fountain south and west of Parker Hall to honor his memory. Here at the fountain are civil engineering professors Joe Butler, Vernon Gevecker and "Skip" Carlton.

Bohn Fountain

MINER SPORTS TRAGEDY

The alarming number of serious injuries and deaths during games was another factor in the drive to reform football. MSM experienced that tragedy in 1920 with the death of Eddie Bohn, who was the quintessential college hero. Hailed as one of the most popular men on campus, the athletic, 6-foot, 3-inch Bohn had lettered in football, basketball, and track. His teammates had selected him as the captain of both the basketball team and the track team. Bohn also belonged to several clubs and Kappa Alpha fraternity. On November 6, 1920, the Miners were at Jackling Field playing the football team from Warrensburg Normal. Bohn had already scored a touchdown and kicked both an extra point and a field goal when he received a punt and headed down field. When tackled by two Warrensburg players, Bohn remained on the ground. Eventually, with the help of teammates he went to the sidelines where he "insisted that he was not seriously hurt." However, a local physician examined him and concluded that the fifth vertebrae in his spine had been fractured. His KA brothers took him to their house and then his family took Bohn home to St. Louis where he died two days later in a hospital. On Tuesday, November 9, the campus held "a mass meeting of faculty and students" where they collected funds for a monument for Bohn. Within a year the campus had a water fountain south and west of Parker Hall to honor Bohn's memory.

In 1972, defensive back Kim Colter became the first of over 100 Miner Academic All-America selections.

ACADEMIC SUCCESS

There are few indicators of how well athletes performed in the classroom compared to the general student population until the late 1920s. In 1928, the campus registrar reported that the football team had a grade point average below that of the campus average, but that the basketball team performed much better than the general student population. Four decades later, athletes collectively out-performed the general student body, with nearly 40 percent making the honor roll. Fullback Bob Nicodemus had four consecutive semesters with a 4.0 GPA, and in December 1968 he was one of only 11 NCAA Division II football players in the nation to receive a post-graduate study scholarship. Among the 33 at all college levels, Nicodemus, a mechanical engineering major, had the highest cumulative GPA at 3.96.

For the next half century Miners excelled as scholar-athletes. In 1986, for example, women's cross country and men's swimming led the way, as Miners made up over a third of all-conference scholar-athletes. Their sterling success allowed Chancellor Martin Jischke to quip at a board of curators meeting that "Miner athletes pass calculus as well as the football." In 1952, the College Sports Information Directors of America began selecting Academic All-Americans. Beginning with football defensive back Kim Colter in 1972, over 100 Miners had been named Academic All-Americans by 2019, which placed Missouri S&T athletes fifth best in the nation among Division II institutions.

This record of excellence drove coaches on the recruiting trail to bring in talented student-athletes that are also able to perform in the classroom. For example, the 2013 women's track and field team had the best cumulative GPA (3.66) among all Division II teams. While not all Miner athletes reached these levels of excellence, it became part of the culture of the athletic program to seek athletes who were motivated to succeed academically as well as athletically.

MISSOURI S&T ALL-TIME ACADEMIC ALL-AMERICA SELECTIONS

Baseball

Brandon Cogan, 2008–09, 2009–10
Eric Cummins, 2002–03
Andy Hall, 2011–12
Steve Hopkins, 2003–04
Lee Voth-Gaeddert, 2011–12

Basketball

Jennifer Cordes, 1989–90
Ross Klie, 1976–77
Bryce Foster, 2013–14*
Jamie Martens, 1997–98
Jeff Mitchell, 1991–92
Dave Moellenhoff, 1985–86
Nick Ulrich, 2015–16
Todd Wentz, 1983–84
Brian Westre, 2001–02, 2002–03, 2003–04

Football

Bo Brooks, 2017–18, 2018–19
Kim Colter, 1972–73
Landon Compton, 2017–18
Bret Curtis, 2016–17
Cole Drussa, 2004–05
Mark Diamond, 1991–92
Brian Gilmore, 1994–95, 1995–96, 1996–97
Randy Hauser, 1982–83
Don Huff, 1991–92, 1992–93
Paul Janke, 1980–81
Deshawn Jones, 2017–18, 2018–19
Curt Kimmel, 2001–02, 2002–03
Eivind Listerud, 1993–94
Brian Peterson, 2012–13
Jim Pfeiffer, 1987–88, 1988–89
Bob Pressly, 1982–83
Tom Reed, 1986–87
Phil Shin, 2005–06
Chad Shockley, 2010–11

Golf

Brian Pankae, 1996–97

Soccer

Caleb Collier, 2012–13
Trent Doerner, 2011–12
Anna Fink, 2014–15, 2016–17
Dan Gravlin, 2006–07
Timmy Kenny, 2013–14
Ryan Lawhead, 2014–15, 2015–16
Denise McMillan, 2000–01
Ryan Muich, 2011–12
David Murphy, 2017–18
Chris Shaw, 2003–04

Swimming

David Calcara, 2007–08
Mark Chamberlain, 2007–08
Miguel Chavez, 2015–16
Bill Gaul, 2004–05, 2005–06, 2006–07*
Stuart Mossop, 2016–17, 2017–18
Jack Pennuto, 2002–03, 2003–04*
Tim Samuelsen, 2017–18
Andrew Schranck, 2012–13
Andy Shelley, 2005–06, 2006–07
Keith Sponsler, 2013–14, 2014–15, 2015–16*

Track & Field/Cross Country

Mary Ann Bradshaw, 2013–14
Taylor Cippichio, 2013–14
Allen Ernst, 2009–10
Kim Finke, 1996–97
Matt Hagen, 1998–99
Kate Hamera, 2002–03, 2003–04
Adriel Hawkins, 2013–14
Dan Hellwig, 2011–12
Jordan Henry, 2007–08, 2008–09
Becca Kueny, 2005–06, 2006–07
Katlyn Meier, 2014–15
Tyler Percy, 2015–16
Lucas Rosenbaum, 2017–18
Adam Stensland, 2012–13
Joseph Vellella, 2013–14

Volleyball

Jennifer Costello, 2011–12, 2012–13*
Lauren Flowers, 2017–18
Krista Haslag, 2015–16
Hayley Wright, 2013–14

* Also named Academic All-America of the Year selections.

Through a gift from successful alumnus Daniel C. Jackling, MSM added these concrete bleachers to the athletic field in 1909.

CHALLENGES TO ATHLETIC SUCCESS

Winning seasons eluded most Miner teams. Indeed, football, baseball, men's and women's basketball, softball, women's soccer, and volleyball all had more losing seasons than winning ones. At times these teams had little depth, particularly in the first six decades of the 20th century. Injuries to a key player or two could doom a season. For example, in 1916, after three successful seasons, the Miner football team had only 20 players. Several got injured, including their great halfback Jack Imlay, who suffered a broken leg in the opening game and missed the rest of the season. The team finished with only one win.

Through the early 1960s, depth was a problem for the football team. In an interview with sports writer Harold Tuthill of the *St. Louis Post-Dispatch*, veteran coach Gale Bullman explained that the 1963 team was the smallest he had had at MSM. "Of 33 players, we will lose eight or so, leaving us with 22 or 23, and you can't compete" in the MIAA with such low numbers. He believed the problem was because "most kids who have been preparing for engineering in high school have not been athletes." In addition, tuition and fees at MSM were higher than at other state schools. Bullman concluded that MSM might have "to drop the sport, maybe for a couple of years."

While most colleges historically had not offered athletic scholarships, the Miners were behind when that became a reality. Athletic directors through the early 1960s could only assist athletes with offers of employment on campus, but few positions were available. Gale Bullman did help athletes from all sports with financial need by offering rooms in Jackling Gym. For about 15 years after the end of World War II, athletes could stay in rooms around

The campus opened Jackling Gymnasium in 1915.

the basketball court and indoor swimming pool. This helped about two dozen athletes every year, men who became known as the "Jackling Jocks." Under Chancellor Merl Baker, the campus allocated funds to the athletic department in the mid-1960s so that the coaches could offer some scholarships. However, it was rare for a coach to be able to offer the number of scholarships allowed under NCAA regulations because the cost of attending UMR and S&T was higher than most of the schools that the Miners played.

For most of the school's history, athletic facilities were inferior to those of the teams the Miners played. In 1891, the board of curators did provide funding for "an athletic field ... enclosed and graded for the benefit of the students," which furnished "ample space for base-ball, foot-ball and lawn tennis." By 1903, there were some temporary bleachers. Two years later, professor of metallurgy William Garrett, "with the aid of some enthusiastic students ... constructed a level and well-banked track, and two good jumping boxes." There was also a temporary gymnasium behind the chemistry building.

In 1909, successful alumnus Daniel C. Jackling gave $1,500 to improve the athletic field and add concrete bleachers. Appropriately, the school named it Jackling Field. There was enough funding to convert an old wood shop into a 1,300-square-foot field house with showers and room for storage. When the Miners began playing intercollegiate basketball in 1909, they had a gymnasium on the second floor of Mechanical Hall.

The biggest improvement in facilities came in 1915 with the opening of Jackling Gymnasium. The ground floor had a 20-foot by 50-foot swimming pool and locker rooms; the second floor had a 70-foot by 90-foot gymnasium; and the gallery above the gym had a running track and limited seating for basketball games.

Over the next half century, there were few upgrades to the facilities, but in 1967 the Miners opened a new football stadium, eventually named Allgood-Bailey stadium, and two years later began playing basketball in a new multi-purpose building, eventually named the Gale Bullman Building.

Initially, coaches sought to schedule "teams which will increase the standing of our team with the leading colleges of our state and adjoining states." Consequently, for the first three decades of the 20th century, Miner teams played against squads from much larger universities. For example,

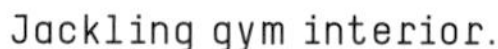

Jackling gym interior.

Richard Boyett was one of the "Jacking Jocks," the athletes who found accommodations in the Jackling Gymnasium while Gale Bullman was athletic director.

between 1900 and 1932 the football team played 41 games against Missouri, Arkansas, Colorado, Illinois, Oklahoma, Oklahoma State, Southern Methodist, Texas A&M, and Vanderbilt. Those teams consistently were bigger, and they had greater depth. In the 1928 game with the University of Arkansas, "the Miners were out weighted more than 25 pounds per man." A decade later, they were even smaller. The Miner linemen averaged 170 pounds and their running backs 140 pounds. Remarkably, they won nine and tied one of those 41 games against major powers, including six wins over Arkansas.

Still, MSM diligently sought entry into a conference with comparable athletic programs. "The admission of the Miners to the M.I.A.A.," the editors of the *Missouri Miner* explained, "would give them an opportunity to be matched against teams of their own class, and they would not then be forced to play such teams as Texas A. & M., Illinois U., Arkansas U. and Oklahoma, all of which are usually far out of the miner's class."

The inability to provide adequate scholarship support to athletic programs, inadequate facilities, and competing teams "beyond their class" posed significant challenges to success for Miner teams. The most consistent factor, however, was the campus's academic demands. The work load was heavy, and the curriculum was challenging. Through the 1920s, most of the degree programs required the completion of between 172 and 197 credit hours. While the number of hours dropped over time, most degrees still required at least 130 credit hours in the 21st century. Consequently, athletic schedules had to accommodate academic schedules. When the editors of the *Rollamo* explained why the basketball team won only three games 1951, they noted, "Perhaps the poor record is due to the heavy scholastic schedule which the students at this school must carry in comparison to the somewhat lighter schedules of the other teams in the conference." In 1961, *Kansas City Star* sports writer Fritz Kreisler explained that head football coach Gale Bullman "waits to see who shows up for practice, because afternoon laboratory classes run until 5 o'clock. The same group of boys rarely show up on consecutive days." As Tony Kaczmarek recalled his playing days from the 1980s, "we only practiced seven hours a week. I spent more time studying for one test than I did in a week's worth of football practice." Football coach Charles Finley told a reporter for the *St. Louis Post-Dispatch* in 1980, "You just can't go out and get the average student to play football here, because he won't cut it. It's really a challenge to play varsity sports and get through school here."

Top: The 2011 volleyball team finished with 24 wins and a trip to the NCAA tournament.

Center: The 1986-87 women's basketball team won 19 games, including two over Division I opponents.

Bottom: The 1967 rifle team won first place in the International Intercollegiate NRA Sectionals.

GREAT TEAMS

Despite these obstacles, there were many successful Miner teams. The 2006 softball team had a record of 33-10. The 2011 volleyball team, led by First Team Academic All-American Jennifer Costello, finished 24-10 and played in the NCAA tournament. Under Mary Ortelee, the Miners' most successful women's basketball coach, the 1986–87 team, after only winning six games the previous year, finished 19-8, including wins over two Division I foes. The 2007–08 women's basketball team ended the year with a record of 24-7, including two wins in the NCAA Great Lakes Regional tournament, before losing to eventual national champion Northern Kentucky. The 2016 baseball team won 39 games, were West Division conference champions, and won four games in the NCAA Midwest Regional tournament. The 2018 football team finished 10-2 and won the second bowl game in school history and the first in 68 years. The 1975–76 men's basketball team won the MIAA conference title and became the first team to play in the NCAA tournament. The men's golf team won the MIAA conference title and the Midwest regional tournament and placed 11th nationally in 1969. Several times the Miner rifle team had success, notably in 1967 when it won first place in the International Intercollegiate NRA Sectionals, and three members of the team were invited to try out for the U.S. Olympic team.

FRONT ROW, left to right: Richard Vogeler, Robert Hill, Wilford Pomeroy, John Peery. BACK ROW: MSG William D. Meredith, coach, Carl Duffner, Charles Foster, Charles Ellison, Samuel Curtis, SFC Orvil E. Parker, asst. coach.

'67 Rifle Team

The UMR Varsity Rifle Team, under the fine leadership of Master Sergeant William Meredith and Sergeant First Class Orvil Parker, completed another successful season outshooting such teams as Oklahoma State, Kansas State, University of Missouri at Columbia and Wichita State. One of the most outstanding accomplishments of this year's team was winning first place in the Fcurth Annual Smallbore Rifle Tournament held at UMR. Twenty teams and eighty-two individual teams fr

The Miners had three truly great teams between 1980 and 2008. Charles Finley had the best run of any football coach in the school's history. He led the Miner program for 20 years beginning in 1972. Between 1977 and 1985, Finley's teams won 70 percent of their games. The 1980 team was 10-0 and finished the season ranked 10th in the NCAA Division II. Their rushing defense was the best in the country. Finley was the MIAA Coach of the Year, the Kodak District VI College Coach of the Year, and finalist for national Coach of the Year. The 1995–96 men's basketball team compiled the best record in the school's history with 25 wins and only six losses. Coach Dale Martin's Miners were the MIAA champions, won the MIAA conference tournament, and hosted the NCAA Division II Regional tournament, winning their first game but losing the championship game to North Alabama. In 2008, Coach Doug Grooms' Miner swimming team finished second in the NCAA Division II championships. This highest finish by any S&T team in a national competition featured nine school-record performances, and all 13 team members earned All-America honors. In addition, the College Swimming Coaches Association of America named Grooms national "Coach of the Year."

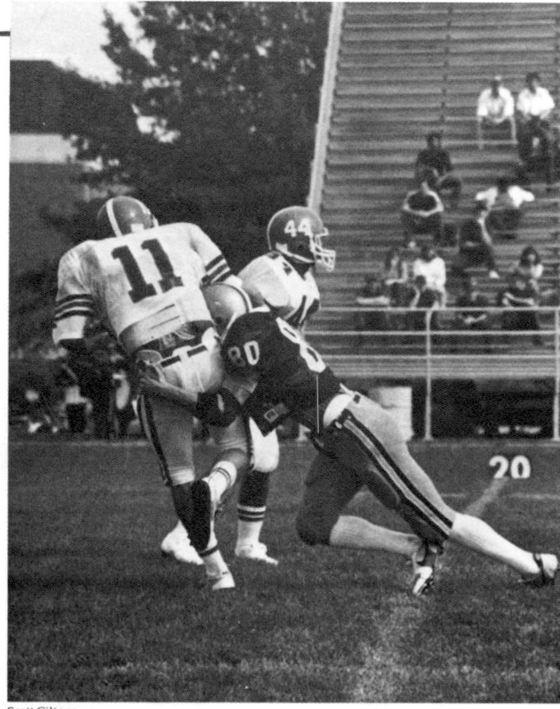

Scott Giltner

Defensive end John Frerking records another sack as he drops the SEMSU quarterback for a loss. Frerking also handled the punting duties for the Miners this year.

Head Coach Charlie Finley views the action from the sidelines.

Doug Richardson

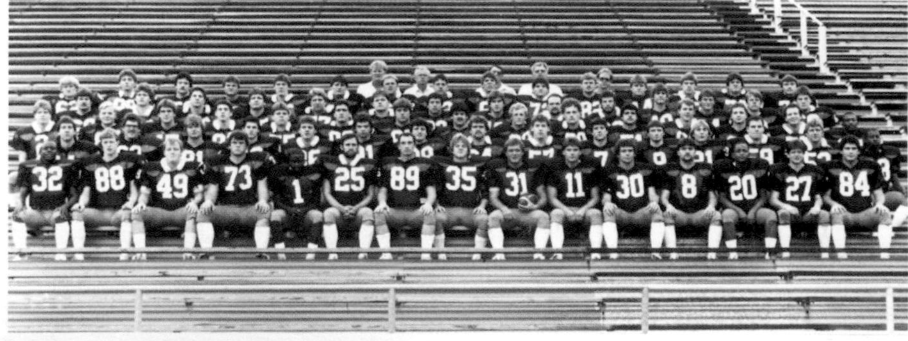

First Row: K. Curry, R. Caruthers, T. Schamel, B. Gorham, L. Flowers, M. Pitsch, A. Jeffers, T. Mueller, B. Andrzejewski, J. Kaczmarek, M. Schafer, B. Bradley, T. Gaines, D. Daring, J. Gregorich, Second Row: B. Haug, G. Gillam, T. Lay, Third Row: T. Kaczmarek, S. Wynn, P. Kaufman, S. Smith, T. Anstine, G. Stock, P. Schmidt, R. Stringer, A. Skoog, S. Posadzy, P. Ryan, J. Frerking, S. Finke, T. Knollmeyer, W. Thompson, Fourth ... Suellentrop, E. Wiegand, Fifth Row: V. Mitchell, T. Jones, G. Lansford, D. Andrzejewski, J. Perry, J. Hirlinger, R. Pogue, D. Goldner, J. Pfeiffer, B. Arthaud, J. Schnefke, D. Brumm, S. Cramer, C. Boone, Sixth Row: Asst.

Above: Between 1977 and 1985, Charles Finley's football teams won 70 percent of their games including a 10-0 season in 1980.

Left: The 1995-96 squad had the best men's basketball record in school history, winning 25 games, the conference tournament, and one game in the NCAA regional tournament.

GALE BULLMAN
Department Chairman
Assistant Professor of Physical Education, 1937.
A.B. 1925, West Virginia Wesleyan;
LL.B. 1929, Washington.

CHESTER BARNARD

THE MSM Intramural Program and the Varsity Swimming Team all fall under the direct supervision of Coach Chester Barnard, a man who has contributed much to the ever expanding school athletic program. Through his efforts the intramural program of this school is ranked among the best, and by his able coaching the Swimming Team has established a record for winning performance.

1

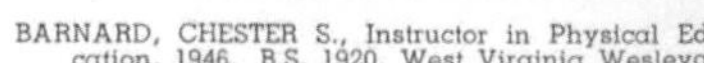

BARNARD, CHESTER S., Instructor in Physical Education, 1946. B.S. 1920, West Virginia Wesleyan.

2

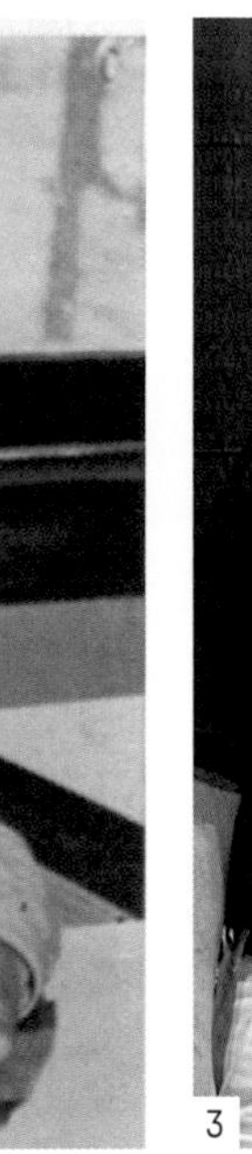

3

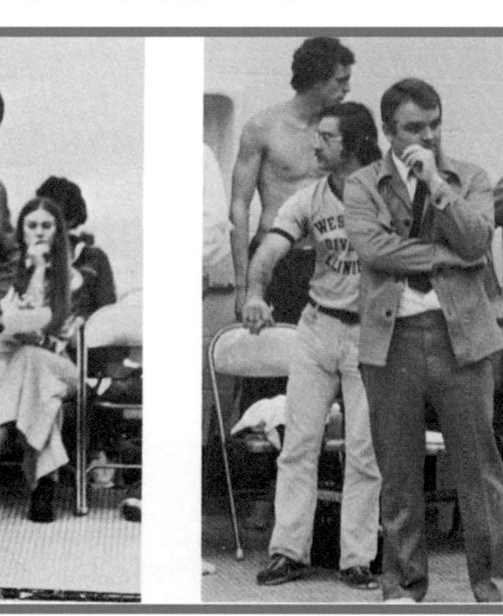

4

1: Swimming coach Chester Barnard's 1948 team won the conference title.

2: Miner swimmers won two-thirds of dual meets during coach Burr Van Nostrand's 11 years as coach.

3: The 2008 Miner swim team finished second in the NCAA Division II championships and head coach Doug Grooms, pictured here on the right with athletic director Mark Mullin, was named "Coach of the Year" by the College Swimming Coaches Association of America.

4: Robert Pease, here in a jacket and tie, won six conference titles as Miner swim coach.

MINER SWIMMERS

Swimming was the most consistently successful Miner athletic program. The editors of the 1932 *Rollamo* proudly announced that MSM was the first college in Missouri to add swimming as an intercollegiate sport, and it enjoyed decades of championships. Because MSM was one of the few colleges with intercollegiate swimming, it was often difficult to schedule meets, and some years the Miners had no competition. Between the end of World War II and 1954, Chester Barnard was the swimming coach. His 1948 team won the conference title, and the following year the team was 6-1 in dual meets. After Barnard's death in 1954, Burr Van Nostrand became the swimming coach. In his 11 seasons, the Miners won two-thirds of their dual meets, and in 1967, the College Swimming Coaches of America cited him for "outstanding contributions to collegiate swimming." Robert Pease elevated the performance of the program even further in the 1970s as the Miners became the premier swimming program in the MIAA conference. Besides winning six conference titles, two dozen of his swimmers became All-Americans.

In 1985, Mark Mullin accepted the head coaching position at UMR. A native of Danville, Kentucky, Mullin had been the swimming coach at Northeast Missouri State University (now Truman State University) for four years before accepting the UMR position. In his 12 years as swim coach, Mullin's teams won nearly 80 percent of dual meets, seven regional championships, and a third-place finish in the NCAA Division II national championships in 1998. His swimmers were just as successful in the classroom. In 1991 for example, the UMR swim team was "the top Division II academic team." Between 1998 and 2019, head coach Doug Grooms' swim teams finished 13 times in the top 10 at the NCAA Division II championships, and team members earned over 300 All-America honors.

Left: Dallas (Kirk) Thorn, who played two seasons in the late 1970s, was the only Miner women's player to average 20 points a game.

Middle: Goalie Lisa Frumhoff was an All-American in soccer in 1983.

Right: Krista Haslag was named three times to All-America teams between 2012 and 2015.

GREAT MINER ATHLETES

There were many outstanding female athletes. Dallas (Kirk) Thorn, who played for the women's basketball team in the 1977–78 and 1978–79 seasons, was the only player to end her career with a scoring average of 20 points a game, a feat she accomplished in both of her years at UMR. Becca Alt, who played on the Miner softball team between 1995 and 1998, is in the top 10 of many offensive categories and leads in career batting average, hits in a season, and most stolen bases in a season and in a career. Lisa Frumhoff was selected to the All-America soccer team in 1983. In 2013, Sandra Magnus, one of Frumhoff's teammates and one of three Miner astronauts, was one of only 48 student-athletes nationwide selected to commemorate the 40th anniversary of Division II athletics. In addition, she was named the previous year as one of the 40 most influential women in college athletics on the 40th anniversary of the enactment of Title IX. Between 2012 and 2015, Krista Haslag was named three times to the All-America team in volleyball. Tamara McCaskill was the all-time leading scorer in women's basketball. Through 2019, McCaskill had the most points and field goals, was fifth in free throws and sixth in rebounds, and was on the All-Great Lakes Valley Team in basketball three times. In addition to leading the 2007–08 squad to a record 24 wins, she earned All-America honors in track and field. In the high jump, McCaskill finished third in the NCAA Division II in 2009 and second in 2010.

Several men's basketball players had extraordinary years, including John Sturm, who averaged over 22 points a game in the 1958–59 season, and Ken Stalling, who averaged nearly 26 points a game 15 years later. Curtis Gibson and Duane Huddleston, high scorers in the 1980s, both earned third-team All-America honors. Between 2000 and 2004, Brian Westre ended up as the all-time leader in blocked shots and the second all-time leading scorer and rebounder. Bill Jolly, the all-time leading scorer for the Miners, also made the most three point shots and free throws. He was on three all-conference teams and was an All-American after the 1992–93 season.

Among the host of All-America swimmers, Zlatan Hamzic and Tim Samuelsen won national titles — Hamzic in the breaststroke in 2009, and Samuelsen in the 1000-freestyle and 1650-freestyle in 2018. In the mid-1980s, Jon Staley established four school records in diving, and between 2014 and 2017, Jon Glaser established three Miner records in freestyle swimming. In track and field, the Miners were strong in the pole vault for several years. Between 1990 and 2016, Tyson Foster, J.R. Skola, Lucas Handley,

1: Tamara McCaskill was the all-time leading scorer in women's basketball and earned All-America honors in track and field.

2: Sandra Magnus, who played soccer at UMR, was named one of the 40 most influential women in college athletics on the 40th anniversary of Title IX. She later became one of three Miner astronauts.

3: John Sturm averaged over 22 points a game during the 1958-59 season.

4: Zlatan Hamzic won a national title in the breaststroke in 2009.

5: Bill Jolly, number 11, was the all-time leading scorer for the Miners and an All-American in 1993.

6: Brian Westre, number 44 in the team photo, was the all-time leader in blocked shots and the second all-time leading scorer and rebounder for the Miner basketball team.

Jordan Henry, Peter Hollenbeck, Dan Hellwig, and Ryan McGuire all produced All-American performances. In 2006 and 2007, Tyrone Smith finished second in the nation in both indoor and outdoor competition in the long jump, giving him All-America status. Smith was both the regional field event "Athlete of the Year" for the 2006 indoor season and the GLVC "Male Athlete of the Year." After graduating, Smith competed in the Olympic Games in Beijing, London, and Rio de Janiero.

The 2010 men's soccer team had two All-American players — Spencer Brinkman and Pat McNamee. In the 2016 and 2017 seasons, Eli Miller set several offensive baseball records, including the best career batting average of .385, most career triples, and the most stolen bases in a season, and had the fourth-most runs batted in for a season. Between 2009 and 2012, pitcher Zack Gronek had the most career wins and strikeouts and the fourth-best earned run average. Beginning in 1941 with lineman Ed Kromka, 13 Miner football players — Kromka, Frank Winfield, Merle Dillow, Bill Grantham, Eivind Listerud, Cole Drussa, Joe Winters, Ashton Gronewold, Bryan Crider, Eddie Rascon, Chris Emesih, Will Brown, and Deshawn Jones — were named All-Americans. Among the multitude of record holders, Gronewold tops many record categories: most points in a career; most receptions in a season; most receptions in a career; most receiving touchdowns in a game, season, and career; and most all-purpose yards in a game, season, and career. Among many other accolades, Gronewold was named Great Lakes Football Conference's "Offensive Player of the Year" and was selected to several All-American teams.

1: Jon Glaser, first on the left in the first row, set three Miner records in freestyle swimming.

2: Tyrone Smith was an All-American, Great Lakes Valley Conference Male Athlete of the Year in 2006, and a competitor in three Olympic Games in the long jump.

3: Best overall batting average was among Eli Miller's many records as a Miner.

4: Ashton Gronewold, a record holder in many categories for receivers, was named to several All-American teams.

5: Deshawn Jones was one of 13 Miners named to All-American football teams between 1941 and 2019.

Departs to Play Arkansas Team

TIGERS HELD SCORELESS

MINERS "MISSOURI'S BEST TEAM"

M. U. Fails to Score

ROLLA WINS

ROLLA WITH LEWIS' TOE

Rollo Expect Close Game

BIG GRIDIRON WILL MAR PIKERS-ROLLA GAME

WASHINGTON IS BEATEN BY ROLLA

TIGERS BEATEN

MINERS TO TACKLE "MISSOURI'S BEST TEAM" IN MINE

ROLLA DEFEATS ARKANSAS

Juggernaut Crushes Washington University, 19 to 0

Line for the State Football Championship

Rolla Cyclone Hits Arkansas

ROLLA GRIDIRON VICTOR

EDMUNDS POINTS PIKEWAY ELEVEN FOR ROLLA GAME

ROLLA MINERS PLAY STRAIGHT FOOTBALL IN BEATING PIKERS

Edmunds Shifts His Lineup for Game With Rolla

Appeal to Major for Big Game

ROLLA 68, DRURY 0

200-Pound Tackle, Rips Holes In the Myrtle and Maroon's Defense

MINERS WILLING TO MEET COLLEGE TEAM HERE DEC. 5

ROLLA OVERWHELMS ARKANSAS ELEVEN

ROLLA EASILY BEATS ARKANSAS ELEVEN

They Call Them the Miners Because They Manage to Dig Up So Many Stars

Mines Team

Gameness Is a Billiken Feature

Miners Trounce Tigers 9 to 0

ROLLA MINERS HIT DRURY IN THE EYE

Rolla Ju

ROLLA EMISSARY CALLS AT C. B. C.

$1,000 OFFER MADE TO ROLLA FOR GAME WITH C. B. C. HERE

Formidable Rolla Machine Crushes Washington U. Team on Muddy Field by the Score of 19 to 0

ROLLA AND C. B. C. TO PLAY NOV. 26

ROLLA MINERS ONLY PILED-UP 104 POINTS

Contest One-Sided

ROLLA REFUSES TO PLAY C. B. C.

Coach Rolla Football Team

ROLLA ANNIHILATES KIRKSVILLE, 150-0

WITH BLAND OUT, BILLIKENS HOPE TO HOLD MINERS

Bland Named in Rolla Lineup Against the Billikens

Famous Back Selected to Play Here on Turkey Day

Billikens' Best Eleven Will Face Rolla

Billikens Swamped 33 to 0 by Rolla's Sweet-Going Eleven

Twists Tiger's Tail

ROLLA MINERS ARE STATE CHAMPIONS

ROLLA DEFEATS ST. LOUIS U. TEAM

Miners State Champions

Miners Easily Pile Up Score on Blue and White

St. Louis U Has Big Job on Hand

ROLLA SHOULD CRUSH ST. LOUIS

BILLIKENS MEET STARS

540 to 0

The Miners' Record for 1914.

Left: The 1914 Miner squad easily defeated all opponents, including the University of Missouri and the University of Arkansas. The editors of the *Rollamo* put together a collage of all the glittering headlines about the team.

Below: Tom Kelly, who became the new Miner football coach in 1914, had been an assistant coach under the legendary Amos Alonzo Stagg at the University of Chicago.

THE GREATEST MINER TEAM

The 1914 football team was the greatest Miner team and one of the best in college history. The previous year, the Miners had a strong football team that won six games to one loss and a tie. Among their victories was a decisive 14-0 win over Oklahoma A&M and a 60-0 thrashing of Saint Louis University. A reporter for the *St. Louis Post-Dispatch* called it "the worst defeat" in the home team's history. The MSM team's only loss that year was 44-14 to the University of Missouri. The Miners had two excellent transfer players: Clark C. Bland and Walter Kiskaddon. Bland, the son of a local businessman, had attended Central College in Fayette, Missouri. During the Missouri game, he had an 80-yard touchdown run. Kiskaddon had transferred to MSM from Grove City College in Pennsylvania, where he had been the quarterback for three years. However, at season's end coach E.H. McCleary resigned.

Photos from MSM's 1914 victory over the University of Missouri.

MSM Director Leon Garrett, according to Lawrence Christensen and Jack Ridley, believed that "having a great football team" would put "the School of Mines on the map." To accomplish that he hired Tom Kelly, a graduate of the University of Chicago, where he had served as an assistant coach under the legendary Amos Alonzo Stagg and then coached at Muhlenberg College in Allentown, Pennsylvania. In addition to about a dozen returning lettermen, Kelly recruited several freshmen players, notably William McCartney from Webster Groves. Most important, however, Kelly brought lineman Charles Copley from Muhlenberg College. After one season with the Miners, Copley, who had been a star lineman for Muhlenberg, went on to play professional football with the Massillon Tigers in the Ohio League and then the Akron Pros and Milwaukee Badgers. A sports writer for the *St. Louis Post-Dispatch* described Copley as a "battering ram"; he weighed 200 pounds while most linemen of that era weighed about 175.

Kelly also found out that two stars for the University of South Dakota had been ineligible for the 1913 season because they had left school with incomplete grades before the fall 1912 semester ended. He persuaded halfback John Imlay and lineman Walter Askew to join the Miners, and they registered for classes in mid-September 1914 as freshmen. Imlay was 22 and Askew was 21. Both players had been on the South Dakota team that defeated the University of Minnesota in 1911.

The 1914 team easily defeated all nine opponents; the only score against their vaunted defense came from a pass interception. The University of Missouri and the University of Arkansas were among

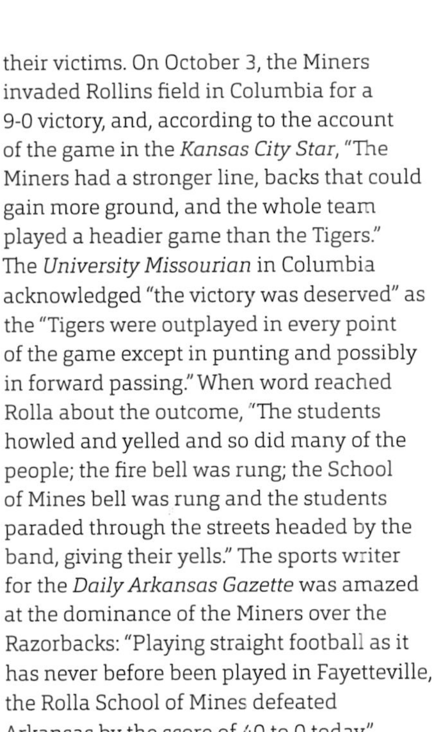

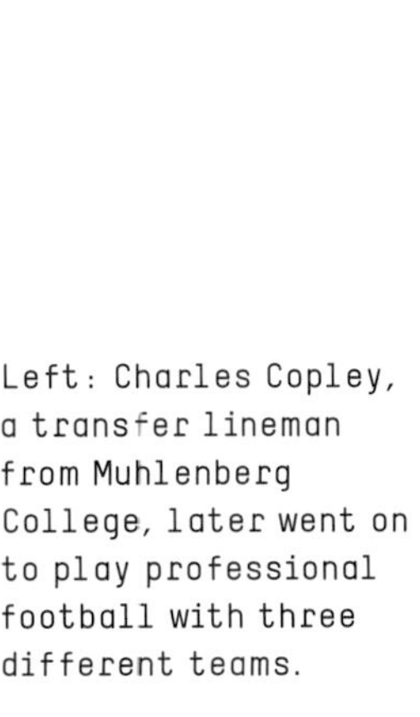

their victims. On October 3, the Miners invaded Rollins field in Columbia for a 9-0 victory, and, according to the account of the game in the *Kansas City Star*, "The Miners had a stronger line, backs that could gain more ground, and the whole team played a headier game than the Tigers." The *University Missourian* in Columbia acknowledged "the victory was deserved" as the "Tigers were outplayed in every point of the game except in punting and possibly in forward passing." When word reached Rolla about the outcome, "The students howled and yelled and so did many of the people; the fire bell was rung; the School of Mines bell was rung and the students paraded through the streets headed by the band, giving their yells." The sports writer for the *Daily Arkansas Gazette* was amazed at the dominance of the Miners over the Razorbacks: "Playing straight football as it has never before been played in Fayetteville, the Rolla School of Mines defeated Arkansas by the score of 40 to 0 today."

Some of the scores were truly stunning: Miners 87, Kansas School of Mines 0; Miners 104, Pittsburg Normal 0; and Miners 150, Kirksville Osteopath 0. After the Miners defeated Washington University 19-0, the article in the *St. Louis Republic* revealed, "The only man able to stop the Rolla attack was Umpire Homer Thomas, who showered the visitors plentifully with penalties at critical times. Rolla lost 150 yards at the hands of the officials, who penalized the Pikers fifteen yards."

As the season was ending, the coach and players for Christian Brothers College in St. Louis asked for a post-season contest to determine the champion of Missouri. Despite a petition from the MSM players to the faculty, an appeal to the board of curators, and support from Rolla residents and *The Rolla Herald* newspaper, the MSM faculty voted not to sanction the game. The two teams played anyway, and the December 5 contest was "lopsided" from the start. Indeed, as a *St. Louis Post-Dispatch* sports writer described the action, "at no time during the game did C.B.C. prove anything like equal to its adversary." The Miners won easily, 26 to 7.

Despite the team's triumph, the MSM faculty was unforgiving. On December 7, they voted to suspend for the rest of

Left: Charles Copley, a transfer lineman from Muhlenberg College, later went on to play professional football with three different teams.

Center: William "Mac" McCartney, a freshman running back on the great 1914 team, later contended that some of the players had been paid by community fans of the team.

Right: Walter Askew was a transfer lineman who had played at the University of South Dakota.

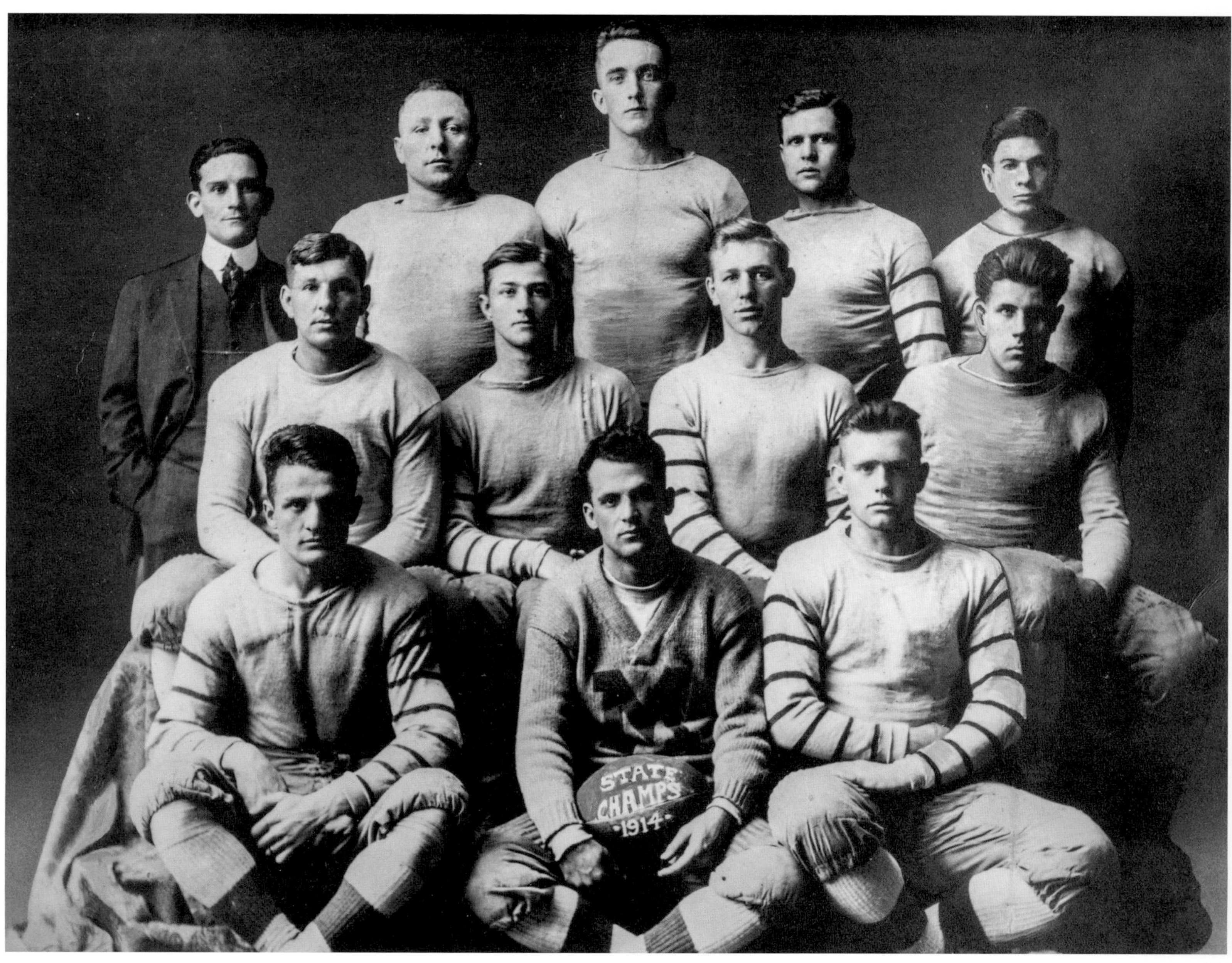

The 1914 Miner football team.

the academic year all the players who participated in the game. The players could individually petition the faculty to be reinstated, however, and several were in 1915.

Almost all contemporaries who saw the 1914 Miners concluded that it was the best team they had ever witnessed. It was a constant refrain among the state's sports columnists, and other coaches acknowledged how dominant the Miners were that year. Indeed, the legendary Knute Rockne, who was beginning his career at Notre Dame as an assistant coach, saw the Miners play and called them "the most powerful team I ever saw." The *Philadelphia Inquirer* truly engaged in hyperbole, calling the 1914 team the "world's champion."

While they were impressed with this Miner team, many at the time and later questioned the legitimacy of some of the players. The author of a letter to the editor in the *University Missourian*, a Columbia newspaper published by the journalism school, claimed, "It is an open secret that some few of the Miner squad are not even pretending to take a full course here and expect to leave as soon as the football season ends." In November, questions emerged in the press specifically about "Pitt" Bland and Charles Copley. Indeed, neither of them returned after the season. There were also rumors that Rolla residents, eager for a winning team, paid some of the players. William McCartney, who was a freshman on the team, later reported that some of the players got $100 a month. All the players got special accommodations during the fall semester. They lived in what usually was the Director's Residence, and Coach Kelly set up a training table to make sure that they got "proper nutrition." Because of these irregularities, Saint Louis University decided not to schedule the Miners for the following season, citing "the fact that Rolla did not adhere to any sort of eligibility rules during the past football season."

GREATEST MINER ATHLETE

John Logan Imlay, better known as Jack, was among the players with a questionable background, but he was the best athlete ever to compete for the Miners. In 1910 and 1911, Imlay was a star running back at Northern Normal and Industrial School in Aberdeen, South Dakota, before transferring to the University of South Dakota. An Aberdeen newspaper characterized Imlay as the "best backfield man ever seen in the state." When he transferred to MSM, Imlay was a man among boys. He scored 30 touchdowns in the 1914 season. Obviously, it helped to have a talented line to block for him, but his success was fundamentally a result of his natural abilities. Besides football, Imlay was a track star. In a track meet against Washington University in 1916, for example, Imlay won the 100-yard dash, the 220, and the long jump. For good measure he also placed second in the shot put. He set the school record in the 100-yard dash with a time of 10 seconds.

Predictably, the editors of the *Rollamo* were over the top with praise for the great running back. As they wrote in 1916, "he is without doubt the classiest, fastest and best halfback turned out in the West, in many years, and it would not be saying too much to say, in the country."

Outsiders were equally impressed. In his account of the Miner game with C.B.C. in December 1914, W.R. O'Connor wrote in the *St. Louis Post-Dispatch*, "above all towered Imlay, the lithe lightweight who steps higher and runs faster than anybody in the Missouri Valley." It seemed to O'Connor that "Imlay's bones must be made of steel, his muscles of wire, while in each heel is concealed 60-h.p. engines that hit on six cylinders without a miss. Despite the mud and the enemy, he got away time and again for long runs and was downed only when more than one man nailed him." Illinois football coach Bob Zuppke scheduled the Miners for a game in 1915. His squad, like the Miners in 1914, gave up only one touchdown during the season. Although Illinois dominated MSM for virtually the entire game, winning 75-7, Imlay received a kickoff during the third quarter and ran "through ... the entire length of the field for a touchdown." After seeing that, Zuppke later said that Imlay "was as great" as the legendary Illinois star Red Grange.

Jack Imlay, a running back for the 1914 team, was the best athlete to play for the Miners. In 1914 he scored 30 touchdowns and set records in track and field events. Illinois coach Bob Zuppke later claimed that Imlay "was as great" as the legendary Illinois running back Red Grange.

The Rolla Herald.

ROLLA, MISSOURI, THURSDAY APRIL 13, 1933

INSPIRATION IN WORD, POEM AND SONG

GOOD FRIDAY TO BE OBSERVED AT CHRIST CHURCH (EPISCOPAL)

Good Friday Musical At Methodist Church

EASTER SUNRISE PR

Trout Placed in Little Piney River

Seed Loans Made To Phelps County Far

Big Day In Rolla

Cardinals Played Rolla

LEGAL BEER ON SALE

Cards Drub Rolla, 11-2, to Close Tour

$10,000,000 Tax Already Brought In By 3.2 Beer

WHOLESALE GROCERY FIRST

Community Club Over KM

Left: Headlines in *The Rolla Herald* note the "Big Day" in Rolla when the St. Louis Cardinals played a local squad.

GREATEST DAY IN MINER SPORTS

Friday, April 7, 1933, was the biggest day in sports history for MSM. The University of Arkansas came to Rolla for a track meet. The Miners nearly upset the visiting Razorbacks at Jackling Field, winning the mile run, two-mile run, half-mile relay, mile relay, 880-yard run, 120-yard high hurdles, and the 220-yard low hurdles. Yet, they came up just short in total points, with 67 to Arkansas' 69.

That early afternoon meet, however, was the prelude for a sports first in Rolla. The St. Louis Cardinals, wrapping up the spring training season, had played a game in Springfield and stopped off in Rolla on Thursday evening and stayed at the Hotel Edwin Long. They had agreed to play a semi-pro team from Rolla headed by former major league catcher Wally Schang. Recognizing the significance of the big sports day, MSM Director Charles Fulton sent a memo to all faculty declaring April 7 a holiday and canceling all classes.

The game attracted a crowd of over 1,000 people who came not only from Rolla, but also, according to *The Rolla Herald*, "from St. James, Newburg, Salem, Steelville, Cuba, Licking, Houston and other places." Most of the Cardinal regulars were in the lineup, and they did not disappoint the fans. Frankie Frisch and Pepper Martin both had triples, and Joe Medwick, the Cardinals' big slugger, had a single, double, and triple as St. Louis won 11-2.

Below: Spalding's official baseball guide for the Cardinals, 1934.

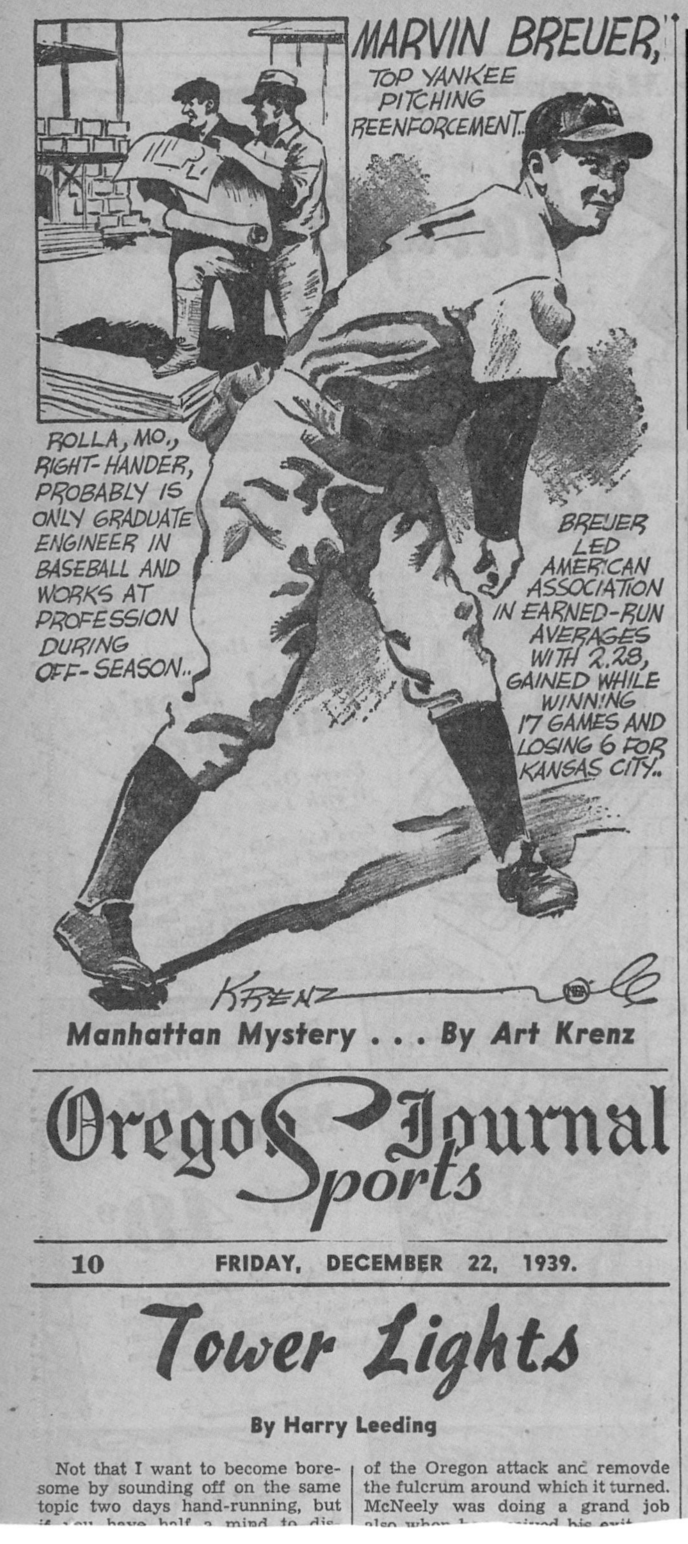

MARVIN BREUER,
TOP YANKEE PITCHING REENFORCEMENT..
ROLLA, MO., RIGHT-HANDER, PROBABLY IS ONLY GRADUATE ENGINEER IN BASEBALL AND WORKS AT PROFESSION DURING OFF-SEASON..
BREUER LED AMERICAN ASSOCIATION IN EARNED-RUN AVERAGES WITH 2.28, GAINED WHILE WINNING 17 GAMES AND LOSING 6 FOR KANSAS CITY..
KRENZ

Manhattan Mystery . . . By Art Krenz

Oregon Journal Sports

10 FRIDAY, DECEMBER 22, 1939.

Tower Lights

By Harry Leeding

Not that I want to become bore-some by sounding off on the same topic two days hand-running, but

of the Oregon attack and removde the fulcrum around which it turned. McNeely was doing a grand job

The reports will include e

reports under the co-ordination the irrigation division of t United States soil conservati service at Medford, are the Unit States forest service, national pa service, Oregon State college, O gon state highway commission, other federal, state and pri agencies.

Reports of the various ce will be radioed or wired to ford, where R. A. Work, ass irrigation engineer, will co and edit them, then forwar material to The Journal.

Terms Described

In describing snow con Work advises, this terminolo be used:

Packed snow is settled which will support the w skiers.

Normal packed snow which will support skiers, them to sink from one inches.

Icy-packed snow will c support skiers on the sur senting a hard, unbreak

Soft snow is unpacked skiers will sink more inches. Further classifi include such terms a

Marvin Breuer, who graduated with a degree in civil engineering, pitched against the St. Louis Cardinals in the 1933 game and then went on to pitch for the New York Yankees in the major leagues.

There was a significant MSM role in the game. Swede Carlsen, who had played football for the Miners and was on a minor league team in Iowa, was the starting pitcher for the semi-pro team. Marvin Breuer, who graduated in 1935 with a degree in civil engineering, relieved Carlsen. Breuer later pitched professionally for the New York Yankees between 1939 and 1943. Finally, Elmer Kirchoff was the second baseman for the Rolla team. He was an outstanding football and basketball player for the Miners, but MSM later declared him ineligible in 1934 because he played for a professional baseball team while still competing in college sports. He coached at MSM for a couple of years before pursuing a minor league baseball career.

The brightest moment of this big day for many was not the track meet or the baseball game. April 7, 1933, was the first day that Americans could legally drink alcohol again, ending the nation's long experiment with Prohibition. Ads appeared in the Rolla newspapers for Blatz Beer, "the beer you've been waiting for! Now it is ready and waiting for you." As one man who attended the Cardinal game explained, "It is not so much the beer that I want as it is my rights restored. I do not believe the American people will ever be led again into the mad folly of trying to dictate a man's appetite." A close track meet against a major college team, the chance to see the St. Louis Cardinals, and legal beer. "All in all," *The Rolla Herald* reported, it "was a happy day in Rolla."

ELIGIBLE PLAYERS

The problem caused by Elmer Kirchoff, as well as the questionable status of a few of the players on the great 1914 football team, demonstrate the difficulty in determining eligibility of athletes in the early decades of Miner sports. In the early 20th century, as historian Ronald A. Smith has shown, "each college determined for itself what eligibility rules it would use." Some schools used graduate students and alumni, others used non-degree-seeking students, and many had "ringers" who had no interest whatsoever in pursuing a degree. One historian dubbed the latter as "itinerant athletes" who would "appear magically on a college campus in time for the fall season, and quietly disappear after the final game."

Miner teams in the 1890s included faculty members. Indeed, Lawrence Christensen and Jack Ridley discovered that "professor of mining and metallurgy Harry K. Landis played end and captained the 1893 football team." This obviously was a concern to Director George Ladd, who in 1901 reported to the board of curators, "I am glad to say further that the members of the team which represents the School this year are all absolutely bona fide students." Yet, three years later, the faculty voted to put two athletes on probation for playing "baseball with other teams than that of the School of Mines."

On December 14, 1914, in the wake of the controversial football game the Miners played with C.B.C., the faculty defined eligible status. No student would be "eligible to play on any athletic team" unless they were taking and passing at least 12 credit hours, and at least two weeks prior to every game the athletic director had to provide to the faculty a list of all eligible players on the team.

In 1931, the faculty were more definitive in determining the eligibility of MSM athletes. To be "a bona fide student," an athlete "shall have met the entrance requirements of this institution," "shall not be on probation," and "shall be doing passing work in at least 10 credit hours." Further, "participation in any athletic contest not under the supervision of his college except during the regular vacations, shall render a student ineligible for the remainder of that semester."

1

3

Miner athletics through the years.

1: An early baseball team (1907).

2: A 1980s swim meet.

3: 1950s football at Jackling field.

4: Women's soccer (2008).

5: Men's cross country team (2016).

6: Women's basketball in the mid-1970s.

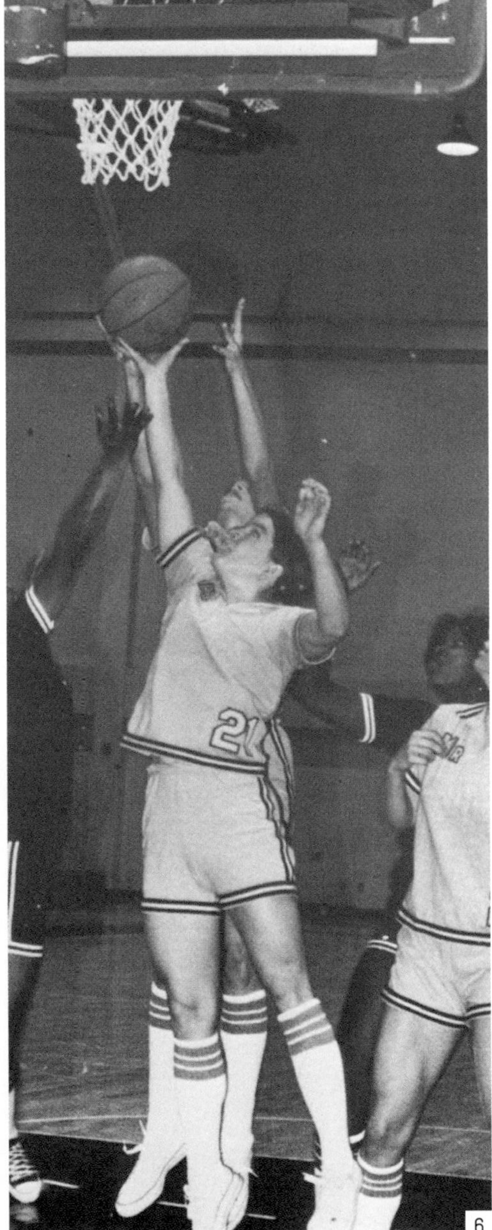

CONCLUSION

In *Campus Life*, her influential study of colleges, Helen Lefkowitz Horowitz argued that "athletics became public relations events to bind to the school the large community of students, alumni, friends, and politicians." Horowitz's analysis partly explains the importance of Miner athletics. Yet, former Miner athletes like Keith Bailey, Mark Franklin, Tony Kaczmarek, Kim Colter, and Paul Stricker took away different lessons from their experiences. They developed enduring relationships with their coaches that lasted far beyond their playing time. They quickly learned that academic success and athletic success were mutually beneficial. They found that intercollegiate sports represented an opportunity to have meaningful interactions with someone unlike themselves. Team sports, particularly after 1950, became a bridge to a more diverse campus experience. Also, as Stricker has noted, athletes understood that they competed not just to represent themselves but something greater — their team and the institution. Finally, for the truly committed athlete, Colter has argued, intramurals and club sports were no substitute for intercollegiate play, as practices were more intense and outcomes more meaningful. The Miner teams, whether in 1914 or in 2014, were an outlet for those who loved to compete.

CHAPTER 8

MINER PRANKS

Chicago Sun-Times columnist Neil Steinberg claimed, "There is something glorious about a college prank." In his book-length study of college mischief, Steinberg concluded, "In the narrow world of university life, so routine, so programmed and often — like life in the real world — too dull to tolerate, a prank shakes things up, breaks the tedium, and gives hope for a life filled with hidden, delightful possibility."

Miners have been all about shaking things up, particularly given the campus's rigorous programs of study. Their pranks largely fall into one of three categories: pranks against professors and administrators, pranks against fellow students, and pranks causing general mayhem. There was also a good bit of unruly behavior in the mix, particularly at athletic events in the 1960s.

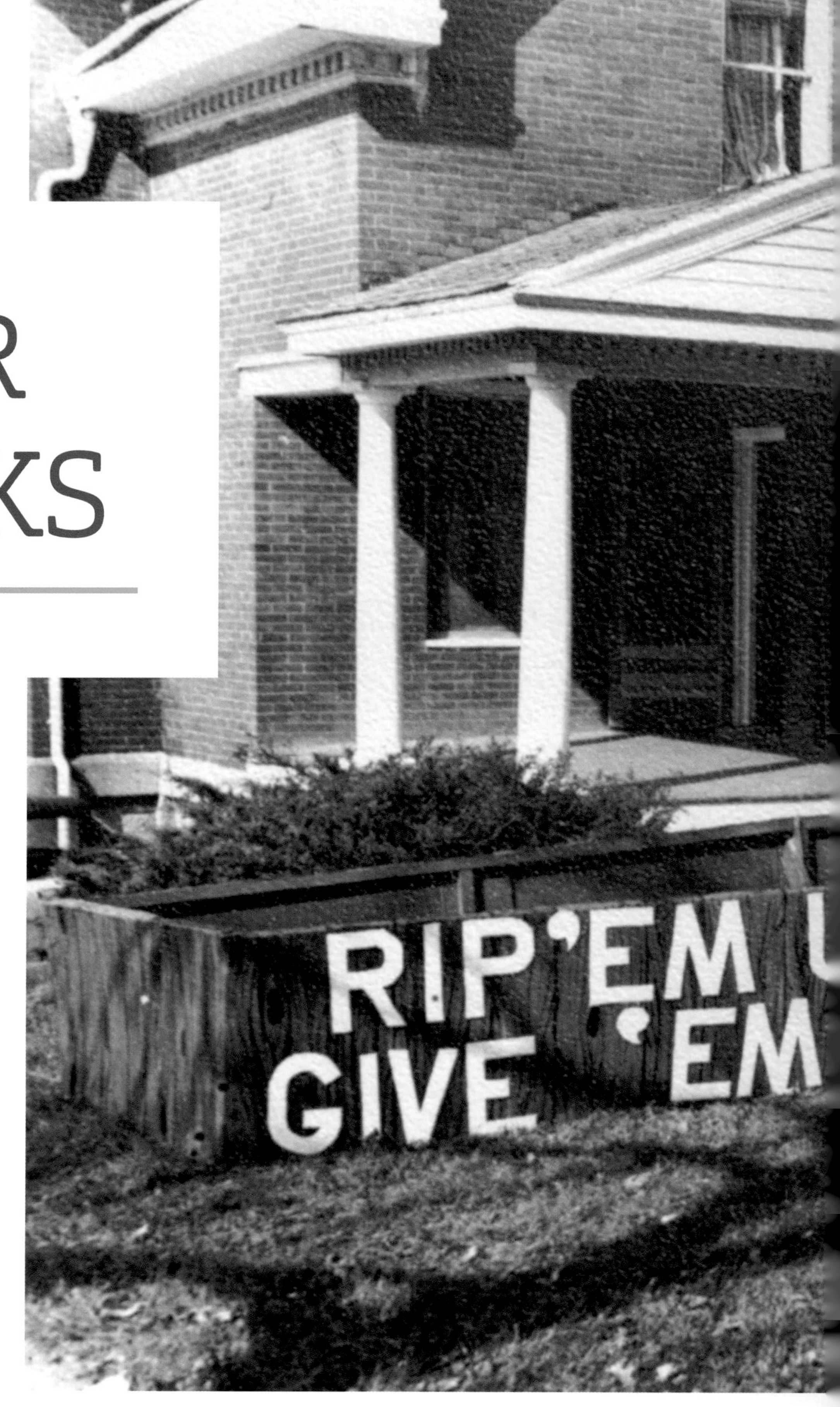

Tau Kappa Epsilon showed some humor as the Miners battled the Central Missouri State Mules at the 1967 Homecoming.

Welcome
Alumni
P-TEAR'EM UP
HELL MINERS!

William Echols, MSM director from 1888–91.

PRANKS ON ADMINISTRATORS AND PROFESSORS

Folklore scholar Simon Bronner has argued that college students across the nation saw "'pulling a prank' in public view" as "empowering" and noted that "pranks aimed usually at the faculty and administration needed to show brazenness and at the same time creativity." He also found that "farm animals figure prominently in pranks," perhaps "to indicate the disconnection of library-bound professors from the outdoors."

Students at MSM were most eager to pull pranks on professors and administrators in the late 19th and early 20th centuries, and they were indeed creative with animals. Director William Echols (1888–91) was one of the earliest targets. His office was in the northwest corner of the third floor of the Rolla Building. Those who recalled the incident years later remembered that it took place on a Halloween night, but could not remember if it happened in 1889 or 1890. About 20 students walked to a nearby pasture, roped a calf, and led it back to campus. One account of the prank said the students "hoisted" the calf up to a third-floor window, but according to a second account, they took it up the west stairs, "twisting" its tail as they urged it on. Regardless of how they got the calf to the third floor, the students left it locked in Echols' office overnight. The same night the miscreants took apart a lumber wagon, reassembled it on the first floor of the Rolla Building, and filled it with a cord of wood. When the director arrived at his office the next morning, he "was greeted by the hungry lowing of a young bull."

An illustration that ran in the 1908 *Rollamo* of George Dean's horse, Calculus.

Mathematics Professor George Dean was one of the students who had participated in this escapade and enjoyed regaling students about it until, according to historians Lawrence Christensen and Jack Ridley, he "walked into his office one morning to find an assortment of livestock occupying the premises." Dean no longer boasted about his exploit, but that did not stop students from pulling more pranks on "Old Prof." One morning, students went early to his classroom and coated all the chairs with lard. In the early 1900s, Dean had a horse, appropriately named Calculus, and buggy that attracted the eye of some of his students. One Halloween they removed the wheels and tossed them into the woods outside town. They also bought some green paint and painted Calculus's ribs green.

Civil engineering Professor Elmo Golightly Harris also had an encounter with an animal in his office. During the administration of Director George Ladd (1897–1907), some of Harris's students seized a burro that had wandered onto the campus. While Harris was lecturing in a classroom on the second floor, the students forced the burro up one flight of stairs and down the hall, where they saw that Harris had left his office door wide open. Once they had the animal in the office, the students shut the door. When Harris returned, he discovered, as Ladd later wrote, that the burro had "made effective use of his time." The burro had "chewed up papers, cleared the desk of its appurtenances, smeared the floor with dung, trampled in it, and kicked it about." An "indignant" Harris demanded that Ladd should not only determine who was responsible, but also should expel them from the university. Ladd took a different approach. He identified the ringleader of the group who, "fearing expulsion," begged for mercy. Ladd granted it, but made him and his followers "thoroughly clean,

scrub, and put in order the office," "pay for all damage done, which included a broken chair," and apologize to Harris, an approach that ultimately pleased the latter.

Yet, students targeted Harris again. In 1905, he had built a new home across the street, directly west of the students' club house (which later became the residence of directors, deans, and chancellors). Prior to having a concrete sidewalk poured, "Harris had installed a double row of two-inch planks" from the street to his porch. His wife hosted a social gathering with "many ladies" of the community after several days of heavy rain. Some students, who had observed the arrival of the women, waited until the party was well underway before removing all the planks and piling them behind Norwood Hall. Once the affair was over, "the women, dressed in their best clothes, had to wade through deep mud."

Again, an indignant Harris demanded that Ladd act immediately. Ladd hired a young man to enroll as a new student and become a "good mixer" to learn the identities of the culprits. After a few days, Ladd's ringer submitted a list of 17 names. At an assembly of faculty and students in the chemistry building, the director called out their names and told them to not only return the planks, but also "place every one of them in its proper position." They readily complied amid the "hysterical laughter and cat-calls" of their fellow students. Ladd later recalled that "Professor Harris was satisfied, and went so far as to congratulate me on the way I had handled the case."

Constructed in 1889, "The Club House" provided dormitory rooms for 30 young men and dining hall services for twice that many. Known as the Chancellor's Residence today, this building has been the home to the chief executive of campus since 1905.

A common theme in campus pranks over the years involved putting animals in inappropriate places. One Halloween night, Director William Echols (1888–91) was the target of one of those pranks. A group of students managed to lead a calf to the third floor of the Rolla Building and left it locked in Echols' office overnight. When Echols arrived at his office the next morning, he "was greeted by the hungry lowing of a young bull." That same night, those students took apart a lumber wagon, reassembled it on the building's first floor, and filled it with a cord of wood.

Paul Worsey, professor of mining engineering, was the target of a prank involving explosives.

In the early years of Prohibition, students developed creative ways to obtain alcohol. Some learned that Director Charles Fulton kept several bottles of wine in the basement of the director's residence. One Thanksgiving, a handful of students, likely with the help of one of Fulton's daughters, broke into the residence and took several bottles. When they learned that faculty members were going to have parties, students also often went to the professors' homes, waiting for the opportunity to surreptitiously enter and steal the punchbowl.

While most of the pranks against faculty and administrators were in the earliest years of the campus, there were a few exceptions. In the mid-1980s, Paul Worsey, then an associate professor of mining engineering, became a victim. Worsey's research focused on explosives, and two of his graduate students designed a remarkable and relevant prank on their professor. The three men had been pulling a few small-scale pranks on each other for some time, but when the two students — Scott Giltner and Robert A. Sickler — learned that Worsey would be out of town for a weekend, they broke into his office and booby-trapped it with over 50 pull-string explosives. The devices could make a lot of noise, but only had about the same amount of powder as a firecracker.

When Worsey arrived for work the following Monday, he found his office door slightly ajar with a string attached. Suspecting that his office was booby-trapped, he left to get a pair of scissors to cut the string. Meanwhile, a custodian pushed open the door to clean the office, and there was a sharp pop. When Worsey returned he discovered that virtually everything had a taped pull-string explosive attached — his chair, the blinds on his window, the filing cabinet drawers, his books, and the trash can. Once they were sure he was in his office, his two graduate students called Worsey, and, of course, the phone was booby-trapped as well. Worsey, who loved pranks, enjoyed their creativity, and they all had a big laugh about the "explosive" prank.

In 1987, Professor Michael Patrick, writing in the *Alumnus*, reminded all that chancellors still faced pranks. "For a number of years," he noted, "Sigma Nus have hosted a champagne tea for alumni during Homecoming. When Homecoming was over, they deposited the empty bottles on the fence around the Chancellor's Residence — leaving a complimentary full bottle for the Chancellor."

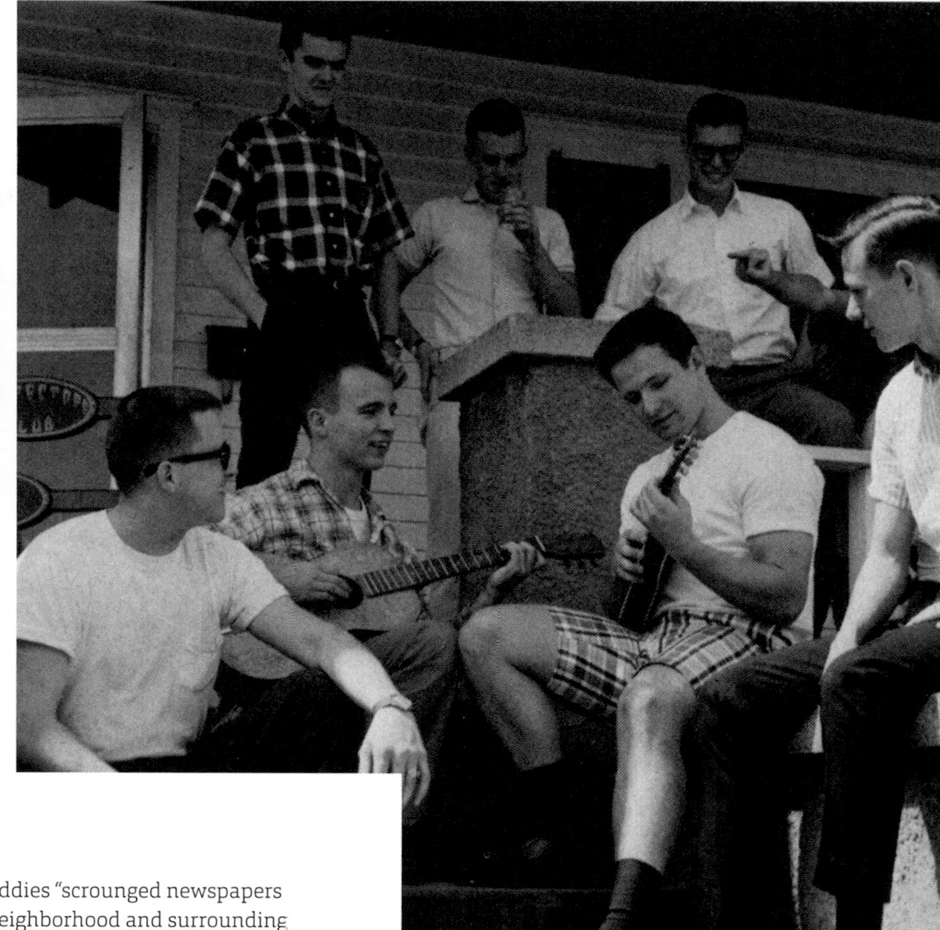

The Prospector's Club, one of the off-campus eating clubs, was the scene of a prank involving a chocolate pie loaded with laxatives.

PRANKS ON STUDENTS

In 1922, three students pulled off a delightful prank on their buddies during a "beer bust." In defiance of Prohibition, the students took a keg of beer just outside of Rolla along the Frisco railway. Three of them, however, did not join their friends immediately. They secured a couple of shotguns, and two of them dressed up as "robbers." The third "got a quantity of red ink." The two with shotguns hid in tall grass across the railroad from where the others were enjoying the beer. The third member of the conspiracy finally arrived, ambling along the railroad tracks. Just as he turned to join his friends, the other two stood and fired their weapons. The victim "yelled as though shot," collapsed, and "spilled red ink all over himself." Some at the beer bust rushed to his aid, but most fled "as fast as possible." Still believing that their groaning friend was mortally wounded, some of them carried him back to Rolla for medical treatment. The next day those who had been present at the beer bust were "crestfallen" to learn about the exquisite prank their three friends had executed.

Going away for the weekend often provided "friends" the opportunity to do something to a person's room. As one scholar has written about college students, they love to bring "disorder to the order of things" in friends' rooms. When Joe Chott, a 1966 graduate in electrical engineering, found out that a friend was going to be gone for a couple of days, he and his buddies "scrounged newspapers from the neighborhood and surrounding stores" and then spent hours crumpling the newspapers before "completely filling his room, floor to ceiling, wall to wall, with the crumpled newspaper. When he opened the door to his room, he was stunned to see the wall of newspaper that dumped on him." Ah, friends. Wayne Hopkins, a 1967 graduate in mechanical engineering, had a roommate who had had a long Saturday night of drinking. When his friend awoke on Sunday morning, Hopkins persuaded him that he had slept for 24 hours and he "sent him off to a test he hadn't studied for."

Just off campus there were eating clubs well into the 1960s. The Prospector's Club was one of these establishments. Martin T. Bruns, a 1963 graduate in electrical engineering, recalled that about 1960, a student who rented a room at the club had gotten into the habit of stealing pies that the club's cooks had baked and then "set out to cool." The cooks' solution was to bake "chocolate pies loaded with laxatives." Soon after everyone noted that the student "disappeared for a couple of days with a bad case of diarrhea." That solved the problem. As Bruns remembered, "No more pies went missing."

Bells and horns were popular devices for pranks against fellow students and the campus in general. In the 1890s, Joseph Campbell, a local banker and a member of the university's board of curators, gave a silver bell to MSM. This "Victory Bell" was at the top of the Rolla Building, and two students came up with a creative way to

use it to irritate people. They attached a wire to "the rotating wheel of the college bell, which was in the belfry," and ran the wire all the way over to Norwood Hall. At night they pulled the wire and the bell started clanging, confusing all, including the head of building and grounds.

In fall 1956, three members of Sigma Phi Epsilon wanted to do "something big to really shake" up the fraternity house. One night they saw a window slightly ajar at an elementary school and decided to go in and take the school bell. They placed it under the floor boards and for a couple of months were able to interrupt study hours with intermittent ringing of the bell. When the administration decided to tear down the old Jackling Gymnasium so that the campus could have a new library, Philip Brave, a 1967 graduate of mechanical engineering, found the horn used during basketball games. As Brave later recalled, he and his roommates "hid it in a tree next to the sidewalk, ran wires up to our second story room, and waited for unsuspecting guys to walk by." They "saw guys fall to their knees" or "drop books ... all while we were bent over in laughter behind our window."

Firecrackers also were favorite devices for pranks. In May 1966, Lawrence Mikelionis, who graduated the following year with a degree in chemical engineering, was sleeping when some graduating seniors tossed firecrackers into his room. Mikelionis and his roommate decided to retaliate. They knew the identity of the culprits, so they snuck into their house and in the common bathroom, "planted several M-80s, suspending them with string and using lit cigarettes for fuses." They raced back home but still were able to hear "loud explosions" and later learned "that the seniors were literally blown out of bed."

Water sometimes played a key role in a prank. Dan Booher, a 1980 civil engineering graduate, lived in Holtman Hall, which was across the street from the Pi Kappa Alpha fraternity house. In the dormitory's laundry room there was an ice machine. "Pike" pledges frequently would walk over and use the street entrance to the laundry room carrying ice chests to steal ice for fraternity parties. Whenever dorm residents saw them sneaking over, they would yell, "Pikers," a signal for all to grab their trash cans, race to the bathroom, and fill them with water, which they dumped on the pledges' heads, all the while

Above: Three members of Sigma Phi Epsilon, shown here in 1956, stole a school bell, placed it under the floor boards, and rang it to bother their fraternity brothers.

Below: A couple of students tied a wire to the "Victory Bell" atop the Rolla Building and rang it from Norwood Hall to irritate the campus community at night.

yelling, "Pikers Suck!" Such exchanges were not unusual given the development of the annual Greek-Dorm water fight.

Occasionally, the pranks moved beyond the humorous to the genuinely dangerous. Such was the case in fall 1992 at Thomas Jefferson residence hall. Students made some bombs that they tossed either from windows or balconies. All the bombs involved the use of two-liter bottles. In some cases, students filled the bottles with water and dry ice. In other cases, the students added Drano. Altogether there were 21 bombs. In one instance, a student tossed one at a pizza delivery driver. In a second instance, according to the *Missouri Miner*, "University Police arrived at the scene ... and experienced eye and nose irritations due to the poisonous fumes." The investigation of the bombings involved the campus police, the Rolla police, and agents from the Federal Bureau of Alcohol, Tobacco, and Firearms. Several students eventually confessed to their involvement in the bombings.

Right: Annual Greek-Dorm water fight in 1981.

Below: Members of Pi Kappa Alpha, or "Pikes." Holtman Hall residents would, in the late 1970s, dump water on Pike pledges who stole ice from the residence hall for fraternity parties.

Above: Daniel C. Jackling, MSM's most famous alumnus, climbed to the top of the Rolla Building and replaced the American flag with "a pair of girlie panties."

Above right: The power plant smokestacks. In the early 1970s, Professor Jim Bogan persuaded two students to scale one of the smokestacks and spray-paint the words "sheep" and "goats" near the top.

GENERAL MAYHEM

In the early 1890s, a handful of MSM students decided it would be fun if they could replace the American flag atop the pole on the Rolla Building with "a pair of girlie panties." Daniel C. Jackling, who became the campus's most celebrated alumnus, volunteered to make the attempt. Assuming that everyone had left campus for the night, Jackling climbed up the exterior of the building, carefully using the "projecting brick corners" to make it to the top. After replacing the flag with the panties, Jackling opened a roof hatch and slid down inside the building. However, he encountered the building's custodian, Bob Dickerson, and took off. As he later recounted the story, Jackling explained that, in the pitch dark he "tried to jump over the pig sty that once stood across the walk running down to Park Street." However, unbeknownst to Jackling, Dickerson had nailed some boards across the 'sty' and when Jackling leaped to get over it, "he hit the boards and was 'knocked cold.'"

Pranks in high places were not uncommon on campus. In the early 1970s, two Miner football players accepted a challenge from Professor Jim Bogan. After reading William Blake's treatment of the parable of the sheep and goats, Bogan challenged Kim Colter to climb one of the 175-foot smokestacks at the campus power plant and spray-paint the word "sheep" and then on the opposite side, the word "goats." Colter took on the challenge. He scaled to nearly the top of the smokestack and painted the word sheep. Then he persuaded teammate James Chatman to do the same for goats. The words remained on the stack for quite a while.

Rolla theaters were the sites of several pranks. Fred W. Erdmann, a geological engineering major who graduated in 1967, enjoyed caving, and one day he collected some bats. That night he took the bag of bats with him to the Ritz Theater, which was screening a horror movie. When a vampire appeared on screen, Erdmann opened the bag and, as he recalled the incident, "the bats flew right at the projector, magnifying them 1000x on the screen." Erdmann never forgot the "screams and laughter that ensued." One student in the mid-1960s "set off an entire string of firecrackers in the Uptown Theater," a prank that sent "patrons running for cover." "Crashing," or crowding a movie theater without buying a ticket, was a more common prank. This most often happened in the 1920s and 1930s following a Miner football victory. There was little theater managers could do to stop this practice. Although, according to Lawrence Christensen and Jack Ridley, "one inventive manager solved the problem one cold wintery evening by shutting off the projector and the furnace and opening the doors, literally freezing out the 'crashers.'"

Downtown Rolla streets were not immune to Miner pranks. In March 1945, Miner student Fred Richardson and five accomplices turned on the town's only stoplight at 8th and Pine streets. The police eventually arrested Richardson and Bill Bennett, who was the editor of the *Missouri Miner*. The police had Richardson in custody in the city hall building, "unwatched and incommunicado," when "a large group of Miners broke" in and released Richardson. He voluntarily returned the following day and paid a $25 fine. However, a forgiving Rolla City Council, in "a special vote," had the charges dropped.

Remarkably, a year later there was another incident involving the stop light. For a pep rally to mark the start of the Miner football season, some students stopped a lumberyard truck, removed some lumber, and started a bonfire under the stoplight. Leo Cardetti, a 1952 petroleum engineering graduate, explained, "We started this bonfire ... and then we started this snake dance down the street." The crowd picked up "anything that could be used as fuel for our fire. Anything in our way — including hand-made wood lawn furniture and ornaments — we would just pick and take with us." The *Missouri Miner* staff chided them for their vandalism. They recommended that if a fire is needed to promote school spirit, "something other than the stoplight at the city's principal intersection should be ignited."

Building walls as a prank was appropriate for an institution known for its prowess in civil engineering. After a heavy snowfall in the mid-1970s, students spent a weekend building a snow wall extending from Parker Hall to the mechanical engineering building. The students reinforced the snow with wire and rebar (steel rods with ridges used to reinforce concrete). They also poured water on it to freeze solid their formidable wall, all of which made it quite a challenge for the physical plant crew to knock down.

Many students recalled the construction of a brick wall across Pine Street. As students left the Uptown Theater after a 7 p.m. show, they saw a large pile of bricks that were to be used to construct what became the Pine Street Building. As John Smith, a 1951 graduate in civil engineering, recalled, "All the boys decided it would be a good idea to build a wall." They constructed a four-foot-high wall that extended across Pine Street, and it took city crews several days "to undo what the hundreds of Miners did in just one hour."

Halloween always prompted pranks beyond the annual burning of an outhouse in front of the director or dean's residence on 11th Street. On a Halloween night in the 1920s, students dismantled a heavy freight wagon that MSM used to move equipment around campus. They took all the pieces to the roof of Norwood Hall and reassembled the wagon. At many campuses across the nation, it was common for students to construct mock graveyards to lampoon their professors or members of competing fraternities. At one Halloween at MSM, however, students took trucks and jeeps to a county cemetery and returned with real tombstones, which they placed on campus.

The types of pranks on campus were limited only by one's imagination, spirit of spontaneity, or consumption of alcohol. In the 1930s, students got attention by riding a horse across campus. Two decades later, driving a car across campus raised eyebrows. Fraternities were given to pulling pranks on each other. For example, in the late 1940s, members of one fraternity took the plaques and trophies from other fraternity houses and switched their locations. A half century later it became the practice for the pledges of Sigma Phi Epsilon, as Brian Call, a 1997 graduate of mechanical engineering, described, "to drag the large rock in their front yard to another fraternity so their members would have to drag it back."

Occasionally, even campus employees pulled pranks. On April 1, 2014, the home page of the campus's website was taken over by "Doge," a Shiba Inu dog "known for its raised eyebrows and captioned internal monologues." April Fool's Day pranks on college websites are fairly common, but the S&T antics of 2014, and the use of this popular internet meme, garnered the campus notable publicity and even led *Wired* magazine to claim that S&T "just won April Fool's Day."

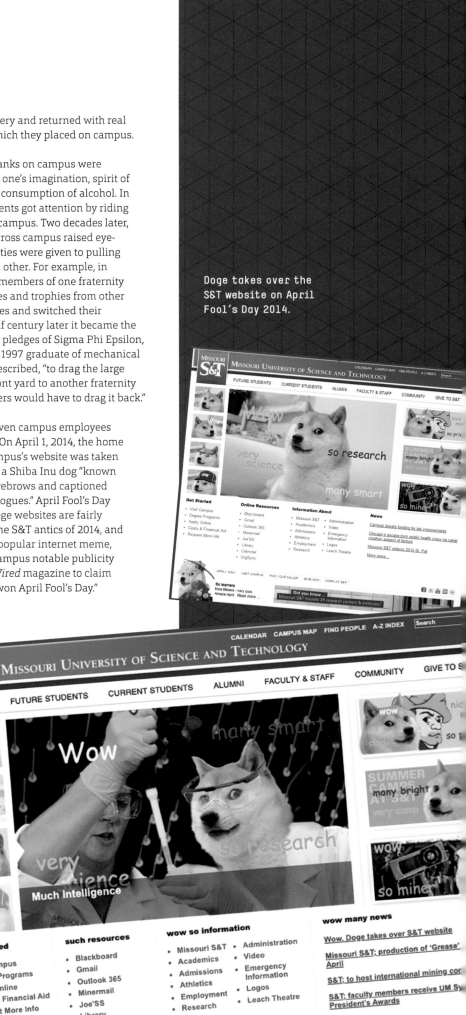

Doge takes over the S&T website on April Fool's Day 2014.

Pine Street in downtown Rolla in the early 1960s.

UNRULY MINERS

At times, Miners went far beyond pranks and engaged in destructive behavior. Lawrence Christensen and Jack Ridley identified such an example in their history of the campus:

In April 1964, 200 to 300 students assembled at Eighth and Rolla streets, blocking traffic and taunting police officers and passersby. Just past midnight, the crowd moved northward along Rolla Street, traveled east on Ninth and began stopping traffic on Pine. Next the mob hastened toward the high school. Rolla police and four state troopers intercepted them there, and the students retreated to the campus, dispersing at 1:30 a.m. The next evening an estimated 600 Miners gathered on Highway 63 between Eighth and Ninth streets. They soaked a tractor tire with kerosene, set it on fire, and sent it rolling down the street. Next, they derailed a boxcar, tore down a goalpost, and damaged the stands at the high school before dispersing.

Miner students gained a great deal of attention for their unruly behavior at UMR athletic contests in the 1960s. In early 1966, the editor of the student newspaper at Southeast Missouri State College (now Southeast Missouri State University) slammed the Miners following a basketball game between the two schools. "We do not question in any way the fans' right to make noise — and at this the Miner fans are the champs." However, the editor was critical of "the pure harassment to which visiting teams are subjected at Rolla. There surely can be no moral justification whatever for the frequent and loud four-letter words aimed at the visitors before, during and after the games — in fact, the locals have one organized yell which features a four-letter noun." The visiting team and the officials were "subjected to a constant booing during the game, even during the introductions." There also were instances of the Miner fans throwing "refuse and pennies onto the playing floor as a gesture of disapproval." The editor admitted, "We have seen trash thrown on other courts, but never as frequently as at Rolla." The editor speculated that such boorish behavior was best explained by the fact that UMR had "an over adrenalized student body which must find some outlet for its leisure time energies."

Because the withering criticism of Miner fan behavior continued the following year, Lou Moss, the assistant director of student personnel, wrote a letter to the editor of the *Missouri Miner*. "In the past year or so," Moss explained, "this school has received some very harsh criticism from friends, alumni, and from other schools concerning the conduct of our students at intercollegiate sports contests." He noted that "the most flagrant violation of good manners is the obscene cheering practiced by individual students and even by groups of them." He called upon the fans to stop all the "odious

Keith Browne, vice president of the M Club in 1968.

yells" at athletic contests, a behavior that he contended would prevent UMR from winning "the full respect" it deserved. The bad behavior led school officials to take the identification cards of students guilty of "riotous behavior." Still, in fall 1968, at a meeting called by the student personnel office with fraternity and independent leaders, students learned that the behavior of Miner fans had led to "some slight trouble scheduling games" and, more importantly, administrators believed "that the reputation of the school was at stake."

Two years later, it was evident that the situation had scarcely improved. Keith Browne, who was the vice president of M Club, wrote a letter to the editor of the *Missouri Miner*. "The rinky-dink remarks thrown at officials and opposing teams by spectators," he wrote, "is very 'small time,' and the athletic teams of this school don't want to be known as 'small time' competitors." Over time, Miner students did moderate their behavior at athletic contests, but for a few years they were the bad boys of the Missouri Intercollegiate Athletic Association.

Pranks diminished over time, but most students had embraced them not just because they were fun, but also because they provided opportunities, like hazing, to initiate new students in the ways of the campus. They also served to deflate the self-important among them and occasionally reminded the faculty and administration that their control over students was not absolute.

PAGE 4 THE MISSOURI MINER

Miner Editorials, Letters, and Fe

Student Speaks Out On SEMS Editorial

Dear Editor,

The following is an editorial from the *Capaha Arrow*, the school newspaper of the Southeast Missouri State College at Cape Girardeau. The editorial seems to refer directly to the February 5, basketball game between the Miners and SEMS. There was no mention of the author's name, however he does deserve credit for a well written article.

SPORTSMANSHIP?

Even though it may sound like sour grapes, we feel that it's time for someone to say a word about the situation in athletics at University of Missouri Rolla.

It used to be that visiting teams at Rolla suffered the many obscene and humiliating abuses by Miner fans as a necessary evil, since they were pretty sure of winning the game in any case. Rolla teams, you will remember, used to be beyond even the help of their fans.

Nowadays, with the improving caliber of sports at Rolla, you can't be sure of winning even on your home facilities, and the crowd factor there has become more of a deciding factor.

We do not question in any way the fans' right to make noise — and at this the Miner fans are the champs. Nor do we believe, given the present rules and interpretations in basketball, that fans anywhere will ever be happy with the refereeing of a game. As sad as the situation is, there will always be booing.

But we think that at least here in the MIAA, Commissioner Roy Brown might undertake to find ways to eliminate the pure harassment to which visiting teams are subjected at Rolla. There surely can be no moral justification whatever for the frequent and loud four-letter words aimed at the visitors before, during and after the games — in fact, the locals have one organized yell which features a four letter noun.

Referees and visitors, subjected to a constant booing during the game, even during the introductions, would be more than human to not feel the hostility and are on an unsound psychological footing when character — and even ancestry — are being assaulted by the more seedy of the rowdies.

We think that Commissioner Brown might also recommend to officials that the tossing of refuse and pennies onto the playing floor as a gesture of disapproval be immediately brought to a halt, by more frequent use of the technical foul call. We have seen trash thrown on other courts, but never as frequently as at Rolla. This is not only juvenile, but dangerous to players on both teams.

Coaches and players have been understandably silent in this entire matter, since not only would complaints sound like sour grapes, but they must also go back again and play next year. One feels confident that any public complaint by any of the teams visiting Rolla would assure an even "warmer" reception at the next visit. We are confident, in fact, that some new and ingenious indignity for our own squad will result from this particular article. Since things could not be much worse, however, we feel it is time for someone to speak up.

It is easy to sympathize with the administration at Rolla, which must oversee a large enrollment composed of nearly all males. Such a situation necessarily produces an over-adrenalized student body which must find some outlet for its leisure time energies. The carnival, "come-as-you-are" atmosphere of UMR athletic events serves the purpose nicely.

We do not wish in any way to inhibit the great school spirit and all-around good time that Rolla fans evidence at their home games. In fact, the general spirit is, in many ways, to be envied.

But UMR's athletic program is growing up, to the point where athletic teams there will probably soon be vying for top spots in the standings. The men of Rolla should take it upon themselves to eliminate their own crudities. If they cannot, then league officials should take whatever steps are necessary for protection of referees and visiting players.

This article makes one good point: its criticism against trash throwing onto the courts is well taken. However, its reference to Miner "crudities" and "obscene and humiliating abuses" is not as bad as the author makes it out to be. I can recall instances where the obscenity at many home football games was from the visiting team. When parents or girls are in Rolla, the Miners' actions can be considered outstanding.

The editorial also refers to the appearance of the Miners at the games as a "carnival, 'come-as-you-are' atmosphere." The 'proper' dress at basketball games at SEMS is slacks, dress-shirt, and tie. I suppose if one were trying to impress somebody this would be a proper and obvious way to do it.

The editorial points out that the enthusiasm and spirit at Miners' basketball games is something to be envied. I think Southeast Missouri State College for crediting us with at least one good trait.

Sincerely,
Steven W. Bisel

Young Service Eases Ca

Prior to the establishment of a Technical Services Office here on campus, the University of Missouri at Rolla suffered from a sore need of printing and reproduction facilities. Printed matter that is necessary to a modern and efficient university had to be sent to the Technical Service of the University of Missouri at Columbia or to private printing firms located in Rolla and St. Louis. Now that we have our own printing facilities here on campus, printed matter is made readily available in a minimum of time.

The Technical Service Plant is housed currently in Building T-11, which is adjacent to the Old Chem Building at the west end of campus. They have the ability to make photographic plates directly from prepared copy. The plate can be transferred directly to one of the two Itek Offset presses. Also, the plant has line-up table facilities for composing and laying out copy, production desks and benches, a Varityper machine which can produce different types of boldface letters for headlines and styles ranging from Gothic Old English. They also have darkroom arrangement and ca a good supply of paper of vari sizes and descriptions. The s vice is equipped to handle m printing jobs that the Univers has to handle. Not only are u versity printings done for the a ministration and various depa

Employees of the Techni Service Office are shown usi one of their two presses.

ments, but work is also done organizations and fraternities very reasonable rates.

The Technical Service Pla was set up under the direction

The Missouri **MINER**

UNIVERSITY OF MISSOURI AT ROLLA

THE MISSOURI MINER is the official publication of the students of the University of Missouri at Rolla. It is published at Rolla, Mo., every Friday during the school year. Entered as second class matter February 8, 1945, at the Post Office at Rolla, Mo., under the Act of March 3, 1879.

The subscription is $1.25 per semester. This Missouri Miner features activities of the Students and Faculty of U. M. R.

Editor-in-Chief	Don Flugrad
	706-B E. 12th — 364-6182
Business Manager	Charles Hansen
	500 W. 8th Street — 364-9993
Managing Editor	Larry Yates
Make Up Editor	Frank Fix
Copy Editor	Bob Fick
Secretary	Charles Painter
Features Editor	Ray Behrens
Photographer	Ron Altman
Advertising Manager	Tom Sauer
Circulation Manager	Jerry Adams
Ass't Managing Editor	Darrell Pepper
Ass't Make Up Editor	Bob Mildenstein
Sports Editor	Jim Weinel
Proofreader	Steve Tocke

NOTICE!

Be sure to read the two page insert in this week's Miner, presenting the needs of the school. We urge you to mail this section home, let your parents know exactly what the University of Missouri at Rolla needs to carry out its job of educating the state's youth.

On the

of The

BY

It's "reminisce time," so and movie watchers draw nea favorites of all our earlier year

Lets begin with Batman a news everywhere. Just a few this famous pair appeared, and 'longer than *Gone With the W* once ran for some fifteen wee our neighborhood theaters. W of you younger seniors, but sti and excitement.

Do you remember when radio creations? Or when th with his mysterious laugh? W lion dollar expense account?

Saturday was always the f It began bright and early with right into the Buster Brown Sh No morning was complete unt had each solved some threat usually a toss-up between mov that comic pair of Laurel and

I'm sure that your memor of those great old shows that agents or James Bonds then, a back on it now, I wonder how?

1966 ENGINEERING GRA

The "harassment" of visiting teams to Miner basketball games prompted a critical editorial in the campus newspaper at Southeast Missouri State College in 1966.

CHAPTER 9

MINER SCANDALS

Colleges and universities that last for 150 years often face scandals that mar their reputations. Such has been the case with Miner history. Several incidents between 1873 and 1979 attracted media attention across the country, in stories that linked MSM or UMR with tragic or infamous developments. Fortunately, the campus quickly recovered from the negative press coverage, but for a time a duel, a murder, an infamous "Freshman Smoker," an armed robbery, a political riot, a Halloween tradition that got out of hand, and Cold War espionage brought the campus attention it did not seek.

MO. SCHOOL OF MINES, Rolla. ...Teacher
Center row: John Holt Gill ('74) - Ada Hill
This copy by Dr. Clair V. Mann, Rolla,Mo.,

> *"... a duel, a murder, an infamous 'Freshman Smoker,' an armed robbery, a political riot, a Halloween tradition that got out of hand, and Cold War espionage ..."*

The duel took place near the staircase at the right side of the Rolla building, shown here in 1886.

Peter Blow, shot in an 1873 duel, is on the far right in the back row.

V. Abert, center) with clas
John W. Pack ('74) - Thoma
Blow (was shot in duel).
er Mrs. J.B.Harrison) - Col
annie Hoskinson - Lola Shaw
6, 1967.

THE "DUEL," APRIL 7, 1873

The legislation creating land-grant colleges and universities required military training for male students. The federal government also supplied weapons for college armories. At the Missouri School of Mines, civil engineering Professor James W. Abert, a Civil War veteran, became the instructor for Company G of the University Battalion established in January 1873. The battalion stored its muskets, bayonets, and swords in an "armory," which was a room on the third floor in the northeast corner of the Rolla Building.

On Friday, April 4, 1873, Cadet John W. McCown violated the rule that required all cadets to wear gloves before entering the armory. When Sergeant Peter Blow, a fellow student, tried to remove him, the two got into a scuffle, and McCown grabbed a sword saying, "Now try it." By then other students had gathered and broke up the fight. Encouraged by his friends, McCown concluded that his honor required him to challenge Blow to a duel. A friend delivered McCown's written challenge to Blow, who chose not to accept it. Friday night McCown bought a pistol from another student, and when he heard that Blow would not bring a weapon to campus (although he had one in his room), McCown told friends that he would make Blow "fight or back down." On Sunday, friends saw McCown raise the pistol while boasting "that he could put five holes through him at that distance."

On Monday morning, a little before 8 a.m., Blow told a friend that he would "see some fun this morning," explaining "McCown has to lick me or I will lick him." When McCown arrived, Blow called him around to the southeast corner of the Rolla Building, where the janitor and a student were talking on the steps. Blow and McCown began arguing, and when the latter pulled the pistol from his back pocket, Blow tried to grab it, but fell on the muddy ground, cutting his hand on the pistol, and McCown fired a bullet into Blow's left cheek. Blow got up and tried again to grab the weapon as McCown fired a second time, wounding Blow in the chest. Blow was able to get up and walk into the building, where he collapsed on the floor. Faculty members gathered as two doctors arrived and "pronounced the wound serious, but not necessarily fatal, and advised that Blow be taken immediately to his room." Abert took the wounded young man in his carriage. Fellow students went along to watch over him.

Rolla Herald-

A DEMOCRATIC NEWSPAPER DEDICATED TO THE

VOLUME XXXV. ROLLA MISSOURI, THURSDAY,

A DOUBLE TRAGEDY.

The Citizens of Rolla Stand in Horror.

J. S. Croswell Shoots Miss Mollie [Pow]ell and Afterwards Commits Sui[cide]

A tragedy has been enacted in our midst within the past few hours that is horrifying to our people in the extreme.

Last Monday night J. S. Crosswell, instructor at the School of Mines, shot Miss Mollie Powell through the heart and killed her almost instantly.

Miss Mollie Powell invited three of her intimate friends among them J. S. Crosswell to take dinner with her Monday evening, the occasion being her nineteenth birthday. After dinner Miss Powell had her trap brought around and she and the three gentleman took a drive around the city and returned about half past eight o'clock at which time two of the gentlemen bid adieu, leaving Mr. Crosswell who went to sit awhile. Mrs. Powell and all of the family were seated in the back parlor and Mr. Crosswell and Miss Mollie joined them. The hours soon passed in conversation, and one by one the children said good night until the hour of eleven when all had retired except Mrs. Powell, Miss Mollie and Mr. Croswell.

Up to this hour Croswell had been engaged in conversation, chiefly with Mrs. Powell, and Miss Mollie who was a little tired had gone in the front parlor, and was reclining on a lounge and was half asleep. At 11 o'clock Mrs. Powell announced that it was bed time, and as Mr. Croswell was very intimate at the house, she informed him that it was time for him to go, and she went into the front parlor and aroused her daughter and kissed her good night. She too told Mr. Croswell that he must go and Mrs. Powell left the parlors, went up stairs to retire, expecting her daughter to follow immediately.

She had been in the room about eight minutes when she heard a scream and she went down stairs and found the door leading from the parlors into the hall which as a rule, always remained open, closed. As she was partially undressed she opened same just a little and asked, "Mollie was that you that called?" and Miss Mollie rushed to the door, exclaiming, "dont go in there: he will shoot you: he has shot me." Mrs Powell thinking what she said was all in jest, started to go in the room as her daughter passed her to ascend the stairway and at ...nt she saw the man ... front door into the ... stantly turned and saw ... about to fall on the stairway and she caught her and laid

He entered into the employment of the School of Mines as instructor in shopwork and drawing in September, 1900. Some time after his arrival in our city he began paying attention to Miss Mollie Powell. His attentions increased and soon became devoted. He sought Miss Powell's hand, but she positively refused to marry him. She

A stunned Rolla community read about the murder-suicide in *The Rolla Herald-Democrat*.

MSM Director Charles P. Williams took McCown to the sheriff's office, where he was released from jail after someone posted a $600 bond on his behalf. Meanwhile, friends and family of Blow's from St. Louis came to Rolla and took him home so that he could recuperate there. The faculty expelled McCown and voted that because Blow had assaulted McCown on April 4, he would lose his rank as a non-commissioned officer. Less than three weeks after the shooting, Blow was back on campus, playing baseball. He hit a triple and as he made it to third base, Blow coughed up the bullet that St. Louis physicians had deemed too dangerous to remove. He continued his studies at MSM, but did not graduate. However, he had a successful career in mining and lived until 1945. Although the faculty had expelled McCown, according to local historian Clair V. Mann, they "examined" the young man "for fitness and ability" and deemed him acceptable for an appointment to West Point, where there is no record that the academy admitted him.

The "duel" gained attention in the St. Louis and New York newspapers because Blow's uncle, Henry T. Blow, was a wealthy St. Louis manufacturer and former congressman who had recently served as the U.S. ambassador to Brazil. Because both young men had guns, the editor of the *Rolla Weekly Herald* chose to use the violent confrontation on campus as "another argument against the practise {sic} of carrying concealed weapons, a practise {sic} that cannot be too strongly condemned."

THE MURDER, SEPTEMBER 23, 1901

A revolver also played a role in another campus scandal. In the fall 1900 semester, Joseph Simons Croswell, a graduate of the Massachusetts Institute of Technology, joined the MSM faculty as an instructor in shop work and drawing. Although George Ladd, the campus director, concluded that the new faculty member had a "distant and uninviting attitude" toward almost all in the small community, Croswell fell in love with Mollie Powell, the 18-year-old daughter of the late Walbridge Powell, who had been the owner and editor of the *Rolla New Era* newspaper. According to newspaper accounts, Croswell became "a persistent suitor," even though Powell "invariably rejected" his marriage proposals.

On September 23, 1901, Powell invited Croswell and three MSM students to her 19th birthday party. They mainly talked about her plans to move to St. Louis to study music. After dinner, one of the students left, but Powell, Croswell, and the other two students went for a ride around Rolla in the family "trap." Once they returned to the Powell home at about 8:30 p.m., the two students returned to campus, but Croswell remained. Powell's mother and siblings joined Croswell in a pleasant conversation. Eventually, the younger children went to bed, and Powell went to the front lounge to take a nap.

At 11 p.m., Powell's mother told Croswell that it was time for him to leave and went upstairs to get ready for bed. However, Croswell went to talk to Powell. Moments later, her mother heard a gunshot and then a scream from her daughter. She raced down the stairs, encountering her daughter, who was trying to come up the stairs, explaining that she had been shot in the chest. Powell's mother sent her son Frank to get a doctor, and on the way the boy told "several business men on their way home" what had happened. They ran to the Powell house, but arrived to discover that Powell had collapsed and died in the upstairs hallway. The men did find a nearly empty chloroform bottle next to the lounge downstairs where Powell had been resting, but the shooter had fled.

Meanwhile, word spread quickly. News reports that followed over the next few days documented the frenzy in the community as the "fire alarm sounded, the whistle at the power house was blown and telephone bells were rung, and shortly after midnight streets were filled with indignant citizens." As authorities began to organize a search for

Croswell, Ladd "called the students together, and told them that they were welcome to join in the search, but by no means to use any violence." They went down every street, and a few went on horseback along all the county roads in a fruitless search. At 7 a.m., Mayor Edwin Long "called a mass meeting of citizens and students," where Sheriff John W. Cooper "swore them in as deputy sheriffs for the purpose of making an arrest." Croswell had been hiding in the woods, but as the "posse" closed in, he shot himself in the chest. When the first two men reached him, they realized that the revolver's flash had caught his clothes on fire. They extinguished the fire, but it was too late to save him.

The reporter who the *St. Louis Post-Dispatch* sent to cover the story learned that the "prevalent feeling" in Rolla was "one of sorrow and pity." Anger had turned to grief for the loss not just of the young woman, but also of Professor Croswell. This became evident when those who had pursued Croswell the previous day "gathered about his coffin on the railway station platform" to participate in a memorial service. The community had experienced a "double tragedy." It had lost a talented and "attractive" young woman from one of Rolla's leading families and a promising new faculty member at the School of Mines.

THE FRESHMAN SMOKER, APRIL 5, 1924

While tragedy defined what happened in the duel and murder, embarrassment defined the response in 1924 to a notorious Freshman Smoker. There had been smokers on campus for several years. Traditionally, after humiliating the freshmen in the annual "Freshman Fight" early in the fall semester, the sophomores would make amends with a smoker in Jackling Gymnasium. The event featured boxing and wrestling matches, singing, jokes, and plenty of cigars and pipes of tobacco. The freshmen would reciprocate with a similar event later in the academic year. The character of the smokers began to change in 1920. During the December 3 event, "the main drawing card of the evening" was a troupe of "cabaret dancers" from St. Louis. Their performances, according to the *Rollamo*, prompted "several hundred fervent sighs."

In the subsequent three years, the freshmen in charge of entertainment also brought female dancers from St. Louis, prompting some community critics to share their concerns with Director Charles Fulton about the "immoral dances." In 1922, Clair V. Mann, a new faculty member on campus, attended the Freshman Smoker and was appalled. Mann wrote to Fulton that he had attended the November 13, 1922, event "in company with a number of other members of the Faculty." Mann had heard that the show would be "spicey" and hoped that if enough faculty members attended they might be "an influence restraining any unduly rough performance." However, he was "extremely mortified and ashamed" at what he saw. He wanted to convey his "unqualified disapproval and condemnation of the affair." Not wanting to offend the campus leader, Mann focused upon what happened after Fulton left at about 11 p.m. The scantily clad women performed "a very low down, vulgar hooch dance." Mann charged that the only "legitimate place for such things is on the floor of the brothel." Although he admitted that he had been free "to leave the building" whenever he chose, Mann ended by saying that he had been humiliated to have to witness "such primary, beastlike indignities."

Top: Clair V. Mann, a new faculty member in the early 1920s, sent reports of "immoral" smokers to Director Charles Fulton.

Bottom: MSM students, critical of Mann for reporting on the smoker, believed that Director Charles Fulton was on their side in the controversy.

Right: Illustration portraying a Freshman Smoker evening entertainment.

Fulton read the complaints, but thought the best course was to defer the matter to the faculty, who decided that future smokers could not include female entertainment. Knowing this, leaders of the 1923 freshman class decided at first not to have a smoker, but later yielded to the pressure of upperclassmen and the *Missouri Miner* staff. A February 4, 1924, editorial had chided the freshmen for not organizing "that usual seductive affair known to the students as the Freshman Smoker." In response, the freshmen eventually produced what prominent MSM alumnus Walter Remmers called the "Freshman Smoker escapade" of 1924. Because of the stories that had emerged following the previous four smokers, there was substantial interest in what would take place on the evening of April 5, 1924. Hundreds of MSM students, some high school students, eight faculty members, and some of the community's leading residents, including Mayor C.L. Woods, attended the event. A few, like Mann, worried that he would view another example of campus-sanctioned "immoral" entertainment. However, most assuredly attended out of prurient interest, and they were not disappointed.

There were several eyewitness accounts of what happened that evening, and all were in essential agreement. It began innocently enough with the traditional boxing and wrestling. Then, however, "Bobby West and her five dancing dollies" from St. Louis began singing "cabaret songs," all "of a lewd nature," while performing "lewd hoochy-hoochy dances," often sitting on the laps of the spectators, and occasionally drawing the students into their dances. At one point, the students conducted an auction of one of the dancer's outfits. A reporter for the *Missouri Miner* described the auction: "Prominent members of the Miner Board, as well as the students and citizens of the town desiring souvenirs of the occasion, did not leave the scene of activities wanting." Indeed, "one prominent gentleman of this institution" also participated. When the auction ended, the dancer "still had the smile and an earring." During the concluding dance, the Jackling Gym "echoed with sighs as of souls in distress," and "after a series of intricate steps our Lady Godiva was hied away and thus the show endeth." After the show, six or seven students followed the dancers into their dressing room, and another "forty or fifty men climbed up to the windows of the room outside. After breaking the glass to the windows, they stood watching the 'dressing.'" As the five dancers walked toward their hotel, "at least 60 men" followed and "indulged in loud and lewd talking."

The reactions to the show were swift. A "citizen of Rolla" wrote to University of Missouri President Stratton Brooks explaining, "The faculty members, as a rule, do not attend these functions, with a few exceptions, and those who do go have not the authority to stop these objectionable parts of the program." This individual, "heartily ashamed that a building of the School of Mines should be turned into a common dance hall," called upon Brooks to stop these types of events. Letters also came Fulton's way. A group of faculty told the director that they had asked the chairman of the student discipline committee to punish those in charge of the event, but that the faculty member had declined to do so. Thus, they implored Fulton "to take this means of bringing the matter to attention of the faculty yourself."

Perhaps with Brooks's prodding (he announced that he would be traveling to Rolla on April 9), or more likely, the salacious account of the smoker that appeared in the April 7 *Missouri Miner*, Fulton called a meeting of the faculty policy committee for April 9. They, likely with President Brooks in attendance, moved swiftly, voting to "indefinitely" suspend the

Five Men Frosh Are Suspended

ROLLA, April 10—Five members of the freshman committee which arranged the annual smoker of the state school of mines here were suspended today because the program contained too much jazz music and refreshments The faculty wanted dignity.

The strains of "pappa went away" and several other dance pieces which the authorities considered improper livened the smoker.

One of the editors of the school paper, the Missouri Miner has been suspended and several of his associates removed from the staff as a result of the picture printed in the paper which if tilted in a way would give an illusion of something the faculty didn't want to be in the aper. The faculty would not make public the names of the disciplined students.

Top: University of Missouri President Stratton Brooks journeyed to Rolla to announce the punishment of the students responsible for the scandalous 1924 Freshman Smoker.

Bottom: Civil engineering Professor T.G. MacCarthy faced the charge that he assisted in the "disrobing" of one of the dancers at the Freshman Smoker.

Right: News of the students' suspension made area papers.

Dr. C. H. Fulton
M. S. M.

THE MISSOURI MINER.

Missouri School of Mines and Metallurgy, Rolla, Missouri.

Vol. 10, No. 31. Monday, April 7, 1924. Price, 8 Cents.

KEMPER AWARDED GOLD BASKETBALL.

Second One Awarded in History of School.

Claude L. Kemper, captain and center of the 1924 quintet, was recently awarded a gold basketball, in recognition of the four years which he has played on the basketball ttam. He is the second man that has ever been awarded a gold basketball, Signer being the first one. Kemper and Signer were teammates on the championship five of two years ago, which swept everything before them.

Starting in as a regular in his freshman year "Kemp" has developed into one of the best players that ever wore the colors of the Missouri School of Mines.

Being mentioned for All-State honors three years out of four is an honor that is aspired to by many, but attained by few. Kemper being one of the few that has attained such recognition. As a center, he has never been outjumped consistently in any one game. Securing the tip-off from DeBernardi, all-American center of four years back, is but one of his achievements. He has also received complishments in his long line of all-State honors in football last year. being placed at left end on the mythical eleven.

"Kemp" will receive his degree in mining this year, and he is leaving in a short time for Chile, South America.

The passing of Kemper marks the passing of a real athlete. A hard fighter, a quick thinker and a clean player, his loss will be keenly felt.

BASEBALL SEASON FORMALLY OPENED.

Chase for H. & S. Cup Underway.

The annual intra-mural baseball series has opened with a big bang, and is sure to bring about several closely matched contestants for the trophy cup, donated by Harvey and Smith. Gentle spring sunshine and balmy breezes have indicated that spring is here; the inclement weather gone and Jackling Field ready to accomodate the lusty (some are rusty,

Continued on Page Five.

FROSH FLING SMOKER.

Annual Fracas Now But a Memory.

After weeks of preparation, the annual Freshman Smoker was made an accomplished fact last Saturday night at Jackling Gym. Due to the fact that the tissue wrappings had been put on the bleachers until the basketball season re-opens, the main floor was filled with chairs, but there wasn't a soul who complained about not seeing enough. In fact all of us saw everyhing, unless we were a bit modest, and raced homeward before the grand finale. There was some evidence of a lack of co-operation among the class members, but the entertainment committee's deeds o'ershadowed all these minor details.

Championship of Phelps County Decided.

The fracas opened at 8:30, and from then until eleven it was bigger and better from all stand points, more particularly the optical.

The fore part of the evening was devoted to a varied athletic exhibition. No one starred much, and there was little interest except in the 125-pound match for the championship of Phelps County, between Ralph Adams, "Pride of Rolla," and "Tutti" Fruit, of the Frosh. Both wrestled manfully for some minutes, and neither seemed to have an advantage. Adams claimed a foul when Fruit tore his trunks, and Adams' second threw

Continued on Page Five.

LETTERS AWARDED IN BASKETBALL AND WRESTLING.

Men Receive Coveted "M."

At a recent meeting of the Athletic Association, five men were awarded the coveted "M" in basketball, and one was awarded an "M" in wrestling. The men who obtaintd the prized letter in basketball are: Captain Kemper, McClelland, Campbell, Arra and Riske, while Sammy Craig received his letter in wrestling.

"Duke" Arra, guard on this year's five, was elected to the captaincy of the 1925 quintet. Altho this was "Duke's" first year as a regular on the team, he played a consistent game all year, and is deserving of the honor which his teammates have conferred on him. "Duke" should make a real leader, and we hope his captaincy will be capped with a championship five

PROF. BROWN IS AUTHOR OF NEW U. S. G. S. PAPER.

The Library is just in receipt of Water Supply Paper 497, United States Geological Survey, on "The Salton Sea Region, California," by John S. Brown. This is one of a series of papers on the desert regions of the United States, the purpose of which is to supply general information of value to travelers in a region in which the lack of good water is an ever present menace.

After brief descriptions of the early history, climate, flora, fauna, physiography, geology and mineral resources the main part of the volume is given over to an exhaustive study of the water supplies of the region. This includes descriptions of surface and ground water supplies; types of desert watering places; surface indications of water; suggestions to travelers exceptionally detailed road logs with notes on water, general supply points, character of ... information useful ... and finally, the work ... tailed descriptions ... more important loc... cial reference to a... quality and amount ...

Mr. John S. Brow... an M. S. M. graduat... now handling the w... Geology at the instit...

Several *Missouri Miner* staff members were removed from the student newspaper after publishing a salacious account of the Freshman Smoker.

five freshmen who were the "responsible agents" for entertainment at the smoker that included "improper dancing." They also voted to suspend the editor of the *Missouri Miner* and removed several of the staff for the rest of the semester. In addition, they agreed that there would be no more freshman smokers. Fulton called an assembly for all students so that Brooks could speak to them. According to Walter Remmers, who was there, as Brooks announced the suspension of their classmates, the students booed and hissed at the university president.

In anticipation of statewide press interest in this scandal, some faculty members crafted a short news release about their actions and sent it to *The Rolla Herald* and five newspapers in Kansas City and St. Louis. The *St. Louis Post-Dispatch* followed up with an interview with Fulton. Their account characterized the smoker as "an unusually entertaining affair" because the dancers violated a campus rule barring "the presence of women at a 'stag' affair." Contradicting all the reports that had come to his desk, Fulton told the *St. Louis Post-Dispatch* that "the dancing was not so highly improper in itself," rather the faculty committee suspended the students for violating the rule against having females at the event. Fulton then sent letters to the parents of the suspended students, explaining the decisions by the faculty, noting that they had disregarded the rule that having women as part of the smoker entertainment was not allowed.

Predictably, students were outraged at the faculty and community response to their smoker. Two days after the faculty had issued their punishment of the *Miner* staff and freshmen responsible for securing entertainment for the smoker, signs appeared along campus sidewalks.

The signs suggest that the students believed that Fulton had sided with them. "We are for Dr. Fulton" and "Chuck is our Chief" were on some signs, and they obviously had discovered that Professor Mann was the leading informer about what had happened at the smoker. They labeled him as "Sherlock Holmes Stool Pigeon" on one sign and wrote "To Hell with Mann and the Mudslingers" on another. As he walked down the hallway of Norwood Hall to his classes that day, Mann had to read the following messages on signs: "Purity Mann," "Jesus Mann," "Beware of Wild Wimmen and Prof. Mann, Miners." Before being ousted, the *Miner* staff published an editorial on April 7 critical of the judgmental Rolla community, comparing it to the mythical Gopher Prairie featured in Sinclair Lewis's 1920 novel *Main Street* about small town narrow-mindedness. The editorial criticized Rolla residents, "particularly women," who "delight in making one appear indecent, immoral, unconventional, and what not, from the most trivial of rumors."

A month later, the board of curators' executive committee, which was responsible for the management of the campus, learned that "some instructors participated in the disrobing of a dancer" and they focused upon T.G. MacCarthy, assistant professor of civil engineering. Fulton wrote to him asking for an explanation. An embarrassed MacCarthy, clearly the "prominent gentleman of this institution" the *Missouri Miner* noted in their account, gave a full account of what happened. He denied "disrobing or removing any wearing apparel of a dancer whatsoever." He said that the freshmen announced that the dancers wished to hand out souvenirs and they called MacCarthy's name to participate. He contended that he tried to flee, but the students assured him "nothing out of the way" would happen. Actually, all he did was accept "a large safety pin ... which upon removal in no way unfastened any of her wearing apparel." Given his explanation, unlike the students, the professor faced no sanction.

ARMED ROBBERY IN BUTTE, MONTANA, 1925

Early on the morning of July 6, 1925, George Forsythe, accompanied by his driver, Henry Reigger, and Reigger's wife, got into his car at the Columbia Gardens amusement park three miles outside of Butte, Montana. It had been a good July 4 weekend, and Forsythe, who managed the property, was taking nearly $5,000 for deposit in a downtown bank. As they approached the bridge leading from the amusement park, Forsythe and Reigger saw a Ford coupe blocking the way. Two young men, Mark Mills and Harold Seifert,

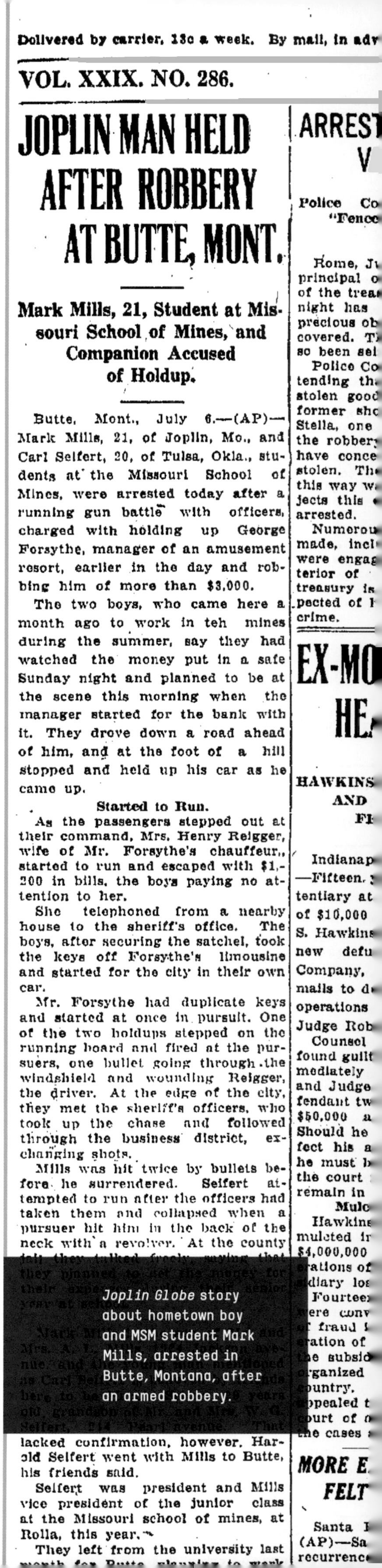

Delivered by carrier, 13c a week. By mail, in adv

VOL. XXIX. NO. 286.

JOPLIN MAN HELD AFTER ROBBERY AT BUTTE, MONT.

Mark Mills, 21, Student at Missouri School of Mines, and Companion Accused of Holdup.

Butte, Mont., July 6.—(AP)—Mark Mills, 21, of Joplin, Mo., and Carl Seifert, 20, of Tulsa, Okla., students at the Missouri School of Mines, were arrested today after a running gun battle with officers, charged with holding up George Forsythe, manager of an amusement resort, earlier in the day and robbing him of more than $3,000.

The two boys, who came here a month ago to work in teh mines during the summer, say they had watched the money put in a safe Sunday night and planned to be at the scene this morning when the manager started for the bank with it. They drove down a road ahead of him, and at the foot of a hill stopped and held up his car as he came up.

Started to Run.

As the passengers stepped out at their command, Mrs. Henry Reigger, wife of Mr. Forsythe's chauffeur, started to run and escaped with $1,200 in bills, the boys paying no attention to her.

She telephoned from a nearby house to the sheriff's office. The boys, after securing the satchel, took the keys off Forsythe's limousine and started for the city in their own car.

Mr. Forsythe had duplicate keys and started at once in pursuit. One of the two holdups stepped on the running board and fired at the pursuers, one bullet going through the windshield and wounding Reigger, the driver. At the edge of the city, they met the sheriff's officers, who took up the chase and followed through the business district, exchanging shots.

Mills was hit twice by bullets before he surrendered. Seifert attempted to run after the officers had taken them and collapsed when a pursuer hit him in the back of the neck with a revolver. At the county [illegible] lacked confirmation, however. Harold Seifert went with Mills to Butte, his friends said.

Seifert was president and Mills vice president of the junior class at the Missouri school of mines, at Rolla, this year.

They left from the university last [illegible]

Joplin Globe story about hometown boy and MSM student Mark Mills, arrested in Butte, Montana, after an armed robbery.

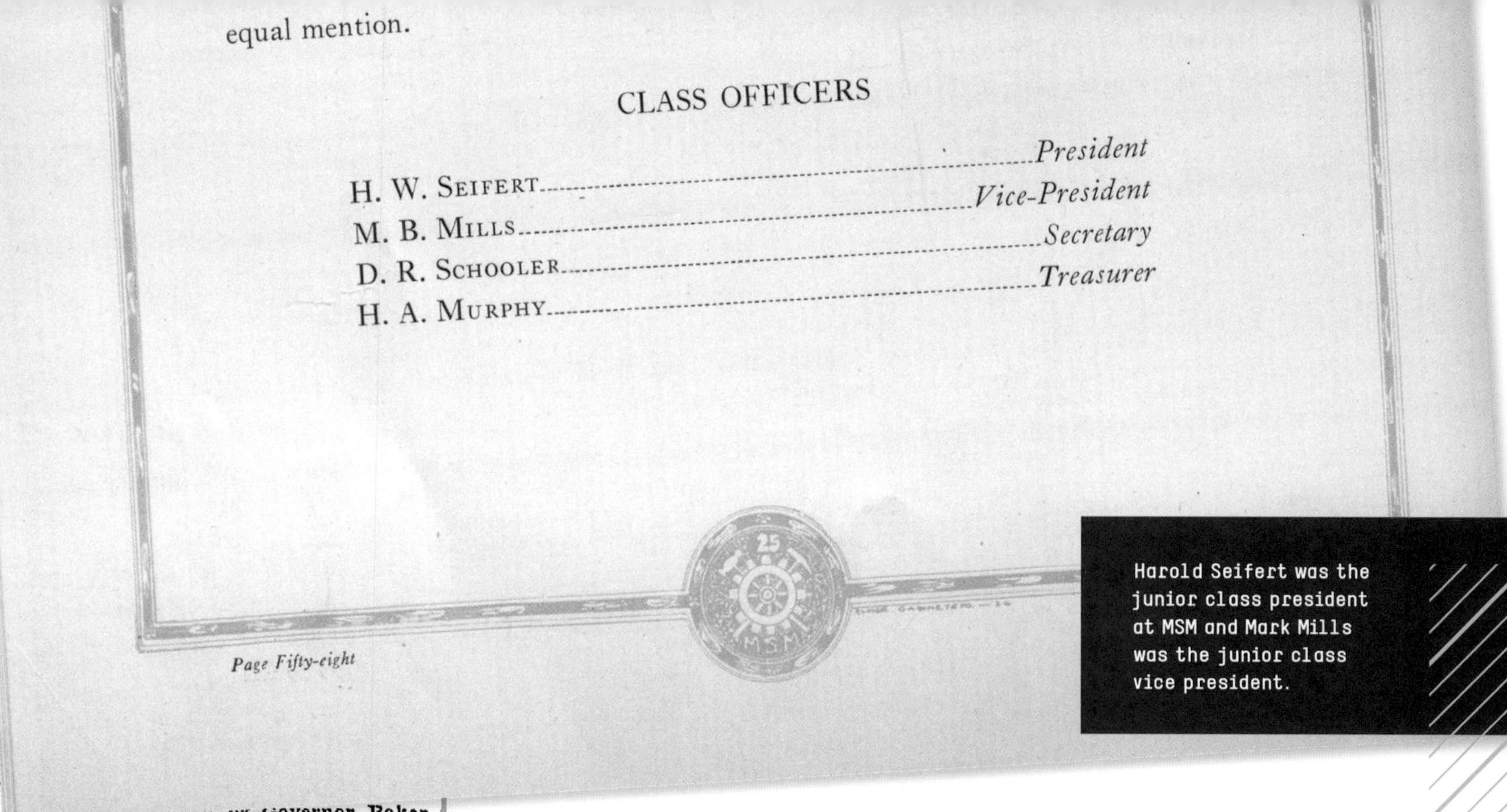

equal mention.

CLASS OFFICERS

H. W. Seifert .... President
M. B. Mills .... Vice-President
D. R. Schooler .... Secretary
H. A. Murphy .... Treasurer

Page Fifty-eight

Harold Seifert was the junior class president at MSM and Mark Mills was the junior class vice president.

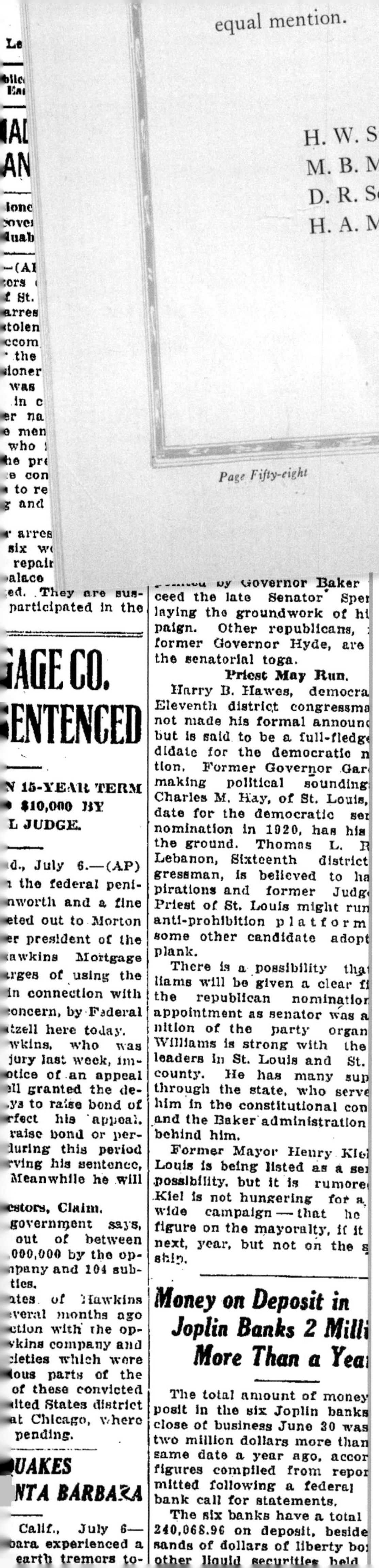

GAGE CO.
SENTENCED

N 15-YEAR TERM
$10,000 BY
L JUDGE.

d., July 6.—(AP)
the federal peni-
nworth and a fine
eted out to Morton
er president of the
awkins Mortgage
rges of using the
in connection with
oncern, by Federal
tzell here today.
wkins, who was
jury last week, im-
otice of an appeal
ll granted the de-
ys to raise bond or
rfect his appeal.
raise bond or per-
during this period
rving his sentence,
Meanwhile he will

estors, Claim.
government says,
out of between
,000,000 by the op-
npany and 104 sub-
ties.
ates of Hawkins
everal months ago
ction with the op-
kins company and
cieties which were
ous parts of the
of these convicted
ited States district
at Chicago, where
pending.

QUAKES
NTA BARBARA

Calif., July 6—
bara experienced a
earth tremors to-

ceed the late Senator Spen
laying the groundwork of hi
paign. Other republicans,
former Governor Hyde, are
the senatorial toga.

Priest May Run.

Harry B. Hawes, democra
Eleventh district congressma
not made his formal announc
but is said to be a full-fledge
didate for the democratic n
tion. Former Governor Gar
making political sounding
Charles M. Hay, of St. Louis,
date for the democratic se
nomination in 1920, has his
the ground. Thomas L. R
Lebanon, Sixteenth district
gressman, is believed to ha
pirations and former Judg
Priest of St. Louis might run
anti-prohibition platform
some other candidate adopt
plank.

There is a possibility tha
liams will be given a clear fi
the republican nomination
appointment as senator was a
nition of the party organ
Williams is strong with the
leaders in St. Louis and St.
county. He has many sup
through the state, who serve
him in the constitutional con
and the Baker administration
behind him.

Former Mayor Henry Kiel
Louis is being listed as a se
possibility, but it is rumore
Kiel is not hungering for a
wide campaign — that he
figure on the mayoralty, if it
next year, but not on the s
ship.

Money on Deposit in Joplin Banks 2 Milli More Than a Yea

The total amount of money
posit in the six Joplin banks
close of business June 30 was
two million dollars more than
same date a year ago, accor
figures compiled from repor
mitted following a federal
bank call for statements.
The six banks have a total
240,068.96 on deposit, beside
sands of dollars of liberty bo
other liquid securities held

their faces covered with handkerchiefs and revolvers drawn, ordered all three out of the car and demanded their money. While Mrs. Reigger, daring them to shoot her, dashed away with $1,500 in her purse, Forsythe handed over several bags of silver coins totaling nearly $3,200. When the two bandits returned to their vehicle, Forsythe and Reigger decided to give chase, twice ramming the coupe; all the way into Butte they exchanged gunfire. As Seifert drove the coupe, Mills jumped onto the running board and fired at their pursuers. One round shattered the windshield and wounded Reigger in the ear, but he kept going.

Meanwhile, Mrs. Reigger called the sheriff's office, and as the two cars approached Butte, sheriff's officers took up the chase. According to the *Butte Daily Post*, it was "a thrilling gun battle through the streets of the city before they were captured by a combined force of police and sheriff's deputies." In the hail of bullets fired during the chase, Mills squeezed off about 20 rounds while suffering wounds in the hip and shoulder.

The next day, the two young men appeared before District Court Judge Jeremiah Lynch without legal counsel, and both pled guilty to robbing Forsyth. Judge Lynch sentenced them to no less than 12 years and no more than 30 years of hard labor at the state prison in Powell County, Montana.

Besides the details of the "daring daylight holdup" that one reporter claimed "furnished Butte with more excitement than any other crime in the city's history," what caught most reporters' attention was the background of the two culprits. Both were students at the Missouri School of Mines and Metallurgy, where Seifert served as president of the junior class and Mills as vice president. The two had been active in a range of student activities. Besides serving as junior class president, Seifert was circulation manager of the *Missouri Miner*, a cadet first sergeant in ROTC, and a member of both the Missouri Mining and Metallurgical Association and Quo Vadis. In addition to serving as class vice president, Mills performed in two campus theatrical productions in 1924 and 1925 and was a member of Pi Kappa Alpha fraternity, the Missouri Mining and Metallurgical Association, the professional engineering fraternity Theta Tau, and Sigma Gamma Epsilon, an honorary society for earth sciences. Notably, he was the only ROTC member to qualify as an expert pistol shot, which explains why he jumped on the running board of the car to shoot at their pursuers. In a letter to Montana Governor John E. Erickson, Director Charles Fulton explained that the reputation of the 20-year-old students "was distinctly good. We are quite at a loss to understand their actions in Butte in view of their record here."

However, the boys' record in Rolla was not as clean as Fulton intimated. Once apprehended, Seifert and Mills explained their criminal action. "'One night,' Mills explained, 'we got drunk and stole a car from the school. We saw that it would take us out West cheaply and we made the trip for about $20.'" While Mills' version suggested spontaneity in the theft, three

Seifert and Mills had stolen a shotgun belonging to mechanical engineering professor R.O. Jackson (pictured) before leaving Rolla for Butte, Montana.

months earlier the two young men, in anticipation of stealing a vehicle, actually had stolen the license plates from a car that Fulton had purchased for his daughter. In addition to their two revolvers, the young men also had stolen a shotgun that belonged to R.O. Jackson, a professor of mechanical engineering. The two had planned on working in the mines in Montana to pay for their senior expenses. As Mills told Butte authorities, "With us it was a question of hard work and more debts or a year of easy life that could be devoted completely to study." Moreover, as Fulton's secretary explained, the two young men were "gloriously in debt."

They did get work at the Black Rock mine outside Butte for three weeks but concluded that they would not be able to make enough to pay off their debts and cover all their expenses in their senior year. Having dropped by the Columbia Gardens amusement park a few times and noting the great business there, Mills and Seifert had decided to rob the place.

Once incarcerated, however, the two became model prisoners. Warden A.B. Middleton later noted that Mills and Seifert "served but a few days behind the walls" because he learned that they came from "good families" and the young men "realized the mistake they had made." He assigned them to the motor vehicle department of the prison where, during their incarceration, Mills and Seifert "handled over a million and a half dollars." Seifert also worked in the prison hospital and helped survey a water line for the state's school for the blind. Moreover, within days of their imprisonment, several people began advocating for a reduction in Mills' and Siefert's sentences. Mills' parents and Seifert's mother visited the two MSM students a week after their imprisonment. A month after the robbery, George Forsythe, after meeting with the families of the young men, appealed to Governor Erickson to pardon Mills and Seifert. Director Fulton joined in the effort in October. In 1926, the Mills and Seifert families, Forsythe, Judge Lynch, and Governor Erickson all appealed to the State Board of Pardons for a reduction in the sentences of the two young men. The members of that board complied, reducing the sentences to a minimum of four years and a maximum of eight years, a decision that made Mills and Seifert eligible for parole on July 7, 1927.

Because he was so impressed with their behavior in prison, Warden Middleton took them to Butte in his "chauffeur-driven" car for their release when they gained an early parole on June 30, 1927. He even called upon Fulton to "re-instate" them at MSM. Fulton declined to do so, but Colorado School of Mines admitted Mills, where he earned a degree in mining engineering and quickly got a job with an Arizona copper mining company. Seifert found work with a steel company in Mexico City, and within two decades he had become the general superintendent of several plants. He later helped found Alumino Industrial Mexicana. Seifert retired in 1958 and did consulting work before returning to Rolla to complete his degree requirements in 1965. Five years later, Seifert gained a full pardon from the Second Judicial District in Montana. Seifert and Mills vindicated Warden Middleton, who concluded upon their release that the two had "proven themselves honest and reliable and I am positive that they will never make a mistake in the future as they have in the past."

Although Mills and Seifert turned their lives around, their actions in 1925 produced the biggest scandal in the campus's history. When Harry Nowlan, petroleum geologist in Tulsa and president of the Miner Alumni Association, learned about their robbery, he worried that news of the crime would reflect badly not only on the two students, but also upon "our good school." Indeed, newspapers from Butte and Boston to St. Louis, New Orleans, and New York City covered the robbery, always noting the robbers' connection with the School of Mines.

THE ALLISON RIOT, MAY 20, 1950

A scandal of a different type occurred a quarter century later. Emery Allison, state senator from Rolla, decided to announce his candidacy for a U.S. Senate seat during a rally in Rolla scheduled for May 20, 1950. Described in *Time* magazine as "an Ozark country lawyer, a Baptist, Mason and Legionnaire, and the plodding cigar-smoking 56-year-old president pro tem of the Missouri state senate," Allison had the endorsement of President Harry Truman and was eager to get his campaign underway. The party's leader in the state senate for the previous five years, Allison had been a supporter of the separation of MSM from the control of the president of the University of Missouri, and he had supported a $500,000 appropriation for a new mechanical engineering building.

The Phelps County Young Democrats formed a torchlight parade beginning at Eighth and Rolla streets and proceeded to the high school football field on 10th Street. Rumors had surfaced during the day that some MSM students might try "to break up the rally." Indeed, some students had made anti-Allison signs. According to one news report, shortly before the parade began, several MSM students "took some of the torches from the Allison-for-Senator committee's truck, and formed a rump torchlight parade" following the larger parade. When the roughly 200 students reached the football field, where nearly 4,000 Allison supporters awaited the start of the rally, some of the MSM students rushed to the stand where the high school band was going to give a short concert. They knocked the instruments from the high school students' hands, and most in the band fled. At this point, Allison's supporters sought to stop the MSM students. One, local businessman Cecil Herrmann, suffered a laceration on his forehead during the fray. The Rolla police force and Missouri State Highway Patrol finally restored some order, but Police Chief Rowe Fort suffered a heart attack in the effort. Throughout Allison's speech, the MSM students "heckled" him "with cat calls, boos and cries of 'Down with Allison.'" When it was all over, the Rolla police arrested two of the student demonstrators.

Two days later, the two students pled guilty to the charge of disturbing the peace, and Police Judge Doug Harvey fined them each $25. Almost 200 students and residents watched the proceeding in the city hall courtroom. When the students left the courtroom, one of them, Val Steiglitz, passed the hat and collected enough to pay the fine for both young men, who also faced probation for a year from the faculty discipline committee.

An abundance of theories bounced around town about the cause of the "riot." Some thought supporters of Thomas Hennings, Allison's rival for, and eventual winner of, the Democratic nomination for the Senate, prompted the demonstration. Allison just chalked it up to normal "collegiate rowdyism." However, the two arrested students told Judge Harvey that they had participated because they did not believe that Allison had supported MSM sufficiently in the Missouri Senate.

Whatever the cause, the editor of the *Rolla Daily Herald* worried about the negative impact on MSM's image when "stories of the unwarranted rowdyism" went "out over the press association wires to all parts of the country." There was good reason for his concern. Drawing upon Associated Press and United Press International wire service reports, reporters across the country came up with striking headlines for their stories, all with Rolla datelines. In the *Omaha World-Herald*, it was "Senate Campaign Opened by Brawl." Readers of the *San Francisco Chronicle* saw "Truman Man's Rally is Disrupted." The *Richmond (Virginia)*

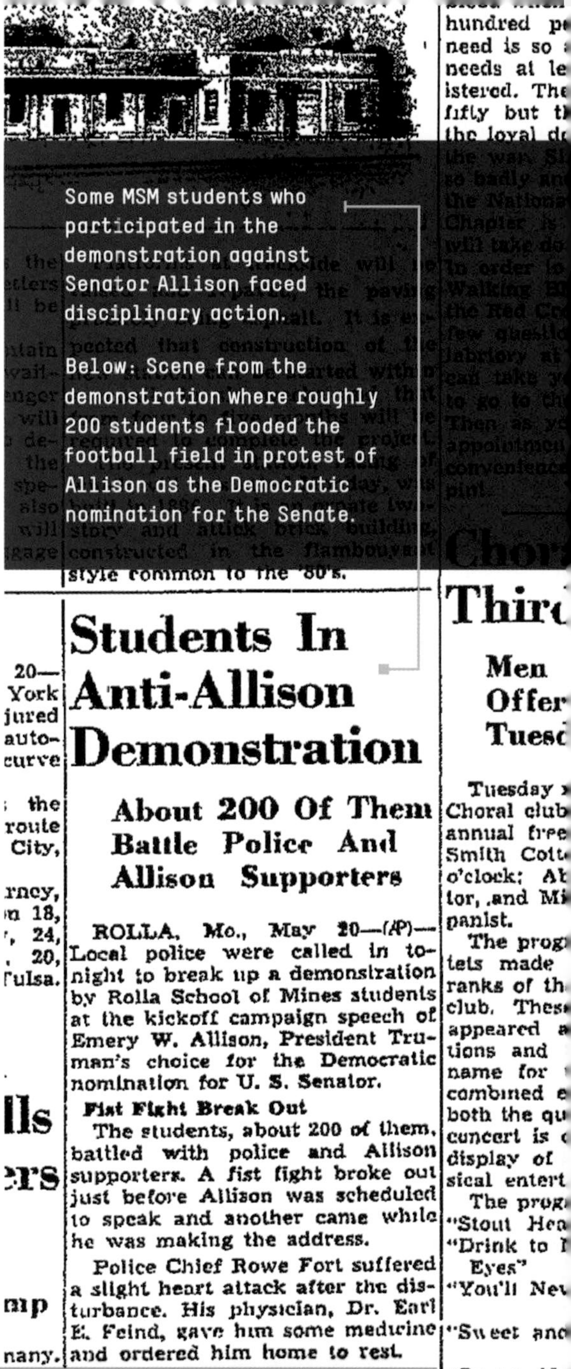

Students In Anti-Allison Demonstration

About 200 Of Them Battle Police And Allison Supporters

ROLLA, Mo., May 20—(AP)—Local police were called in tonight to break up a demonstration by Rolla School of Mines students at the kickoff campaign speech of Emery W. Allison, President Truman's choice for the Democratic nomination for U. S. Senator.

Fist Fight Break Out

The students, about 200 of them, battled with police and Allison supporters. A fist fight broke out just before Allison was scheduled to speak and another came while he was making the address.

Police Chief Rowe Fort suffered a slight heart attack after the disturbance. His physician, Dr. Earl E. Feind, gave him some medicine and ordered him home to rest.

Some MSM students who participated in the demonstration against Senator Allison faced disciplinary action.

Below: Scene from the demonstration where roughly 200 students flooded the football field in protest of Allison as the Democratic nomination for the Senate.

Times-Dispatch led with "Truman's Choice for Senate Stirs Near-Riot at Rally," and the headline in the *Jefferson City Daily Capital News* read, "Two Fined after Rolla Fracas."

The *Rolla Daily Herald* editor also was "sorry ... that a demonstration of 'mob violence' had to be perpetrated when this community was host to ... more than two dozen state legislators." Professor Clair V. Mann understood that someone in the crowd heard a couple of state legislators say "that, if this was the kind of education being dispensed at Rolla, they intended to question Dean Wilson when he next came before the Legislature asking for maintenance funds."

Below: After taking appropriate precautions, an outhouse was set ablaze outside the Chancellor's Residence.

Opposite: Dean Curtis Laws Wilson addresses students after they set fire to an outhouse in front of the dean's residence.

THE HALLOWEEN RIOT, OCTOBER 31, 1959

Fortunately for the campus, legislators did not punish MSM in the next legislative session for this riot, and the campus evaded national scrutiny for almost another decade. However, on October 31, 1959, another riot by MSM students gained attention throughout the Midwest. For several years, MSM students had taken a break from studies to celebrate Halloween. As one student explained in 1958, "this is one of the few times that the students at MSM are allowed to let their hair down and get rid of the nervous tension that comes from attending a school such as MSM." The tradition involved bringing an outhouse to 11th and Rolla streets, in front of the dean's residence, and setting it ablaze. At the end, Dean Curtis Laws Wilson would offer a few remarks. Occasionally, things got a little out of hand. In 1958, for example, some of the MSM students walked from the dean's residence to the Kroger grocery store, stole pumpkins, and began tossing them at cars and a Trailways bus. They then took pumpkins to the Ritz Theater on Rolla Street and threw one through the theater marquee.

Things truly got out of hand, however, in 1959, when several hundred students participated in a destructive riot following the burning of the outhouse. Following the annual outhouse-burning ritual, someone yelled, "Let's go downtown." After failing to break into the Ritz Theater, several hundred young men marched west to Highway 63 at Eighth Street. There, they tried to build a barricade to block the traffic. They stopped when a Rolla police officer fired a couple of shots in the air. Heading downtown, they picked up a small sports car and put it on the sidewalk on Pine Street across from the Hotel Edwin Long. Along the way, this mob, growing in size, tore down, mutilated, or stole several street and stop signs. They continued east to Rolla High School, where they broke off the goal posts, ripped out some seats, and knocked down the snow fence. Returning downtown, someone threw a rock through a window at City Hall, and as they passed the "Frisco station" they took a couple of the baggage wagons. Upon reaching 10th and Pine streets, the mob started a large bonfire and threw one of the baggage wagons into the blaze. Several of them, who had been to Jackling Field, brought a ticket booth which they tossed into the fire. They then turned on several fire hydrants downtown. The police called the fire department, and the firemen not only put out the fire, but also turned off the hydrants. Near the Woolworth store, several in the mob picked up a car with several passengers inside and placed it on concrete blocks they had taken from a construction site. Police officers struggled to maintain any semblance of order. Several of them got hit by eggs thrown by the students. One officer, chasing a student who was throwing rocks, fired three rounds into the ground behind the rapidly escaping culprit. Police Chief

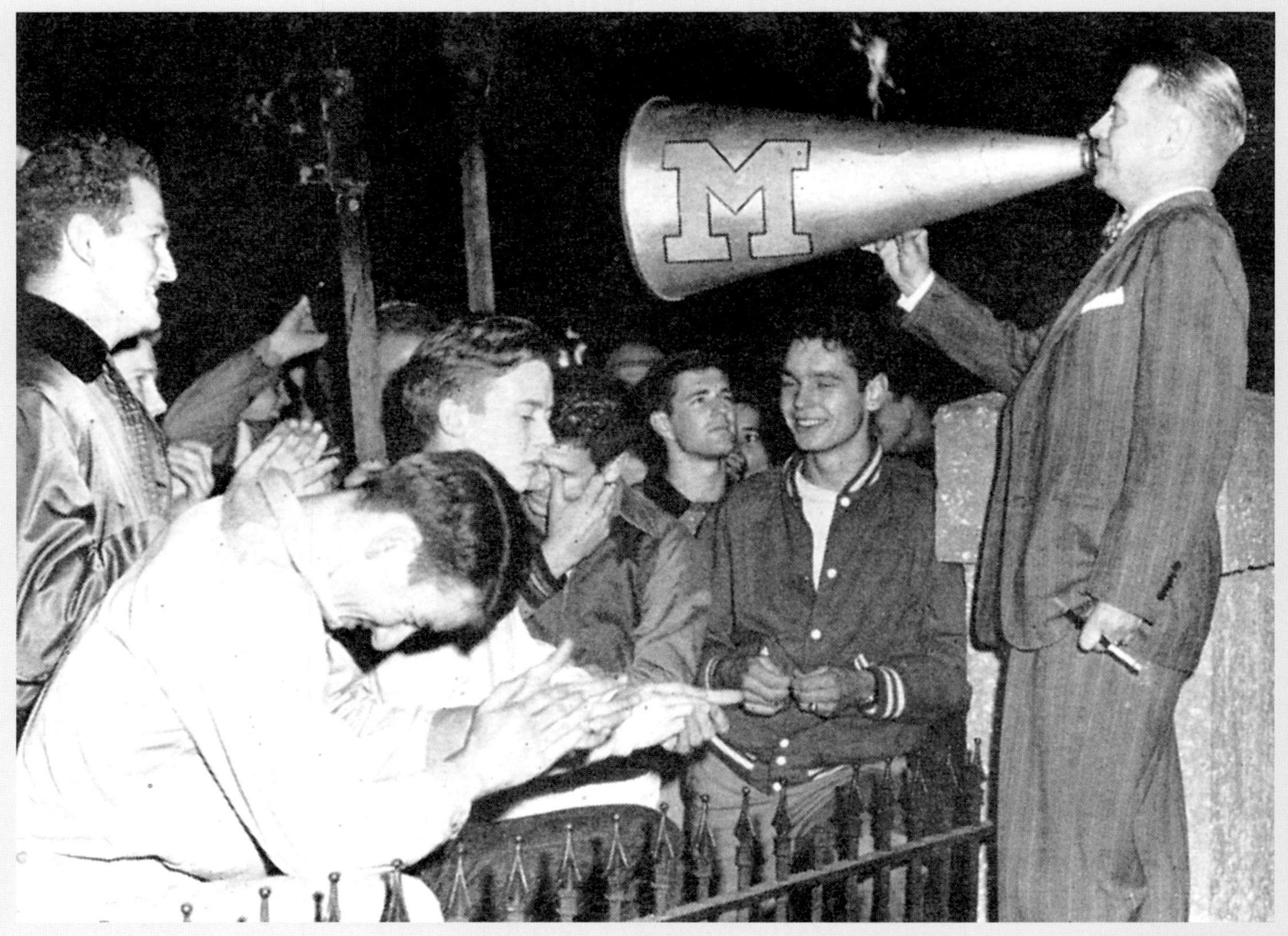

George Pruett called Troop I of the highway patrol for assistance, and while he awaited their arrival, Pruett had the firefighters turn their high-pressure hoses on the students. When four highway patrol cars arrived, the officers joined the Rolla police in writing down about 200 names of students, and the violent incident finally concluded.

The damage was considerable. Pruett called it the worst riot he had seen in his career and estimated the property damage to be "in the thousands of dollars." Besides the damage at the high school football field, about $400 worth of destroyed street signs, the burnt baggage wagons, and the broken window at City Hall, the mob damaged several automobiles, smearing them with paint, kicking in their sides, or letting out the air in their tires. Students also stole many of the downtown businesses' advertising signs. Two police officers were slightly injured by rocks thrown by the students. Professor Leon Hershkowitz, who had just taken over the duties of assistant dean a few weeks earlier, tried to persuade the students to leave, but they poured ketchup on his head. When local State Representative Gene Sally called upon them to desist, they shouted him down.

"This is one of the few times that the students at MSM are allowed to let their hair down and get rid of the nervous tension that comes from attending a school such as MSM."

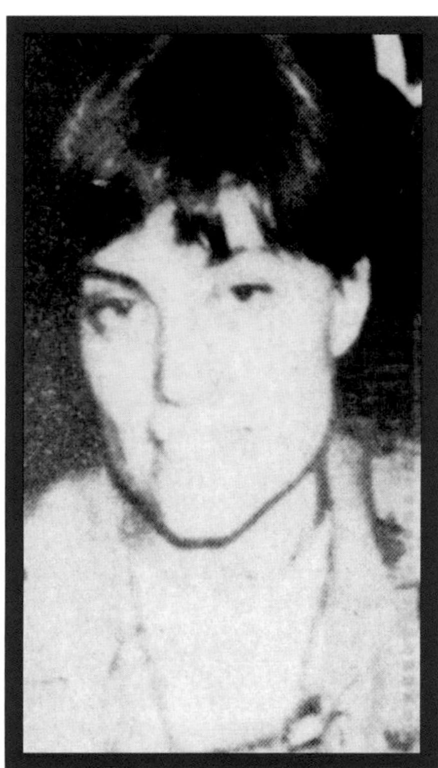

After her mysterious departure from Rolla, authorities determined that sociologist Ingrid Deich had been an East German spy.

"There are certain edges and corners in people's lives which are not always straight."

Dean Wilson told the press that he believed most of the people in the mob were not MSM students. One fraternity member, fearing that the campus fraternities would get most of the blame, contended in a letter to the *Missouri Miner*, that "there were also Rolla High boys and soldiers, as well as many independents." However, Representative Sally, the Rolla police, and the highway patrol, according to *The Rolla Herald*, "reported that nearly all of the mob was composed of Missouri School of Mines students."

Most importantly, as with all scandalous behavior associated with MSM, the *Rolla Daily News* worried that out-of-town newspapers would report the incident "entirely out of proportion." It did not take long for most newspapers in Missouri and the Midwest to publish eye-catching headlines about the riot: "Students at Rolla Riot, Cause Damage in Thousands," "Officials at Rolla Investigate Wild Night of Rioting," "Students Stage Riot at Rolla," and "School Seeks Rolla Rioters."

THE EAST GERMAN SPY, JANUARY 29, 1979

The Cold War between the United States and the Soviet Union involved the University of Missouri-Rolla in an extraordinary story of the mysterious disappearance of a faculty member and international intrigue in 1979. On January 18 of that year, Werner Stiller, a case officer for the East German intelligence agency known as the Stasi, crossed into West Berlin. In his defection to the West, Stiller brought a case of microfiche of nearly 20,000 pages containing the identity of dozens of East German agents in Western countries. According to political scientist Joseph Fitsanakis, "The Stasi is believed to have recalled an additional 40 operatives from several Western countries as a precaution in response to Stiller's defection." Indeed, Markus Wolf, the head of the foreign intelligence division of East Germany's State Security Ministry, later explained, "Our immediate task was to warn" Stiller's "contacts and agents."

Eleven days after Stiller's defection, Ingrid Deich, assistant professor of sociology, who was teaching her "Energy and Society" class at 1:30 p.m. in the Humanities-Social Sciences Building, heard a knock on the door. She stepped out and had an animated conversation with a man. Although Deich returned to finish the class and another in the next hour, she told department chair Erwin Epstein that she was ill and would miss that day's scheduled department meeting. No one saw Deich the following day, and she did not come to campus to teach her Wednesday classes. Epstein tried to get in touch with her Thursday and Friday morning with no luck. Ingrid lived in a house just three blocks from campus with her husband Werner, who most assumed was the man who had interrupted her class. Epstein finally contacted the Rolla police department. According to the *St. Louis Post-Dispatch*, when they entered the residence, police officers discovered that everything appeared "orderly and secure, with no signs of foul play," although they did find "three chairs pulled away from the dining room table." Apparently aware of the defection of an East German spy, acting police chief Gary Ozment asked the FBI if the Deichs had been involved in "undercover intelligence." Rumors later surfaced that Werner Deich had emptied a satchel into a dumpster on campus on January 29.

Whether true or not, the couple was never again seen in Rolla. Only a few personal possessions and one of their cars were missing on January 31. Eight days later, Deich sent a telegram from Mexico City to Epstein explaining that she had left Rolla to be with her husband who allegedly had a new position as a researcher for Mexican population policy. On February 27, Epstein received a letter of resignation from Deich, indicating that she had had to choose between her work and her marriage.

Deich had two degrees from the Freie University in West Berlin. That is where she had met her husband. With a Ph.D. in history, Werner found a job at the University of Missouri-Columbia, where he studied West Germany's nuclear research program while Ingrid began work on a Ph.D. in sociology. When Werner failed to get tenure, the couple moved to Rolla, where Ingrid got a job at UMR teaching sociology courses on energy policy. In her 1986 memoir, Deich said the culture of the campus was "a mixture of miners' pride and miners' masculinity, early-capitalistic entrepreneurial drive and a spirit of inventiveness." She was dismissive of the "professors and students" whose thinking had not progressed beyond the era of "free competition." A Marxist sociologist, Deich struggled with the conservative students who opposed "all manifestations of state regulation." Deich also recalled being frustrated with the "Rolla professors who called the shots" because they somehow "equated sociology with 'socialism.'"

Despite her frustrations with the situation on campus, Deich was attracting external support for her research. According to her dissertation director, Deich's "academic specialty was science policy, particularly federal governments' involvement in planning industrial policy." At the time of her disappearance, the National Science Foundation was about to award her a grant for her research on industrial policy and would have enabled her to examine some "moderately classified material."

The FBI quickly concluded that there was "only one reason a person flees from the West to the East and leaves a refrigerator full of food." Six years later, a spokesman for the West German Interior Ministry who talked to a reporter for the *Columbia Daily Tribune* had little doubt about the role Werner and Ingrid played in the Cold War: "The Deichs disappeared about 10 days after Stiller came across the border, and they went from the states via Mexico to the GDR (German Democratic Republic)." A professor of political science at the University of Missouri-Columbia explained that the Deichs had "made several trips between Missouri and Europe. The presumption in most circles is that they were providing courier service."

When contacted in the 1980s by a reporter, Deich would neither confirm nor deny her status as an agent for the East German government. At one point she said, "'I have to laugh. I don't have to say that. I won't." Yet, she obliquely added, "There are certain edges and corners in people's lives which are not always straight." Researchers still link this former spy and the Rolla campus. Thirty-five years after her mysterious departure from Rolla, a former University of Missouri-Columbia professor, studying the Stasi, noted that Werner and Ingrid "both had worked for (Stasi leader) Markus Wolf but were forced to flee when Werner Stiller defected to the West."

21ST CENTURY INCIDENTS

In the 21st century, three incidents occurred on campus that brought unwanted media attention to the university.

In 2007, a graduate student from India, Sujithkumar Venkatramolla, entered a lab in Butler-Carlton Hall armed with a knife, claiming to have a bomb, and carrying a bag of white powder that he claimed was anthrax. Police responded and an investigation determined that there was no bomb, and the white powder was confectioner's sugar. Venkatramolla was charged with making a terroristic threat and deported to his native India.

In May 2011, a high-speed police chase that began in Waynesville, Missouri, about 30 miles southwest of Rolla, ended on campus when a suspect, who had been shooting at his law enforcement pursuers, crashed his car between the Havener Center and McNutt Hall. The suspect entered McNutt Hall and exited the north side of the building, ditched his firearm under a parked vehicle, and escaped on foot. A manhunt ensued, and the campus was put on lockdown. The suspect was captured hours later near Edgar Springs, Missouri, south of Rolla, driving a car he had stolen in Rolla.

During racial unrest at the University of Missouri-Columbia in November 2015, an anonymous user posted on the social media app Yik Yak a threat to "shoot every black person I see" on the Columbia campus. Authorities traced the message to Missouri S&T student Hunter Park, who had posted the threat from his room in Thomas Jefferson Residence Hall. Park pleaded guilty to making a terroristic threat and was sentenced to a three-year suspended sentence and five years of probation. Park's action spurred a copycat threat by a former student, Tyler J. Bradenberg, who took to Yik Yak to threaten a similar act of violence on the Rolla campus. Bradenberg, too, was charged with making a terroristic threat.

That MSM, UMR and Missouri S&T continued to go about the endeavor of promoting student success during these scandals and incidents is a testament to the vitality and strength of the institution. Moreover, that there were few Miner scandals over the institution's 150-year history reflects well on the general character of the faculty, administration, staff, and students on the campus. Scandals grab our attention because they are so rare.

CHAPTER 10

MINER RELATIONS WITH CENTRAL ADMINISTRATION

In 1946, Daniel C. Jackling, the most renowned graduate of the Missouri School of Mines and Metallurgy, characterized the relationship of the Rolla campus to the University of Missouri's main campus in Columbia in a manner that has endured. Jackling contended that too often MSM had been "simply a stepchild receiving only the scraps and crumbs from the family table."

Many others have used family metaphors to describe the relationship of the Rolla campus to the university's presidents and the board of curators. In 1891, Director William H. Echols (1888–91) described MSM as "a forlorn foundling ... despised by the mother institution." But, the "stepchild" characterization has been the longest lasting.

Jackling was not the first to use it, as is clear in a 1937 issue of the *Missouri Miner*, which complained that MSM too long had "been considered more or less as an undeserving stepchild of Missouri University." Following Jackling, many, including former university presidents Elmer Ellis (1955–66) and James Olson (1977–84), have characterized the Rolla campus as the "unwanted stepchild" of the Columbia campus.

Among schools of mines and metallurgy, the one in Rolla had a unique origin. As other states began instruction in mineral engineering, they either added degree programs at an existing institution or established a separate mining school. Because MSM was a division of the University of Missouri, its directors and faculty rarely had much control over their destiny. Some university presidents through the 1950s viewed MSM as a costly mistake for higher education in fiscally conservative Missouri. As James Olson, a late 20th-century president of the university, noted, "The people of Missouri have never supported their University in a manner commensurate with its need, let alone their expectations for it." Because of that reality, and a belief that instruction in mining and metallurgy should have been established in Columbia, some university leaders chafed at the appropriations that went to the Rolla campus, given that the Columbia campus had granted degrees in civil engineering as early as 1856 and had established a school of engineering 21 years later. Most university presidents through the early 1940s sought to move the well-established programs in mining, metallurgy, and civil engineering, and nascent programs in mechanical, electrical, and chemical engineering, to Columbia or at least restrict the offerings at Rolla to mining and metallurgy. When the Rolla campus became a part of the University of Missouri System in 1963, its leaders continued to struggle to define the institution's identity and gain a sense of autonomy.

A Biography of Daniel Cowan Jackling

Daniel Cowan Jackling '92

When Merritt A. Yeater '87 permitted a curious young farm boy to take a look through his surveyor's transit while starting to practice his profession in civil engineering near Sedalia, Mo., he started a train of events that resulted in developments which doubled the world's supply of copper. After this experience with the surveyor's transit, Daniel Cowan Jackling decided to be an engineer. He came to MSM from which Mr. Yeater had graduated in '87 and received his degree in Bachelor of Science in Chemistry. Mr. Jackling's outstanding accomplishments have brought him recognition from practically all of the major engineering societies. His loan fund, known as the Jackling Loan Fund, which he established in MSM with the avowed intentions of making it easier for young men of modest circumstances to obtain an education, has, since its establishment, aided about one-third of all of the graduates at MSM in securing their education and won the undying appreciation of these graduates. These loans have been repaid almost all without exception and the interest payments have substantially increased the total amounts made available by Mr. Jackling, showing that these young men appreciate what the fund has done for them and have helped keep it available for future generations.

Jackling Field, where the Miners play their football games, was likewise made available through Mr. Jackling's generosity and Jackling Gymnasium on this field was named in his honor.

Mr. Jackling received his degree in '92. He received his Metallurgical Engineer's in 1900, and in 1933 in a colorful ceremony held at a special assembly in the auditorium of Parker Hall, he was granted the honorary degree of Doctor of Engineer.

Before coming to MSM he had started in Missouri State Normal School, now Central Missouri State Teachers College, at Warrensburg. Space will not permit the recreating of Mr. Jackling's many accomplishments and the many honors that have been bestowed upon him. His biography is briefly given in the following paragraphs.

As did many others, famed alumnus Daniel C. Jackling characterized MSM as a "stepchild" to the Columbia campus.

[illegible] a corporation executive, was [illegible]on Township, Bates County, [illegible]l Lydia Jane (Dunn) Jackling. [illegible] Virginia Jolliffe of San Fran- [illegible]om 1891 to 1893 as Assistant [illegible] Metallurgy in the Missouri [illegible] to 1896 he was Chemist and [illegible]eek District in Colorado, and from 1896 to 1900 he was in charge of construction and operation of the metallurgical works of the Mercur Gold Mines.

He was on active service of the Staff of Gov. J. H. Peabody as a Colonel of the Colorado State National Guard from 1903 to 1904. From 1909 to 1913 he was Colonel on the staff of Gov. William Spry of Utah. In 1909 he was Utah Com-

D. C. Jackling receiving the honorary degree of Doctor of Engineering from President Walter Williams of the University of Missouri Dr. C. H. Fulton (left)

Ray Consolidated Copper Company, Chino Copper Company, Nevada Consolidated Copper Corporation, Gallup American Coal Company and the corporate subsidiaries of these, including the Nevada Northern Railway Company, Bingham & Garfield Railway Company and Ray & Gila Valley Railroad Company. He held similar offices also with the Butte & Superior Mining Company, Alaska Gold Mines Company, Granby Consolidated Mining Company, American Zinc, Lead & Smelting Company, Mesabi Iron Company, and numerous other industrial corporations of lesser importance. He also served as a director of Braden Copper Company and director of mining operations of the Kennecott Copper Corporation. He was retired as an officer and director of all the foregoing industrial corporations named during or before 1942 except the Mesabi Iron Company, of which he remains president and director. During the stated period he also served as a director of the Chase National Bank, 1916–1924.

A leading figure in professional organizational affairs, Mr. Jackling was president in 1938, director in 1925–28 and 1938–41 of the American Institute of Mining and Metallurgical Engineers. He was councillor of the Mining and Metallurgical Society of America in 1939–41; president of the Missouri School of Mines Alumni Association from 1932 to 1933.

He is a Fellow of the American Society of Mechanical Engineers and is a member of the American Chemical Society, the Western Society of Engineers, the American Institute of Electrical Engineers, the Newcomen Society of England, American Branch, and life member of the American Association for the Advancement of Science.

In 1904 he was awarded the active service Gold [illegible] the Colorado State National Guard.

His professional distinctions include such honors as: Gold

TURF BATTLES THROUGH 1935

In the early years, this sense of being the "tail to the University dog," another Jackling characterization, was most evident in the neglect of the campus by university leaders. Following President Daniel Read's eloquent endorsement of MSM at its formal opening in November 1871, he (1866–76) and his successor Samuel Laws (1876–89) paid scant attention to the Rolla campus. In fact, Laws did not even visit Rolla during his presidency. In part, this neglect was due to the sad state of affairs at MSM. The student body annually averaged fewer than 100 through the early 1890s, and many of those admitted were not ready for the challenges of a college curriculum. In an attempt to maintain enrollment, according to Director Walter "Buck" Richards (1893–97), "everyone who wished to enter was admitted." It seemed to some — including one state legislator — concerned about the "heavy expense" of educating so few, often mediocre, students, that it might be best to close MSM. Many in Rolla feared that rather than eliminating instruction in mining and metallurgy in the state, degree programs in those disciplines would be moved to Columbia. A reporter for a newspaper in nearby Iron County wrote in 1884 that "friends of the institution" expected "that sooner or later an open effort would be made" to move MSM to Columbia.

There was good reason for such fears. Four years earlier, Laws had unsuccessfully tried to move the technical degree programs in Rolla to Columbia in exchange for the teacher education program, then called the Normal Department. President Richard Henry Jesse (1891–1908) was the most consistent advocate of moving MSM. As he explained to his successor A. Ross Hill (1908–21) in 1913, "I have prayed many a prayer for twenty-odd years that this University might be consolidated." Believing that dividing the University "into two pieces" had been a mistake, Jesse urged Hill to push the consolidation. The latter agreed with Jesse, and, according to George Ladd, MSM director from 1897 to 1907, Hill wrote to Ladd in 1909, "If you will keep out of the State and keep hands off, we can move the School to the University ... and take care of it nicely at Columbia." However, Ladd refused, as he had emerged as the most formidable challenge for presidents Jesse and Hill.

Ladd dramatically improved the campus in his decade as director. Because of his skillful lobbying of state legislators, state appropriations for the campus more than tripled. He also nearly tripled the number of faculty members to meet the demand of a nearly 50 percent increase in students. Ladd added Mechanical Hall and Norwood Hall, as well as two wings and another floor to the Chemistry Building. Moreover, he spent a great deal on landscaping and sidewalks to improve the campus's appearance. Ladd also consistently resisted any efforts by the board of curators to limit program offerings on the Rolla campus. As far as Jesse was concerned, Ladd fundamentally ignored him. When the MSM director resigned in early 1907, Jesse wrote, "the School of Mines during Dr. Ladd's regime have paid very little attention to the President of the University, in fact none at all." Indeed, when Ladd stepped down, Jesse did not find out until he saw a report in the newspapers.

A Board of Visitors, appointed by Governor Elliot Major, bolstered the hopes of President Hill. In early 1915, the board members recommended moving the programs offered in Rolla to Columbia, and that "an industrial and home economics school" be established in Rolla. Following the issue of that report, Hill appeared before the House Committee on Education and acknowledged that he "had drawn a bill providing for the removal of the School of Mines to Columbia."

In the wake of efforts to move their campus, interim Director Durward Copeland and A.L. Baysinger, the Rolla member of the board of curators, drafted a bill to permit MSM to expand its degree offerings to include chemical engineering, electrical engineering, and mechanical engineering. Local representative Frank Farris introduced the bill and in defending it, according to press reports, "made a bitter personal attack on President Hill and the board of curators and charged them with treating the School of Mines unfairly." Moreover, Farris claimed that Copeland had come to Jefferson City "at his (Farris') request to present this matter to the committee but that President Hill had ordered him to go home and stay there." Because Farris made little progress in the House, Carter Buford, who represented Rolla in the Senate, introduced the bill in that chamber, where it passed easily, followed by an equally lopsided margin in the House.

After Governor Major signed the Buford Act, Copeland quickly approved plans for MSM to offer degrees in chemical, electrical, and mechanical engineering. However, the board of curators refused to comply with the new law, and the board's president, former Governor David R. Francis, informed campus officials that they could not mail MSM catalogs that included the new degree programs. The local postmaster,

Top: Believing that the establishment of MSM had been a mistake, University of Missouri President Richard Henry Jesse consistently sought to consolidate MSM's degree programs with those in Columbia.

Bottom: Unlike his two predecessors, interim University of Missouri President John Carlton Jones sought to develop a harmonious relationship between MSM and the president's office.

Above: Once the governor signed the Buford Act, interim Director Durward Copeland swiftly approved plans for MSM to offer degree programs in chemical, electrical, and mechanical engineering.

Below: University of Missouri board of curators during a 1946 meeting (left to right) Roscoe Anderson, John H. Walpers, Frank C. Mann, Stratton Shartel, Harold J. Moore, Allen McReynolds (board president), University of Missouri President Frederick A. Middlebush, Leslie Cowan (board secretary), David W. Hopkins, James A. Potter.

Booker H. Rucker, a long-time supporter of MSM, refused to obey. Meanwhile, in a speech before the City Club in Columbia, Hill pushed the Board of Visitors' earlier recommendation declaring "that he and the curators favored the removal of the School of Mines to Columbia, but not until the State was ready to use the Rolla buildings for a large new institution for industrial education." A State Supreme Court ruling that sustained the Buford Act finally resolved the controversy.

Conflict was not always the relationship between MSM and University of Missouri officials. Lewis Young (1907–13), who followed the combative Ladd as director, later recollected a cooperative spirit with Presidents Jesse and Hill, although the latter rejected the MSM attempt to begin a ceramic engineering program. Moreover, John Carlton Jones (1922–23), Hill's interim successor, sought to set a new tone with MSM Director Charles Fulton (1920–37). As an article in the *Missouri Miner* explained in 1922, "no matter how many ideas or attempts to move the School of Mines from Rolla to Columbia," Jones and Fulton agreed "that instead of discord and jealousy between the two schools, there should be harmony and cooperation." In fact, "as far as they are concerned the old bogy of the removal of the School of Mines from Rolla is dead." That spirit largely prevailed under the leadership of Stratton Brooks (1923–30) and Walter Williams (1930–35), Jones' successors.

THE FREDERICK MIDDLEBUSH ERA, 1935–54

However, during the administration of Frederick Middlebush (1935–54), the longest-serving University of Missouri president, everything changed. Formerly the dean of the School of Business and Public Administration on the Columbia campus, Middlebush emerged as a truly assertive president. Allen P. Green, a strong supporter of MSM who dealt frequently with Middlebush in the 1940s, characterized him as "a stubborn Holland Dutchman," a man of "such a nature that you must be forceful" in dealing with him. Middlebush bluntly told Fulton, for example, that he, like Hill, believed that the School of Mines was "an educational mistake" for Missouri and "felt compelled to continue and administer the School" only "because of the requirements

Above: During his two-decade tenure as University of Missouri president, Frederick Middlebush consistently sought to limit MSM degree programs to mining and metallurgy.

Below: Director William Chedsey was dismissed in 1941 by President Frederick Middlebush because he challenged the president's efforts to limit degree programs in Rolla.

of Missouri law." Throughout his tenure as president, Middlebush sought to restrict MSM programs to mining and metallurgy. In part, Middlebush had to find ways to cut spending because of diminishing appropriations from the state government during the Great Depression. That reality drove him to pursue a policy dictated by the principle that "the University should never expand its program at the expense of a high standard of quality," meaning that he worked to avoid a duplication of degree programs.

More importantly, Middlebush drew upon conclusions included in an external review of the MSM degree programs that he had authorized. Middlebush asked A.A. Potter, the dean of engineering at Purdue University, and H.C. Parmalee, editor of *Engineering and Mining Journal*, to visit MSM and provide a thorough assessment. They visited with Fulton and most department heads, and toured the campus with a focus upon the laboratories. Potter and Parmalee concluded that the faculty and labs in mining, metallurgical engineering, ceramic engineering (which had been added in 1926), and, to a lesser degree, chemical and civil engineering, were adequate. They recommended, however, that "consideration may well be given to the consolidation of the offerings of degree granting curricula, at Columbia only, in electrical and mechanical engineering." Those teaching in the latter two programs, like newly arrived Stuart Johnson in electrical engineering, agreed that MSM had a "pretty pedestrian program," not worthy of accreditation.

Two years later, the *Biennial Report of the Board of Curators* concluded that MSM should have a remarkably narrow focus. It should "train engineers for work in the Mineral Industry" and "conduct investigation and research for the Mineral Industry of Missouri." In 1941, the board's view of MSM's role in the university, and, by implication the view of Middlebush, had not changed. Board members issued a document stating that MSM "was originally established as a specialized institution whose work was confined to the fields indicated by its name." Further, board members asserted that the 1915 Buford Act had been ill-advised because it had led to "unnecessary duplication" of programs.

Given this perspective, it is not surprising that Middlebush and board members were diligent in limiting the breadth of offerings at MSM. Because of the constant challenge in obtaining state appropriations for the university's operation, they believed that they were being good stewards of the funds available.

Yet, the constant efforts from Columbia to constrain MSM frustrated Charles Fulton and he stepped down in 1937. Middlebush selected William Ruel Chedsey (1937–41), a mining engineer on the faculty at Pennsylvania State College, as the next director of MSM. A reference letter for Chedsey played a key role in Middlebush's selection of a director he believed would carry out his agenda for MSM. Pennsylvania State College President Ralph Dorn Hetzel described Chedsey as belonging "to that school of leadership which wins support and following by virtue of tact and sympathetic dealing. He is not a driver." Believing that he had found a competent, but compliant, leader for MSM, Middlebush sent an offer letter to Chedsey the following day. Middlebush made it clear in writing to Chedsey after the latter's acceptance of

"... belonging 'to that school of leadership which wins support and following by virtue of tact and sympathetic dealing.'"

the position that he expected his new hire would not expand offerings in engineering, but rather "that under your leadership the School of Mines and Metallurgy may move forward to the point of where it may again be rated as one of the outstanding schools of mines and metallurgy in the country."

Chedsey followed Middlebush's mandate in one important regard. The new director eliminated majors in several disciplines, including English, economics, and biology. However, contrary to Middlebush's vision for the campus, Chedsey sought accreditation for mechanical engineering and chemical engineering and gained legislative support for the construction of a chemical engineering building. Chedsey's independence led to his dismissal. As F.M. McDavid, the president of the board of curators, explained, Chedsey is "well educated and a fine gentleman, but he was unable to co-operate with the curators and the president. He just was not fitted to the exact job." Middlebush replaced Chedsey with Curtis Laws Wilson (1941–63), who historian Jack Ridley has argued "shared the president's views of the role of the School of Mines." Middlebush gave Wilson the title of dean instead of director to make his position comparable to the men who headed the divisions of the university on the Columbia campus.

Following his dismissal of Chedsey, Middlebush, with the approval of the board of curators, became an intense micro-manager of the Rolla campus. An executive committee of the board had always been charged with monitoring the MSM budgets and the activities of campus directors, yet most presidents had not been particularly intrusive in MSM's internal affairs. Middlebush and the board of curators, however, decided that changes were needed. They replaced the MSM policy of "permanent" department heads with chairmen "appointed annually by the President ... upon recommendation" of the MSM dean. They also replaced the campus registrar with the university registrar who became responsible for the admission of all students, with the help of an assistant registrar on the Rolla campus. In addition, the president "integrated" the business office at MSM with the "general business office of the University." Believing that Directors Fulton and Chedsey had not hired the most capable faculty members, Middlebush even took "a strong personal hand in the selection of senior faculty." For example, Harold Q. Fuller, who began at MSM in 1947 and later became chair of the physics department, interviewed first with Wilson, but then had to travel to Columbia where both Middlebush and Graduate Dean Harry Bent interviewed him.

Besides the determination of university officials to limit what MSM could offer to students, many of the faculty, students, and Rolla residents believed that university presidents and board members had consistently treated the Rolla campus unfairly in the distribution of resources. For example, in 1932, Joe Butler, chair of the civil engineering department, conducted a study of faculty salaries in Columbia and Rolla and presented to a general faculty meeting evidence that full, associate, and assistant professors at the University of Missouri made more than those at MSM. Four years later, almost all MSM faculty members signed a petition to the board of curators asking "That the salaries of the faculty members of the Missouri School of Mines beginning January, 1937, be placed on the same scale as the faculty members at the University of Missouri at Columbia." Graduate Dean Bent later vividly recalled their anger. He wrote that "the faculty at Rolla always felt that it was discriminated against." In particular, "they felt that their salaries were lower and that they were not quite appreciated."

In 1938, in a front-page editorial, the *Missouri Miner* staff argued that for many years "there has been a considerable amount of agitation at Missouri University against the School of Mines. It has been claimed that it is useless and costly to maintain a separate school at Rolla and that if it were moved to Columbia the efficiency would be greatly increased because a smaller faculty would be required to teach the engineering students. It has been claimed that the courses at Rolla are a duplication of those at Missouri University, and therefore are a useless waste." This "attitude" had led, in the previous decade, to discrimination in financing "to the extent that the salaries paid the professors [in engineering] run, man per man, from $200 to $2,400 per year more at Missouri University than at the School of Mines. While building programs have been in progress at all of the teachers' colleges and the University, nothing was added to the MSM campus." On the last point, the students were largely correct. In the 1930s, the board of curators authorized 14 buildings for the Columbia campus, with most of them "paid for entirely by state funds," but only one, Harris Hall, completed in 1940, for MSM.

There was an abiding sense in Rolla that Middlebush was intent upon marginalizing MSM, not just in limiting curriculum and in discriminatory funding, but also in the

Civil engineering professor Joe Butler's 1932 study revealed that professors on the Columbia campus made higher salaries than those on the Rolla campus.

dismissive way he dealt with the campus. He did not visit the campus until his third year in office, and when he traveled to Rolla through the early 1940s, it usually was only to attend commencement. Allen P. Green recalled that Middlebush "would drive to Rolla at graduation, arrive five minutes before the ceremonies, say howdy and go to the platform. Then, when the ceremonies were over, he would step in his car, say goodbye and be off."

THE SEPARATION MOVEMENT

Frustrated by the actions and inactions of officials in Columbia, MSM partisans, over time, pushed efforts to separate from the University of Missouri. In the early 1880s, a Lebanon, Missouri, newspaper advocated the separation of MSM from the University of Missouri. Between 1889 and 1895 there was a series of legislative efforts to separate MSM from the University of Missouri and name it the Missouri Institute of Technology. A few faculty members advocated separation in the 1930s, but the most significant effort took place in the following decade.

In 1941, two developments triggered an attempt in the state legislature to sever the connection between the MSM campus and the president's office in Columbia.

"... an emancipation proclamation ... that 'seeks to free the institution from the unfriendly, stifling influence of President Middlebush.'"

Resentment on campus grew throughout the year over Director Chedsey's dismissal. Many felt that he had not been treated fairly by Middlebush, and students were outraged that the president and board of curators had refused to make appropriations for a dormitory a priority in their funding request to the state legislature. While the Columbia campus had been able to add both a men's and women's dormitory in the 1930s, demands on the Rolla campus for its first dormitory since the short-lived Club House in the 1890s went unheeded. For generations, students had rented rooms from homeowners in Rolla, but the construction of nearby Fort Leonard Wood, an Army training base, dramatically increased demand for housing, as did the growing enrollment on campus. While it was not his top priority, Chedsey sought funding for a dormitory, a move opposed by Middlebush. During the spring 1941 semester, over two-thirds of the students signed a petition in support of funding for a dormitory, and approximately 300 drove to Jefferson City to march in a demonstration at the Capitol Building with placards reading "We Want a Place to Sleep" and "We Want a Dorm." They delivered their petition to Governor Forrest C. Donnell, all to no avail.

Activists in Rolla formed the Association for the Advancement of the Rolla School of Mines and immediately condemned Middlebush not only for opposing the dormitory funding, but also because, they contended, he had "never addressed the faculty or students nor acquainted himself with the needs of the institution." Indeed, the group called for Middlebush to step down as president.

Emery Allison, Rolla's representative in the state senate, who had introduced a funding bill for the MSM dormitory request, shortly afterward introduced a bill to have the director of the campus report not to the president, but directly to the board of curators. Allison called the bill "an emancipation proclamation for the administration of the School of Mines and Metallurgy at Rolla" that "seeks to free the institution from the unfriendly, stifling influence of President Middlebush." The staff of the *Missouri Miner* wholeheartedly supported the senator's lla Herald.

ESTABLISHED 1866

Phelps County's leading newspaper with wide circulation that spreads the doctrine of genuine Democracy.

ERALD, THURSDAY APRIL 3, 1941 NUMBER THIRTY-EIGHT

M.S. M. FRIENDS CONDEMN CURATORS ACTION

St. Louis Globe-Democrat April 1

Stating a crisis exists at the Missouri School of Mines and Metallurgy at Rolla, Mo., because of the lack of housing facilities for students and the requested resignation of William R. Chedsey, director of the institution, a resolution condemning the action of the Board of Curators of the Missouri University and the policy of the university's president, was adopted by the Association for the Advancement of Missouri School of Mines and Metallurgy at a meeting last night at Bryan Mullanphy School.

The resolution, according to Ray F. Rucker, chairman, condemns the curators, who "have been guilty of unbecoming conduct in lobbying against efforts in the General Assembly to obtain appropriations for an emergency building" for housing students; calls attention of Gov. Donnell and members of the Assembly to the "objectionable policy on the part of the president of the university with respect to the administration of the school of mines," pointing out he has never addressed the faculty or students nor acquaint ed himself with the needs of the institution and "has displayed prejudice in handling the dismissal of Director Chedsey."

Continuing, the resolution, according to Rucker, recommends the president, Frederick A. Middlebush, be relieved and returned to teaching duties and urges that the Governor fill three vacancies on the board with persons "known to be without prejudice and who will dedicate themselves sincerely to te institution."

Rucker who is superintendent of the Aluminum Ore Company, East St. Louis and a graduate of Rolla, said the problem is to get facilities at the school so the students can live co[illegible]ably. (The association is working to obtain an appropriation of $150,000 from the Legislature for a dormitory.) He said civil housing facilities are insufficient, especially since the influx of the military.

Turning to Chedsey's dismissal he said the "director (of the School of Mines) never knows how long he will retain his position" under present arrangements.

School Of Mines Students March On State Capital

Students of the School of Mines, being aroused over efforts to emasculate the institution and to hinder its usefulness, went in a body to Jefferson City last Monday to express their indignation against university authorities, and at the same time to appeal to Gov. Donnell and the Legislature for help.

The following account taken from the Post-Dispatch tells the story:

JEFFERSON CITY, March 31. —Several hundred students and friends of the Missouri School of Mines and Metallurgy took over the capital today in a typically collegiate demonstration, urging the Legislature to approve a $150,000 appropriation for a new student dormitory at the school.

The students, after driving 60 miles from Rolla this morning, gathered at the front steps of the Capitol with signs and placards, pointing out that the dormitory was needed because of the housing shortage at Rolla resulting from the influx of thousands of persons connected with the construction of Fort Leonard Wood.

Headed by the school's R. O. T. C. band, the group marched up High street, to the Missouri Hotel, where many members of the Legislature stay when in Jefferson City, then returned to the Capitol. At noon a committee of students presented a petition to Gov. Forrest C. Donnell requesting funds for the dormitory. The petition was signed by about 700 of the 900 students of the school.

Gov. Donnell spoke briefly to the student demonstrators, assembled on the first floor of the rotunda.

"I am much pleased to receive this petition," the Governor said. "It is striking evidence of the interest the student body is taking in one of the great institutions of the Sate. I am aware of the fine reputation your institution has, not only in Missouri, but throughout the United States.

"I assure you this petition will receive earnest, careful and honest consideration, not only by the Legislature but by the executive department of the State Government."

The students cheered Gov. Donnell. The student committee went with the Governor to his office for a short conference. Students on the committee included Armin Fick, Oscar Muskopf, Alden Hacker and Robert Sexton of St. Louis.

In the line of march was a small automobile, carrying an overflow load of about 12 passengers riding on the running boards, hood and fenders. A large sign held above the machine said: "If you think we are crowded, come to Rolla.' '

Other placards declared: "We want a place to sleep," "Standing room only" and "We want a dorm."

Spectators who lined the parade route were most amused by a series of signs, which said:

"Once I went to Rolla Tech,
"Till they built the Army Camp,
"Then I went out on my neck,
"That is why I am a tramp."

The $150.00 appropriation for the dormitory was written into the omnibus appropriation bill by the Senate and later removed by a conference committee. The Senate rejected the committee report last week and the matter is pending before the Legislature.

The Rolla School of Mines, one of the outstanding institutions of its kind, is a department of the University of Missouri. Senator Emery W. Allison of Rolla charged in a recent debate on the proposed dormitory appropriation that the University Board of Curators was attempting to "kill off" the School of Mines. Other charges have been

MSM students organized a march on the State Capitol in 1941 to demand appropriations for a dormitory.

president of the university . The sign said: "Quit beating arou[illegible] (Middle) bush."

ROLLA SCHOOLS GET INCREASE

To Employ Two Additional Teachers

The second and final appropriation of state funds for the school year of 1940-41 reached Mr. F. A. Germann, Rolla District Treasurer this week for the year 1940-41 showed only an increase of 5.8 per cent over that for 1939-40. This increase was slightly below the average increase of 6.85 per cent for the schools of the entire state and furnished the district $1,416 additional funds. This amount will about offset the cost of adding two teachers this year, one for part time in Junior High School and librarian in Senior High School, the other for an added teacher to relieve crowded conditions at West Elementary. While this apportionment was heralded by the press last week as the largest total school apportionment ever made in Missouri, it actually gave each district but little additional funds above last year. It represented 98.68 per cent of the minimum guarantee of the 1931 school law, not the maximum as both the United and Associated Press indicated last week. Sufficient funds have never yet been available to pay the minimum guarantee of the 1931 school law, but this year's apportionment very nearly reached this minimum.

According to the provisions of this school law, apportionment above 100 per cent of the minimum would be made on the basis of the number of teachers in each school and their educational qualifications. Rolla school authorities are very well pleased with the plan of distribution under the present 1931 school law.

The three largest cities of the state are dissatisfied because their large valuations and consequent local taxing ability automatically reduces their share of this state apportionment. These cities are urging pasage of House Bill 419 designed to give them a very much larger share of the state

In 1941, the *Missouri Miner* staff called for MSM's separation from reporting to the University of Missouri president.

effort, explaining, "The dormitory issue and the forced resignation of Dr. Chedsey has again vividly brought out to the School of Mines the dead weight that has been holding the school down for 50 years — its constitutional affiliations with the University of Missouri. Now is the time when those affiliations can be partly broken loose."

Allison could not muster the votes to gain a separation of MSM from the president's office, but the concerns and complaints about dominance from Columbia continued. When Governor Donnell selected a Board of Visitors to inspect the University of Missouri in 1942, he selected Allen P. Green to chair the board. Green, the successful owner of the A.P. Green Fire Brick Co. in Mexico, Missouri, had attended MSM in the 1890s, and with other refractory businessmen, had not only urged the campus to offer ceramic engineering, but also had provided funding for some of the early ceramic labs.

Green attempted to improve relations between the Rolla campus and community and the president's office. He met with leading Rolla residents who had been critical of the board of curators and President Middlebush to learn about their fundamental complaints. They were angry about the low appropriations for the MSM campus, the discussions about the president "taking away some of the degrees and work at the School of Mines and putting them in Columbia," and their belief that

What To Do About A Dormitory?

Now that the "Omnibus Bill" seemingly has been declared dead, what is the School of Mines going to do about housing for its students? Killing the bill does not relieve us of the problem of where we are going to live next year. Now is the time to solve that problem if it is to be solved. If it isn't solved we all know only too well what the predicament will be next fall. 12,000 people will be living in a town that is equipped to hold only five or six thousand. Shall we fold our hands and sigh about it? WE'RE ENGINEERS. Supposedly resourceful and creative people. Five years from now most of us will be handling projects much bigger than the building of a dormitory. Should the dropping of the bill stop us now?

There are two courses we can follow to get a dorm. One is to talk to the Board of Curators and convince them that we have to have appropriations from the state, and that it is up to them to get us the money. They are supposed to be looking toward the welfare of this school. With our parents organization and the student body both clamoring for a dormitory, we can make it hot for them if they don't get us one. Leaders of the "Student Movement" are working on this angle. Mr. McDavid has promised them that he will hear their plea at a curator's meeting this week if the Board can be called together. By next Monday we should know something of what we can expect from the Curators. Let's hope they will give ample consideration to the evidence presented.

If this doesn't bring results we still won't have to admit defeat. The school has the power to float a bond issue and build a dormitory itself. This has often been done by other schools, and it didn't take an Army camp to prompt them to do it. It's true that someone would have to be prodded along before it would be done. Director Chedsey is not in a position to get it done. BUT STUDENTS AND PARENTS ARE, AND THERE'S PLENTY OF REASON WHY WE SHOULD!!

Do Your Part In Keeping The Issue Alive!!

The dormitory issue and the forced resignation of Dr. Chedsey has again vividly brought out to the School of Mines the dead weight that has been holding the school down for 50 years—its constitutional affiliations with the University of Missouri. Now is the time when those affiiliations can be partly broken loose. The issue is before the public eye enough to have it drawn to a head.

Senator Allison has introduced a bill to the legislature that will give us a president who has powers equivalent to those of President Middlebush, and who is not responsible to him. This will be sufficient separation if there are several members on the Board of Curators who will help fight our battles. The "Association for the Advancement of MSM" has sent a resolution to the governor asking the rectification of this.

What is the individual student's job? Simply this. If you happen to know anybody who has a drag with the governor or any legislator, write him and ask him to exert pressure in having the bill passed by the legislature and the resolution given consideration by the governor. Do it now! We need immediate

Asser
C. A.
Dis
Resc
Form the att Board School dismiss Middleb Univers to Gov. bers of of stud and oth adopted Associa of the
The submitt
WHE tain m Curator souri a of Dire has cre souri S lurgy a confusi and ma develop life of
THE SOLVE for the souri S lurgy, Missour the unl conduct Board gainst pending of Miss Mines a building attentio fact th tors, na member tee of Metallu solemn the we that in same T cally d W. All of the Metallu in priv souri, for the
We f attentio to the Assemb not de Preside Missou bush, w

Allen P. Green, who owned the A.P. Green Fire Brick Co. in Mexico, Missouri, served as chairman of a Board of Visitors that inspected the University of Missouri in 1942. In the photo above, Green (left) congratulates M.H. Thornberry, with President Frederick A. Middlebush (center) and MSM alumnus Karl F. Hasselmann (right).

Middlebush and the board members were still considering "moving the School of Mines to Columbia." In other words, they believed that "the Curators were trying to ruin the School of Mines." A complicating factor, Green learned, was their "inborn desire to fight at the drop of the hat and if necessary, borrowing the hat to drop." After meeting with Middlebush, Green believed that one of the biggest challenges was getting the president to change his attitude toward MSM. He needed to "unbend a little and thaw a little"; otherwise, the situation would not become "much better."

In early 1943, Green arranged a meeting with leading Rolla dissidents, Middlebush, the president's secretary Leslie Cowan, and Tom K. Smith, who headed the executive committee of the board of curators for the Rolla campus. It seemed to Green that the Rolla men were ready "to bury the hatchet and work with the University authorities," and all parties seemed to agree that they had "wiped out many of the differences that existed."

American participation in World War II diverted almost everyone's attention, including the critics of Middlebush and the board of curators. At war's end, however, the anger and recriminations returned, this time led by a small but vocal cohort of faculty members. Clair V. Mann, chair of the engineering drawing department and primary author of the first history of the campus, led this group of dissidents. Supporters included electrical engineering Professor Floyd H. Frame, modern languages Professor Oscar A. Henning, geology Professor Garrett A. Muilenburg, and chemistry professors Karl K. Kershner and Clarence J. Monroe. For three years, it seemed to outside observers there was "a lamentable degree of turmoil in the faculty" in Rolla. Some blamed Dean Wilson, who they claimed deported "himself in a high-handed way" and ran "things to suit himself without consultation with other than a handful of his favorites." They also charged that Wilson complied too easily with Middlebush's effort to restrict the degree programs on the MSM campus.

Left: Dean Curtis Laws Wilson had both critics and defenders among the faculty during the 1940s "separation" crisis.

Below: Professor Dudley Thompson was one of Dean Wilson's critics, believing that the latter was an authoritarian leader.

Opposite: Professor Clair V. Mann was dismissed by Dean Wilson as chairman of the engineering drawing department after growing weary of Mann's constant criticism.

Chemical Engi
Departme

The Chemical
found in every I
trial organizatior
ing in the devel
improvement of
ducts. His duties
him in the execu
ment, research, d
plant and equip
plant constructio
tion, process con
nical sales. In a
will be in the mic
making every ef
duce better livi
the application
Engineering and
There are un
portunities for
who is willing t
fundamental t r

Dudley Thompson
Department Chairman
Professor of Chemical Engi-

Daniel C. Jackling, who many consulted about the campus's challenges in the 1940s, concluded that both Middlebush and Wilson, the men "responsible to the State for the constructive and dignified supervision and direction of the institution's operations have been delinquent in the proper exercise of their stewardship." Four years into Wilson's administration, Jackling remained "skeptical ... about his possession of either the attributes or experience essential to executive responsibilities and direction." Once Wilson had survived the tumultuous 1940s, some on the campus, like Dudley Thompson, a chemical engineer who became dean of faculties and interim chancellor, believed that Wilson suffered from a "Napoleonic Complex," and that he had become an "authoritarian" leader who wished to always be in control. Yet, Wilson had supporters on campus, notably his Assistant Dean Rex Z. Williams, who characterized his boss as a real fighter and determined that "nobody was going to chase him out."

Others attributed the problems to the "small perpetual clique of disgruntled self-seekers" on the faculty who offered nothing but "continued vociferous misgivings." Some of them had opposed Director Fulton as well, at one point seeking a no-confidence vote. Those who criticized the faculty dissidents focused their attention upon Mann, who Wilson thought had a "perverted mind" and who Allen P. Green concluded was "screwy" and "verging on unbalanced mentality," a man intent upon "devoting his time to throwing poison around the country." Wilson grew weary of Mann's criticisms, and fired him as chair of the engineering drawing department.

When Allen McReynolds became the presiding officer of the board of curators, he authorized an investigation into the "faculty insubordination" at MSM. In January and May of 1946, the executive committee of the board conducted over 20 lengthy interviews of faculty members and concluded that Mann and his supporters were working to undermine Wilson. During the interviews, Mann, Frame, and Muilenburg admitted that they had drafted an anonymous, widely-circulated 27-page indictment of Wilson, Middlebush, and the board of curators. With a report based upon those interviews in hand, in their spring 1946 meeting, board members gave Mann the "opportunity to resign, which he did." After Wilson also urged Middlebush to do something about the other dissenters, the board drew upon the 1946 report to take action against Mann's five strongest supporters. In 1948, it concluded that professors Frame, Henning, Muilenburg, Kershner, and Monroe were "leaders of a group that lets its desire for autonomy interfere with its loyalty to the school." Middlebush told Wilson to inform the five that they would retain the status of tenured professors and their salaries, however, the board of curators had ordered their transfer to the Columbia campus. All five resigned rather than move. Despite their resignations, some, notably Mann, remained busy. Mann sent "evidence" of what he perceived as Wilson's and Middlebush's malfeasance to the North Central Association of Secondary Schools and Colleges, Engineers Council for Professional Development, and the Association of University Professors.

Professor Clair V. Mann, with four of the five other dissident faculty members, all of whom resigned after they were ordered to transfer to the Columbia campus in 1948. From left to right are Oscar A. Henning, Karl K. Kershner, Floyd H. Frame, Garrett A. Muilenburg, and Mann. Clarence J. Monroe is not in the photo.

"After Wilson also urged Middlebush to do something about the other dissenters, the board drew upon the 1946 report to take action against Mann's five strongest supporters."

102 *History of School of Mines and Metallurgy*

PROFESSIONAL DEGREES GRANTED, 1921-1941

Year	*Mining Eng.*	*Met. Eng.*	*Civil Eng.*	*Mech. Eng.*	*Elect. Eng.*	*Chem. Eng.*	*Ceramic Eng.*	*Gen. Science*	*Total*
1921	7	2	1	..	..	..	..	..	10
1922	3	2	4	..	..	..	..	..	9
1923	5	1	..	1	..	..	..	..	7
1924	4	2	1	2	1	1	..	..	11
1925	6	2	1	..	..	1	..	..	10
1926	3	..	..	..	..	..	..	..	3
1927	12	1	..	..	..	4	..	..	17
1928	4	..	1	..	..	..	..	..	5
1929	1	2	..	..	..	2	..	..	5
1930	7	2	3	..	..	..	..	..	12
1931	2	2	2	..	1	2	..	..	9
1932	1	1	8	..	..	..	..	..	10
1933	1	..	3	..	..	..	..	..	4
1934	4	..	4	..	..	1	..	..	9
1935	7	1	5	..	1	..	..	..	14
1936	3	..	..	..	..	..	1	..	4
1937	1	..	4	..	..	1	..	..	6
1938	6	..	5	..	..	..	..	..	11
1939	5	..	3	..	2	..	..	..	10
1940	2	..	1	1	..	..	..	..	4
1941	3	1	..	..	..	3	..	..	7
Totals...	87	19	46	4	5	15	1	..	177

CHAPTER VII

DEAN CURTIS LAWS WILSON

and

THE PRESENT MISSOURI SCHOOL OF MINES

1941—1946

The present Dean, Curtis Laws Wilson, who has so efficiently and successfully administered the School of Mines' affairs for the past five years, assumed his duties on August 1, 1941. Dr. Wilson for twenty years previously, was affiliated with Montana School of Mines, at Butte, Montana, and for thirteen years served as Professor of Metallurgy and headed the department at that institution.

Dean Wilson was born and reared in Baltimore, Maryland, and was graduated from the Baltimore City College in 1916. He then moved to Montana where he was graduated from the Montana School of Mines in 1920. After service for a year with the Anaconda Copper Company at Butte in various capacities, Dr. Wilson joined the faculty of the Montana School of Mines as instructor in Metallurgy, and was later advanced to the position of head of that department.

In 1928, after twenty-seven months of study in Europe, Wilson was awarded the degree of Doctor of Philosophy, Magna Cum Laude, from the University of Goettingen, in Germany.

Dr. Wilson was active in civic and community affairs at Butte, and in problems of a statewide character. He was particularly prominent in the fight against tuberculosis, and served as First Vice-President of the Montana State Tuberculosis Association.

In addition to his service to the state in the realm of civic affairs, he was likewise prominent in the professional engineering societies. His membership included the American Institute of Mining and Metallurgical Engineers, the American Chemical Society, and the Montana Society of Engineers. He served for one year as chairman of the Montana section of the American Institute of Mining and Metallurgical Engineers.

Dean Wilson was also well-known as the author of numerous articles in the field of Metallurgy. At the time of his appointment, in 1941, he had in the hands of his publishers, a book dealing with the metallurgy of copper.

The MISSOURI MINER for September 17, 1941, was dedicated to the new dean. As an expression of best wishes from the students, the MINER had this to say: "We hope that your stay here will be

(103)

History of the University of Missouri School of Mines and Metallurgy **was written by Professor Clarence Roberts (below) in 1946 to help commemorate the campus's 75th anniversary.**

There were even competing interpretations of the history of the campus available to the partisans of the 1940s. With his wife Bonita, Clair V. Mann had published a mammoth history of MSM in 1941, titled *The History of Missouri School of Mines and Metallurgy*, which was an unrelenting attack on university presidents and members of the board of curators for their "hostility and indifference" toward MSM. History professor Clarence Roberts, however, published a shorter history of the campus, titled *History of the University of Missouri School of Mines and Metallurgy*, as part of the campus's 75th anniversary celebration in 1946. Roberts argued that since Wilson's appointment there was "a new spirit of cooperation and mutual friendliness" between Rolla and Columbia. He praised "the interest, efforts, and loyalty displayed by" Middlebush and argued that "Dean Wilson without doubt, will rank as one of the greatest administrative heads in the history of the school."

All the agitation on the Rolla campus had an impact on Fredrick Middlebush, who slowly began to change his attitude toward MSM. Allen P. Green explained that during the dinner he had arranged for the president with some Rolla community "die-hards" in early 1943, "they went after Middlebush so strong that he couldn't deny any of their statements." Thereafter, he changed his behavior when visiting Rolla. Instead of just showing up for graduation ceremonies and abruptly leaving, "he spends the day and a night, goes hunting and fishing with them. He has addressed the various clubs and the Chamber of Commerce and really I think he is trying to do better." Middlebush even made a pilgrimage to visit Daniel C. Jackling in San Francisco where he "admitted freely that in times past the University administration had not been as cooperative ... as it should." While he also pointed out that the MSM "administration had not worked as harmoniously with the parent institution as the legally prescribed relationship envisioned," Middlebush promised the

powerful MSM alumnus that he would not "restrict the School of Mines in any way in its province as an engineering college or in the provision of finances or facilities."

Remarkably, after all his skillful diplomatic work for over four years, Green drew a surprising conclusion in late 1947. In a letter to Jackling, Green reported that Wilson believed that during "this or the next session" of the legislature, there will be a bill "separating management of the School of Mines from the University, and thinks it may carry. I am beginning to feel that, that might be the best thing for the School, give it a strong Board and have an independent institution. I don't think the institution is getting the cooperation it should from the University Curators. They seem to feel that the University comes first and that Rolla is just another interest like the Agricultural Experiment Station."

Green was also reflecting a reality that had been established a year earlier. Booker H. Rucker, state representative from Rolla, polled 1,000 alumni and over 500 current students. Well over 80 percent of both groups favored "immediate separation of MSM from MU." Yet, some of the most successful alumni were deeply divided over this prospect. Jackling, whose views all seemed to respect, wrote in early 1946, "I have never suggested ... that the School of Mines should be autonomous in its relationship with the University; but I do insist that it should have a larger degree of independence in freedom from ulterior machinations originating at the University."

The following year, he wrote, "I have always thought that the School of Mines should have an administration separate, but not necessarily wholly independent, of the University." After reading scores of letters and reports about MSM, Jackling concluded, "Rolla has not been getting the cooperation that it should from the University Curators" and he doubted that the campus would ever get "fair treatment."

Other prominent alumni disagreed. James L. Head, a 1916 MSM graduate who served as vice president of the alumni association in the early 1940s, wrote that the "antagonism" between Columbia and Rolla had been "very much overplayed," and that it was time for supporters of MSM to understand that "rugged individualism and a spirit of aggressive independence so dear to our hearts as 'Miners' have in 75 years got us exactly nowhere." In 1948, as sentiment continued to build for separation, Karl Hasselmann, president of the alumni association and successful Texas oil man, asked MSM alumnus Mervin J. Kelly, research director and soon to become the president of Bell Labs, to complete a thorough study of the situation at MSM and make a recommendation on the separation question.

After three months of visiting with Wilson, many faculty members, Rolla residents, prominent alumni, Middlebush, and officers of the Engineering Council for Professional Development, Kelly praised the board of curators, Middlebush, and Wilson, as well as the faculty. Specifically, he believed

Above: Alumni Association President Karl Hasselmann (left), President-elect Mervin J. Kelly, and Mrs. F.C. Schnenberger. In 1948, Kelly, a prominent alumnus soon to be president of Bell Labs, conducted a study of the Columbia-Rolla conflict and concluded that separation would not be in the best interests of MSM.

Below: Karl Hasselmann, a respected MSM alumnus, strongly opposed the separation effort of the late 1940s.

Rolla Lumberman Collapses in House Chamber

Frank Powell, Rolla lumberman, collapsed in the House chamber last night after speaking before a House committee for a bill to put control of the school of mines at Rolla instead of at Columbia.

He was taken to St. Mary's hospital and a heart specialist was called.

Powell, 64, is brother-in-law of Howard Katz, former business manager of the school of mines.

When he started to speak before the committee he said his son had asked him not to come because his heart "had been acting up recently."

Just before he quit he told the committee with a grin: "And I heartily endorse every-

Above: Rolla businessman and MSM graduate Frank B. Powell died shortly after speaking on behalf of a bill to have the MSM director report directly to the board of curators and not the University of Missouri president.

Below: University of Missouri President Elmer Ellis followed the pattern of Frederick Middlebush in seeking to limit the expansion of graduate degree programs at MSM.

that the president had worked diligently to improve the faculty and funding for MSM. Contrary to earlier studies, for example, he found little difference in the faculty salaries in Rolla and Columbia and, exclusive of funding for buildings, he concluded that between 1935 and 1947, "the appropriations per student at Rolla has been larger than the appropriations per student at Columbia." In the end, Kelly recommended "that the Alumni Association strongly support the present setup — the School as an integral part of the University."

As the alumni association leadership diligently made a case for maintaining the status quo in early 1949, Representative Rucker introduced a bill, similar to Allison's eight years earlier, that would have required the board of curators to appoint a director for MSM who would report not to the university president, but to the board. Rucker argued that Middlebush had too much control over MSM and, drawing upon that well-used metaphor, believed the campus was still little more than a "step child of MU." At a March 23 hearing on the bill in Jefferson City, both sides brought large delegations to testify. Opponents of the bill included several Rolla businessmen and alumni who argued that the supporters actually represented "a very small group" in Rolla, but the supporters, including Clair V. Mann and Floyd Frame, argued, in the words of Rolla businessman John Powell, that Middlebush had tried "to restrict Rolla in every way" as he sought "to build up the College of Engineering at Columbia." There was a dramatic moment when John's father, Frank B. Powell, a 1906 graduate of MSM and "widely known lumber man," suffered a stroke after speaking on behalf of the bill. The elder Powell, "who had been ailing with a heart condition for some time," died the next day in a Jefferson City hospital. While Rucker's bill survived two readings, he failed to get sufficient support in a May vote on the bill. This was the last effort to separate MSM from the control of the university president.

Middlebush remained in office until 1954, but his successor, Elmer Ellis (1955–66), continued the Middlebush approach of close control of the Rolla campus. For example, in 1957, Ellis chided Wilson for offering too many courses that attracted fewer than 15 students. More irksome for many at MSM was the MU graduate dean's control over graduate study on the Rolla campus until 1965. Graduate Dean Harry E. Bent believed that MSM had too few faculty with doctorates and the requisite research records to offer quality Ph.D. programs. Hired by Middlebush in the 1930s, Bent had the same goal of preventing duplication of programs that existed on the Columbia campus. As he explained to Wilson in 1959, "The idea that your major emphasis should be in the fields of Ceramics, Mining, and Metallurgy seems quite obvious."

Ellis similarly resisted efforts to expand the number of Ph.D. programs at MSM. In 1962, Wilson wrote to the president supporting a faculty policy committee recommendation that MSM offer Ph.D. degrees in chemistry, electrical engineering, civil engineering, mechanical engineering, and nuclear engineering. He argued that without the Ph.D. degree, faculty members in those departments would leave MSM. Ellis rejected the argument, trotting out an often-used rationale. If the Rolla campus began offering duplicate Ph.D. programs such actions would "lower the quality" of all programs at both campuses and such an action would further dilute precious resources. He told Wilson to pursue cooperative degree programs.

Perhaps most telling of the University of Missouri's administrative control of MSM was an incident involving a bill for $34.37. In 1955, Wilson hosted a dinner at a local restaurant for the accreditation committee from the Engineers Council for Professional Development. The dinner for eight people cost $34.37 with a tip, but Ellis's Vice President Leslie Cowan called Wilson to remind him that reimbursement could only be $3.75 per person, or no more than $30, and he would not authorize payment, leaving Wilson to beg Ellis to reimburse him.

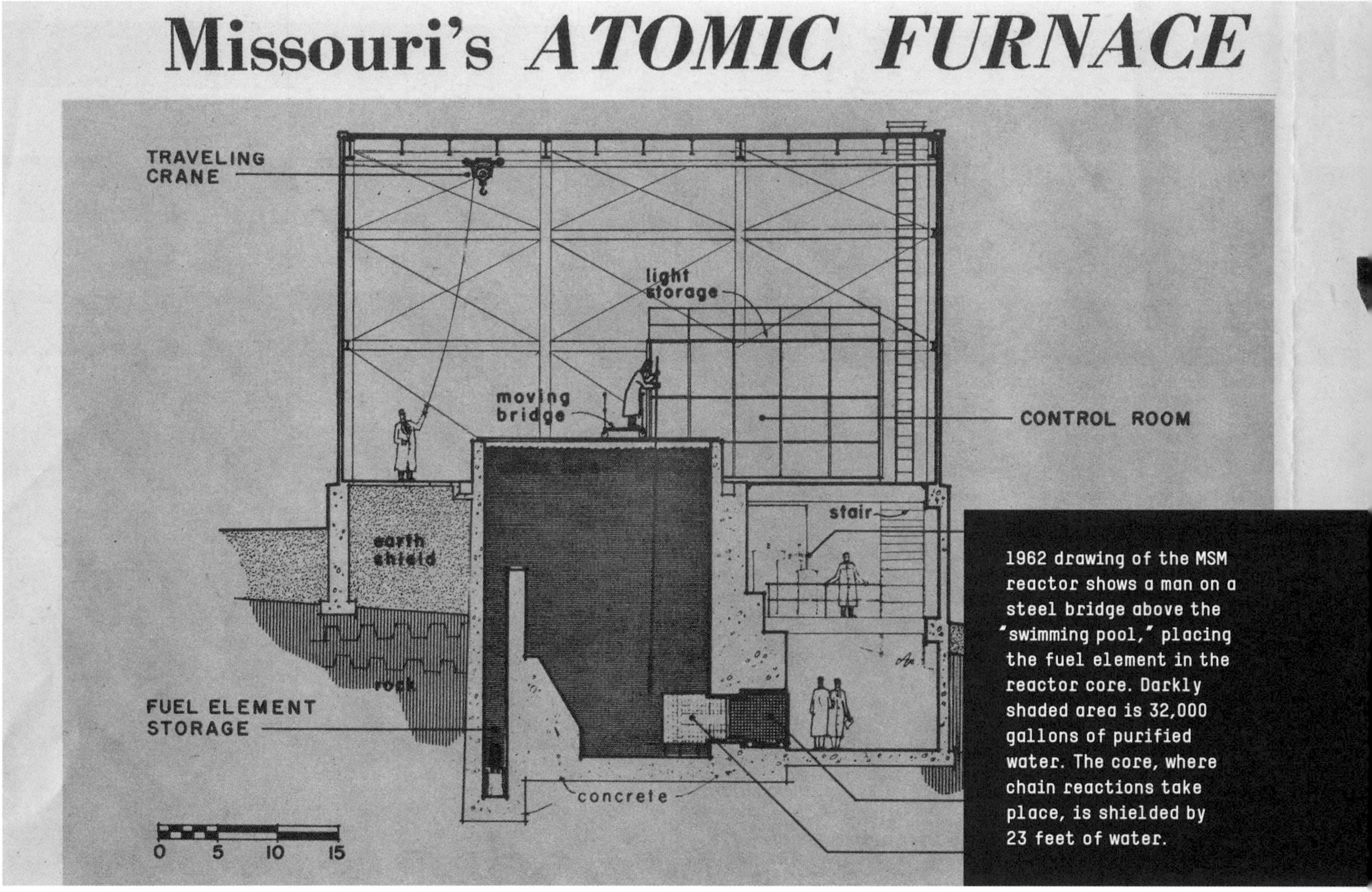

Missouri's *ATOMIC FURNACE*

TRAVELING CRANE

light storage

moving bridge

CONTROL ROOM

stair

earth shield

rock

FUEL ELEMENT STORAGE

concrete

0 5 10 15

1962 drawing of the MSM reactor shows a man on a steel bridge above the "swimming pool," placing the fuel element in the reactor core. Darkly shaded area is 32,000 gallons of purified water. The core, where chain reactions take place, is shielded by 23 feet of water.

While Ellis remained as controlling as Middlebush, he was more supportive with resources for the Rolla campus. In his first three years as president, Ellis lobbied state legislators for appropriations for eight new buildings for the campus, and the faculty got their largest salary increases in MSM's history. Also, here and there, he did support what James Olson has called "a broadened mission for MSM." Specifically, he permitted nuclear engineering to become an option of metallurgical engineering in 1956. Also, "in 1960, with a grant from the National Science Foundation, MSM established a Computer Center, providing the basis for its development into a leadership role in computer science. Missouri's first nuclear reactor was dedicated on campus in 1961, and construction of a Materials Science Research Center was begun in the last days of the Wilson administration." When state legislators appropriated funding for a University of Missouri research center, they did not specify whether it should be in Columbia or Rolla. To further energize the research activities at MSM, Ellis chose the Rolla campus.

For all university presidents, the challenge had been how best to restrain "mission creep" on the Rolla campus while at the same time giving the faculty at MSM a sense of autonomy. In most cases, they erred more on the side of the former than the latter.

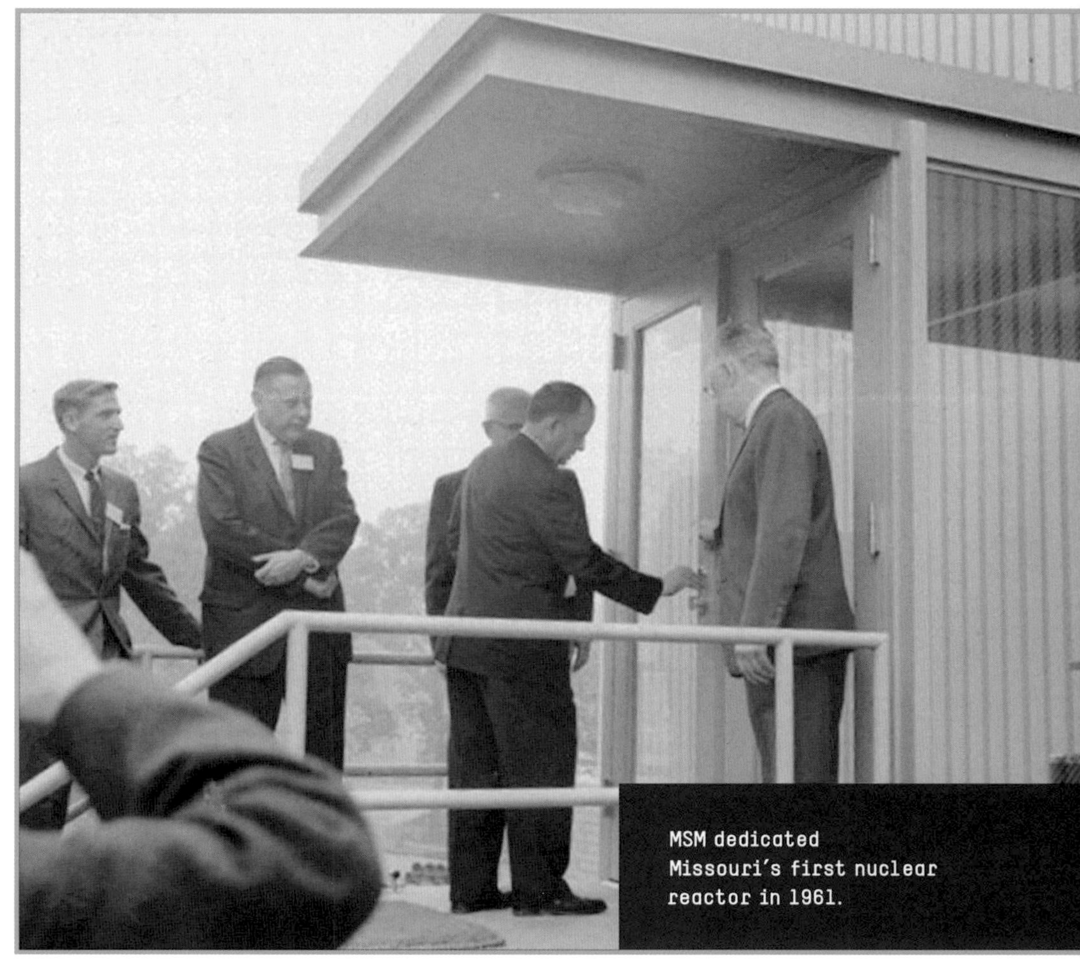

MSM dedicated Missouri's first nuclear reactor in 1961.

Asks for Loyalty to Whole M.U. System

Dear Alumni,

One bright October Saturday afternoon this fall, the Miners won their football game on the day of their first use of their new stadium facility. That same afternoon the Tigers of Columbia lost a hard fought encounter in California. I happened to be on the Rolla campus that evening and a number of staff members sought to console me over the fact that my team had lost while theirs had won. I was quick to respond: "But you're wrong! One of my teams lost and one of my teams won."

The point is, of course, that as President of the University of Missouri my heart, my hopes, my aspirations are no more centered in Columbia than in Rolla. Be it physics or football, I have an undivided allegiance to all campuses of the University of Missouri and the future of that institution as one great University. Each of its campuses has much to contribute to the strength and potential of every campus, and we must all join hands, as a state-wide academic team, to bring high quality education to young people in whatever community our flag flies.

Under the Constitution of Missouri the University is governed by a single board; its management is the ultimate responsibility of a single president. Working with four chancellors it is my hope that I can assure careful coordination of activity and the achievement of efficient, noncompetitive, but mutually sustaining use of the resources made available to us.

I can well understand that those of you who associate your college experience with the pleasant Ozark campus in Rolla will always have a particularly warm spot in your heart for that place and its traditions.

I would hope that in the years ahead you will find additional satisfaction and excitement in giving your active allegiance and support to the *whole* University of Missouri.

John C. Weaver
President
University of Missouri

3

In a 1966 letter to UMR alumni, new University of Missouri President John C. Weaver called upon them to support the new university system as well as UMR.

BECOMING PART OF THE UNIVERSITY OF MISSOURI SYSTEM

As Elmer Ellis neared the end of his presidency, he turned his attention to establishing a university system. According to James Olson, who carefully researched the origins of the UM System, Ellis understood that "Kansas City and St. Louis were the two largest cities in the United States without public institutions of higher education." Moreover, Ellis concluded "that the university needed a presence in the two cities if the university were to play an effective role in a state steadily becoming more urban." Built upon the nearly 125-year-old Columbia campus and the nearly century-old Rolla campus, Ellis drew in the private University of Kansas City and a community college created by a St. Louis school district to establish the University of Missouri System in 1963.

University systems were relatively new. The hope in states that adopted systems was to determine the allocation of diminishing legislative appropriations in a rational way, to coordinate degree program offerings, and, where needed, to reduce duplication while improving educational standards of all programs. Ellis and his successors, along with the board of curators, had to decide how their system would function: as one university with four campuses or as a federation of semi-autonomous campuses. The advantage of the former approach was more rational strategic planning. The advantage of the latter approach was that it afforded each campus greater opportunity to draw upon its unique culture in strategic planning and, thus, have more control over its destiny. John Weaver recalled that when he became president in 1966, it did not take him long to determine that alumni and faculty of the newly named University of Missouri at Rolla favored the latter approach as they were "pretty sensitive about their independence."

Regardless of which model the UM System adopted, the four campuses would have the advantage of essential shared services and system resources. For example, having a general counsel office at the UM System to serve all the campuses eliminated the need for individual campuses to establish a similar office. In addition, as interim President Mel George explained to the UMR Academic Council in 1984, when the Rolla campus experienced a significant drop in enrollment in the early 1970s, "Rolla had a lot of protection from the University system." George made it clear that one of the essential roles of the UM System was to "somehow insulate any campus against those enormous enrollment swings."

Initially, Ellis struggled with some key questions: Should the president of the system also serve as the chancellor of the Columbia campus? Should the president have his office on the Columbia campus? Should staff from a campus serve simultaneously on the system president's staff? Initially, Ellis decided in the

Merl F. Baker (right) became UMR's first chancellor under the new University of Missouri system. He and student William A. Crede (left), editor in chief of the *Rollamo*, look over the yearbook in front of Parker Hall.

affirmative on all those questions, but his successor John Weaver (1966–70) reversed those decisions. He separated the two offices, moving to a new office in University Hall and not mixing campus staff with system staff.

The Rolla campus made the transition with a new leader. Wilson retired in 1963, and Ellis selected Merl F. Baker (1963–73) as the next dean for MSM. Baker was a mechanical engineer at the University of Kentucky, where he had led the Kentucky Research Foundation. When the campus changed its name to the University of Missouri-Rolla, Ellis elevated Baker's title to that of chancellor, the title all subsequent leaders of the Rolla campus have held.

Board of curators members made it clear to President Weaver that they wanted the "one" university model. Indeed, in several documents between 1967 and 2018, the board of curators affirmed its commitment to the concept of "the University of Missouri" as "a single institution with four campuses, each of which is a component of the whole." To institute that approach, board members instructed Weaver to develop a long-range plan for the UM System. While Weaver knew that he could not have "indefinite duplication of everything among the campuses," he largely let the four campuses develop degree programs if they already had the "financial resources" to fund them. However, Weaver occasionally blunted campus efforts. For example, he prevented UMR from developing a degree in biology because the campus had only one biologist, and "he was in the Chemistry Department."

Weaver's successor, C. Brice Ratchford, and the board of curators were disappointed in the 1968 10-year plan that had emerged. It seemed to them like a "pie in the sky" set of plans that would be hopelessly underfunded. Ratchford concluded, for example, that UMR was simply unrealistic believing that it could develop graduate programs in the arts and sciences.

UMR Enrollment Down 530

President Ratchford To Seek Revamp Of Academic Programs

Under the leadership of President C. Brice Ratchford, the University of Missouri is continuing a school-wide re-evaluation of programs and goals, it was announced Friday at the meeting of the Board of Curators in Rolla.

According to Dr. Ratchford, a program has been underway for the past year, studying ten major areas of the university system. Under this program, each of the four campuses will be responsible for redefining its role and scope within the system. This is to be completed by December of this year.

A re-appraisal of the academic programs will follow, with a five-man evaluation committee. This committee will review the existing academic endevors on all levels. Special interest will be given to the continuation, relocation, adjustment, iniation, or termination of many doctoral and professional degree programs.

Over a three year period, the committee will study the quality, appropriateness, significance, need, cost, and the potential for change and improvement of every program. Results of these studies and appraisals will be forwarded to the Academic Planning council and members of the curators by 1974.

The final step of the program will be to make improvements on the administrative structure of the University.

Dr. Ratchford termed this "A time of opportunity for higher education;" and stated, "I am extremely confident that this reappraisal will be good for the University and the State."

Also at the meeting, the final on-campus tally of students for the fall semester was announced, with the four campus system boasting 46,395 students, an increase of 543.

Broken down by campus, the figures reveal: on the Columbia campus, 21,942, an increase of 261; on the Kansas City Campus, 9,510, a gain of 305; in St. Louis, 10,188, up 507; and in Rolla, 4,755, a decrease of 530.

Regarding the decline of 530 students here in Rolla, President Ratchford cited several factors which may have contributed to the decrrease. It was felt that the current publicity given to the projected surpluses of trained engineers has discouraged some prospective students from entering the science or engineering field. Dr. Ratchford also noted that the decrease in graduation requirements from 142 to 132 hours was responsible for many students being able to reduce the amount of time they needed to spend on campus.

In the graduate programs of the University, enrollment dropped 360. The number of freshmen also declined, showing a decrease of 279; however, the undergraduate enrollment increased 680.

Concerning the present wage-price freeze, and its affect on University salaries, Dr. Ratchford explained that the University was in the dark about as much as the average person. He pointed out that the administration gets its information in the same way as the

(Continued on Page 6)

At a meeting of the Board of Curators under the leadership of President Bruice Rutchford of the University of Missouri, it was decided to continue re-evaluation of Academic programs and goals.

When Weaver departed to take the job as president of the University of Wisconsin, the board of curators named Ratchford (1971–76) as interim president and the following year, on a five-to-four vote, named him president of the University of Missouri. Determined "to maintain the concept of a single university on multiple campuses" as mandated by the board, Ratchford embarked upon the most far-reaching planning effort in the history of the UM System. After meeting with administration and faculty leaders, Ratchford sought a plan that would eliminate or at least minimize duplication of programs. Because it involved an assessment of all degree programs, Ratchford concluded that he had to take "a completely top-down approach."

During the October 1971 board meeting in Rolla, Ratchford announced that "each of the four campuses will be responsible for redefining its role and scope within the system." This "Role and Scope" approach would be a three-year study of "the quality, appropriateness, significance, need, cost, and the potential for change and improvement of every program" on all four campuses.

Ratchford issued an early draft of the plan at the December 1971 board meeting. "No campus shall be complete in itself. The University must be a genuine association among all campuses." UMR would have a limited mission, "largely that of serving as the University's center for programs in basic engineering and in some of the sciences." Specifically, UMR "would be the University's center for advanced study in basic engineering; would offer a limited range of undergraduate studies in the liberal arts; would in partnership with the St. Louis campus be the center for graduate

In 1971, University of Missouri President C. Brice Ratchford, believing it essential to use a "completely top-down approach," implemented a strategic plan called "Role and Scope."

study in the earth sciences; and would be a community college for the region, providing associate degree programs as feasible."

Baker was critical of Ratchford's approach, one that Baker believed involved too much of "a central mandate without participation" from below. Upon the release of the first version of "Role and Scope," students and faculty in Rolla protested and circulated petitions calling for changes. According to a January 1972 editorial in the *Missouri Miner*, "The main cause for concern at UMR is the liberal arts program." The fear was that the campus's "liberal arts would degenerate to a junior college curriculum with no B.A. degrees offered." On the Columbia campus, "1,400 attended a protest rally" and "the *Maneater*, Columbia's student newspaper, called for Ratchford's dismissal."

Undeterred, Ratchford proceeded with "Role and Scope." In May 1972, the plan had greater detail, but was still grounded on the fundamental principles of "one" university with diminished duplication: "The University will be comprehensive and each campus shall have some unique responsibilities, especially at the advanced professional level. Each will have a range of programs, but it is not intended that each campus will be comprehensive in scope." Most alarming to the Columbia campus was the decision on doctoral programs: "Administration of doctoral programs will be through a well-consolidated structure involving qualified faculty from each campus. One campus will normally be selected as an administrative center." In some doctoral programs, the designated department was not in Columbia because several of the doctoral programs on that campus got "low ratings."

After many months of program reviews, including the use of external consultants, the board of curators adopted the plan in August 1974. In the end, in the face of significant opposition from the campuses, there were few changes in what the four campuses offered, and almost none of the degree programs were scheduled for "reduction or elimination." In the process, Ratchford later acknowledged, "we made no progress toward the goal of increased cooperation." Indeed, he ultimately concluded after the "Role and Scope" fiasco that "nobody" really knew how to do system planning well. Yet, system planning continued with a new major effort usually following the appointment of each new president. However, most presidents had learned the lesson about the challenges of top-down planning from the "Role and Scope" episode and called upon chancellors to develop priorities for their campuses.

Missouri's political realities also made fully implementing the "one university" concept challenging. When he arrived as the new UMR chancellor in 1986, Martin Jischke quickly concluded that it was

When he became UMR's chancellor in 1986, Martin C. Jischke (above left, with UM System President C. Peter Magrath) quickly realized that each of the four UM System campuses had their own political constituency, a situation he said would make it difficult to see the system as "one university."

While serving as president of the University of Missouri, C. Peter Magrath (right, with UMR Chancellor Martin C. Jischke) believed it would be a mistake to micro-manage the campuses.

1

2

Chancellor John Park led the campus effort in winning a Missouri Quality Award.

Opposite: University of Missouri presidents Manuel Pacheco (1) and Gary Forsee (2) believed that strategic planning should begin at the UM System level, but that each campus should have goals reflecting their strengths.

unlikely that a system as envisioned by those who established the UM System could become fully functional. He saw that each campus had a local political constituency that focused upon advancing the interests of their institution. Jischke's perception is reflected in the work of political scientist Jeannette B. Welch, who wrote in 1995, "Each branch of the university, and even each school, has its own loyal supporters and alumni, as well as legislators, who are more loyal to it than to an abstract entity known as the University of Missouri."

Presidents' interpretations of their role in the system have varied over time. As former UMR Chancellor Merl Baker described Ratchford's approach, "Brice wanted to get things done, and the faculty was supposed to do it." James Olson (1977–84), who followed Ratchford into the presidency, had served under him as chancellor at the University of Missouri-Kansas City. Those two experiences led Olson to conclude in his memoirs that "effective presidential leadership required" a different approach. A president had to "resist the temptation to micro-manage the vast enterprise for which he had ultimate responsibility."

C. Peter Magrath (1985–91), who followed Olson, agreed. Acknowledging that most campuses distrusted the system president's office and that he had no constituency other than the board of curators, Magrath did not believe that he was in charge. Given that understanding of his circumstance, Magrath believed it would be a mistake to micro-manage the campuses. Later presidents Manuel Pacheco (1997–2002) and Gary Forsee (2008–11) offered a variation on that theme. They wanted each campus to understand that they had integrity on their own and that they should determine what they did best and what they wanted to be. To them, strategic planning began at the system level, but each campus would have goals reflecting their strengths. At Rolla, that meant engineering and the sciences.

Underlying the approaches of Magrath, Pacheco, and Forsee was a belief articulated by Olson "that decisions should be made as close to the action as possible." Indeed, in 1993, Olson wrote, "As the system matured, successive presidents had increasingly delegated authority to the chancellors." The UMR campus reflected that reality in its 1978 self study which it submitted in support of its request for reaccreditation. From the inception of the University of Missouri, the self study authors noted, "The one university concept has proceeded with an increasing coordination of educational programs, the centralization of certain services and offices needed by each of the four campuses, and an increasing spirit of cooperation among and between the campuses." Yet, decentralization had accompanied that development not only at the system level, but also at the campus level, where there had been "a concerted effort ... to decentralize the decision-making and operational processes from the campus central administration and to establish a meaningful degree of autonomy for its division administrators, especially the school and college deans."

Interested in knowing how best to govern the UM System, Magrath called on Charles E. Knight, the CEO of Emerson Electric, to study the system and recommend any needed changes. In response, Knight urged Magrath and the board of curators to accelerate the decentralization process, which pleased faculty members in Rolla. In a 1986 Academic Council meeting, they anticipated that "administrative control and other activities of the Central Administration" would "be increasingly carried to the individual campuses" and they welcomed the movement "toward more autonomous campuses."

Chancellors at UMR and S&T believed that the decentralization of authority gave them great latitude in running their campus and determining what to focus upon in their administrations. As he wrestled with the problem of defining UMR's role in the UM System, Martin Jischke (1986–91), for example, focused upon giving UMR a stronger statewide identity as "Missouri's Technological University." John Park (1992–2000) used the strategic planning process to aggressively and successfully pursue a Missouri Quality Award, believing that would demonstrate that UMR went about its job following the performance criteria of quality management and continuous improvement as established for the Malcolm Baldrige National Quality Award. To broaden the campus's academic portfolio, Gary Thomas (2000–05) successfully gained approval of several new academic programs, including environmental and architectural engineering and business administration. John F. Carney III (2005–11) made the boldest moves in eliminating the academic colleges at UMR to streamline the administrative structure and then gained approval of a name change for the campus. He believed, like Jischke, that the UMR name suggested only a regional identity, and he promoted a name (Missouri University of Science and Technology) that reflected the distinctive nature of the campus, one separate from the UM System. When she learned that President Timothy Wolfe (2012–15) was going to require campuses to submit comprehensive strategic initiative proposals to get additional state appropriations, Cheryl Schrader (2012–17) led a thorough, aggressive, and successful campus strategic planning process. In the first year alone, it led to the UM System favoring S&T over the other three campuses, providing $4.5 million in new strategic funding largely to bolster Ph.D. programs. The board of curators also granted a request from interim Chancellor Christopher Maples (2017–19) to label S&T a "highly selective" admissions institution. This provided the campus another distinction from the three other campuses, which were all rated as "selective."

Besides developing their diplomatic skills in dealing with UM System presidents, vice presidents, and members of the board of curators, chancellors in Rolla always had to deal with the challenge of the "flagship" campus in Columbia. When university systems emerged in the 1950s, typically the senior campus gained the designation of "flagship campus," but that did not happen in Missouri. That was a concern for the faculty and administrators of the largest and oldest campus in the system, many of whom had opposed the idea of a university system. For nearly a century they had bemoaned the resources going to the Rolla campus, and they envisioned more challenging financial times with new campuses in Kansas City and St. Louis. Their perspective was not unique. As Mark G. Yudof, who served as president of the California system, has explained, typically, "the flagships felt threatened by the wannabes and their advocates."

Moreover, according to Ratchford, the Columbia faculty looked upon the other three campuses as "branch schools" and "*This* was the university." Paul Nagel, his vice president for academic affairs, agreed. He recalled that the Columbia campus saw the other three campuses as "little satellites out there beeping around the Mother Country." While the designation of the Columbia campus as the "flagship" did not reside in the university's collected rules, presidents and chancellors of the other campuses have had to deal with the Columbia campus's embrace of that concept. As late as 2018, the Columbia campus catalog referred to Mizzou as "Missouri's flagship university."

There were also occasional discussions of a "flagship model" for the UM System, a model that would include the president of the university also serving as the chancellor of the Columbia campus. President Elson Floyd (2003–07) briefly promoted this idea, and in 2018 President Mun Choi (2017–), senior administrators, and members of the board of curators considered but rejected a "flagship style system." Instead, the curators affirmed the one university system concept, one that embraced the idea of one system with four distinct universities. Moreover, the board of curators decided to use the designation of "university" rather than "campus" to acknowledge that each institution had developed a greater degree of autonomy than branch campuses in other university systems.

When MU Chancellor Alexander Cartwright was named president of the University of Central Florida in March 2020, however, the board of curators appointed Choi to serve as interim chancellor of the Columbia campus in addition to his role as UM System president. The appointment also came as all four system universities were moving classes online and sending students home for the remainder of the semester due to the coronavirus pandemic. The pandemic was one of the factors that caused the board in July 2020 to make permanent Choi's appointment as president of the UM System and chancellor of the Columbia campus. The board also created a Council of Chancellors, chaired by Choi, to "meet monthly to address challenges and opportunities."

For 150 years, the leaders of the Rolla campus reported to a president in Columbia. Directors, deans, and chancellors have worked with presidents who supported their campus, demeaned their campus, or just ignored their campus. Their fundamental dilemma has been to determine how best to negotiate the fine line between being a strong advocate for MSM, UMR, or S&T as they sought to establish a separate identity for their campus, while acknowledging when they needed to abide by what was best for the overall university. Clearly, the Miner relationship to central administration has been and will remain the most significant enduring challenge for chancellors at Missouri S&T.

1: Chancellor Gary Thomas gained UM System approval for several new degree programs.

2: Interim Chancellor Christopher Maples gained UM System approval to designate S&T a "highly selective" institution.

3: Chancellor John F. Carney III not only eliminated the academic colleges on campus, but also successfully pushed an effort to change the name of the campus to Missouri University of Science and Technology.

4. In July 2020, UM System President Mun Choi was appointed chancellor of the Columbia campus, taking on a dual role discussed for decades.

5: Chancellor Cheryl Schrader completed a comprehensive strategic planning process that led to substantial increases in funding from the UM System.

1

MISSOURI
S&T
2

3

4

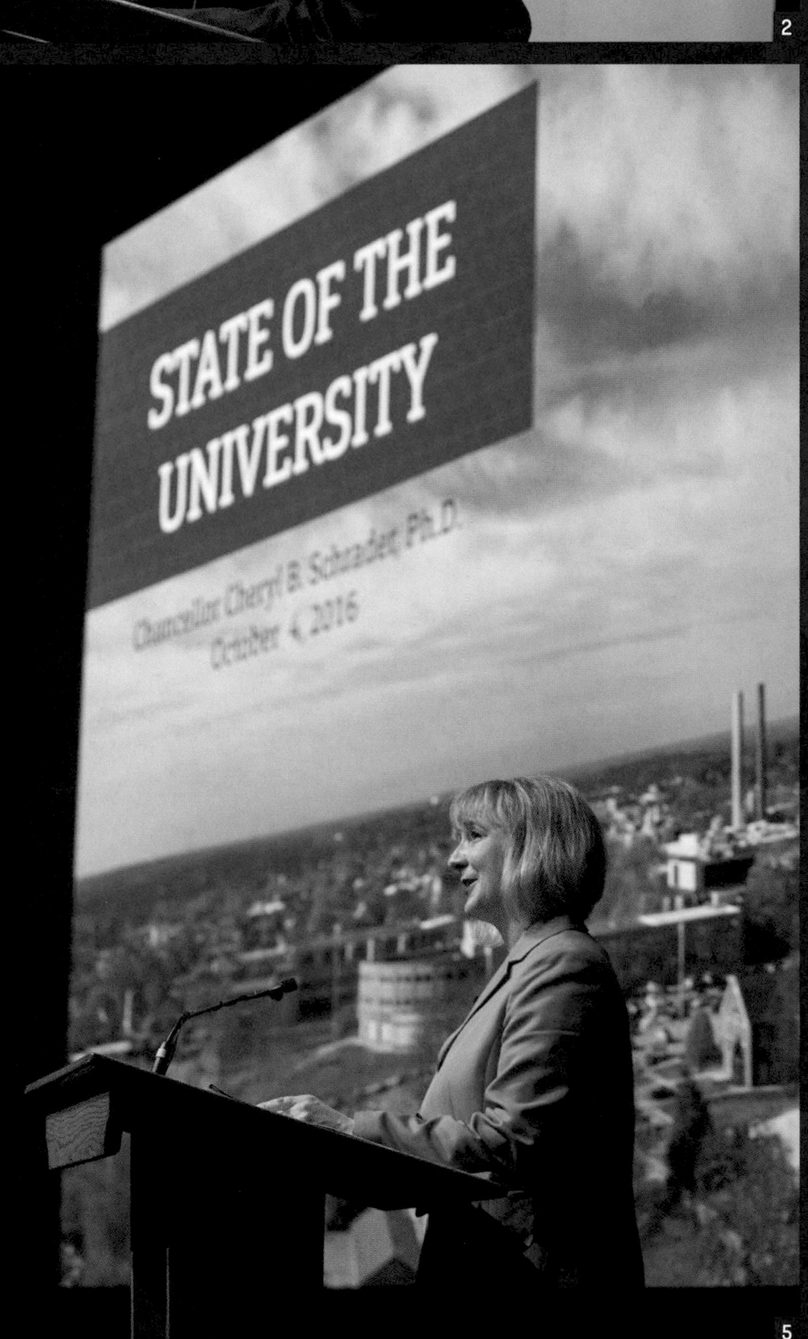
STATE OF THE
UNIVERSITY
Chancellor Cheryl B. Schrader, Ph.D.
October 4, 2016
5

CHAPTER 11

MINER IMPACT

The nearly 75,000 Miner alumni include not just miners, metallurgists, and engineers, but also scientists, entrepreneurs, lawyers, teachers, professors, military officers, philanthropists, and political leaders. Their collective impact has been incalculable. Yet, it is possible to gain an appreciation of the magnitude of their achievements by focusing upon the contributions of a few notable graduates: Daniel C. Jackling, Gary White, and the many Miners who played critical roles in the American space program.

PAGE SIX. THE MISSOURI MINER.

JACKLING TO BUILD U. S. EXPLOSIVE PLANTS.

$90,000,000.00 To Be Expended.

The heart of every friend of the School of Mines will swell with pride as they read the following dispatch from Washington:

Washington, D. C., Dec. 15.—Daniel C. Jackling, of San Francisco, managing director of a group of copper mines producing a large percentage of the copper of the United States, and one of the best known industrial executives in the country, will take charge of the building of the Government's explosive plants.

He will act directly under the authority of the Secretary of War by whom he is appointed.

There is contemplated the expenditure of over $90,000,000 in the erection of explosive plants for the United States Government for the purpose of supplementing the present output of private manufacturers, which, it is calculated, will not be sufficient to meet the Government's future needs.

The St. Louis Republic of Sunday, in commenting upon the number of St. Louisans and Missourians that had been called into the Government service to help Win the War, said:

President Woodrow Wilson has drafted the biggest business men in the United States to organize and direct the business management of the war.

Industrial captains, technical experts and practical men of the most intensive training have volunteered their services to the Government.

$100,000 Man Gives Time to Government for $1.

Daniel C. Jackling, a Missourian by birth, has just been called to Washington to serve the Government as a copper and mining expert. Jackling is rated the greatest copper man in the world. He is giving his services to the Government for the duration of the war for the sum of $1.00.

Jackling succeeded John Hayes Hammond as mining expert to the Guggenheims of the American Smelting Company. He was earning something like $100,000 annually when he retired from the ranks of salaried men to become director in a dozen Western mining, railroad and banking corporations.

It has not been announced in just what capacity Jackling will be used at Washington, but the boys whom he used to teach chemistry and metallurgy at the Missouri School of Mines at Rolla are satisfied his position will be a most important one.

Daniel Cowan Jackling is one of the best known mining engineers in the world. The Utah Copper Company is his crowning achievement. Jackling organized this company in 1903, and has been managing director ever since

Jackling's Rise Like Arabian Nights Story.

Jackling was born near Appleton City, Bates County, Missouri, in 1869. He is a son of Daniel and Lydia (Dunn) Jackling. Educated at Warrensburg Normal and the Missouri School of Mines, he became assistant professor of chemistry and metallurgy of the latter school.

Cripple Creek, the great Colorado gold and silver camp, coaxed young Jackling away from Rolla in 1892. In 1896, when he was placed in charge of the construction and operating department of the Consolidated Mercur gold mines of Utah, Jackling remained with the Mercur mines until 1900. Then he discovered a new process of extracting copper from the discarded ore. This process brought fabulous wealth to the Utah Copper Company, and made it one of the greatest copper properties of the world.

Jackling's history reads like an Arabian Night's dream. After he became a millionaire he returned to Rolla, and donated Jackling Field to the School of Mines. Jackling relinquished the following positions to serve the Government:

Vice-president and managing director Ray Consolidated Copper Company of Arizona, and Chino Copper Company of New Mexico; director, Nevada Northern Railway Company, Alaskan Gold Mines Company, Bingham & Garfield Railway Co., Ray & Gila Valley Railway Company; president. Utah Light and Power Company; director, General Petroleum Company of California: vice-president Utah State National Bank; director, Salt Lake Security and Trust Co., Utah Hotel Operating Company, and Utah Fire Clay Company, and Chase National Bank, New York

Jackling's address of recent years has been Hobart Building, San Francisco.

From the Front.

Dear Lady:
Thank you for the socks;
They were some fit;
I wear one for a helmet,
And one for a mitt.
I would like to meet you
When I have done my bit,
But where in the deuce
Did you learn to knit?

Capt. F. E. Dennie is spending a few days in Rolla.

The staffs of both the *Missouri Miner* and the *Rollamo* frequently included stories of Daniel C. Jackling's many accomplishments.

Left: An original plaque from Jackling Gymnasium now hangs in Hasselmann Alumni House.

Above: Daniel C. Jackling, an 1892 graduate, became known as a pioneer of open-pit copper mining in the early 20th century.

Below: Jackling Gymnasium, completed in 1915, was razed in 1965 to make way for the new library.

DANIEL C. JACKLING

Daniel C. Jackling, the orphaned school boy from Sedalia, Missouri, who graduated from MSM in 1892, became one of the premier mining engineers in the nation over his 50-year career. In 1926, at a gala dinner in New York's Waldorf Hotel, the Mining and Metallurgical Society of America awarded Jackling its prestigious gold medal. One of the speakers that evening called Jackling "the greatest mine-operating executive the world has ever known." Four years later, James W. Gerard, who had served on the New York Supreme Court and as ambassador to Germany, proclaimed that Jackling was one of "the 59 rulers of America." He argued that men like Jackling, Henry Ford, and John D. Rockefeller, because of their "wealth and important industrial positions," were the "actual power behind the throne" in American political life. In 1932, the American Association of Engineering Societies bestowed upon Jackling its highest honor, the John Fritz Medal, which put him in truly elite company. Previous recipients of this honor, dubbed "the highest award in the engineering profession," included Lord Kelvin, George Westinghouse, Alexander Graham Bell, Thomas Edison, Guglielmo Marconi, and Herbert Hoover.

From a poor Missouri farm family, Jackling worked his way through a year of study at the State Normal School in Warrensburg before transferring to MSM in 1889. Jackling enrolled in preparatory courses because, as he later acknowledged, he was "not sufficiently advanced to enter the freshman year of any technical course." However, despite working as a student for chemistry professor Cuthbert Conrad, Jackling was able to graduate in 1892 with a degree in metallurgy. He remained at MSM for a year to teach chemistry, but then headed west where for two years he worked in Colorado and Utah "as a miner, assayer, mill hand and metallurgist in several mining camps." He certainly looked the part. As one contemporary described Jackling, he was "a big, bluff, strapping, red-faced fellow" who "looked like a miner."

While designing and building a gold mill for an investor in Mercur, Utah, Jackling began to explore the possibilities of mining copper ore in nearby Bingham Canyon. As famed financier Bernard Baruch explained, the canyon had a "cavernous gulch of mineralized porphyry rock. Tests showed that this porphyry was impregnated with copper, but the ore was so low in grade that no one seemed to feel that it could be mined profitably." According to Jackling's calculations, each ton of ore would yield 39 pounds of copper. Like his contemporaries, he knew that the traditional underground "tunnel and shaft method" could never yield a profit with the ore having only a two percent copper content. He thus proposed an open-pit approach similar to what had been recently introduced in the Mesabi Iron Range in Minnesota.

PAGE 2

Students Aided by Ten Loan Funds

There are ten different loan funds at the School of Mines from which students may borrow money. These funds have been made available through the generosity and interest of friends and alumni of the school. Some of the funds provide short-term loans of small amounts to assist students who face unexpected expenses which they cannot meet at the moment, but which they can handle after a reasonable delay.

Other funds provide money to enable students to complete their college education while not planning on repayment of the loan until after graduation. From this latter type of fund students may borrow amounts up to as much as a thousand dollars, although the average loan is considerably less. The various loans carry interest rates which vary from as much as 4% per annum downward to interest-free loans. In some cases endorsement of financially responsible persons is required, while in others security is provided by an assigned life insurance policy, and in some cases no security of any sort other than the borrower's signature is required.

In general, a student's borrowing capacity is not very great during his Freshman year and he should not anticipate using the loan funds, other than for short-term emergency loans, during his Freshman year. It is possible for a Sophomore to borrow with a date of repayment after graduation, but such cases are unusual and such loans are not approved except in very unusual cases. During the Junior year the student's borrowing capacity is much greater, but even in that year it is better for the student to conserve his borrowing capacity for his last year or Senior year.

The largest loan fund is the Jackling Fund which was provided by D. C. Jackling, an alumnus of the school. This fund has been in operation since 1909 and has provided almost 1400 loans to students. Other loan funds include the Lawrence R. Hinken Fund, The Fred Fisher Fund, the Alumni Association Loan Fund, the Women's Auxiliary AIME Fund, the Missouri Eastern Star Fund, the Campus Veterans Association Loan Fund, the Rolla Lions Club Loan Fund, the Phi Kappi Loan Fund, and the American Society of Mechanical Engineering Loan Fund. The Lawrence R. Hinken fund was provided by Mr. Hinkin who is an alumnus of the school. The Fred Fisher fund was provided by the family of Mr. Fisher who was a faculty member at the School of Mines prior to his death. Money for the other funds was provided by the organizations whose names are used in describing the funds.

The total amount of money in all of the loan funds is approximately $46,000. A typical year's business shows approximately 300 loans granted, amounting to about $23,500.

All of the school's loan funds are administered by the Business Office under the direction of a faculty loan fund committee of which the Assistant Dean is chairman. This committee receives applications and acts upon them. The Business Office handles all of the business transactions once the loans have been approved by the Loan Fund Committee.

There have been many students who have been able to complete their education at the School of Mines primarily because of the existence of the loan funds, and it is anticipated that this condition will continue down through the years to come.

The greatest impact of Daniel C. Jackling's generosity to the campus came in the form of the Jackling loan fund.

Jackling attracted enough investors to incorporate the Utah Copper Co. in 1903. He continued the underground mining approach until he could implement the open-pit method three years later using high explosives and steam shovels to strip both ore and waste. Railroad cars transported the ore to a mill a few miles away, "where the copper was separated through a flotation process and turned into a concentrate."

The transformation was rapid. By 1908, as historian Charles K. Hyde noted, Jackling "had eight steam shovels and seventeen steam locomotives at work."

The impact of the Jackling approach was extraordinary. In the 12 years following the introduction of steam shovels at the Bingham Canyon Mine, the Utah Copper Co. produced a staggering "billion and a quarter pounds" of copper. By 1963, the total reached 16 billion pounds. At Jackling's death in 1956, his method of processing low-grade copper ore "accounted for more than 60 percent of the world's copper production," according to an article in the *Sacramento Bee*. Historian Timothy LeCain, who has written the most comprehensive study of Jackling, concluded that by the time Jackling retired in 1942, "his Bingham mine and its many imitators had essentially guaranteed the nation would enjoy cheap copper for decades to come, an accomplishment with indisputably profound social and economic consequences."

The state legislature in Utah paid homage to Jackling and his impact on their state by placing a nine-foot bronze statue of him in the state capitol building rotunda. The mere size of the Bingham Canyon mine is an even more impressive monument to Jackling's impact. A half-mile deep and over two miles from rim to rim, the world's largest open pit mine, according to Timothy LeCain, is "unquestionably . . . among the biggest single human-made artifacts on the planet," one that astronauts can see from earth's orbit.

Like many Americans who gained great riches in the late 19th and early 20th centuries, Jackling flaunted his wealth, estimated at $25 million in 1918. A year earlier, Jackling leased the entire top floor of the Hotel St. Francis in San Francisco. And in 1926, he and his wife moved into the even-more luxurious Mark Hopkins Hotel, where they had the top floor converted into a penthouse, which they rented for $1,250 a month.

When Jackling traveled domestically, he did so in a private luxurious rail car. He also loved to travel the world and in 1913 acquired a 267-foot-long yacht to do so in great comfort. As far as journalists could determine, the *Cyprus* was either the fifth- or sixth-largest private yacht in the world. Only the likes of Fred Vanderbilt, wealthy director of the New York Central Railroad; J.P. Morgan Jr., son of the banking baron J.P. Morgan; and

Miners at play on Jackling Field (1909).

Over the years, Jackling shared his success with MSM. In 1909, he gave $1,500 to cover the cost of improving the campus athletic field. More meaningful, in the same year he started the Jackling Loan Fund with a $1,000 gift and regularly added to that figure. By 1951, his support had assisted 1,400 students. Jackling commissioned Jonas Lie to paint 10 scenes of the Bingham Canyon mine, one of which he donated to MSM in 1928. Most importantly, he left $300,000 in his will to 10 universities. Both MSM and Brigham Young University received the most — $100,000 each.

Jackling's successes reflected not just the technical expertise of Miner alumni, but also the drive many of them had to start businesses. In a 1994 issue, the *MSM Alumnus* magazine focused upon their collective entrepreneurial spirit by identifying 250 alumni who had founded over 1,000 companies altogether. Civil engineers had founded the most, with over 250, followed by mechanical engineers, who had founded 200, and electrical engineers, who had founded over 150.

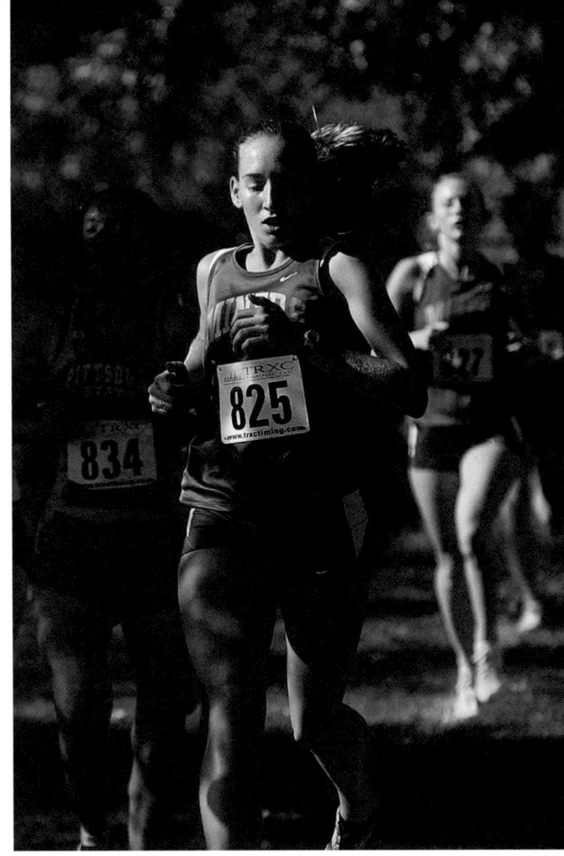

Above: Jackling Jocks Invitational (2014).

Below: Jackling Introduction to Engineering Summer Camp (2019).

James Gordon Bennett Jr., the publisher of the *New York Herald*, could top him. The massive vessel, with two 4,000-horsepower engines, could travel at 19 knots. It took a crew of 50 to serve the many guests he took along on trips. It included 10 bedrooms, each with a private bath. Journalist Millie Robbins wrote shortly after Jackling's death, "the real eye poppers were in the lavish furnishings." There was a "music room, with an open fireplace," "Java teak" paneling, and "Tibetan mahogany" lining the library walls. "Another room was stocked with enough huntin,' shootin,' and fishin' gear to equip a couple of first-rate sporting goods shops."

Jackling eventually commissioned Santa Barbara architect George Washington Smith to design a Spanish Colonial Revival mansion befitting one of the world's most successful mining executives. Smith produced a two-story, 30-room, 17,000-square-foot house with 14 bedrooms on a 90-acre estate located in Woodside, California, midway between San Francisco and San Jose. Along with nearly 21,000 shares of Kennecott Copper stock (Kennecott had purchased Jackling's Utah Copper Co. in 1936), the mansion was a substantial part of his $9 million estate when he died in 1956. Steve Jobs, the Apple guru, purchased the mansion, but had it demolished, arguing that it was "one of the biggest abominations of a house" he had ever seen.

Jackling also attracted his share of critics. Some disparaged him for being "uncompromisingly anti-union." Indeed, in a violent 1912 strike, he drew upon "an 'army' of company deputies" and "professional strikebreakers" to prevent the Western Federation of Miners from organizing the workers at the Bingham Canyon mine, and he never agreed to a contract with unions while he ran the business.

Criticisms of the massive open-pit mine's impact on the environment were more common. Kennecott Copper spent years addressing the "blasted eco-system" caused by decades of open-pit mining. Beyond the pollution of bodies of water and aquifers, smoke from the mine's smelter polluted the air in Salt Lake City. Reclamation efforts continued through the second decade of the 21st century, and reclamation costs were substantial. Some critics like historian Timothy LeCain were particularly harsh. LeCain charged that the responsibility for the "radically scarred and transformed landscapes" of America "lies with Daniel Jackling and the invention of mass destruction technology during the twentieth century."

Above: White co-founded Water.org with actor Matt Damon to work toward solving the world's water crisis.

Below: After graduating with two degrees in civil engineering, White began his career with Catholic Relief Services in New York.

GARY WHITE

In its 2011 list of the 100 most influential people in the world, *Time* magazine included actor Matt Damon and civil engineer Gary White, who had teamed up to address the challenge of "a lack of clean water and sanitation" in many parts of the world. While his endeavors were in a dramatically different field, White's accomplishments were as consequential as Jackling's.

In 1981, White graduated from O'Hara High School in Kansas City, Missouri, a school that instilled in him a deep sense of social justice. As a teen he had been interested in mathematics and science, and when he considered colleges, he knew UMR to be "the" engineering school in Missouri, which made his selection of a university easy. He quickly felt at home in the civil engineering department because professors like Paul Munger and Jerry Bayless were committed to their students. Professor Bobby Wixson, who was the director of the Center for International Programs, introduced White to civil engineering alumnus Gary Lee. A 1971 graduate, Lee had become involved in the Partners in the Americas development program after meeting Wixson at a conference in Washington, D.C. In the early 1980s, Lee had assisted a health clinic associated with Project Hope by drilling wells along the Amazon River to provide clean water.

White also met a Methodist minister named Fred Lamar, who had been the director of the Wesley Foundation at UMR in the late 1960s and early 1970s before becoming the chaplain at Depauw University. In 1984, White joined Lamar and Depauw students on service projects in Guatemala, where they built a dormitory to house people who were taking classes and receiving health care services. There he saw children walking with buckets to a communal drum to get water for their families. He later recalled that this was his epiphany moment: "I can still clearly see the little girl who brought the water and sanitation crisis into striking focus for me. She had a determined expression on her face as she dipped her can into a rusty barrel of contaminated water. Heaving the can into her arms, she walked alongside a stream of open sewage back to her shack. At that moment, I knew what my life was going to be about — bringing safe drinking water to people living without it."

Inspired by the experience, White told a reporter for the *Missouri Miner* that he hoped civil engineering students at UMR could organize such an effort. White's remarks reflected the start of a philosophy that guided his actions over the next three decades, one influenced by his high school experience and interactions with Lee and Lamar. White hoped a UMR program of service projects would provide "a heightened awareness for the students of the problems in developing countries, a realization by the students of the demand

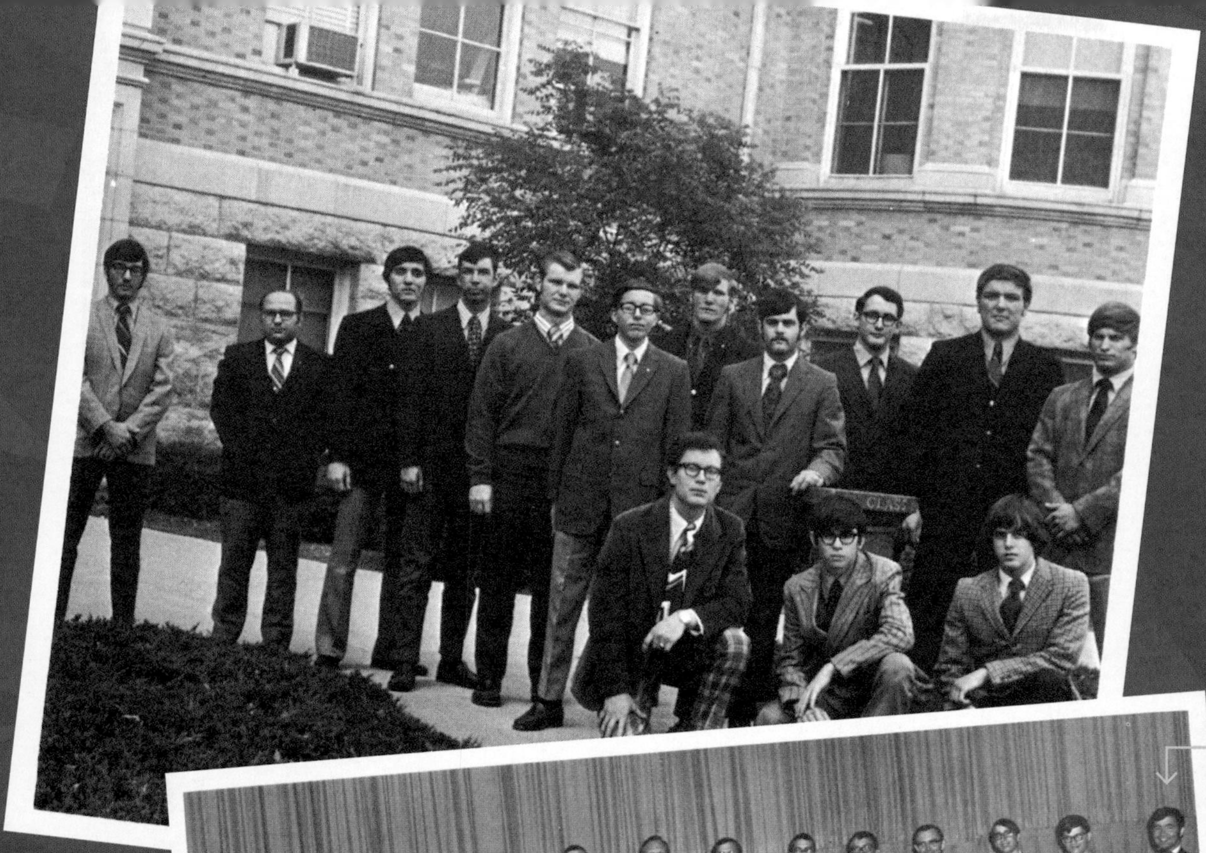

Top left: Gamma Alpha Delta thanked Fred Lamar for his help in service activities (1971).

Middle: Fred Lamar had served as the campus minister for the Wesley Foundation, shown here in 1971, at UMR in the 1960s and 1970s. Lamar was one of Gary White's inspirations for his life work.

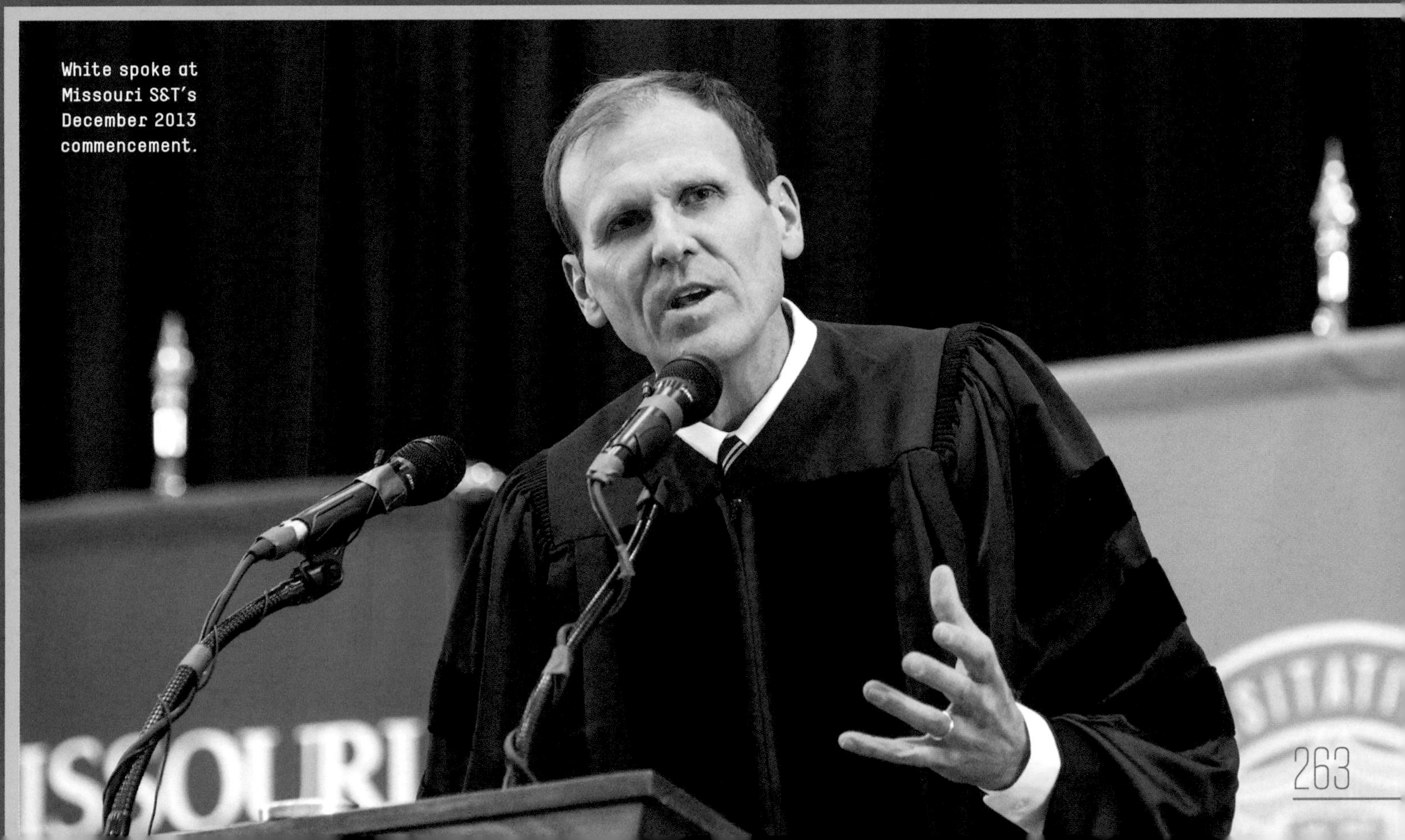

White spoke at Missouri S&T's December 2013 commencement.

Gary White partnered with actor Matt Damon to establish Water.org in 2009.

for engineering in third world countries, and a positive impact in a developing country."

After earning both a bachelor's and master's degree in civil engineering from UMR, White moved to New York to work with Catholic Relief Services, becoming the manager of its Latin-American programs before heading to Chapel Hill to work on a Ph.D. at the University of North Carolina.

With like-minded students he created WaterPartners, a non-profit agency established to improve access to safe water and sanitation. According to journalist Beckie Strum in *Barron's* magazine, White quickly "made himself one of the leading experts" on "tackling the world's water and sanitation crisis." Indeed, leading philanthropic foundations like Pepsico and MasterCard consulted with White on how they could best contribute to the effort.

In 2008, White met Matt Damon at the Clinton Global Initiative. Damon similarly had been interested in promoting greater access to fresh water. He had been the co-founder of H20 Africa but his organization lacked the deep technical experience that White had developed. The following year the two men merged their organizations into Water.org. Damon's celebrity status was critical in giving the organization visibility and in attracting funding while White was developing innovative and effective ways of enabling people to connect to water systems.

The enormity of the challenge drove White and Damon's aggressive effort. A 2017 World Health Organization report revealed that over two billion people had neither "safely managed water" nor "basic sanitation services." Moreover, they discovered that the burden for water collection fell "disproportionately on the women and the girls" in families and, as a consequence, many girls around the globe could not attend school "because they're scavenging for water for their family." Yet, White knew that there was sufficient water on the planet for all. As he explained in 2013, "If every person in the world who currently lacks a safe water supply secured 50 liters of water for daily use, it would take a mere fraction of 1 percent of the world's water resources to provide it."

White had discovered that in many parts of the developing world, people, like those he met in Honduras, relied upon water vendors. It was not uncommon for them to pay a quarter of their income for water. His approach, a sharp departure from traditional philanthropy, was to use the funds raised to make loans of $50 to $200 to individuals, as he explained in 2013, so that they could "gain access to the water or sanitation systems." Then, "as loans are repaid, they can be redeployed to additional people in need of safe water, reducing the need for subsidies." Nearly 100 percent of those who borrowed money repaid their loans.

White and Damon also established WaterEquity and WaterCredit to encourage investors to support "microfinance institutions" in developing regions with an emphasis on "social impact above financial return." Further, they became regular participants at development conferences like the annual World Economic Forum in Davos, Switzerland. To further promote their mission, the duo frequently appeared on morning television and radio network news programs, cable news networks, and late-night talk shows.

Through Water.org White had a greater impact on the world than any other Miner. He helped about a million people in Africa, Central America, and South Asia in the organization's first three years, but the momentum built rapidly. By 2019, the total had reached one million additional people each quarter as White accelerated his efforts to reach his goal of helping provide "universal access to safe water and the dignity of a toilet."

As Daniel Jackling's entrepreneurial success illustrated a trend shared by many Miners, White's extraordinary accomplishments highlighted another important trend. Gary Lee, who had an early impact on White's thinking, continued with significant service. He was involved in helping recover the water system after the massive 1985 earthquake in Mexico City and had assignments with the World Bank to work on projects in Panama, Guatemala, and Nicaragua. Alumni like Richard Arnoldy, a 1969 civil engineering graduate, chaired MicroFinancing Partners in Africa, and Farouk El-Baz, who played such a big role in the Apollo space program, helped the Egyptian government determine the locale of groundwater under the desert. Indeed, reflecting back on a career of monumental achievements, El-Baz said that he derived the greatest satisfaction in helping "find water for the people who needed it the most." The campus, led by civil engineering Professor Richard Stephenson, established a student chapter of Engineers Without Borders in 2005, just three years after the international organization was founded. The Missouri S&T chapter, the first EWB chapter formed in Missouri, has worked on water quality projects in Bolivia, Ecuador, Guatemala, and Honduras.

missouri m

Wednesday, Feb. 5, 1986 University of Missouri-Rolla

Twenty Pages

Engineering students aid developing countries

By Mella J. Sage
News Editor

Gary White, a senior majoring in civil engineering at UMR, recently returned from Guatemala where he participated in a project that uses college students to aid developing countries.

White went to Guatemala with a group from Depauw University who built a dormitory in a small village. "The dorm was built to provide a place to stay for people who come to the village for classes and health care services among other things," said White.

White's participation in the Guatemala project is the first step in what is hoped to be a program that will enable several students to participate in similar projects. "Presently, we are working through Depauw University because they are established in this type of program," said White. "But, eventually, we hope to make a networking system that an international agency could contact that would in turn put them in touch with qualified students who are interested in a particular area," he added.

Also working on this program are Dr. Jerry Bayless, acting chairman and associate professor of civil engineering at UMR; Dr. Paul Munger, professor of civil engineering and director of the Institute of River Studies at UMR; and Dr. Bobby Wixson, dean of International Programs and Studies at UMR. These three, along with White, have been working on this program since last fall. "We tentatively hope to send 8 to 12 studends on a similar project in Jan. 1987," said White. "A proposal will be submitted to the American Society of Civil Engineers (ASCE) requesting them to begin funding of the program in Jan. 1987. If it succeeds, it, along with a little fund raising by the students participating in the program should allow sufficient funding so that there will be no out-of-pocket expenditure by the student," said White.

The program is chiefly for civil engineering students due to the nature of the work. A civil engineering course will be required in the fall for those who will be participating in the tentative project in Jan. 1987. "We hope to have the students who will be participating in the program chosen by the end of this semester," said White.

The benefits of the program, according to White, are: a heightened awareness for the students of the problems in developing countries, a realization by the students of the demand for engineering in third world companies, and a positive impact in a developing country.

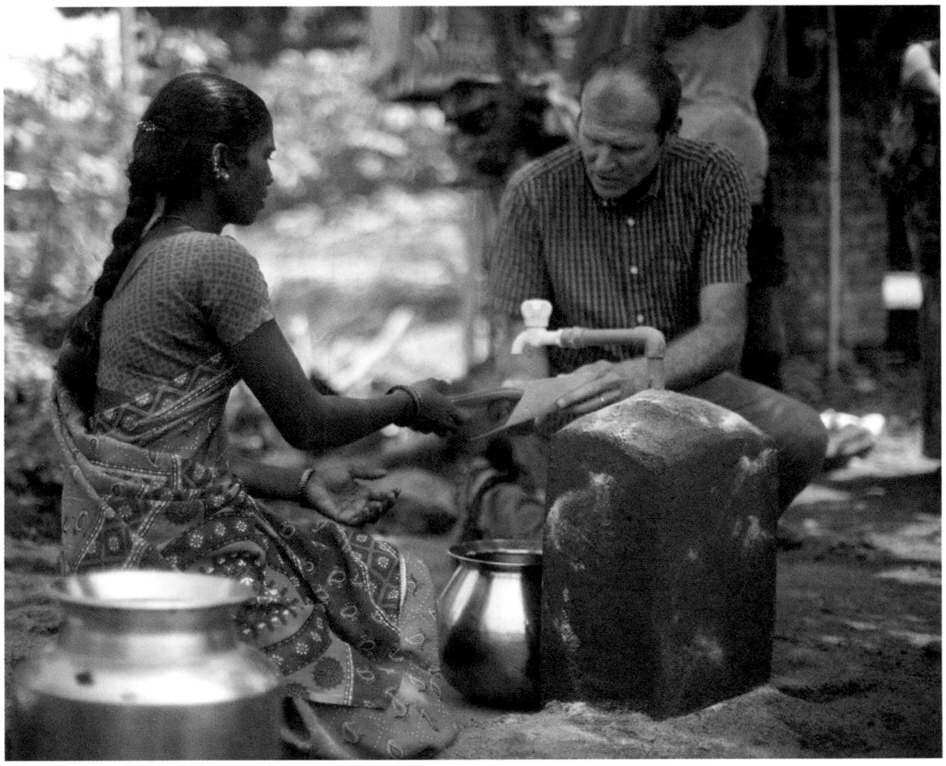

Above: After a service project in Guatemala, Gary White called upon UMR engineering students to join in this effort.

Left: Water.org's efforts have allowed millions of people to gain access to safe water and sanitation systems.

Above: A 1941 MSM graduate, Demarquis Wyatt joined NASA in 1958, and eventually became deputy director to Wernher Von Braun, who was in charge of long-range planning.

Right: George Mueller (center) and mission officials following the successful *Apollo 11* launch.

Below: A 1939 MSM graduate, George Mueller was in charge of human space flight for several years in the 1960s.

THE MINER CONNECTION WITH NASA

The Soviet Union's 1957 launch of a satellite named *Sputnik* prompted President Dwight Eisenhower and congressional leaders to push for the creation of the National Aeronautics and Space Administration (NASA) a year later. Two of its missions were to expand "human knowledge of phenomena in the atmosphere and space" and to develop "vehicles capable of carrying instruments, equipment, supplies and living organisms through space." Miners were involved in the space program from the agency's earliest days.

Demarquis Wyatt, who had earned a degree in mechanical engineering from MSM in 1941, worked at the National Advisory Committee in Cleveland during World War II. In 1945, Wyatt became head of a research section devoted to testing aerodynamics in supersonic wind tunnels. He joined NASA in 1958 as the technical assistant to the director of space flight programs. Three years later, Wyatt became director of programs with the responsibility of developing financial control programs. He also served as assistant administrator for programming. Late in his tenure at NASA, Wyatt became deputy to Wernher Von Braun, who was in charge of the agency's long-range planning, a post Wyatt held until his retirement in 1973. He was hailed as one of the "pioneer administrators" at NASA when he died in 1996.

George Mueller, who graduated from MSM in 1939 with a degree in electrical engineering, played a critical role in the success of the Apollo program. When he died in 2015, most of the world's press characterized him as "a coolly decisive engineer, scientist and administrator who was given much credit for enabling NASA to meet President John F. Kennedy's manned moon-landing timetable."

After graduating from MSM, Mueller went on to earn a master's degree at Purdue and a Ph.D. at Ohio State, both in electrical engineering. He worked for a time at the Bell Labs in New Jersey and on the faculty of Ohio State University before joining Ramo Wooldridge Corp., where he worked on missile guidance systems.

In 1963, Mueller became an associate administrator at NASA and was in charge of human space flight through 1969. To more effectively manage the burgeoning space program, Mueller placed the management of three centers under his office in Washington, D.C.: the George C. Marshall Space Flight Center in Huntsville, Alabama; the Manned Space Center in Houston, Texas; and the John F. Kennedy Space Center in Cape Canaveral, Florida.

Ron Epps and the Columbia (STS-1) flight control team.

Farouk El-Baz, who earned both a master's degree and a Ph.D. in geology, joined NASA in 1967 and served as secretary of the landing site selection committee for the *Apollo 11* flight.

He oversaw not only the conclusion of the Gemini program (space flight with two astronauts), but also the successful moon landing of *Apollo 11*. Before stepping down, Mueller became an advocate of what journalist Robert Z. Pearlman called "an orbital workshop," one that could be served by a "reusable transportation system." Thus, Mueller is credited with the idea of *Skylab* and the space shuttle.

Ron Epps, a 1967 physics graduate, spent 39 years with NASA. His initial work was as a technical advisor on the recovery of the spacecraft after Apollo flights. For a dozen years Epps was a flight dynamics officer at Mission Control, and he trained astronauts preparing for shuttle missions. When he retired, Epps was the chief of Flight Design and Dynamics Division, which supported the shuttle and space station programs. In reflecting on his experiences at NASA, Epps emphasized the achievements of the Apollo program, which he called "a technical marvel." Indeed, he did not believe that "any group of talented individuals has ever done so much for the country outside of wartime."

Farouk El-Baz was one of the "talented individuals" Epps mentioned. El-Baz had a bachelor's degree in geology and chemistry from Ain Shams University in Egypt. With support from the Egyptian government, he traveled to Rolla, where he obtained both a master's degree (1961) and a Ph.D. (1964) in geology.

After teaching a year at Heidelberg University in Germany and another year working for an oil company, El-Baz joined NASA in 1967, where he began work on the Apollo program. Specifically, he was secretary of the landing site selection committee for the *Apollo 11* mission in 1969, and his team was responsible for determining the ideal landing site for that historic mission. He gained popular notoriety through the HBO series *From the Earth to the Moon*, which included a segment titled "The Brain of Farouk El-Baz," and the television series *Star Trek: The Next Generation*, which featured a shuttlecraft named the *El-Baz* in his honor.

Several other Miner alumni worked at NASA during the Gemini and Apollo years, notably three electrical engineers. Ronald Lawrence, a 1960 graduate, worked on the Gemini program; Bob Pulley, a 1962 graduate, worked on the guidance and navigation systems of the *Saturn V* vehicle at the Marshall Space Center in Alabama; and Irving Wheeler, a 1964 graduate, was on the launch team for both Apollo and *Skylab*.

Three Miner astronauts gave the campus the greatest visibility. After obtaining a degree in mathematics at UMR in 1973, Tom Akers returned to his hometown of Eminence, Missouri, where he became the high school principal. At the end of a five-year stint in education, Akers joined the Air Force, where he became a missile data analyst, and, after being accepted into

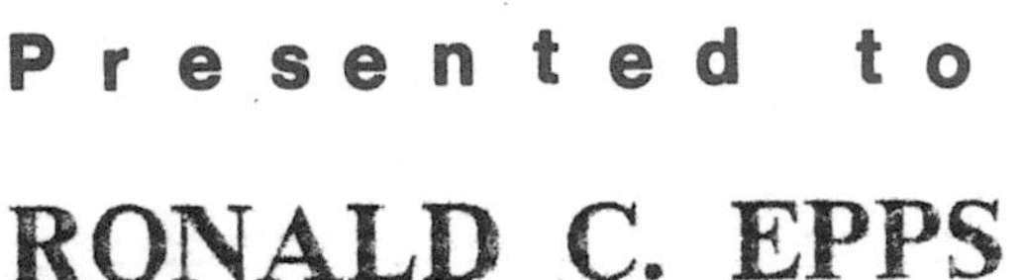

P r e s e n t e d   t o

RONALD C. EPPS

This flag was flown aboard
Space Shuttle **"Columbia"** (STS-1)
April 12 - 14, 1981.
It is presented to you in
recognition of the significant
contribution you made to the
success of the mission.

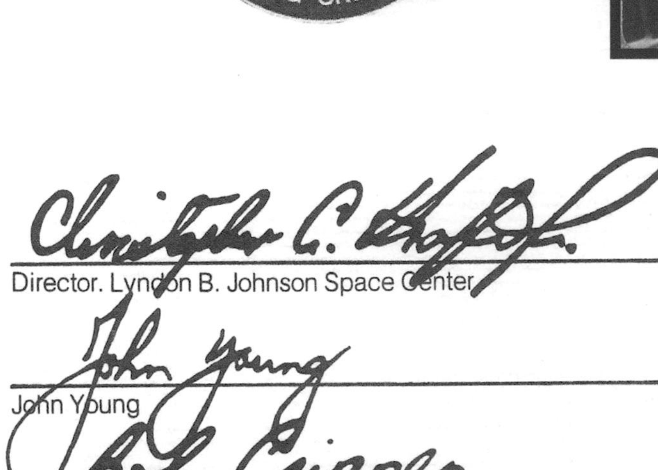

Director. Lyndon B. Johnson Space Center

John Young

Robert Crippen

Opposite: One of many awards of recognition Ron Epps received during his 38-year career with NASA.

Above: Ron Epps, a 1967 physics graduate.

Top right: On the third of his four missions, Tom Akers was part of a team that repaired the Hubble Space Telescope.

Bottom right: Tom Akers, a 1973 mathematics graduate, became UMR's first astronaut.

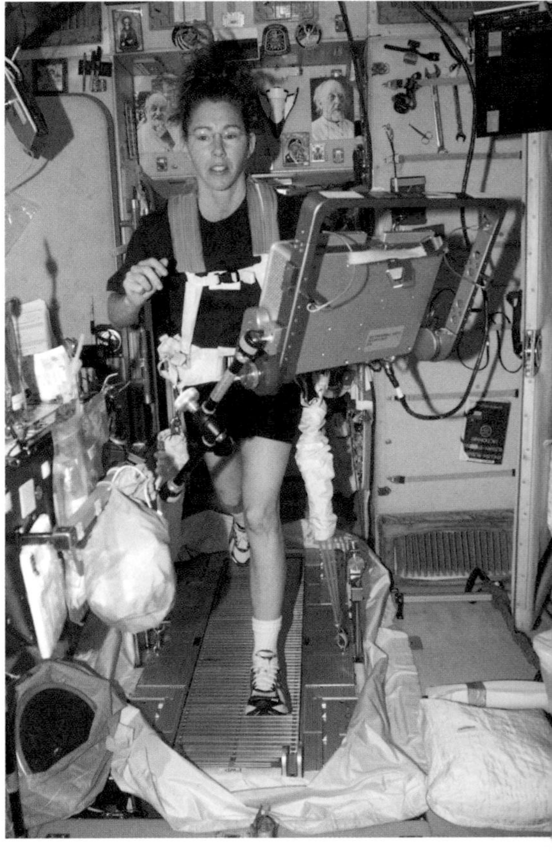

Top left: Janet Kavandi flew on three space flights and served as director of flight crew operations at the Johnson Space Center in Houston.

Above: Sandra Magnus, who earned a bachelor's degree in physics and a master's degree in electrical engineering, maintained a Missouri S&T blog during a four-month-long mission on the International Space Station.

Bottom left: Astronaut Janet Kavandi, who earned a master's degree in chemistry at UMR in 1982, is pictured with President Barack Obama and his family.

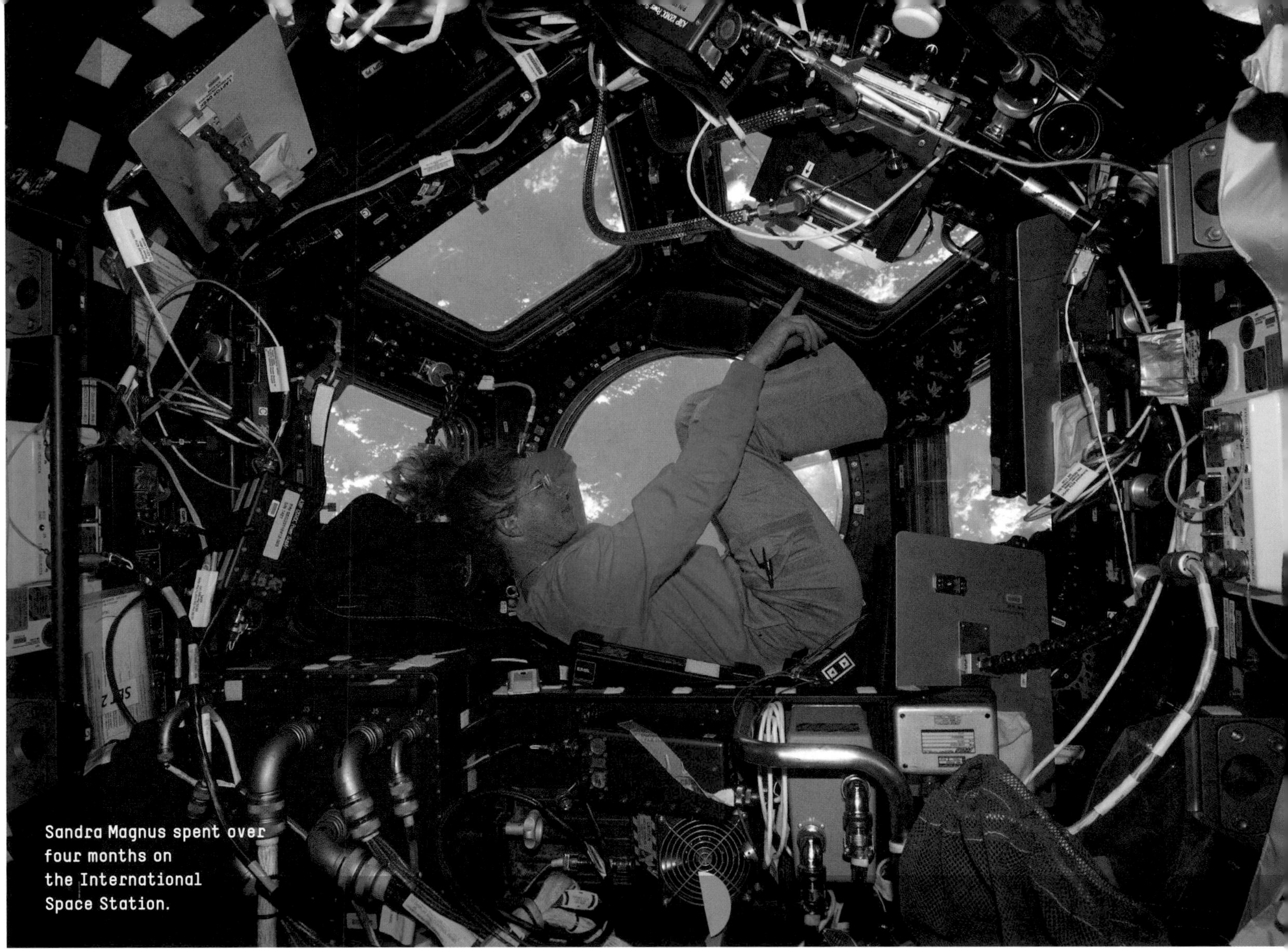

Sandra Magnus spent over four months on the International Space Station.

test pilot school in 1982, flew backseat in F-4s, F-15s, and T-3s as an engineer working on weapons development programs. In 1987, Akers was accepted for the astronaut program and flew on four shuttle missions. In his second mission, Akers was part of the first three-astronaut spacewalk to repair the Intelsat (International Telecommunications Satellite). During his third mission he was part of the team that repaired the famed Hubble Space Telescope. Akers' last mission involved a rendezvous with *Mir*, the Russian space station. He left the astronaut program in 1997 and returned to UMR, first as commander of the Air Force ROTC detachment and then for 11 years as a professor of mathematics.

A graduate of Carthage High School and Missouri Southern State University, Janet Kavandi earned a master's degree in chemistry from UMR in 1982. After working two years at Eagle-Picher Industries in Joplin in battery development, Kavandi moved on to Boeing in Seattle and earned a Ph.D. in analytical chemistry from the University of Washington in 1990. When she applied to be a part of the astronaut corps, fellow Miner Tom Akers was on the interview team. She was accepted in 1994 and subsequently flew on three space flights between 1998 and 2001. Her first was the last docking mission with *Mir*. Kavandi continued to play a critical role for NASA, serving as director of flight crew operations at the Johnson Space Center in Houston and then as director of the John H. Glenn Research Center in Cleveland.

Sandra Magnus received both a bachelor's degree in physics and a master's degree in electrical engineering at UMR before earning a Ph.D. at Georgia Tech in 1996, the year she joined NASA. Between 2002 and 2011, Magnus was on three flights, including a four-and-a-half-month mission on the International Space Station, where she served as a science officer and engineer. During her 50-million-mile voyage, which was focused upon expanding the station to accommodate a six-person crew, Magnus frequently updated a Missouri S&T blog. Shortly after her final flight, which was also the final shuttle mission, Magnus briefly served as deputy chief of the astronaut office before being appointed executive director of the American Institute of Aeronautics and Astronautics.

Sandra Magnus.

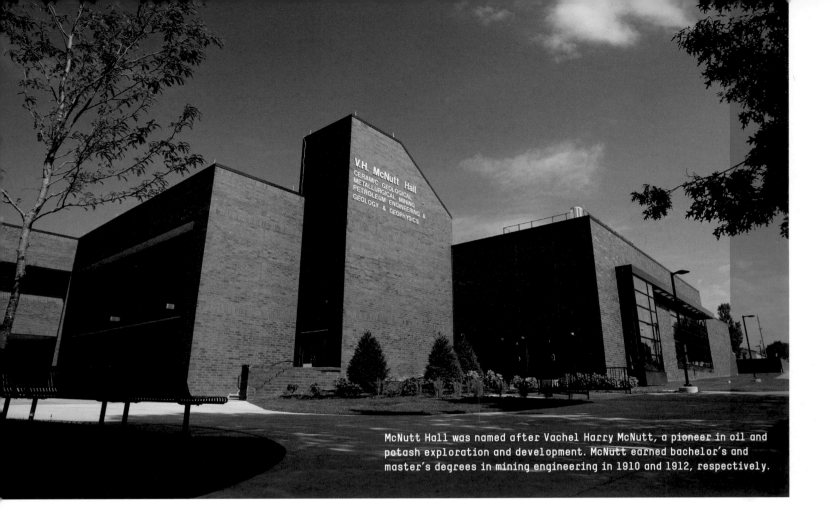

McNutt Hall was named after Vachel Harry McNutt, a pioneer in oil and potash exploration and development. McNutt earned bachelor's and master's degrees in mining engineering in 1910 and 1912, respectively.

Vachel McNutt, who discovered the first commercial potash deposits in the Western Hemisphere, was inducted into the National Mining Hall of Fame.

MINERS WHO MADE AN IMPACT

Gustavus A. Duncan

MSM's first student, Duncan was an 1874 graduate with a degree in civil engineering. Through the late 1920s Duncan was a prominent mine owner and consultant in Minnesota, South Dakota, Utah, and Nevada who secured five patents.

George Easley

Easley graduated in 1909 with a bachelor's degree in mining engineering. In Bolivia, he became a pioneer of tungsten mining and was a consulting engineer for many other mines in Mexico, Central America, South America, and the United States before becoming president of both the Mining and Metallurgical Society of America and the Mining Club of New York.

Hector Boza

A native of Peru, Boza graduated in 1911 with a bachelor's degree in mining engineering. He became one of the leading mine operators in his home country and an important political leader. He served in the cabinet of President Oscar Benavides, as president of the Peruvian senate, and Peru's delegate to the United Nations.

Eva Endurance Hirdler

Hirdler graduated in 1911 with a bachelor's degree in science. Although she had a successful mining engineering career, Hirdler's greatest impact was as a symbol of the unwavering opposition of MSM to grant her a degree in mining engineering even though she had met all the degree requirements.

Mervin J. Kelly

After graduating in 1914 with a bachelor's degree in general science, Kelly earned a Ph.D. at the University of Chicago. In the 1920s, at AT&T Bell Laboratories, Kelly's work on vacuum amplifying tubes led to the first trans-oceanic telephone call. A member of the National Academy of Sciences, he became first president and then chairman of the board of Bell Laboratories.

Enoch Needles

Needles graduated in 1914 with a degree in civil engineering. A partner in a major bridge engineering firm, he supervised the design of several large and movable bridges throughout the country. He served as president of the American Society of Civil Engineers and was a key advocate for the 1956 legislation that created the interstate highway system.

Karl and Marjory Hasselmann.

Above: Eva Endurance Hirdler became the first woman to graduate from Rolla after pursuing a technical course of study.

Below: Mervin J. Kelly, a 1914 graduate in general sciences.

Vachel McNutt

McNutt earned both a bachelor's degree (1910) and master's degree (1912) in mining engineering. Beyond significant oil discoveries in Kansas and New Mexico, McNutt discovered the first commercial potash deposits in the Western Hemisphere near Carlsbad, New Mexico. He was inducted into the National Mining Hall of Fame. His wife, Amy Shelton McNutt, became a major benefactor of UMR.

Walter Remmers

With both a bachelor's degree (1923) and a master's degree (1924) in metallurgical engineering, Remmers was on the faculty at Washington University before working at Western Electric. He spent the bulk of his career with Union Carbide, becoming vice president before retiring. He and his wife, Miriam, provided the funding for the Remmers Special Artist/Lecturer Series.

Harry Kessler

After earning a bachelor's degree in metallurgical engineering in 1924, Kessler developed an improved process for metal casting and became a consultant for foundries around the country. Besides the notoriety of being the nation's leading foundry trouble-shooter, Kessler was known by millions of boxing fans as a referee on the nationally televised "Friday Night Fights" from Madison Square Garden in New York.

Karl Hasselmann

Hasselmann earned a bachelor's degree in 1925 and became a field geologist in Europe for almost a decade. When he returned to the United States, Hasselmann founded Salt Dome Oil Corp. and became a leader in the development of offshore oil fields. He served as president of the Miner Alumni Association, and a bequest from his estate provided funding for Hasselmann Alumni House.

Walter P. Leber

Leber graduated in 1940 with a bachelor's degree in petroleum engineering. In the Army Corps of Engineers for 35 years, Leber served in World War II and Korea. He was the Ohio River Division Commander of the Corps of Engineers before becoming the governor of the Panama Canal Zone in 1967, a post he held for four years.

Robert Bay (right), a 1949 civil engineering graduate.

Bob Brackbill receiving an honorary degree in 1983.

Bob Brackbill

Brackbill graduated with a bachelor's degree in mining engineering in 1942. After serving in World War II with a B-17 bomber group, he became a leader in offshore oil exploration in Thailand and the Philippines. After a 20-year career with Shell Oil Corp., Brackbill became the president and chairman of the board of Texas Pacific Oil.

Robert Bay

A World War II veteran, Bay earned a bachelor's degree in civil engineering in 1949. After serving in the St. Louis District of the Army Corps of Engineers, Bay worked for Laclede Steel Co. where he helped develop a composite steel joist system for the World Trade Center in New York. With Black and Veatch, Bay worked on wastewater systems from Los Angeles to Cairo, Egypt. In 1985, he served as the national president of the American Society of Civil Engineers.

John Toomey

A Navy pilot in World War II, Toomey earned a bachelor's degree (1949) and a master's degree (1951) in mechanical engineering. In 1959, he established VSE Corp., a federal government services company, in

Alexandria, Virginia. His gift of $5 million for the renovation of the mechanical and aerospace engineering building was one of the largest to an academic unit in the campus's history.

Thomas Holmes

After serving in World War II as a Navy pilot, Holmes earned a bachelor's degree in mining engineering in 1950. He went to work for Ingersoll Rand Co., which manufactured industrial machinery, and worked his way up to chair, president, and CEO of the company before stepping down in 1988. He served on the board of directors of several other companies and as interim CEO of W.R. Grace & Co.

Richard Stegemeier

Stegemeier graduated with a bachelor's degree in petroleum engineering in 1950 and began working for Unocal Corp. the following year. He worked his way through the ranks, becoming the chairman, president, and chief executive officer between 1988 and 1995. A leader in discovering new oil fields and the holder of seven patents, he was elected a member of the National Academy of Engineering.

Vernon Jones

Jones, a Korean War veteran, graduated with a bachelor's degree in civil engineering in 1953. His career began with City Service Oil Co., but he later joined Explorer Pipeline Co. where he became president and chief executive officer before moving on to become president of Williams Pipeline Co. and then president of the parent Williams Companies.

Ed Tuck

Tuck, a 1953 graduate with a bachelor's degree in electrical engineering, was a quintessential entrepreneur who started many companies, including serving as the principal in the investment firm Falcon Fund. The holder of a dozen patents, Tuck was a strong supporter of private space flight.

Above: Ed Tuck, a 1953 electrical engineering graduate.

Below: John and Mary Toomey. John earned bachelor's and master's degrees in mechanical engineering in 1949 and 1951, respectively.

Toomey Hall.

Above: Fred Kummer, a 1955 civil engineering graduate.

Below: Delbert Day, a 1958 ceramic engineering graduate.

Below right: The Delbert Day Cancer Institute in Rolla was named in honor of the 1958 graduate and innovator.

Fred Kummer

A 1955 graduate with a bachelor's degree in civil engineering, Kummer founded Hospital Building and Equipment (HBE) five years later. While building hundreds of hospitals across the nation, Kummer also began the Adam's Mark Hotels and Resorts, a chain of two dozen properties that he sold in 2008. Through a lead gift from Kummer, S&T established the Kummer Student Design Center.

Delbert Day

In 1958, Day earned a bachelor's degree in ceramic engineering and then launched a more than six-decade-long academic career. The many accomplishments of this member of the National Academy of Engineering and holder of more than 50 patents include the development of radioactive glass microspheres to treat liver cancer.

Dick Vitek

Vitek earned a master's degree in chemistry in 1958 and became a research scientist for the Atomic Energy Commission and Aldrich Chemical Co. Vitek then founded three companies, including Fotodyne Inc., which manufactured lab instruments for DNA research. He also developed UV imaging instruments that could analyze oil spills as well as a method to test arsenic levels in wine.

Jerry Bayless

After earning a bachelor's degree (1959) and a master's degree (1962) in civil engineering, Bayless served on the faculty for over 50 years. He was the department's advisor to freshmen and transfer students, and assistant to the department chair. He also served as assistant and associate dean of the College of Engineering, all the while becoming an iconic figure on campus known by thousands of students.

Don Gunther

In 1960, Gunther earned a bachelor's degree in civil engineering and went to work for Bechtel, the world's largest construction company. He began by building fertilizer plants but eventually had the opportunity to manage the construction of the massive Syncrude refinery in Alberta, Canada. Before retiring, Gunther directed the international division of the Bechtel Group.

Bipin Doshi

After earning both a bachelor's degree (1962) and a master's degree (1963) in chemical engineering, Doshi worked as a research scientist for Uniroyal, rising to the vice presidency of a subsidiary. In 1988, he purchased Schafer Gear Works in South Bend, Indiana, and remained president and chief executive officer for over three decades while purchasing six other companies.

Left: Bipin Doshi spoke at S&T's 2019 Commencement.

Above: Don Gunther, a 1960 civil engineering graduate.

Below: Jerry Bayless, known by many as "Mr. MSM," "Mr. UMR," "Mr. S&T" or simply as "Mr. Miner," poses with Joe Miner.

Above: Jim Bertelsmeyer, a 1966 chemical engineering graduate.

Right: Chemical Engineering lab in Bertelsmeyer Hall.

Below: Matt Coco, a 1966 civil engineering graduate.

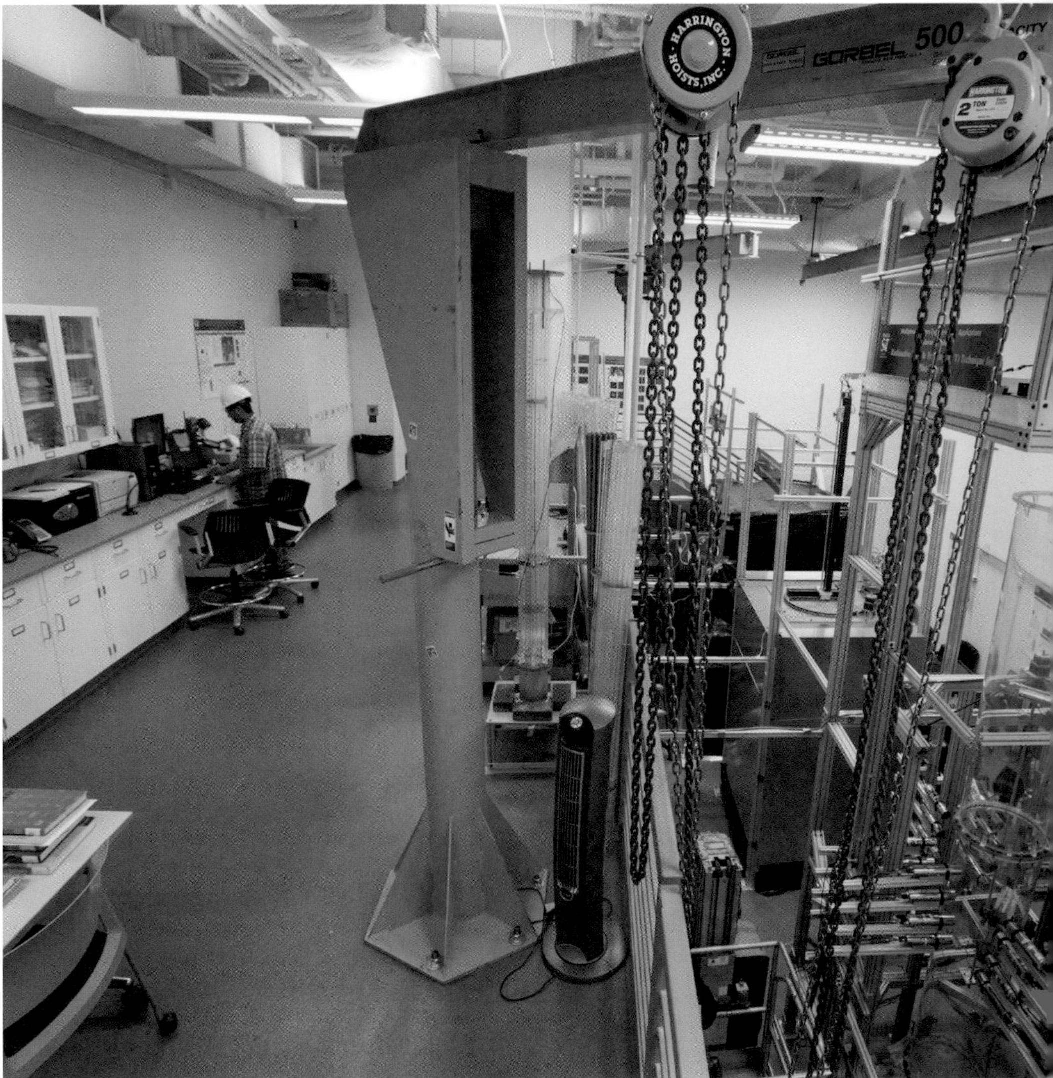

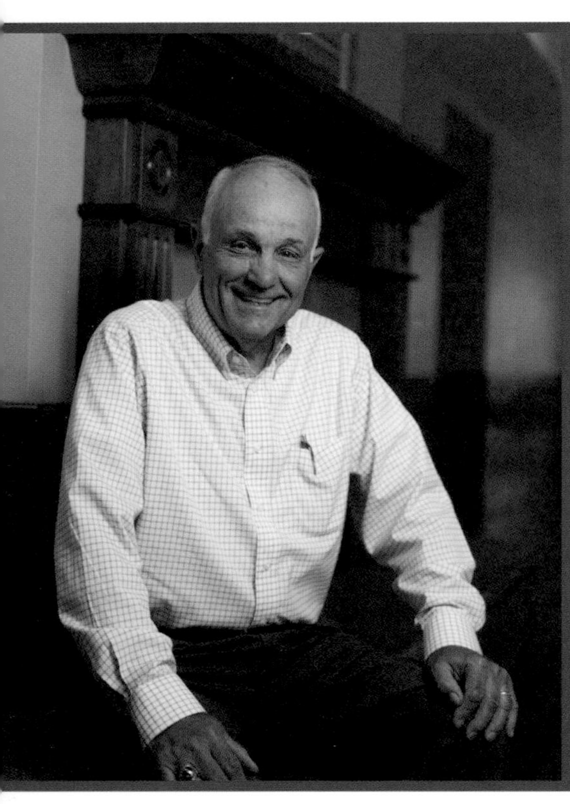

Gary Havener

After earning a bachelor's degree in applied mathematics in 1962, Havener served four years in the Army Corps of Engineers before going to work for an antenna manufacturer in Texas. He became a successful "multipreneur," turning failing companies into successes. He was president of Phazar Corp., a major manufacturer of small cell antenna. Through his lead donation, UMR opened the Havener Center in 2005.

Keith Bailey

Bailey earned a bachelor's degree in mechanical engineering in 1964 and began working for Continental Pipe Line. He joined the Williams Companies in 1973 as an assistant to the vice president. Twenty-one years later, Bailey became the chairman and chief executive officer of the integrated natural gas company that had over 4,000 employees.

Philip Chen

With a 1965 master's degree in mechanical engineering, Chen worked for Xerox Corp. and later for Microtek. A researcher at the two firms, he developed high-speed printers, optical disc drives, and image scanners while he secured several patents. He later established his own company, Avision Inc.

Roger Dorf

Dorf went to work at IBM after earning a bachelor's degree in mechanical engineering in 1965. He eventually held leadership roles in several companies, becoming the general manager and vice president of Cisco Systems Broadband Wireless Group. Helping to take wireless networking to developing nations was the most notable among his achievements.

Opening Week 2017 on the Havener Center lawn.

Jim Bertelsmeyer

A 1966 graduate with a bachelor's degree in chemical engineering, Bertelsmeyer began his career in Conoco's gas and pipeline divisions. He later became president of Buckeye Gas Products before founding Heritage Propane Corp., one of the nation's largest propane companies. He also served as president of the National Propane Gas Association. His $5 million gift to Missouri S&T led to the construction of a new chemical engineering building, named in his honor.

Matt Coco

In 1966, Coco graduated with a bachelor's degree in civil engineering and went to work for St. Louis-based Alberici Constructors. He remained there for his entire career, retiring as vice president of the building division. After working on hundreds of projects for Alberici, Coco volunteered as the project manager on the construction of Hasselmann Alumni House.

Roy Wilkins

Wilkins earned a bachelor's degree in electrical engineering in 1966. He worked for many companies and started one of his own, WilTel, which was a business firm in the Williams Companies in Tulsa. Notably, he used decommissioned gas and oil pipelines to establish a national fiber optic network. Wilkins retired as chairman at Adaption Technologies, a company he co-founded.

Jon Bereisa

With a bachelor's degree (1967) and a master's degree (1970) in electrical engineering, Bereisa went to General Motors and was the systems architect for an extended-range electric vehicle called the Volt. He also directed GM's development of hydrogen fuel technology and the company's application of microcomputer chip technology. He later became the president and chief executive officer of a company called Auto Lectrification.

Gary Havener, a 1962 mathematics graduate.

1: John Mathes, who earned bachelor's and master's degrees in civil engineering in 1967 and 1968, respectively.

2: Dick Arnoldy (left) pictured with Chancellor John F. Carney III.

3: Bob Brinkmann, a 1971 civil engineering graduate.

Right: Eugene D. Jackson shown here with the founding members of the Epsilon Psi chapter of Alpha Phi Alpha.

Above: Joe Ballard, who earned a master's degree in engineering management in 1972.

Below: Gary Forsee, a 1972 civil engineering graduate.

Eugene D. Jackson

One of the founding members of the Epsilon Psi chapter of Alpha Phi Alpha, Jackson earned a bachelor's degree in electrical engineering in 1967. A telecommunications entrepreneur, in 1972 Jackson established the National Black Network, the first Black-owned national radio network. He also became the first Black member of the board of directors of the National Association of Broadcasters.

John Mathes

Mathes earned a bachelor's degree (1967) and a master's degree (1968) in civil engineering. He established John Mathes and Associates, a multidisciplinary consulting firm that dealt with a range of contamination problems from groundwater investigation to hazardous waste projects. After Burlington Environmental purchased the firm, Mathes continued to lead operations through 1992. He also served on the University of Missouri board of curators.

Ted Weise

After graduating in 1967 with a bachelor's degree in electrical engineering, Weise was one of the first employees for a new company, Federal Express. He established the company's hub at the Memphis International Airport. Initially, the start-up used small business jets, but when Weise retired as president and chief executive officer of the mammoth global company, they were using Boeing 727 and 777 planes to carry FedEx cargo.

Dick Arnoldy

Arnoldy earned both a bachelor's degree (1969) in civil engineering and a master's degree in engineering management (1973). During his career he served as president of two major St. Louis construction companies, R.W. Murray and ARCO, which he co-founded in 1992 with fellow Miner alumnus Jeff Cook, who also earned a master's degree in engineering management.

Bob Brinkmann

Brinkmann's first job was with the Illinois Department of Transportation after earning a bachelor's degree in civil engineering in 1971. He then worked for several construction companies before founding R.G. Brinkmann Co. in 1984. In the subsequent quarter century, Brinkman Constructors completed projects worth $3 billion in 30 states.

John Fairbanks

After earning a bachelor's degree in electrical engineering in 1971, Fairbanks went to work for Texas Instruments, which was beginning to develop calculators. In 1987, he and some co-workers from Texas Instruments formed Poqet Computer where they built the first sub-notebook computer using voltage and frequency scaling to save power.

Joe Ballard

In 1972, Ballard earned a master's degree in engineering management. He led a storied career in the U.S. Army, serving as the first African-American commander of the Army Corps of Engineers in 1996. Two years later, the lieutenant general was named "Black Engineer of the Year" at the annual Black Engineer of the Year Awards Conference.

Gary Forsee

A 1972 graduate with a bachelor's degree in civil engineering, Forsee held several executive positions in telecommunications companies, including president and chief executive of Sprint Nextel. His career took a dramatic turn when he became president of the four-campus University of Missouri System in 2008, a position he held for three years.

1: Mariana Rodrigues, a 1980 civil engineering graduate.

2: Joan Woodard, a 1973 mathematics graduate.

3: Jack Dorsey, who attended UMR in the 1990s.

4: Steve Sullivan, a 1989 electrical engineering graduate.

Above left: 2019 Woman of the Year Kathleen Sheppard (front row, third from left) pictured with past award recipients. The award was created by Cindy Tang (above).

Below: Zeb Nash, a 1972 chemical engineering graduate.

Zebulun Nash

Nash earned a bachelor's degree in chemical engineering in 1972 and went on to a career with ExxonMobil, where he held several executive positions including as site manager for its chemical plant in Baytown, Texas. Before beginning that career in 1979, Nash spent two years in the Peace Corps in Kenya.

Joan Woodard

A year after earning a bachelor's degree in applied mathematics and computer science in 1973, Woodard joined Sandia National Laboratories, where she had a 36-year career. Among a host of leadership positions, she served for over a decade as the executive vice president and deputy laboratories director.

Mariana Rodriguez

A native of Peru, Rodriguez earned a bachelor's degree in civil engineering in 1980. She became a higher education leader in Peru, establishing four institutes and universities including Cibertec, Universidad Peruana de Ciencias Aplicadas, Instituto Tecnologico del Norte, and the Universidad Privada del Norte.

Cindy Tang

In 1985, Tang earned a bachelor's degree in economics. She founded an entrepreneurial software consulting firm called Insight Industries Inc. in Wisconsin. She also was an "angel investor" for innovative businesses. Tang also established the Woman of the Year award at S&T.

Steve Sullivan

After earning a bachelor's degree in electrical engineering in 1989, Sullivan went to Hollywood where he became a senior technology officer for Lucasfilm Ltd. He became prolific in developing computer-generated images for films like *Pirates of the Caribbean*, *Iron Man*, and *Avatar*. Three times he won Academy Awards for his work.

Jack Dorsey

Dorsey attended UMR between 1995 and 1997 and then transferred to New York University, later becoming one of the nation's leading internet entrepreneurs. He is the co-founder and CEO of Twitter and the founder and CEO of Square, a mobile payments company. In 2020, Dorsey donated $1 billion to fight coronavirus, support girls' health and education initiatives, and support universal basic income.

MINER IMPACT

The achievements of these individuals illustrate the impact Miners have had in 150 years. Collectively, they have improved the mining and processing of metals, enhanced the nation's infrastructure, uplifted the well-being of humanity, helped ensure a strong national defense, advanced our understanding of the universe, improved our ability to communicate and imagine our world, provided ever-greater cultural opportunities, and advanced higher education, particularly at their alma mater, which gave them their start. Regardless of their major, they were Miners, and they pursued careers to take care of their families' needs, but also they made the world a better place.

EPILOGUE

3

2

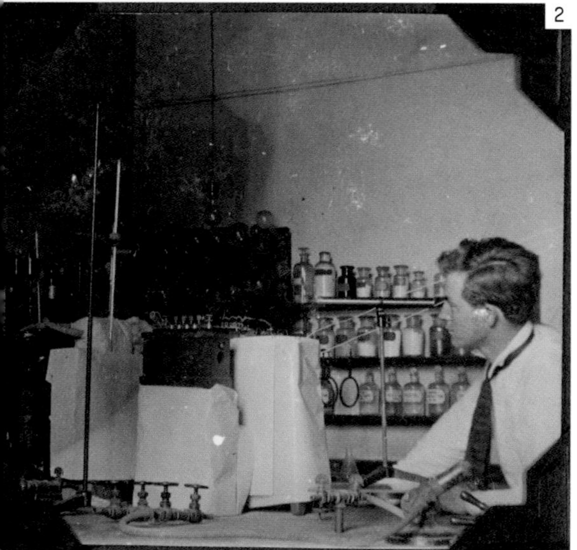

1

The Miner story is one of change and continuity. After 20 years, the small struggling college had only three buildings, 80 students, and six faculty members. Yet, by 1920, MSM had emerged as one the nation's leading mining schools, with more students in mining and metallurgical engineering than any other college. In the five decades after state legislators voted in 1915 to permit the campus to offer electrical, mechanical, and chemical engineering, MSM became ever less a school of mines and metallurgy and ever more a leader in undergraduate programs in engineering. By 1970 only Purdue University awarded more engineering degrees than UMR and the civil engineering department led the nation in undergraduate degrees granted. Five decades after the Miner campus became part of a new University of Missouri System in 1963, S&T had evolved into a respected technological research institution with over 8,000 students and a wide array of undergraduate and graduate programs.

As it celebrates its sesquicentennial, S&T is poised for even greater change. With a vision to become a world-class science and technology university for workforce development, research breakthroughs and economic development, look for S&T to become a U.S. News and World Report top 100 university as well as a Carnegie "Research 1" university while building its total enrollment to 12,000.

This vision received an enormous boost with a truly transformative gift in October 2020. Fred Kummer, a 1955 graduate in civil engineering, and his wife June, a graduate of Washington University's architecture program, made the largest single gift ever to higher education in Missouri. Indeed, it was the third-largest charitable contribution in the United States in 2020. Their $300 million gift will enable the campus not only to establish a college of innovation, entrepreneurship, and economic development, but also to fund scholarships for hundreds of undergraduate students and a fellowship program for Ph.D. students in STEM disciplines, to recruit outstanding new research faculty members, and to fund new research centers.

Amid the impressive changes of the past and the prospect for even more in the near future, some things remain the same at S&T. Campus leaders, faculty, and staff have never forgotten the Miner commitment to the land-grant mission of the university. Providing access to qualified students and helping them succeed is the most important element in the Miner DNA. Indeed, one of the most significant commitments the campus made in 2019 was to improve the retention and graduation rates of its students to record levels. The over 60,000 alumni of S&T, who appreciated the role the campus played in their success, can rest assured that S&T will always be mindful of its laudable heritage of being a student centered campus.

Reflecting upon a truly remarkable past during the sesquicentennial year, S&T and all its supporters can look forward to even an brighter future.

Sincerely,

Chancellor Mo Dehghani

4

5

6

1: Five gentlemen sit on rocks and pose for the camera from a collection of amateur images donated to the university.

2: This photo of a campus laboratory was provided to the University Archives by Benjamin Cody, a 1911 mining engineering graduate. Cody created the first St. Pat's Blarney Stone and in 1962 he was dubbed an Honorary Knight of St. Patrick. After graduation, Cody worked as a sampler for the Arizona Copper Co.

3: The Rolla Building, pictured here in an early campus photo, was originally owned by the Rolla Public School. To the left is the university's second building, a chemistry laboratory known as "Old Chem." It stood on campus until it was destroyed by fire in 1969.

4: Students gather on the campus mall outside Norwood Hall, one of the campus's oldest buildings. Completed in 1903, the building housed the library until 1912 and was the main administration building for years. Today it houses wellness, counseling and career services, international affairs, student affairs, student support and the testing center

5: The Kummer Atrium of Butler-Carlton Civil Engineering Building is part of a renovation completed in 2003 designed to make the entire 143,000-square-foot structure a working laboratory, where even the hallways are designed to teach engineering.

6: Biological sciences graduate student Nada Abokefa works in a newly renovated biology research lab in Schrenk Hall West. Abokefa is a student in Assistant Professor Julie Semon's regenerative medicine lab.

NOTES ON SOURCES

Larry Gragg

Historians begin a research project by reading all of the relevant secondary sources and there are several for a history of MSM/UMR/S&T: Jonas Viles, *The University of Missouri: A Centennial History, 1839–1939 (1939)*; Clair and Bonita Mann, *The History of Missouri School of Mines and Metallurgy* (1941); Clarence N. Roberts, *History of the University of Missouri School of Mines and Metallurgy, 1871–1946* (1946); Frank F. Stephens, *A History of the University of Missouri* (1962); Jack B. Ridley, *Completing the Circuit: A Century of Electrical Education at MSM/UMR* (1984); Jack B. Ridley, *Spanning the Years: Civil Engineering the Rolla Way* (1986); James and Vera Olson, *The University of Missouri: An Illustrated History* (1988); and Diana Ahmad, revised ed. *Spanning the Years: Civil Engineering the Rolla Way, 1871–2003* (2003). *UM-Rolla: A History of MSM/UMR* (1983), written by Lawrence O. Christensen and Jack B. Ridley, is the best of the histories of the campus. The memoirs of three University of Missouri System presidents include discussions of the relationship of the Rolla campus to their office: Elmer Ellis, *My Road to Emeritus* (1988); James C. Olson, *Serving the University of Missouri: A Memoir of Campus and System Administration* (1993); and C. Brice Ratchford, *Memoirs of My Years at the University of Missouri* (1996)

Three critical printed primary sources exist for a history of the campus: the *Missouri Miner* student newspaper (1915–2019), the *Rollamo* student yearbook (1907–2019), and the university's alumni magazine, the *MSM Alumnus/UMR Magazine/Missouri S&T Magazine (*1926–2020). Much about campus life can be found in local newspapers including *The Rolla Herald, Rolla New Era*, and *Rolla Daily News*. Missouri newspapers frequently covered campus developments, notably the *Columbia Daily Tribune*, *Kansas City Star*, *Springfield News-Leader*, *St. Louis Republic*, and *St. Louis Post-Dispatch*.

In addition to these sources is an abundance of unpublished manuscripts, reports, letters and photographs in the Missouri S&T Archives, the University of Missouri Archives, and the State Historical Society of Missouri. The large Clair V. Mann collection, a treasure trove of material accumulated by the longtime MSM faculty member, in the campus archives, is the most important collection of primary sources. Along with his wife Bonita, Mann wrote an unpublished three-volume history of Rolla that includes several sections on the history of the campus: *The Story of Rolla, Missouri to 1974* (1975)

Interviews are critical to an understanding of the evolution of a university, and I have drawn upon many. When Lawrence Christensen and Jack Ridley were researching their history of the campus in the early 1980s, they interviewed almost 50 alumni, faculty, and administrators. Their interviews with Harry Kessler, John Lyons, Robert Moore, Jim C. Pogue, Walter Remmers, and Dudley Thompson were especially useful

I was fortunate to have the opportunity to interview many current and former students, staff, faculty, administrators, members of the board of curators, and state legislators, and they all helped me understand how the institution changed over time: Tom Akers, Keith Bailey, Jerry Bayless, Richard Boyett, Meg Brady, Linda Bramel, Julia Brncic, Dan Brown, Henry Brown, Russell Buhite, Jack Carney, Mun Choi, Matt Coco, Harvest Collier, Robin Collier, Kim Colter, Elizabeth Cummins, Donald Cupps, Robert Davis, Delbert Day, Arlan DeKock, Glenda Dickman, Jim Drallmeier, Farouk El-Baz, Ed Emery, Ron Epps, Dixie Finley, Lelia Flagg, Gary Forsee, Jay Goff, Connie Goodridge, Maurice Graham, Richard Hagni, Floyd Harris, Pamela Henrickson, George Horne, Wayne Huebner, Tseggai Isaac, Irina Ivliyeva, Bill James, Martin C. Jischke, Janet Kavandi, Walter Knecht, Leonard Koederitz, Gary Lee, Suzanna Long, Paula Lutz, Yinfa Ma, C. Peter MaGrath, Sam Mahaney, Shenethia Manuel, Chris Maples, Dale Martin, John Mathes, Greg McClain, Henry Montrey, Mark Mullin, Francisca Oboh-Ikuenobe, Manuel Pacheco, John Park, John Phillips, Cuba Plain, Jerry Plunkett, Gus Ridgel, Jack Ridley, Catherine Riordan, B. Ken Robertson, Cheryl Schrader, Robert Schwartz, Eric Showalter, Philip Snowden, David Steelman, Richard Stevenson, Lynn Stichnote, Laura Stoll, Paul Stricker, Keith Wedge, Gary White, Timothy Wolfe, Kent Wray, and Margaret Zoller

The alumni who completed the questionnaires for the Golden Alumni Reunion Memory Books provided wonderful stories and reflections on their time in Rolla, and hundreds of alumni responded to questions posed by the Miner Alumni Association through *Missouri S&T Magazine*. I read them all, and their recollections informed my conclusions about Miner history.

PHOTO SOURCES

ACME News Photos: 134.1

***Alumnus*:** 39.3(1965); 46.A(1964); 86.A(1979).R(1973); 87(1946); 88.A(1979); 98.B; 103(1959); 104.A(1944); 132.L(1943); 163(1958); 170.B(1996); 173(1969); 186.M(1947); 235(1946); 243(1947); 247.A(1948); 250(1966); 255(2000); 260.L(1951); 267.B(1996)

***Columbia Missourian*:** 28.A

Matt Dunham/AP/Shutterstock: 196.2

Richard Elgin, CE'74, MS CE'76: 169.T

Ron Epps, Phys'67: 269.O

Evan Thayer Studios Inc: 283.B

Fairfax Media: 282.3

***In and About the Missouri School of Mines: The Photography of George E. Ladd Director of MSM — 1897–1907*:** 185.A

Islamic Center of Rolla, Missouri: 44.3

James Memorial Library: 156.R

***Jefferson City Daily Capital News*:** 248.A (March 24, 1949)

***Joplin Globe*:** 226

Kessler, The Millionaire Referee: 37.R

Andrew Layton: 60.R

Library of Congress, General Collections: 202.B

***Macon Daily Chronicle Herald*:** 224.R

Gene McFarland, Econ'70: 93.T.B; 218

McKendree University: 183.B

Miner Athletics: 194.R; 195.1; 196.5; 198; 200

***Missouri Miner*:** 13.L(March 19, 1915); 14.T(March 3, 1971); 42(March 29, 1926); 43.R(May 13, 1970); 76.L(February 24, 1971); 109(October 13, 1993); 133(October 1934); 150(May 11, 1917); 171.A(December 9, 1966). B(October 27, 1967); 172(March 25, 1966); 219.R(February 25, 1966); 225(April 7, 1924); 242(April 8, 1941); 252(October 20, 1971); 258(December 21, 1917); 265.A(February 5, 1986)

Missouri S&T: 23; 24; 25.L; 26.T; 28.L; 32.T.M.BR; 33.TL; 40.B; 57.2.3.4; 60.R; 65.O1.O2; 66; 75.2.3.4; 76.A; 77.T.B; 78.B; 79.1.5; 80.1; 83.A.B; 84.B; 88.L; 89.2; 99.A.ML.MR; 102.2; 108; 127.T; 147.2.3.4.5; 168.3; 174.A.R; 175.T.B.R; 177.A; 179.B; 193.3; 196.4; 205.4; 212; 217; 256.1.3; 274.B; 275.B; 276.A; 277.A; 278.A; 279.B; 281.A.B; 282.1.2; 283.A; **Terry Barner:** 113.TL.MR.BR; **Jesse Cureton:** 113.ML; 205.5; **Rebecca Frisbee:** 81.A; **Sam O'Keefe:** VI; 26.BL; 27.BL.BR; 33.B; 34.4; 44.4; 53.4; 57.5; 65; 67.1; 80.2; 89.1; 107.B; 113.TR.BR; 134.2.3; 143.4; 145; 178; 256.5; 259.L; 261.A; 272.T; 275.L; 276.B; 278.R.B; 279.T; 280.3; 285.4; Back End pages; **Bob Phelan:** 75.2; 78.A; 79.2; 80.3; **B.A. Rupert:** 26.BR; 29.T.B; 33.M; 64.O3.O4; 75.1; 79.3; 85.A; 89.3; 99.B; 107.T; 146.A; 147.1; 160.BR; 183.TR; 263.B; 277.B; 280.1.2; **Terrill Story:** 79.4; **Tom Wagner:** Cover; 33.TR; 53.3; 55; 177.L; 179.T; 246.T; 256.2; 261.B; 277.L; 283.AL; 285.5.6; 286; Back Flap

NASA: 195.2; 266.R; 267.T; 269.A.TR.BR; 270.TL.A.BL; 271.T.B

National Library of Medicine: 72

New York Yankees 1943 World Champions — National Poster Stamp Society: 203.BR

***Oregon Journal of Sports*:** 203.L (December 22, 1939)

Christopher Parr, U.S. Air Force: 39.4

Rob Greer Photography: 275.A

***Rolla Daily News*:** 25.AL

***The Rolla Herald*:** 5.L; 202.L; 229.B; 241

***Rolla Herald-Democrat*:** 132.AR; 222

***Rollamo*:** **1907:** 9.B; 51.2; 121.A; 129.B; 185.B; 204.1. **1908:** 123.L; 124.A; 181.; 208.B. **1909:** 13.B; 71.A; 112.A; 126.R. **1910:** 47.3; 125.B; 155.B; 182.A; 188.T.B; 272.B. **1911:**101.O; 111.B; 118.B. **1912:** 118.A. **1913:** 12.M; 122.AL. **1915:** 197.L.B; 199.L.C.R; 201; 237.A. **1916:** 12.B; 189; 190.T.M. **1917:** 151.A; 152.T.B. **1918:** 140.T.; 153. **1919:** 156.L.; 157.L.R. **1920:** 68.B; 223.R. **1921:** 15.A; 127.B; 158; 176.A.R; 186.T. **1922:** 119; 223.T. **1923:** 236.B. **1924:** 37.B; 58.A; 186.B; 223.B. **1925:** 166.B; 224.T.B; 227; 228.; 247.B. **1926:** 16; 259.B. **1927:** 68.L; 73.R; 129.L. **1928:** 44.2; 71.B; 102.1. **1929:** 100.L; 111.T; 123.T; 128.B; 159.R. **1930:** 149; 162.3; 182.C. **1931:** 70.L; 106.B. **1932:** 85.R. **1933:** 239. **1935:** 67.3; 203. TR. **1937:** 162.5. **1938:** 20.T.; 238.B. **1939:** 266.B. **1940:** 162.1; 165.3; 168.2. **1941:** 125.R; 162.2; 165.1.2; 166.T; 266.A. **1942:** 20.B; 21.T; 162.4.6. **1943:** 166. TR.BR. **1944:** 167.L.A.B. **1945:** 246.B. **1946:** 58.R; 114; 115; 244.O. **1947:** 20.L; 49.T; 84.T; 120; 244.L. **1948:** 91.B; 182.R. **1949:** 238.A. **1950:** 21.M; 168.1; 230.O. **1952:** 67.2; 193.1. **1954:** 94.T; 193.2. **1955:** 67.A. **1956:** 214.A; 248.B. **1957:** 104.O; 126.A.B. **1958:** 135.L; 190.B; 244.B. **1959:** 180; 195.3; 204.3. **1960:** 17.B; 39.2; 51.1; 95.O. **1963:** 159.B. **1964:** 17.R; 112.B; 121.B; 251. **1965:** 213. **1966:** 44.1;

A=Above; T=Top; L=Left; R=Right, M=Middle; C=Center; B=Below/Bottom; O=Opposite

96; 124.R; 135.A. 169.TR. **1967:** 57.1; 169.R; 191.B; 206. **1968:** 49.B; 51.3; 83.TL; 102.3; 159.T; 183.TL; 219.L. **1969:** 22; 25.A; 40.O; 46.AR; 82.T. **1970:** 43.A; 97; 123.A. **1971:** 140.BL; 263.TL.M. **1972:** 34.3; 216.AR. **1973:** 187. **1975:** 184. **1976:** 193.4; 205.6. **1978:** 51.4; 141.A. **1979:** 53.1; 194.L. **1980:** 215.B. **1981:** 215.R. **1982:** 53.2; 98.L. **1984:** 59; 60.A; 82.B; 194.M. **1985:** 192.A. **1986:** 139.AR; 253; 254.T; 262.B. **1987:** 85.R; 191.C; 205.2. **1988:** 142.A. **1989:** 32.BR. **1992:** 195.5. **1996:** 192.L; 230.B. **2003:** 195.6. **2008:** 195.4. **2011:** 191.T. **2015:** 196.1. **2016:** 196.3

Sam Fentress Photography: 276.BR

***San Francisco Chronicle*:** 151.B

1908 University of Missouri *Savitar*: 236.T

***The Sedalia Democrat*:** 229.R

Dan Seifert, Stone House Photography: 81.L

Spectrum: 110.1.2.3.4

S&T Archives: Front End pages; 3(Young Collection, donated by Becky Young (1911–12)); 5.AL.AR.R(Tom Wagner); 6.A.O; 8; 9.T(Benjamin Horace Cody Collection, MinE 1911 (1906–12)); 10.A.L.OT(Tom Wagner).OB; 12.T; 14.B; 15.B(Clair Mann Collection); 18; 19; 21.B; 30.1.2.3.4; 31.1.2.3.4; 34.1.2(Young Collection, donated by Becky Young (1911–12)); 36; 37.T; 39.1(Lelia Thompson Flagg scrapbook); 47.1.2 (Benjamin Horace Cody Collection, MinE 1911 (1906–12)); 48; 54; 62.A.R; 63; 69; 70.T.R; 73.A; 74; 75.5; 92.T.B; 100.B; 106.R; 116; 122.B; 128.A.AR(Young Collection, donated by Becky Young (1911–12)); 129.TR(Tom Wagner); 130; 131; 134.4; 136; 137.A(Benjamin Horace Cody Collection, MinE 1911 (1906–12)).L.B(Benjamin Horace Cody Collection, MinE 1911 (1906–12)); 138(Benjamin Horace Cody Collection, MinE 1911 (1906–12)); 139.AL.B; 140.BR; 141.AL; 142.R; 143.1.2.3.5; 144(TomWagner); 152.R; 154; 155.T; 160.A.TR; 161; 208.R; 209; 210; 214.B; 216.A; 221.L.R; 232; 237.B; 245.R; 249.B; 259.A; 261.L(Benjamin Horace Cody Collection, MinE 1911 (1906–12)); 273.A.B; 274.T; 280.R; 284.1(Young Collection, donated by Becky Young (1911–12)).2(Benjamin Horace Cody Collection, MinE 1911 (1906–12)).3; 289

Steve Jennings Photography: 282.4

St. Louis Mercantile Library: 91.R

***St. Louis Post-Dispatch*:** 249.T

Sumner High School 1950 yearbook: 94.B

University of Missouri System: 254.1.2; 256.4

Water.org: 146.T; 262.A; 264; 265.L

George A. Whiteman family: 164

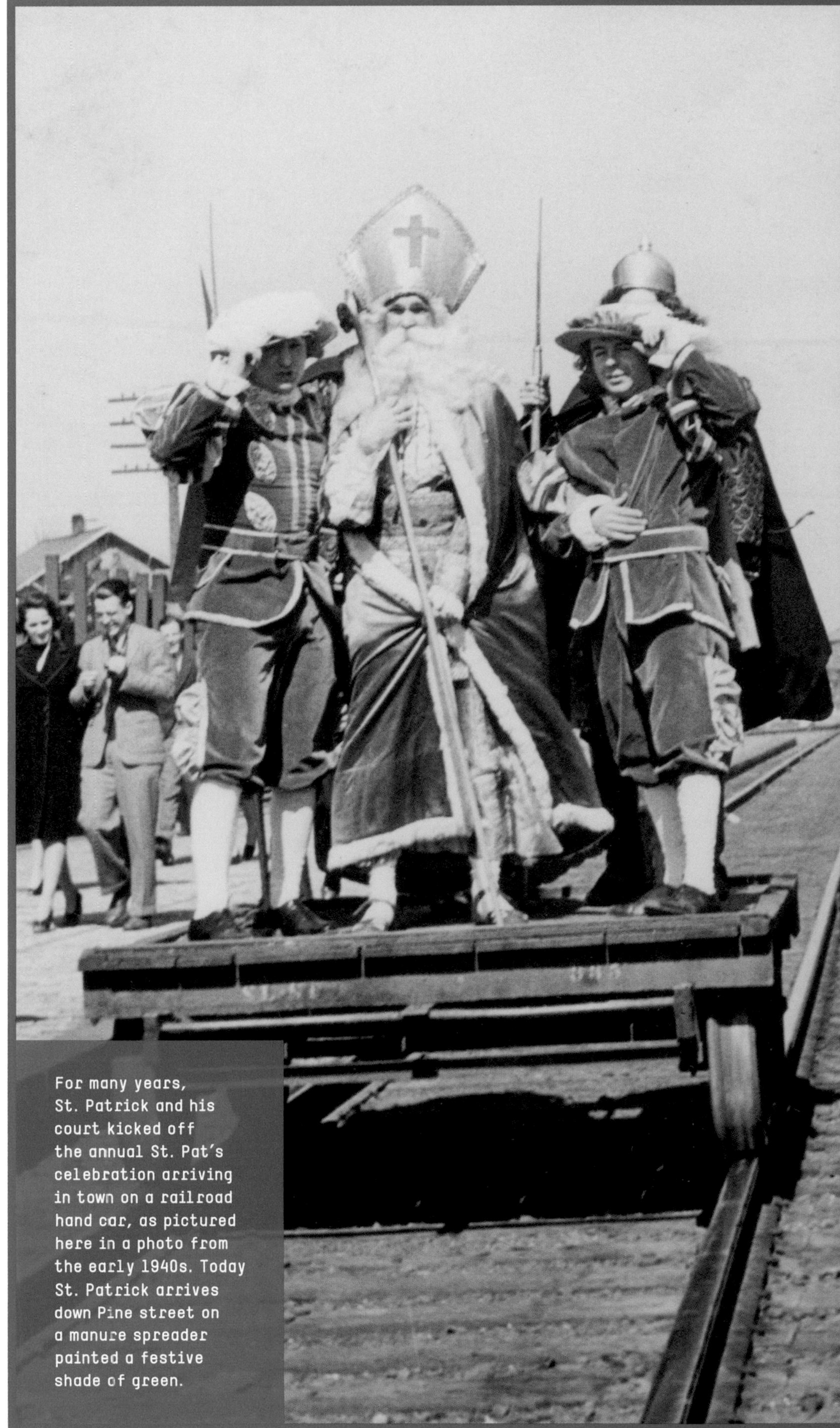

For many years, St. Patrick and his court kicked off the annual St. Pat's celebration arriving in town on a railroad hand car, as pictured here in a photo from the early 1940s. Today St. Patrick arrives down Pine street on a manure spreader painted a festive shade of green.

A=Above; T=Top; L=Left; R=Right, M=Middle; C=Center; B=Below/Bottom; O=Opposite